Splendid Monarchy

Twentieth-Century Japan: The Emergence of a World Power
Irwin Scheiner, Editor

Splendid Monarchy

Power and Pageantry in
Modern Japan

T. Fujitani

UNIVERSITY OF CALIFORNIA PRESS

Berkeley / Los Angeles / London

University of California Press
Berkeley and Los Angeles, California

University of California Press, Ltd.
London, England

First Paperback Printing 1998

Library of Congress Cataloging-in-Publication Data

Fujitani, Takashi
    Splendid monarchy : power and pageantry in modern Japan /
T. Fujitani.
        p.   cm.—(Twentieth-century Japan : 6)
    Includes bibliographic references and index
    ISBN 0-520-21371-8 (pbk : alk. paper)
        1. Japan—History—1868–. 2. Emperor worship—Japan.
3. Monarchy—Japan. 4. Emperors—Japan. 5. Japan—Kings
and rulers.
I. Title.   II. Series.
    DS881.9.J847   1996
    952.03—dc20   95-38543

Printed in the United States of America

08   07   06   05   04   03   02   01   00
9   8   7   6   5   4   3   2

The paper used in this publication meets the minimum requirements of
ANSI / NISO Z39.48-1992 (R 1997) (*Permanence of Paper*). ∞

Contents

Figures and Maps

Figures

Maps

Preface and Acknowledgments

When I began this book well over a decade ago, I had only a general sense of the variety and complexity of issues that would be opened up by the evidently limited topic of state ritual in modern Japan. Initially, I had been inspired by the work of historians and anthropologists working on political symbolism and ceremonials in other contexts, primarily in Europe and the United States, who were arguing that public pageantry or ritual events, far from becoming obsolete with modernity, had in fact experienced an incredible efflorescence during the late nineteenth and early twentieth centuries. These included coronations, processions of heads of state, funerals and festivals to honor national heroes, celebrations of royal or national jubilees, and so many other new ceremonial events, including exhibitions. Although I do believe that it had some important precursors, the book edited by Eric Hobsbawm and Terence Ranger, *The Invention of Tradition* (Cambridge: Cambridge University Press, 1983), which placed the invention of modern national cultures squarely within the period of the formation of mass nationalism and the heyday of imperialism, has by now made such a perspective on national cultural production quite well known. I also knew that the capital cities of these nations had undergone massive transformations in the nineteenth and twentieth centuries as they became prepared to serve as enormous public theaters for the performance of such rites. One had only to think of the rebuilding of Washington, D.C., into a ceremonial city with such landmarks as the Washington Monument and the Pennsylvania Avenue processional route, or the reconstruction of Paris under the direction of Baron Haussmann in the mid–nineteenth century.

I began my research with a suspicion that the political elite in Japan might also have seen the utility of similar types of public pageantry, ceremonial spaces, and monuments, mainly because I had already become convinced that they, like their counterparts in the Euro-American world, had begun in Meiji to fashion various and powerful new mechanisms to reconstitute the common people into active subject-citizens who would participate in the realization of the new nation-state's objectives. It therefore seemed highly unlikely that the Japanese elite would have ignored the potential of public ritual or the symbolic power of capital cities and monuments to naturalize official ideologies and to create a sense of national community. Moreover, I suspected that the Japanese government's leaders, assiduous in their attention to adapting new technologies of rule in the late nineteenth century, must have been impressed by the political possibilities of the ceremonial activity and the more general invention of tradition then taking place in the United States, and in Europe and its dominions.

I found my expectations fully confirmed in the first few months of research as I skimmed general chronologies of historical events, pored over Meiji popular magazines and newspapers, and explored Tokyo's archives and libraries. While that phase of research took some two years, it became evident early on that during the Meiji era (1868–1912) powerful individuals in the Japanese political elite, as well as a vast supporting network of bureaucrats and advisers, had indeed constructed an enormous variety of national and imperial symbols and rituals. These included public pageants and ceremonial sites fully comparable to those I had been reading about in the late nineteenth- and early twentieth-century Euro-American scene.

I first published the results of my research in 1985 in an article entitled "Kindai Nihon ni okeru kokka-teki ibento no tanjō—1889–1912 no Tōkyō" (*Yasō* 14 [February]: 126–40), or "Tokyo and the Rise of National Ceremonies in Modern Japan, 1889–1912." I placed the emergence of what I then called "national events" within the global context of the "invention of tradition," but I also argued that the year 1889 in fact marked an important shift in the dominant style of state pageantry in Japan. Previously, its main form had been the imperial progress, a ritual style that had been recuperated from archaic models for quite modern purposes; but from the time of the Meiji Constitution's promulgation, a host of entirely new pageants, including celebrations of war victories and imperial funerals, weddings, and wedding anniversaries, came to form the core of a more cosmopolitanized system of state ceremonials. I made the additional point that the shift in public ceremonial form was inextricably tied to the reconstruction of Tokyo into a ceremonial center.

Yet over the years I have found it necessary to refine, revise, and branch out my analyses, to grapple if sometimes only in a cursory and suggestive way with issues central to Japanese experiences of modernity that I did not have clearly in mind when at first I naively imagined that there must have been a Japanese version of the "invention of tradition" that took place around a century ago. The topics this book now covers range widely (and admittedly sometimes only briefly) over the many and intricately imbricating dimensions of culture and power that center on the larger topics of modern nationalism, images of the emperor's "body" and imperial family, the system of domination that is known as the emperor system, the gendering of "politics," the emergence of visual and disciplinary technologies that are often associated with modern regimes of power, city planning, the media, modern memory and forgetfulness, and the production of national time. Some of these concerns emerged immediately out of the materials that I discovered and my engagement with them, but many others have been sparked by encounters with the work of other scholars, or by the criticisms, encouragement and suggestions that colleagues and friends have offered.

It is of course impossible to give a full accounting of the numerous people and institutions that have participated (often unwittingly) in the production of this book. Yet I want to acknowledge the major debts I owe, and at least to suggest the work's historicity. Irwin Scheiner was my dissertation adviser at the University of California, Berkeley. His encouragement, criticisms, and good humor have consistently helped me to think through my analyses and in the end to complete the task of writing. In Japan I had the great pleasure of working with Yasumaru Yoshio of Hitotsubashi University. To those who are familiar with his writings, it will be obvious that his views of modern Japanese history have influenced me deeply. As my endnotes indicate, I am especially indebted to him for his sweeping insights into radical changes in elite assumptions of rule that occurred in the late Tokugawa and Meiji eras, and into equally convulsive transformations in the subjectivities of the common folk that took place during that same period. Thomas C. Smith aided me with his knowledge of source materials and his uncommon good sense. Although I would now look critically at the ideological character of what Robert N. Bellah has called the "religious dimension" of national communities such as the United States, I want to acknowledge that many of the interests reflected here were first sparked when I worked with him as a graduate student in history learning classical sociology. Lisa Yoneyama has been my most unfailing supporter, critic, and colleague over nearly the entire life of this project, and in one way or another almost every section of this book bears her imprint.

I spent the academic year 1987–88 as a postdoctoral fellow at the Reischauer Institute of Japanese Studies, Harvard University. At that time I began to read extensively in poststructuralist theory and to consider more seriously how my work might benefit from a more Foucauldian analysis. Also in the summer of 1988 I had the good fortune of meeting Yoshimi Shun'ya, who pointed out that in my 1986 dissertation I had not adequately dealt with the question of the emperor's gaze. In addition, he introduced me to the pioneering book on visibility and power by Taki Kōji, *Tennō no shōzō* (Tokyo: Iwanami Shoten, 1988). These encounters prompted me to think more about the relations among the monarchy, nationalism, and the disciplining of national subject-citizens. The immediate result was an article skillfully translated by Professor Yoshimi, "Kindai Nihon ni okeru gunshū to tennō no pējento: shikakuteki shihai ni kansuru jakkan no kōsatsu" (*Shisō*, no. 797 [November 1990]:148–64), or "Crowds and Imperial Pageantry: Some Thoughts on Visual Domination in Modern Japan." The arguments and most of the text have been incorporated into this book.

My work on the Meiji era slowed considerably when the Shōwa emperor fell gravely ill toward the end of 1988, for I was compelled to think more directly about the present and to consider how the monarchy of the postwar and post–high economic growth era might still be important in the politics and nationalism of Japan today. It quickly became apparent that no simple lines could be drawn between the period of the invention of the Japanese monarchy in the late nineteenth to early twentieth centuries and the present. Most important, I found it necessary to place the monarchy within the context of late capitalism and the "televisualization" of contemporary culture. Yet I was also reminded, especially by the oppositional discourses of feminists and minoritized groups in Japan, of the ongoing relevance of the issues dealt with in this book—in particular the importance of fashioning a historically informed critique of nationalism and the monarchy in Japan. Moreover, it was also at this time, when political struggles over memories of Imperial Japan and the Second World War in the Asia-Pacific region began to intensify, and under much influence from Lisa Yoneyama's work on Hiroshima memories, that I began to feel that the concept

of memory was central to much of what I had be...
point. While the full results of this diversion into t...
lished elsewhere ("Electronic Pageantry and Jap...
peror,'" *Journal of Asian Studies* 51 [November 1...
research is reflected in some important ways in p...

Over the years I have tried to develop a metho...
historicized analysis of culture, particularly the cultu...
during the formation of the modern nation-state. Though still not
entirely satisfactory, the introduction to this book is an attempt to discuss
such a method and to place my project within a historical framework that
posits a major historical break in the relationships among culture, memory, the state, and the individual that begins around the time of the Meiji
Restoration. Harumi Befu gave me an opportunity to present a sub-
stantial portion of this introduction in a conference on cultural nationalism in 1990. The paper was published in a slightly different form as
"Inventing, Forgetting, Remembering: Toward a Historical Ethnography of the Nation-State," in Harumi Befu, ed., *Cultural Nationalism
in East Asia* (Berkeley: Institute of East Asian Studies, University of
California, 1993), 77–106, and it is republished here, with some revisions
and expansion, courtesy of the Regents of the University of California.

In addition to those already mentioned, Herbert Bix, Hirota Masaki,
Irokawa Daikichi, Mellie Ivy, Jung Young-hae, Maeda Ai, Masao Miyoshi, Miyata Noboru, Murakami Shigeyoshi, Nakamura Akira, Ohama
Tetsuya, Shimazono Susumu, Stefan Tanaka, Yoneyama Toshiko,
Yoneyama Toshinao, Yoneda Kenji, Yoneda Mari, Eiji Yutani, and many
others all assisted me in either locating sources or thinking through my
analyses. Harry Harootunian has shown by example and through personal communication how cultural theory can be fruitfully applied to
questions of culture and power in Japan. He also read through the entire
penultimate draft and offered many constructive criticisms. An anonymous reader for the Press pushed me toward greater clarity. A shortened
version of this book appeared in Japanese as *Tennō no pējento*, trans. Lisa
Yoneyama (Tokyo: Nihon Hōsō Shuppan Kyōkai, 1994), and during its
production the editor for the NHK Books series, Michikawa Fumio,
provided many helpful suggestions. I also want finally to let my friends
in the East Bay and my parents know just how valuable and sustaining
their patience, love, and emotional support have been over so many
years.

I have received generous financial assistance from the Fulbright-Hays
Doctoral Dissertation Research Abroad Program, the Japan Foundation,

cial Science Research Council, the Mabelle McLeod Lewis Me-
rial Fund, the Reischauer Institute of Japanese Studies at Harvard
University, and the Santa Cruz and San Diego campuses of the University
of California. Sheila Levine and Erika Büky at the Press and my copy-
editor Alice Falk were skillful enough to both improve the manuscript
and accommodate most of my idiosyncrasies. I thank them all.

Here and throughout this book the personal names of those who reside
or have resided primarily in China, Japan, or Korea are written with the
surname preceding the given name while the reverse order is followed
for all others.

CHAPTER ONE

Introduction

Inventing, Forgetting, Remembering

Today it is not unusual for historians and other histori-cally minded analysts of culture to speak of the relatively recent "in-vention" of some of our most taken-for-granted customs, practices, symbols, ceremonials, and institutions. "Traditional" folk songs, na-tional anthems, flags and costumes, monarchies, and many convention-ally accepted practices have come under a new and critical scrutiny. The pomp of British royalty, "splendid, public, and popular," is now un-derstood to be a construct of the years between the late 1870s and 1914 and not a venerable tradition at all. Bastille Day, it turns out, was not a spontaneous festival originating immediately after the French Revo-lution; rather, it was invented in 1880. In the United States as well, daily worship of the national flag apparently became a regular school practice only in the 1880s, during the great drive to make recent immigrants into Americans. This current focusing on the invented quality of many un-critically accepted traditions, this historicizing of the details of everyday culture, has contributed to a new kind of skepticism about some of our most deeply held notions. Not least of these has been the naturalness or timelessness of the nation and of national identity.[1]

Interestingly, Basil Hall Chamberlain, the learned pioneer in English-language studies of Japanese history and literature, had already made the same sorts of points about invented traditions more than three-quarters of a century ago. In 1912 he published a short, brilliant, but for the most part now long-forgotten essay titled *The Invention of a New Religion*. Chamberlain argued that while Japan's governing elites had begun to convince the Japanese people and the rest of the world

that the "new Japanese religion" of "Mikado-worship and Japan-
worship" was of ancient vintage, they were in fact inventions of extraordinarily modern times. From a critical perspective that sounds
surprisingly fresh today, he maintained that "every manufacture pre-
supposes a material out of which it is made, every present a past on
which it rests. But the twentieth-century Japanese religion of loyalty and
patriotism is quite new, for in it pre-existing ideas have been sifted,
altered, freshly compounded, turned to new uses, and have found a new
centre of gravity. Not only is it new, it is not yet completed; it is still in
process of being consciously or semi-consciously put together by the
official class, in order to serve the interests of that class, and, incidentally,
the interests of the nation at large."[2]

As proof of the newness of this religion Chamberlain pointed out that
Shinto, "which had fallen into discredit," had been "taken out of the
cupboard and dusted" in order to assist in the construction of the
imperial cult. Only in recent years, he noted, had the Shinto priesthood
been allowed to conduct burial rites and marriage ceremonies. Quite
correctly, as we shall see, Chamberlain reminded his readers that historically the marriage ceremony had not been a religious rite at all; as for
the "traditional" Shinto-style marriage, that was a complete invention.
In schools, too, the emperor's portrait had only recently become an
object of worship, and festivals celebrating official imperial holidays
were also an innovation. In fact, despite a glowing emperor-centered
official history filled with "miraculous impossibilities," he asserted that
"no nation probably has ever treated its sovereigns more cavalierly than
the Japanese have done, from the beginning of authentic history down
to within the memory of living men. Emperors have been deposed,
emperors have been assassinated; for centuries every succession to the
throne was the signal for intrigues and sanguinary broils. Emperors have
been exiled; some have been murdered in exile. From the remote island
to which he had been relegated one managed to escape, hidden under
a load of dried fish."[3]

But in his documentation of the apparently amazing gullibility of the
Japanese people, Chamberlain's most acute observation concerned the
credulity of people in general toward cultural inventions. The Japanese,
he reminded his readers, were not the only ones who made up ideas and
then fervently began to believe in them. Jean-Jacques Rousseau, for
example, had simply sat in a forest, invented man in a state of nature,
and then imagined a "pseudo-history of man from his own brain." But,
even more incredible, Rousseau "fanatically believed in this his pure

invention, and, most extraordinary of all, persuaded other people to believe in it as fanatically." In other words, Chamberlain did not assume that the Japanese governors, the manufacturers of the cult of the emperor and of the nation, remained cynical and detached as they busily tried to persuade others of the truthfulness of this new religion. Rather, he concluded that even those who had concocted the new creed had become believers in their own myths.[4]

But how could a religion, so recent a fabrication and so completely alien to the great masses, have come to have such veracity for enormous numbers of people that, as Chamberlain put it, a whole generation was "growing up which does not so much as suspect that its cherished beliefs are inventions of yesterday"? And more surprisingly, how could even the creators of the new ideas have come to believe in their own innovations? Chamberlain's main explanation for the phenomenon of mass belief was that "the spread of new ideas has been easy, because a large class derives power from their diffusion, while to oppose them is the business of no one in particular." As for the second matter, Chamberlain conjectured that the governing elites believed in their own inventions because people in general tend to take up ideas that will further their own interests. Since the Japanese rulers wished to have all the masses come under the sway of the new religion, the result was their belief in that very fabrication.[5]

Chamberlain was probably right, insofar as he went; but he might have gone further in addressing the issue of how it had come to pass that during the late nineteenth and early twentieth centuries the Japanese people, governors and governed alike, learned to forget the invented quality of the modern cult of the emperor and of the nation. Most people must have experienced a massive and sudden case of what Pierre Bourdieu has termed "genesis amnesia." History had somehow produced a forgetting of history, to the extent that recent fabrications had quickly passed into the subconscious area of the seemingly natural and self-evident.[6] For while historians are generally agreed that common folk had little or no knowledge of the Japanese emperor during the Tokugawa period, during the Meiji era and later it became commonplace to think of the flow of time, the organization of political space, and even Japanese culture as converging on that very emperor. Even today high government officials and respected scholars continue to espouse the belief that history and culture for the Japanese people have almost always centered on the imperial institution.[7] And the Constitution of Japan proclaims that "the Emperor shall be the symbol of the State and of the unity of the people." This paradox of emperor-centered nationalism is much like one of the great paradoxes of nationalism itself, in which, as Benedict Anderson has put it, "the objective modernity of nations to the historian's eye" exists alongside "their subjective antiquity in the eyes of nationalists."[8]

I am proposing that we remember—not the entire history of the imperial institution, for such a project, even if it were to be a critical one, would inadvertently contribute to the myth of the imperial institution's continuity. Rather, following a Foucauldian genealogical method that sees the principle of continuity itself as a metaphysical a priori,[9] I want to remember the instant of historical rupture, the moment of the imperial institution's new emergence in modern Japan. Thus my approach is absolutely opposed to the overall project of many new and widely read works on the Japanese emperor that either attempt to produce generalizations about Japanese kingship over time,[10] or explain modern kingship in Japan by resorting to metaphysical assumptions about Japanese mentality.[11] This is not to say that these books do not contain interesting and useful details about the imperial institution in particular historical periods. Moreover, I do believe that insights about kingship in other times and places can be used metaphorically to illuminate the nexus of culture and power in modern Japan. Rather, it is to say that the overall approach of these books—which tends toward hypostatizing and thereby essentializing Japanese kingship or mentality—runs the great risk of mystifying all those forces that came together in the late nineteenth and early twentieth centuries to throw the emperor and the nation onto the center stage of Japan's modern history.

Nationalism and the Emperor in Tokugawa Japan

As a first move in this project of remembering discontinuity, it would be useful to briefly sketch the Tokugawa period as background to the later rise of nationalism and the modern imperial cult. It is obvious to sensible historians today—and it was all too apparent to the Meiji regime's leaders—that during the Tokugawa period the common people had neither a strong sense of national identity nor a clear image of the emperor as the Japanese nation's central symbol. Nowadays Japan appears to form an almost natural political community, with its people possessing a remarkably uniform culture and national identity. Surrounded by the sea and set off at a considerable distance from the powerful cultural influences of the Asian continent, geographical circumstances also seem, at least superficially, to have been congenial to the development and preservation of a unique national culture. Even one of the most thoughtful of Japanese writers argued not long ago that Japan's physical insularity, complemented by "the same language and the same system of gestures[,] has unite[d] the population so that they feel almost as though they were distant relatives."[12] But the strong sense of national consciousness and identity that has characterized the modern Japanese is less a product of natural circumstances that can be traced back in time to the geological formation of the Japanese archipelago than of strategically motivated cultural policies pursued by Japan's modern ruling elites.

During the earlier Tokugawa period, the official discourse on ruling stressed that both society and polity were to be maintained by the accentuation of social, cultural, and even to some extent political differences, not by an ideology of social, cultural, and political sameness. Society was stratified into functionally interdependent but sharply distinctive horizontal estates or statuses—primarily the samurai, peasants, artisans, and merchants. The duty of the ruling elite, the samurai, was to see that rigid status distinctions were maintained so that the organically related parts of the body politic could function harmoniously. One historian of Japan has aptly called this system "rule by status."[13] Society, culture, and politics were also separated into vertical compartments. On the one hand, under a system that has been likened to a "federation,"[14] the political order was institutionally separated into largely autonomous domains, or *han*. On the other hand, particular local cultures characterized by distinct and often even mutually unintelligible dialects contributed to the insularity of local communities from each other within Japan, rather than the insularity of Japan from outside cultural influences.

In short, politics, society, and especially culture under the ideal Tokugawa system of rule were marked by both horizontal and vertical distinctions and separation—a situation that the anthropologist Ernest Gellner has described as being typical of agrarian societies with a literate class of elites and not conducive to the formation of a modern nationalism, which is based upon "an ideal of a single overriding and cultural identity."[15] In his sociological formulation, Anthony Giddens would call this a "class-divided society," one in which "system integration . . . does not depend upon the overall acceptance of symbolic orders by the majority of the population within these societies."[16]

It is certainly true, as some Japanese historians have argued, that the faint glimmerings of a sense of national identity at the folk level did emerge as early as the late seventeenth century in the cities of the Kyoto/Osaka region, that is, in the area near the imperial court. They maintain that at least within this energetic urban environment common people developed a consciousness of distinctly Japanese cultural traits, as opposed to Confucian ones, as well as an awareness of a land of the emperor or of the gods that was distinct from China. As evidence they cite such representative works of popular culture as the writings of Ihara Saikaku and the plays of Chikamatsu Monzaemon.[17] And in his brilliant reading of Tokugawa nativism, H. D. Harootunian has argued that in the early eighteenth century new discourses began to challenge neo-Confucianism's overly simplistic division of society between the rulers and the ruled, between mental and manual labor, because this official discourse had become increasingly incapable of representing "the complexity and plurality of the social urban environment." Tokugawa nativism, in particular, contested the official representation of order while emphasizing that which made "the Japanese irreducibly Japanese—the same and thereby different from the [Chinese] Other."[18]

There were also opportunities for common city folk to learn about the existence of the emperor and his court. For example, during periods of mourning for deceased members of the imperial family there were sporadic public injunctions against the playing of musical instruments (*nari mono chōji*), and official notices of such deaths even reached villages far from Kyoto. Many people, ranging from those in some "outcast" groups to others as diverse as physicians and confectioners, also sought social prestige by claiming connections of their houses with the imperial court. In fact, Amino Yoshihiko has shown that many nonagriculturalists (*hinōgyōmin*) in the even earlier medieval period traced their lineages back to emperors or other imperial ancestors. In 1840, when the Tokugawa system of rule was rapidly breaking down, peasants in Shōnai *han* even talked of the possibility of a direct petition to the emperor and his regent after exhausting other avenues of protest.[19]

Yet all of this points to the existence of only an emergent and geographically limited consciousness of national identity at the *popular* level. When the Meiji rulers ushered in what they called the restoration of imperial rule, many of the common people looked with great expectation to the arrival of a world renewed by the new regime; but this does not mean that they held strong beliefs about either the nation or the emperor. Rather, they longed for a bettering of their lives, for such concrete benefits as the reduction of taxes or the redistribution of land. When their hopes were shattered—by representatives of the state who attacked their religion and way of life, by compulsory education that was costly in terms of tuition and children's labor lost, by military conscription, and by even heavier taxation than they had experienced in the past—they reacted immediately and violently. The first decade of the Meiji era was rocked by a series of violent antigovernment uprisings, some of which—like one in Mie Prefecture in late 1876, touched off by demands for reduced and deferred taxes—began with a specific demand and exploded into wholesale attacks upon the central government itself. In the Mie uprising the rioters attacked all local figures and institutions connected with the central government: headmen (*kochō* and *kuchō*), schools, post offices, and central and local government offices. In the Mikawa region peasants led by Buddhist priests demonstrated their rejection of the new government by spearing and decapitating a government official, then burying him halfway in mud in an inverted position. When some of these rioters called the officials of the national government "traitors to the *kuni,* enemies of Buddhism (*hō*)," they obviously did not mean by *kuni* "nation," as it can mean, but "province."[20]

From the rulers' perspective, a major reason for the instability of the early Meiji government was the inadequacy of the existing popular image of the emperor. Susaki Bunzō, born on Amakusa Island (Kumamoto Prefecture) into a long line of fishermen, and a centenarian at the time he was interviewed in the early 1960s, remembered that one of the major reasons for the reluctance of villagers to become recruits to fight against Saigo Takamori's rebellion in 1877 was that they were not sure who the emperor was. Elderly women were saying, he recalled, that "even though it's said that the emperor's taken the place of the shogun, what kind'a person is he (*dogan hito ja*)? Must be the one in the *kyōgen* play who wears the gold crown and the full-sleeved robe with gold brocade."[21]

A remarkable woodblock print depicting popular images of the emperor on the occasion of his first progress to Tokyo in 1868 reveals that some craftspeople of Edo, where little traditional knowledge of the emperor existed, surmised that he was in fact Shōtoku Taishi, a deity of popular Edo folklore. In "Craftspeople Praying to the Deity Prince

Figure 1. Woodblock print representing Edo craftspeople's images of the
emperor around the time of his first entry into Tokyo. "Shōtoku kōtaishi no
mikoto e shoshokunin ritsugan no zu," 1868. Courtesy of Asai Collection.

Shōtoku," the deity is seen descending on a cloud while Tokyo craftspeople implore him to grant them simple worldly favors (see Figure 1).
A young apprentice woodblock cutter says, "I want to become head
cutter quickly and fill up my belly with tempura and dumplings." The
wife of a tilemaker would like to have something done about her husband: "I pray that my mate be cured of his laziness, that he earn lots of
money, that I have *kimono* for summer and winter, and that we do not
fall in arrears in our rent." A roofer asks "Taishi-sama" to protect him
from falling off roofs and for plenty of work worth "three or four yen"
to come his way. An ambitious carpenter prays for no less than "one
hundred apprentices" and a lifestyle to match. "Please grant this wish,"
begins a plasterer, "that I get work in hundreds of mansions of the
aristocrats and that I'll have nothing to do with such things as tenement
houses (*nagaya fushin*)." A proud woodworker, apparently also a bach-
elor, fancies a sharp saw and the ability to do work vigorously. But that

is not all, for he also wonders if the deity can "fix him up" (*osewa*) with a "wife who can make a lot of money and feed" him. "My son is too good-looking," mourns the mother of a joiner, and "all the young girls in the neighborhood fall for him and he won't begin to work. Since his loafing around just won't do, please prevent girls from falling in love with him."[22]

In general, popular images of the emperor before the Meiji era tended to be nonpolitical and rooted in folk religions, rather than political and representational of the national community. The historian and ethnographer Miyata Noboru has used collections of popular legends of emperors to argue that the belief in emperors and imperial princes, which existed in some areas of Japan, overlapped with folk beliefs in *marebito*—that is, sacred beings who were thought to make visitations on the village world and who supposedly dispensed tangible this-worldly benefits to the people. The common folk believed that these emperors had brought or continued to bring such benefits as the creation of sacred rivers, bountiful and often unique crops (such as chestnuts bearing imperial toothmarks), and protection against various natural or magical threats to crops. Moreover, the *tennō* (emperor) was often fused in the popular mind with another *tennō*, *gozu tennō*, the deity of popular folklore believed to ward off evils and calamities.[23]

During the Tokugawa period, then, Japan was populated by a people separated from one another regionally, with strong local rather than national ties. Horizontal social cleavages also marked off each social estate from the others, thus precluding the development of a strong sense of shared cultural identity. In addition, the common people's knowledge of the emperor, potentially the most powerful symbol of the Japanese nation, was nonexistent, vague, or fused with folk beliefs in deities who might grant worldly benefits but who had little to do with the nation. Thus the leaders of the Meiji regime needed novel and powerful means of channeling the longings of the people for a better world and the inchoate and scattered sense of identity as a people in the direction of modern nationalism.

Mnemonic Sites

The new rulers could and did use speech and writing to explain the centrality of the emperor in national life. From the early

Meiji years, government authorities in the provinces often wrote public notices for the common people about the emperor. An early notice drawn up by the Nagasaki courthouse explained in the easily understood vernacular that "in this land called Japan there is one called the Emperor (*tenshisama*) who is descended from the Sun Deity (*tenshō kōtai jin-gūsama*). This has not changed a bit from long ago and just like the Sun being up in the heavens He is the Master (*goshujinsama ja*)." In the "Official Notice to the People of Mutsu and Dewa" (*Ōu jinmin kokuyu*), the authorities explained the political and religious significance of the emperor in a similar way: "The Emperor is the descendant of the Sun Deity and has been the Master (*nushi*) of Japan since the beginning of the world. All the rankings of the various deities of the provinces, such as 'first rank,' have been granted by the Emperor. Therefore, He is indeed loftier than the deities, and every foot of ground and every person belongs to the Emperor."[24] Such government agents as *senkyōshi* (state propagandists) and later *kyōdōshoku* (national priests), who were appointed in the early Meiji years to preach to the masses, continued to edify the people with homilies. In late 1870 in Kikuma *han*, for example, the local representative of the central government designated two local Buddhist priests as educators (*kyōyushi*). They spoke on patriotism, the worship of national deities, Confucius and Mencius, and the proper method of prayer for worshipping at shrines.

While the central government could not strictly control all the activities of the *kyōdōshoku*, it directed these preachers especially to encourage patriotism and reverence for the emperor and the national gods. The government also instructed them to instill in the people a wide range of values and learning that together were deemed to form a core of knowledge for all Japanese. This knowledge ranged from the moral value of loyalty to international relations and "civilization and enlightenment."

The verbal exhortations sometimes brought completely unintended results. The people in Mikawa, for example, thought that the *kyōyushi*, dressed as they were in unfamiliar green garments and preaching what were to them unusual doctrines, were "Christians" bent on transforming their world. An antigovernment uprising ensued. Since the government appointed local religious leaders as *kyōdōshoku*, appointees often were more interested in using their positions to preach their own particular religious beliefs than in educating the masses about matters of national and political significance. The people also sometimes misconstrued the messages and hence the significance of the official agents.

This happened, for example, when the abbot (*monshu*) of the Nishi Honganji denomination of the Shinshū sect preached in Kyushu. The Shinshū believers treated the *monshu* as the Shinshū religious leader he was by spontaneously throwing money offerings (*saisen*) at him and reciting the Shinshū *nembutsu* prayer to Amida. Nevertheless, by 1880 there were more than a hundred thousand *kyōdōshoku* throughout the nation who expounded on the centrality of the emperor and the gods in national life.[25]

Yet the rulers' attempt to involve the common people in the culture of the national community was not limited to words and preaching. As a result of policies that Chamberlain described as "consciously or semi-consciously put together by the official class, in order to serve the interests of that class," the everyday world of the masses came to be filled with an extraordinary profusion of nonverbal official signs and the dominant meanings, customs, and practices associated with them. In this book I am attentive to two types of what I will call mnemonic sites:[26] that is, material vehicles of meaning that either helped construct a memory of an emperor-centered national past that, ironically, had never been known or served as symbolic markers for commemorations of present national accomplishments and the possibilities of the future.

The first such site was that of ritual. It is not at all difficult to establish that ever since the Meiji Restoration, ritual making has been a central concern of Japan's governing elites. This modern obsession with ritual can certainly be traced back to thinkers of the late Tokugawa era and to the policies of several important domains in that period.[27] But during the Meiji years and later, Japan's governing elites invented, revived, manipulated, and encouraged national rituals with unprecedented vigor. Through rites the rulers hoped to bring this territory, which had been segmented into horizontally stratified estates and vertically divided regions, under one ruler, one legitimating sacred order, and one dominant memory. From an early date the leaders of the Meiji government fostered rites at the tens of thousands of shrines scattered throughout the nation. Through an edict issued on 5 April 1868[28] only months after the restoration, they resuscitated the anachronistic-sounding Department of Shinto Affairs (Jingikan), encouraged rites for the national gods, and attached all shrines and Shinto functionaries directly to the Jingikan. During the course of the Meiji-Taishō period the government established uniform guidelines for rites to be performed at all shrines throughout the nation. The government's specialists on Shinto rituals generally modeled these newly prescribed rites for local shrines on rites performed within the imperial household and thereby gave local rites an imperial and a national significance.[29] Just as they had promised in their early declarations calling for the "unity of rites and governance" (*saisei itchi*), the rulers had made the performance of rituals an inextricable part of governance. Local rites had become politicized as they became sites of official memories, and through them national politics became ritualized.

National holidays were also an invented site or device for the remembrance of a mytho-history which had never been known. In the period through 1945, and even to some extent after the Second World War, Japan's national holidays have expressed the idea that the national community and the imperial institution are coterminous both forward and backward in time. The invention of Japan's national holidays began in January 1873, with the establishment of two holidays: one to celebrate the accession of Japan's first ruler, Emperor Jimmu, and the other to celebrate the reigning emperor's birthday. In November of the same year the government added six holidays, and in June 1878, another two. The ten official national holidays celebrated in the period between June 1878 and 1927 were the following: (1) Empire Festival (*genshisai*, 3 January), which commemorated the descent to earth of the Sun Goddess's grandchild, Ninigi-no-mikoto, and therefore commemorated the beginning of eternal rule over the nation by the Sun Goddess's descendants; (2) New Year's (*shinnen enkai*, 5 January); (3) Emperor Kōmei Festival (*Kōmei tennō sai*, 30 January), which was intended to memorialize each previously reigning emperor and which was therefore replaced by Emperor Meiji Festival (30 July) and Emperor Taishō Festival (25 December) during the next two reigns; (4) National Foundation Day (*kigensetsu*, 11 February), meaning literally the beginning of time, history, or narrative, which commemorated the accession of Emperor Jimmu; (5) Imperial Ancestors' Spring Memorial Festival (*shunki kōreisai*, vernal equinox); (6) Emperor Jimmu Festival (*Jimmu tennōsai*, 3 April), which memorialized Jimmu's death; (7) Imperial Ancestors' Autumn Memorial Festival (*shūki kōreisai*, autumnal equinox); (8) Offering of the First Fruits Festival (*kannamesai*, initially 17 September but moved to 17 October in 1879), which consisted of the offering of the first fruits of the harvest at Ise Shrine and from 1871 at the Imperial Palace's *kashikodokoro*; (9) Emperor's Birthday (*tenchōsetsu*, during Meiji's reign 3 November); and (10) Rice Harvest Festival (*niinamesai*, 23 November), which, although an agricultural festival, had from prehistoric times become associated with the ritualized regeneration of the imperial soul within the reigning emperor. In 1927, the total number of holidays increased to eleven with the addition of Emperor Meiji Day (*Meijisetsu*, 3 November), a holiday commemorating Meiji's virtues.[30]

While the political rituals described above focused on the emperor's material traces, that is, on signs of the emperor's absent presence, the late nineteenth- and early twentieth-century architects of the modern imperial institution also fabricated an enormous number of new rituals performed by the emperor himself. Murakami Shigeyoshi, a tireless compiler of information on religion and politics in modern Japan, has pointed out that the great majority of even those archaic-looking rites performed within the innermost recesses of the palace, the Imperial Household Rites (*kōshitsu saishi*), were invented after the Restoration; moreover, eleven of the thirteen rites performed by the emperor himself had no historical precedents.[31]

In fact, every major political event seemed to warrant the production of some new imperial ritual. On the day after the rulers established the Jingikan in April of 1868, the emperor conducted a specially devised ritual within the Kyoto Palace to set out the basic principles of the regime as outlined in the famous Charter Oath. A few days later he officiated at a military ritual held before the national gods to report a military expedition to the east against the last supporters of the Tokugawa *bakufu* (central government). The ritual makers also refashioned the imperial accession ceremonies, one of which took place in Kyoto (*sokui shiki*, 10 October 1868) and another in Tokyo (*daijōsai*, 28 December 1871).[32]

The most spectacular state ceremonials of Japan's modernity, however, were the great imperial pageants that brought the emperor, his family, and the military and civil members of his regime directly before the masses, and these constitute the main focus of this book. Until the late 1880s, the dominant form of public imperial pageantry was the progress—a style of ritual in which the emperor traveled around the countryside watching and being watched by the people who were becoming the Japanese. These progresses began with a trip from Kyoto to Osaka in the spring of 1868 and then another to Tokyo later that year. Such large-scale progresses continued through most of the first two decades of the Meiji era, taking the emperor as far north as Hokkaido and to the southern tip of Kyushu.

From the late 1880s, however, the Meiji regime's public rituals took on their full-blown modern form, with Tokyo and to some extent Kyoto used as central and open stages for a dazzling new assortment of imperial pageants. All of these were influenced by Western models, even the most archaic looking of them, and some of them—such as imperial weddings and wedding anniversary celebrations—had no precedents whatsoever in the ceremonial vocabulary. The most spectacular pageants of the late nineteenth and early twentieth centuries included celebrations of political accomplishments such as the promulgation of the Meiji Constitution, war victory ceremonials, and imperial funerals, weddings, and wedding anniversaries.

The power of these ceremonials as mnemonic sites may perhaps be gauged from a particularly revealing memoir by the writer Tayama Katai. In his reminiscences of more than thirty years spent in Tokyo beginning in the early 1880s, Tayama recalled the days preceding the most dramatic of the national pageants he was ever to witness, the funeral of Emperor Meiji. The newspapers, he remembered, had informed the public of the emperor's critical illness in late July 1912. Within four or five days an endless stream of people began flowing into the area of the plaza facing the Nijūbashi entranceway to the palace to pray for the emperor's recovery. The following passage describes Tayama's feelings:

His Majesty (*heika*) the Emperor Meiji, Mutsuhito the Great, the Lord of Restoration—as a young child His Highness (*seijō*) grew up through adversity, then overcame numerous difficulties and dangers, finally leading Japan to its exalted level of civilization in the world today. In reflecting on the life of His Highness there was no one who could hold back a flood of tears.

I knew that I would someday have to bid His Majesty farewell. I could not have been alone. Surely all the Japanese people (*kokumin*) must have thought so. The Great Ceremony of Accession, the Rite Transferring the Capital—these I was too young to have seen; but whenever His Majesty's honor guards rode majestically through the streets I always mixed into the crowds of roadside onlookers and beheld his dignified countenance, if only from a distance. Then came the move from the Aoyama Palace to the Imperial Palace, the Rites of Investiture as Crown Prince, and the Grand Marriage Ceremony for our present emperor; at that time my wife and I went all the way out to Akasaka Mitsuke to view it. Yet I had never imagined that the Imperial Funeral would come so soon, before we could take part in the jubilee for the fiftieth year of his reign.

The announcement of Emperor Meiji's death came on a hot, hot, day in late July that I will not forget . . . "Ahh, he has finally passed on."

In thinking this an inexpressible feeling came over me. My mind was filled with a confusion of all sorts of things. The Saigo Rebellion (1877)—my father had died in that campaign. Then came the Sino-

Japanese War. During the Russo-Japanese War I served in a photography unit and saw with my own eyes the splendor of His Majesty's august virtue shine over the Eight Quarters of the World (*hakkō ni kagayaku miitsu*). When I saw the Rising Sun flag glittering from the enemy position at Nanshan in Jinzhou my heart leapt with joy. I could not help but feel that within my blood flowed the warm blood of the Japanese people. Philosophically, I am a "freethinker," but in my soul I am one of the Great Japanists (*dainihonshugi no hitori*) after all.[33]

By the end of the Meiji period the Japanese people had become accustomed to the observance of spectacular public ceremonies marking important moments in the life of the nation. For Tayama the death and funeral of Emperor Meiji brought back a torrent of memories in which these imperial ceremonies, national symbols, national wars, the nation in world civilization, the imperial family, the national monarch, and national sentiments came together in a dizzying circulation of signs and meanings. These memories evoked feelings of love and respect for the emperor, pride in being Japanese, and a sense of communion with other Japanese ("I could not have been alone. Surely all the Japanese people [*kokumin*] must have thought so") and helped overcome ambivalence about his father's death. They left him with the tragic conviction that while a "freethinker," he was in spirit a die-hard supporter of the Japanese empire who could even rejoice in the expansionist enterprise.

Yet imperial ceremonies, the many symbols of which they were made, the space in which they were performed, the sacred places that gave the ceremonies their cosmological meaning—these had not existed in their early twentieth-century forms since ancient times. In fact, many had been created out of whole cloth during Tayama's lifetime.

The invention of Japan's modern national ceremonies was, quite simply, a response to specific domestic and international political forces of the late nineteenth and early twentieth centuries. Before then the open area in front of the Imperial Palace where the Japanese people went to pray for the emperor's recovery had not existed. The Imperial Palace had been an old and dilapidated castle. Nijūbashi, one of the most powerful of Japan's national symbols to which busloads of Japanese citizens still make their pilgrimages, had been little more than an aging bridge. The Japanese had neither a national flag nor an anthem. The great majority of common people did not recognize the emperor as the central symbol of the Japanese nation; nor did they have a sense of national identity. Thus, Tayama's memories—made of national symbols, imperial pageants, strong national sentiments, and adoration of the Japanese monarch—were those of a Japanese who had experienced the modern governing elites' energetic creation of a culture of nationalism.

These imperial pageants, themselves mnemonic sites and vehicles of meaning, tended to generate further signs in the official system of representations. For example, they led to the creation of nationally significant memorial days. Because the promulgation of the Meiji Constitution took place on *kigensetsu*, the Japanese people celebrated 11 February of each year as both Constitution Day (*kenpō kinenbi*) and as the holiday solemnizing the founding of the Japanese empire.[34] The day is still observed today as National Foundation Day (*kenkoku kinen no hi*). In 1917 the annual spring and fall festivals at Yasukuni Shrine were changed to 30 April and 23 October to commemorate the Triumphal Military Review of 1906 and the Triumphal Naval Review of October 1905, respectively.[35]

Written and visual representations of these ritual events also proliferated. They have been the subjects of numerous anecdotal reminiscences of life during the first half-century of Japan's modern regime (for example, in Natsume Sōseki's widely read novel *Kokoro*). And nearly all Japanese are familiar with at least a few of these late nineteenth- to early twentieth-century pageants, not only through written testimonies, but also because impressive visual images of them remain. These include a huge number of colorful woodblock prints and other pictures (such as the paintings in the Memorial Picture Gallery), lithographs, photographs, and commemorative stamps and postcards, as well as reproductions of all the above in places such as school textbooks.

The pageants left permanent imprints on the city as well as on other places in the nation, especially Kyoto. Most important, those directing the rebuilding of the Imperial Palace—with the area in front cleared of nearly all structures in order to accommodate great crowds and ceremonies—timed the completion of the construction to coincide with the Meiji Constitution's promulgation ceremonies; and the Tokyo city government, under the guidance of the central government, built the broad thoroughfares now crisscrossing the Outer Garden of the Imperial Palace (*kōkyo gaien*) as triumphal avenues (*gaisen dōro*) for the Triumphal Military Review of April 1906.[36] Emperor Meiji's funeral site became in 1926 the location for the Memorial Picture Gallery (Seitoku Kinen Kaigakan), the centerpiece of a cluster of Meiji commemorative structures situated in the Meiji Shrine Outer Garden (Meiji Jingū Gaien). Dominating the end of an expansive gingko-lined avenue, it houses some eighty large murals depicting important events in the lives of Emperor Meiji and his consort, Empress Dowager Shōken. Behind the gallery building a camphor tree—or *kusunoki*, surely not coincidentally a homophone of the name of the famous fourteenth-century loyal imperial retainer Kusunoki Masashige—marks the place where the Emperor Meiji's funeral carriage was put out for public viewing following the obsequies. Nearby is a small *enoki* tree commemorating Emperor Meiji's numerous military reviews at what was then the Aoyama Military Parade Field.[37] At Ueno Park the impressive Hyōkeikan edifice (completed 1909), an addition to what was then the Imperial Museum, stands as a monument commemorating the wedding of Crown Prince Yoshihito (Emperor Taishō). The building had been a wedding gift from the citizens of Tokyo.[38] In the southeastern hills of Kyoto the Fushimi Momoyama Mausoleum, completed shortly after Emperor Meiji's funeral, sits in subdued grandeur on the highest point in an expansive imperial forest of native trees and shrubs.

The second type of mnemonic site this book attempts to identify and analyze is, in fact, the material sign on the physical landscape. As in most other newly forming nations, the leaders of the Meiji regime initially found themselves with a fairly meaningless natural terrain, from the point of view of a dominant national memory and discourse. However, through a calculated transformation of the physical appearance of various shrines, buildings, and other public places, they gave new meanings to the acquired territory. On a rather unpretentious level, the people witnessed a veritable wave of "statumania," beginning in 1893 with the erection of a bronze of the national and military hero Ōmura Masujirō. Before that time there had been no tradition of public statuary celebrating national heroes. Japan's rulers also built new shrines to national gods, past emperors, and national heroes and merged, destroyed, or otherwise manipulated shrines that did not contribute to the emperor- and nation-centered memory. An example of the latter was the demotion of the great anti-imperial rebel Taira no Masakado in 1874 from one of two central deities of Kanda Shrine in Tokyo to one of several secondary deities there because of the unfortunate countermemory he represented. A modern monumentalism in the building of gateways (*torii*) to national shrines also dates from the late nineteenth century.[39]

On a much more grandiose scale, Japan's two capital cities (in an administrative sense modern Japan has had one capital, but in a symbolic sense it has had two) and Ise Shrine were manufactured into three of the most important points on what might be thought of as Japan's modern symbolic topography. Kyoto, filled with physical reminders that it had served as the seat of the imperial court for more than a millennium, became a representation of the depth of the imperial institution's historical past. It became the nucleus of the officially prescribed notion of "tradition." Ise Shrine, reconstituted from its importance during the Edo period as primarily a center of a nonpolitical folk religion, gave visible form to the official assertion that both the imperial institution and the nation had emerged out of a past that blended into the "age of the gods." In the final decade of the nineteenth century, Tokyo, physically different in many respects from both Edo and Tokyo of the early Meiji years, had become an official sign of Japan's progress and prosperity. These dominant meanings had not simply existed "out there," as a part of the natural terrain. They were purposely invented, created, as a part of the culture of the modern nation.[40]

Toward a Historical Ethnography of the Nation-State

The production of an official "memoryscape,"[41] located materially in time and space, and indeed the obsessive manufacturing of official culture in general, must be placed within the context of a dramatic transformation in the attitude of the rulers toward the ruled, which began in the late Tokugawa period and culminated in the years following the Meiji Restoration. For most of the Tokugawa period, the governing samurai elite had separated themselves from the governed and ruled under the premise that politics was the special prerogative of their estate. Under this system of rule, as the historian and political scientist Maruyama Masao put it many years ago, "Tokugawa feudal society remained divided into two parts. On the one hand the samurai class functioned as the sole political agents vis-à-vis the common people and took all political responsibility upon themselves. In contrast, the common people, who constituted more than 90 percent of the total population, were forced to 'depend' (*yorashimu*) passively on the given order as no more than the objects of political control. How could one speak of a unified nation when rulers and subjects were rigidly separated socially?"[42]

However, as historians such as Yasumaru Yoshio have noted, the last decades of the Edo period witnessed a radical reversal in the attitude of the rulers toward the ruled. While the samurai political elite under the earlier Tokugawa system had been content with the passive compliance of the common folk, the ignorant masses (*gumin*), the new Meiji rulers began to demand the active spiritual participation of the common people in the realization of national objectives.[43] As I would describe it, they hoped to reconstitute the people into more than simply objects of rule, so that they could become knowledgeable and self-disciplined subjects in the dual Foucauldian sense—that is, subjects who were not only subjected to "control and dependence" but who were also subjects possessed of their own identity by a "conscience or self-knowledge."[44]

This new conception of rule unleashed a torrent of policies aimed at bringing the common people into a highly disciplined national community and a unified and totalizing culture. A kind of cultural terror, understood as being pedagogical, swept through local communities as the state's agents attacked folk religions through the destruction or manipulation of local shrines and the suppression of "irrational" beliefs—whether they were of shamans, diviners, or what were called *inshi,* evil deities—while also instructing them in proper modes of worship. The new rulers preached ideas about "civilization and enlightenment" while also prohibiting numerous folk practices, such as extravagance in festivities, either to gods or Buddhas, or excessive leisure and gambling.[45] From a very early date, in fact, the state's cultural policies reached down to the most mundane level. In Tokyo, for example, the authorities launched aggressive campaigns against mixed bathing, public nudity, and urinating in public (*tachi shōben*). In 1876, the Tokyo police arrested 2,091 people for nudity and 4,495 others for urinating in public.[46] And in what was then called Toyooka Prefecture, the authorities prohibited a seemingly innocuous summer custom, daytime napping.[47]

This attention to the culture of everyday life, I believe, reflected not simply an impatience with the stupidity of the common people but a great faith in their ability to be educated—that is, a conviction that if properly instructed, the formerly despised commoner could become an informed and responsible member of the national community. This of course does not mean that the Meiji state abandoned physical violence as an instrument of social control or that it did not attempt to place limits on the spread of certain types of knowledge. But it is important to recognize that Japan's modern political leaders, no less than their counterparts in the liberal nation-states of Europe and the United States, conceived of the entire cultural apparatus of the modern state as a mechanism for enlightening the masses. Control through official culture was not understood in the negative images familiar to most students of Japan's so-called emperor system—such as shackling, enslaving, blinding, and making submissive, frustrating the development of a modern subjectivity[48]—but rather in positive terms, as a means of sweeping away ignorance, inflexibility, or darkness, and thus as knowledge in the positive sense. For example, in a memorial urging an imperial progress to Hokkaido, probably drawn up in July 1875, Sanjō Sanetomi, then grand minister of state (*dajō daijin*), argued that "the people in remote regions are almost all accustomed to old thoughts and mired in ancient customs" and that the "extension of the emperor's power to the remote regions" would result not only in an increase in "national prestige" (*kokui*) but also in "the advancement of the narrow and inflexible people into enlightenment" (*korō no jinmin yōyaku kaimei ni susumi*).[49]

The Meiji Restoration was thus revolutionary in the sense that such historians of the French Revolution as Lynn Hunt and Mona Ozouf have ascribed to the revolutionary politics of that more famous historical moment. They have argued that a central, if not the central, feature of the French Revolution was its faith in the ability of politics to refashion the everyday life and mentalities of a people.[50] The Meiji Restoration was every bit as revolutionary. For like its French counterpart the Japanese revolution set off a double movement of the "political." By this I mean that while it expanded, once and for all, the shape of the polity so that government became, most preeminently, that of the nation-state, at the same time the Meiji Revolution, propelled by a faith in human plasticity and a new civilizing mission for the state, extended the state's reach into the very souls of the people.

What Yasumaru and others have been writing about is the intellectual background to and the creation of what I call the folklore, in the broad sense of the term, of the modern Japanese regime. I have borrowed the idea of a "folklore of a regime" from the French historian Maurice Agulhon; and by it I refer to that homogenized, official culture fostered by the state, which has included various rites, symbols, customs, beliefs, and practices.[51] These were perhaps even more important to ruling than the formally written down ideas supporting the regime, because they could more easily infiltrate everyday folk life, because they could in many instances be unconsciously inscribed in daily practices and on bodies (for example, in the form of clothing, hairstyles, modes of physical deportment, and the like), and because their recent invention could more easily be forgotten. This folklore contrasted with the conventional folklore of the populace—that is, with the rites, symbols, customs, beliefs, and practices that made up the life of the common people before the rise of the new regime. By its nature the conventional folklore was localized and diverse—heterogeneous, fragmented, and dissonant within itself—thus contrasting with the national, uniform, and totalizing nature of the new folklore. The modern Japanese experience was by no means unique, for wherever ruling elites have attempted to form nation-states, they have fabricated such folklores for their regimes.[52] Whatever else it may also have been, the modern nation-state's eruption into history was thus a cultural emergence, and the method of approaching its history should include a cultural analysis.

Methodologically, we need to begin by subjecting the folklore of Japan's modern regime to the ethnographer's near-obsession with the description and analysis of signs, however trivial they might at first seem. Thus in looking at the mnemonic device of imperial pageantry, for example, we ought to be attentive to the minutiae of ritualized representations, for there we will discover a host of meanings that were apparently congenial to the interests of Japan's modern state—ideas about the sacred, the emperor, the nation, the family, prosperity, tradition, gender, and much else. Official ideologies were meticulously displayed in the multiple scenes of the performances, painstakingly inscribed directly onto the bodies of the emperor and members of his entourage, and brilliantly represented in the mise-en-scènes upon which the symbolic action took place and in the costumes worn by the many actors. Details as seemingly arbitrary as a moustache, a hairstyle, a particular clothing fashion, an intimation of gender, the choice of a mode of transport (ox-drawn wagon, English carriage, or open car, for example)—all these were intentionally fabricated and meaningful signs, together forming systems of signs designed to convey particular messages to the Japanese people and to the world. We must begin by taking these performances as seriously as their creators did, by describing and analyzing their representations with the same recognition of their importance that they took in producing them.

In this I, like many others who have turned toward the study of "rites of power,"[53] follow the lead of Clifford Geertz, who has put the ethnographic approach at the center of his methodology and who has urged us to view the symbolic as an integral and not epiphenomenal dimension of politics. "The real is as imagined as the imaginary," he has said. "The dramas of the theater state, mimetic of themselves, were, in the end, neither illusions nor lies, neither sleight of hand nor make-believe. They were what there was."[54] Yet Geertz's brand of analysis is too assuming of a cultural unity or consensus—both over time and within a political system—so that he prevents us from seeing how those in power serve their own interests by inventing rites, signs, customs, and practices and by constructing dominant meanings.[55]

The bulk of Geertz's work is profoundly ahistorical. His nineteenth-century "theater state" in Bali, for example, does have a dynamic temporal movement—but it is a circular and repetitive one. In this scenario lords and lineages rise and fall in a constant struggle for power, but culturally nothing significant ever changes. Rather, the divine king cult at the heart of his poetics of power turns out to be "an essentially constant cultural form." In fact, Geertz's state theater is not the theater of a particular court at all: it is "a conceptual entity, not a historical one." And with the proper adjustments made for time and space, the model can be used to guide one through all of "Indic civilization in Indonesia and beyond"! The model of *negara*, Geertz claims, "is a guide, a sort of sociological blueprint, for the construction of representations, not necessarily or even probably identical to it in structure, of a whole set of relatively less well-known but presumptively similar institutions: the classical Southeast Asian Indic state of the fifth to fifteenth centuries."[56] Culture, it seems, is not only essentially frozen in time, it is transportable from one place to another.

Here there is no room for a consideration of cultural discontinuity, for a Foucauldian attention to the historical ruptures behind which lie the play of power. While Foucault's genealogical method is based upon a distrust of the seemingly similar over time, Geertz actively seeks out and simply assumes historical continuity. Thus, "Bali in the latter half of the nineteenth century may not have been a mere replica of Bali in the middle of the fourteenth, but it was at least fully continuous with it, a reasonably regular development out of it. . . . No cultural fossil, this tight little island was nonetheless, like Tibet or Yemen, culturally quite conservative."[57] While there is more than a touch of Orientalism here, the same sort of attention to continuity can be found in Geertz's statements about Western cultures. Cultural idioms may differ from place to place, and they may change over time to some extent, but according to his argument, "cultural frame[s]" or "master fictions" construct politics and political leaders, and not the other way around. This is the same everywhere, whether it be "Germany or France, India or Tanzania (to say nothing of Russia or China)."[58]

In short, for Geertz rites of rulers are sensible because they dramatize the cultural values that have been shared by rulers and ruled alike—since who knows when. Rulers are recognized as legitimate because they place themselves in the cultural frameworks that already unify a people. Though culture for Geertz may not be quite the neat, "seamless web of significances" propounded by Max Weber—perhaps, he has argued, it more closely resembles a gangling octopus[59]—it is still a consensual web. Power is in large part actualized through the performance of ideas already in everybody's head.

Yet the production of official culture in Japan during the late nineteenth and early twentieth centuries testifies to the fact that elements in the symbolic dimension of politics can be as much invented as inherited. This is clear, for example, in the area of official culture that has occupied much of Geertz's attention—namely, state pageantry. Though not always successful, political elites in modern Japan manufactured ideas through the manipulation of publicly ritualized imagery, and they were often quite conscious of doing so. Itō Hirobumi, for example, understood that there might be a vast gap between folk culture and the newly created national culture centering on Japan's emperor. In a talk presented to the Survey Bureau for Imperial Household Institutions (*Teishitsu seido chōsakyoku*), of which he had just become president, he explained that with regard to the construction of imperial funerals, popular traditions should not constrain official inventiveness. He concluded, "The imperial household should not by any means emulate the popular customs and practices which have developed naturally in accordance with such religions as Buddhism."[60]

The "folklore of a regime" concept facilitates a move toward a more truly historicized ethnography. On the one hand, by disjoining the cultures of the masses from the official culture at a particular historical moment, it allows us to recognize the historical contingency of the national culture that was imposed by those in power and that now tends to be assumed as natural and timeless. On the other hand, by suggesting the importance of ethnographic detail, it forces us to get at the meanings of rites, symbols, customs, and practices, so that we are not left with a simple functionalist interpretation of the culture of the nation—that is, that culture was invented to foster and reflect a sense of national unity. Such a Durkheimian argument would not be so much wrong as it would be too reductionist, privileging culture's function to the exclusion of its content.

A comprehensive historical ethnography of the modern Japanese regime's folklore would consider all those areas of culture the rulers created, treating them as a result of the decisive shattering of their old perception of ruling the populace through a fragmented rather than unified culture. This book focuses on the invention of the emperor and his traces—that is, the purposeful fabrication of the modern monarch and his cities, shrines, death monuments, commemorative buildings and monuments, pageants, and more. But because the imperial institution has for so many been seen as central to the Japanese nation and culture, this exercise of remembering its invention—which is to say, of dismembering official memories[61]—is also an exercise in the interrogation of nationalism.

Visual Domination

While I have thus far been able only to introduce the topic of the new visibility of the emperor and his signs and traces to the people and have merely touched on the idea of the people's visibility, during the late nineteenth and early twentieth centuries the people too became discernible to the emperor, or his agents. The emperor was not only a visible symbol that could represent the national totality; he was also a sign with an ability to look back at the people. All of the Meiji period's imperial pageants—whether the progresses, which had been modeled on the archaic rites of a reclaimed past, or the late Meiji spectacles, which adopted a new and international ceremonial idiom— helped establish historically unprecedented relationships of sight or visibility between the emperor and the Japanese people.

From one point of view, these public ceremonials made the emperor and his spectacles visible to all the people of the nation. In this relation the crowds viewing the pageantry (that is, the people) were the subjects of sight and the emperor and his ceremonials the objects of their observation. Yet the imperial pageants also coerced the people into becoming objects of the emperor's gaze. In this inverted ocular relationship, it was rather the people who became visible to him as he traveled throughout the country or as he looked upon them from his central location in Tokyo. Imperial pageantry was part of a cultural apparatus that helped fashion Japan's modern emperor into a transcendental subject, one who could be imagined as casting a single and centralizing gaze across all the nation and into the souls of all the people. Put in the obverse, it was a mechanism whereby all the people of the empire—not simply the people of a certain region (for example, in the area around the Kyoto Court) or the members of an aristocratic class (for example, the Kyoto courtiers)—were made visible to one dominating and all-seeing monarch. If this project had been completely successful, and there is no doubt that its successes were considerable, we can imagine the making of a modern citizenry with an interiorized sense of themselves as objects of an unremitting surveillance.

In other words, the great imperial pageants of the Meiji era were central to the construction of a kind of ocular domination in modern Japan, one that was both fully comparable to and yet different from the visual domination that, according to Michel Foucault, emerged in France around the time of the Enlightenment. As is well known, Foucault argued that Jeremy Bentham's model for the penitentiary—with its prisoners made completely visible to an anonymous gaze located in the structure's central tower—was a diagram of modern power. Because the Panopticon's arrangement made the prisoners in their cells visible from one central point in the structure's center while rendering the prison's Overseer invisible, prisoners could never know whether they were being observed. As a consequence they would always have to behave as if they were being watched—that is to say, they would have to internalize their own surveillance. Yet what we must recall about Foucault's postulation was that he was less concerned about the Panopticon as an instrument of the penal system than as a model of modern power that was replicated in practice throughout the social formation.

This is the way that I choose to think about the construction of the visionary emperor in Japan. I believe that Foucault's model explains better than any other how representations or demonstrations of the effects of the emperor's gaze upon the people both diagrammed and helped to produce the suspicion that the nation's subject-citizens might at any moment be objects of surveillance. While certainly not the only apparatus through which the disciplinary society came into being, the image of the seeing emperor facilitated the production of the nation-state as a bordered space of visibility within which the people could imagine themselves as objects of observation. The aspect of pageantry considered here does not so much concern ideologies but rather discipline, a dimension of both the emperor system and modern nationalism that has received scant attention. In this sense my proposed historical ethnography of the nation-state is nothing other than an ethnography of Japan's modernity.

This approach to analyzing the modern monarchy in Japan, like that of remembering its recent invention, forces us to abandon once and for all readings of the monarchy as a sign of the feudal, premodern, or backward. In this respect I consider myself to be among a number of scholars of the so-called emperor system who have begun in various ways to critique the view long espoused by Japanese Marxists of the *kōza* school, as well as modernists such as Maruyama Masao, that treated the prominence of the monarchy in modern history as a reflection of and reason for the incompleteness of Japan's modernity.[62] By resituating the emperor at the center of a modern panoptic regime, as I propose, we see not only that the cults of nation and emperor were created in relatively modern times, but also that what has been called the emperor system, far from being characterized by its "feudal" characteristics, was central to the production of Japan's modernity.

But herein also lies a major difference between my appropriation of a Foucauldian framework and Foucault's own historicization of what he calls the "surveillance society." While he sees the rise of this modern society coming in conjunction with the decline of the monarchy, or at least of "monarchical power," I describe both sorts of power as coming together at the same historical moment in Japan. What I mean by this should become clearer as I proceed, but suffice it to note at this point that it would be wrong to replicate earlier work done on the Japanese monarchy, whether of the Marxist or modernist variety, insofar as they unwittingly accept the post-Enlightenment narrative of historical stages that is also to be found even in Foucault's framework. This narrative, originating in the Western European and North American experiences, reads monarchical regimes as the temporal "others" of the modern, a stage, in other words, that must be overcome in order for modernity and progress to appear in their plenitude.

To be sure, it could be argued that the misrecognition of the Japanese monarchy as feudal or premodern served at a particular historical junc-ture—especially during the 1930s—as a means by which to achieve an exteriority and thereby to enable a critique of the modern regime itself. Yet today such a mode of criticism would be disenabling because it would play into the idea that politically, Japan and its people have never been modern enough. Such a view, though critical of contemporary politics in Japan, would continue to allow the displacement of our discontent with modernity onto a Japanese past called "feudal"; furthermore, it would preclude the possibility of turning the gaze emanating from the modern West back onto itself. Most important, it would keep us from recognizing that the subject-citizen produced by the Japanese emperor-centered regime no longer appears so different from the hero of modern bourgeois civil society, the supposedly autonomous subject that people like Maruyama Masao have so long sought.

In the limited sense that I am placing the Japanese monarchy at the heart of Japan's modernity, it is true that (oddly enough) my position bears some similarity to that of the modernization theorist John Whitney Hall. For in his highly influential essay, "A Monarch for Modern Japan," Hall argued that the Japanese monarchy was not only compatible with modernity, but that it had in fact played an important role in Japan's modernization. Yet at least two irreconcilable differences distinguish my perspective from that of such modernization theorists. First, while mine is critical of the monarchy and the nation-state in Japan, Hall's was a defense of the monarchy against the polemical writings of Marxists and such modernists as Maruyama. In effect, Hall praised the monarchy for its ability to provide social stability—whether in the post-Meiji years or in the years following the Second World War in Asia and the Pacific—and to inspire the Japanese people toward capitalism and democracy. Moreover, his essay was fully compatible with U.S. cold war policy in East Asia and ought to be considered an ideological text that legitimated restitution of the monarchy in postwar Japan in order to hold back a more radical social transformation.

Second, when he did have something mildly negative to say about the monarchy—for example, that it had been used by the right wing in the dark days of Shōwa—this was attributed to "the most traditional and irrational inheritances which the emperor had brought with him out of the Japanese past." Thus in contrast to my interpretation, Hall's is characterized by the attribution of all negative aspects of Japan's nineteenth- and twentieth-century experience to some vaguely understood premodern past. Hall wore the friendly face of liberal-rationalism and was full of confidence about "progress," defined as emulation of the Western capitalist democracies; and he was completely uncritical about national modernity as it had emerged in nineteenth- and twentieth-century Japan, let alone anywhere else. Put differently, within his post-Enlightenment framework of knowledge, or epistemology, and despite attacking them, Hall in fact shared the perspective of the

Marxists and modernists that the tragedies of modern Japan had stemmed from the country, and perhaps even the monarchy, not being modern enough.[63]

◆I◆

My own examination of the monarchy and national modernity in this book is made up of three main parts. Part 1 focuses on the years in which the primary form of state pageantry was the imperial progress. During that time the Meiji political elite constructed the emperor as the roaming Ruler who ministered to the people while integrating the territory under his visible and visibly seeing presence. This was the period when the emperor's court became a court in motion, and it was also the historical moment during which minimal thought was given to fashioning either Kyoto or Tokyo into symbolic and ritual centers. I argue that the emergence of such an understanding of Kyoto's and more centrally Tokyo's potential as centers of national meaning and as public arenas for imperial pageantry set the stage for the decline of the progresses and for the appearance of a new and more cosmopolitan style of public state rituals. Part 2 analyzes these new types of pageants and considers their relationship to the ritual and symbolic spaces on the physical terrain that had been constructed in the first two Meiji decades, and which are also discussed in Part 1. It is in Part 2 that I delve most deeply into the imagery of the modern monarchy; I argue that in the same way that the national landscape contained two capitals, Tokyo and Kyoto, the imperial body was in fact two bodies. Moreover, Tokyo, the center of progress, prosperity, military power, and Civilization, corresponded to—that is to say, was homological to—the masculinized, human, and politically engaged emperor, while Kyoto, the official representation of the past and Tradition, corresponded to the largely invisible, divine, timeless, and transcendent emperorship. Part 3 attempts to look at the newly constructed official world of mnemonic sites and the emperor's panoptic gaze from the point of view of the common people. One of my major arguments here is that however limited the Meiji regime might have been in producing a uniformity of belief or a uniformly self-disciplining population, its successes were considerable. Moreover, the imperial pageants as well as other elements in the regime's folklore certainly succeeded in producing a new sense of national simultaneity—a sharing of time among people who could not possibly have had face-to-face contact.

PART I

National Mise-en-Scène

CHAPTER TWO

From Court in Motion to Imperial Capitals

The place of the Emperor in Shinto should be mentioned. He is considered to be descended from the sun-goddess, Amaterasu-o-mikami. Some people connect Amaterasu with the sun; others say Nichirinsama and Amaterasu-o-mikami are different gods. The bowing of farmers to the east on arising is by some ascribed to reverence for the sun, by others to reverence for the Emperor (whose palace is to the east of Suye). When school children or a group of people at school bow to the east before beginning work on hand, it is definitely toward the Emperor's palace.

John F. Embree, *Suye Mura: A Japanese Village* (1939)

All nations have their sacred places: national cemeteries, monuments to commemorate significant events in the authoritative history, palaces or other official residences of royalty and heads of state, shrines to the gods of the national religion, and public statuary celebrating national heroes. Not only do a nation's subjects experience these sites in everyday life—directly as well as through photographs, paintings, and postcards—they even make special pilgrimages to them. In Japan, for example, school excursions (*shūgaku ryokō*) to such sites as Ise and Yasukuni Shrines, the Imperial Palace, Kyoto, and other points of interest highlighted in the official national history began as early as the 1880s and became a customary practice in nearly all elementary schools by the turn of this century.[1] And by the time the Japanese Empire had extended its reach into the South Pacific, groups of imperial subjects intent on taking in the national sights came not only from the ends of the Japanese archipelago but from as far away as the islands of Micronesia. Typically, a sight-seeing tour of local elites from the "South Seas" (Nan'yō) included pilgrimages to Yasukuni and Meiji Shrines, a walk down the fabulously modern Ginza Avenue, a visit to Nijūbashi, the "Double Bridge" leading into the Imperial Palace, a guided walk around the walls of the palace, and a round of *banzai*s to the emperor.[2]

The capital cities of most modern nation-states hold an extraordinarily large number of such sacred sites. Filled with objects of national significance, they form prominent points, or central landmarks, on what might be called a symbolic national topography. Moreover, in addition to dominating the symbolic dimension of national landscapes, the great capital cities of the world have also served as central arenas for the staging of national ceremonies.

During the nineteenth and twentieth centuries the governing elites in Europe, America, and elsewhere transformed their capitals into grand symbolic and ceremonial centers. Their style of city planning was characterized by the strategic siting of massive public buildings, expansive processional avenues, axial approaches to monuments and plazas, riveting scale, and enveloping greenery. In fact, in that age of rising nation-states a sort of international rivalry in the display of national power and prestige through urban architecture and space swept through Paris, Madrid, St. Petersburg, Vienna, Berlin, Rome, and Washington.[3] Washington, to take one example—with its center dominated by the Capitol, White House, and Washington Monument and unified by the Mall and the Pennsylvania Avenue processional route—began to take shape only in the latter half of the nineteenth century. In the 1830s, it had been "little more than an overgrown village spread loosely over its enormous site and dotted here and there with large but unrelated public buildings."[4] Even London, a capital often thought to be exceptional in its lack of attention to this style of city planning, experienced considerable embellishment during the late nineteenth and early twentieth centuries through the large-scale construction or rebuilding of national buildings and monuments.[5]

This wave of capital city reconstruction sent reverberations to places as far away as New Delhi and Canberra. Edwin Lutyens, the primary architect of New Delhi, designed the city with a long processional route that provided magnificent vistas of such monuments as the All-India Memorial Arch, the Jaipur Column, and above all the Viceroy's House perched atop Raisina Hill.[6] Though Canberra has never completely fulfilled the 1913 vision of its architect (the American Walter Burley

Griffin) as a majestic, monumental city, crowned by the purely symbolic Capitol Hill, it too bears the basic imprint of this modern style—a fact that was recently brought home by the opening of Australia's new Parliament House on Capitol Hill, which incidentally was timed to coincide with the two hundredth anniversary of British settlement. One architectural historian has explained the original vision: "Like the acropolis at Raisina, Capitol Hill was intended to be profoundly symbolic: although not meant to house the mechanism of government, its building was to serve as a ceremonial and archival center, commemorating Australian achievements and representing an emotional and spiritual focus of national life."[7]

Present-day observers of Tokyo have often remarked on the singularly unimposing appearance of Japan's capital, especially when compared to such cities as those mentioned above. The monumental architecture and the well-ordered avenues, they claim, are lacking; and the core of the city is conspicuous by its relative emptiness, the Imperial Palace's walls concealing the place which ought to display meaning most openly.[8] In typical fashion, the French semiotician Roland Barthes has observed that while Tokyo is similar to the vast majority of Western cities in its concentric design, it is aberrant in having a center which is empty rather than full of meaningful things. Thus Tokyo is described as a paradoxical city, one which is "built around an opaque ring of walls, streams, roofs, and trees whose own center is no more than an evaporated notion, subsisting here, not in order to irradiate power, but to give to the entire urban movement the support of its central emptiness, forcing the traffic to make a perpetual detour." Tokyo, in short, is deemed to have a structure quite different from cities consonant with "Western metaphysics."[9]

And yet, such views of Tokyo, which transform the city into an exotic abnormality, obstruct an understanding of Japan's capital as a city with a history in which its center has indeed been filled with meaning by a conscious governing elite. Though its appearance may not conform to modern Western standards, this fact should not deter us from understanding the enormous symbolic power of the city on its own terms. In the late nineteenth and early twentieth centuries it too became a place filled with significant monuments clustering around the core of the capital; and it too began to serve as a central arena for the performance of dramatic national ceremonials.

However, it is true that just after the Restoration of 1868 it was not by any means evident to Japan's modern rulers that Tokyo had, or for that matter needed, a symbolic and ceremonial dimension. There was confusion as well about what was to become of Kyoto, the ancient imperial capital. This is certainly not to say that the new government's leaders were inattentive to the symbolic and ritual dimension of politics, for they vigorously encouraged the building or refashioning of a host of shrines around the country to honor national gods, past emperors, and exemplary heroes. Moreover, Ōkubo Toshimichi and other powerful figures within the government launched the youthful Emperor Meiji (fifteen years old at the time of the Restoration, according to Western reckoning) on a series of stately progresses through the countryside.

This chapter's first section considers the rather startling fact that the new national leaders seemed almost totally unconcerned about reconstructing Tokyo into a visually impressive ceremonial and symbolic site during the first decade and a half or so of the Meiji period. This was in large part because the imperial progress or tour, rather than public ceremonials that might be performed in the capital, was the primary form of state pageantry. In fact, and this is the second issue to be taken up, I argue that the ideas of *sento*, transferring the capital, and *junkō*, the imperial progress, were inextricably intertwined in a much more ambitious attempt to construct the emperor as a Ruler who could both be seen and who could see the people and the land. This project privileged the urgent matter of getting the emperor out and in front of the people scattered throughout the realm rather than building Tokyo into a monumental city. The third issue concerns Kyoto. During approximately the first Meiji decade, the new leaders overlooked the possibilities offered by Kyoto as a symbolic center even more than they neglected Tokyo. Yet an awareness of its importance as the primary material site of the imperial memory—that is to say, the site of the imperial household and hence of the nation's past—began to appear at least by the early 1880s. Kyoto was then increasingly incorporated into the national ritual and symbolic topography. The chapter's fourth section discusses the new understanding of Tokyo and some of its most significant physical transformations, and in the last section I make a few final observations about the production of Japan's modern ritual and symbolic topography.

Tokyo as Temporary Court (*anzaisho*)

In 1898, Tokyo's citizens celebrated the thirtieth anniversary of the establishment of Japan's capital at Tokyo with the "greatest festival since the promulgation of the Meiji Constitution."[10] The occasion itself was splendid. The central ceremony took place in a specially constructed pavilion located on the Palace Plaza. Its highlight was an appearance of the emperor and empress, with an extolment of their virtues and praise for the establishment of the capital at Tokyo. Following this, various groups with moving displays paraded across the plaza and through the city, providing entertainment and articulating the significance of the event in more spectacular form. Some paraders masqueraded as members of a *daimyō* procession or as shogunal ladies-in-waiting. They evoked memories of the glorious days of the feudal lords in Edo. Others among them gave a more nationalistic, even jingoistic tone to the event. Two thousand marchers dressed as sailors pulled floats depicting a cannon and a warship. Still another group pulled a float carrying a figure of Yamato Takeru, the legendary military hero and imperial prince. Comic storytellers (*rakugoka*), with obvious reference to Japan's victory in the 1894–95 war with China, presented their rendering of the Peach Boy (*Momotarō*) legend: after squirming out of a gigantic peach, their hero Momotarō went on to conquer Demon Island and returned gloriously home with war treasures.

Tokyo's citizens did not limit their celebrating to the Palace Plaza as they put up arches, *torii* (shrine archways), and a variety of displays throughout the city. Most of these displays had nationalistic themes. In Kanda and Shin-Yoshiwara, for example, one could find figures of Jimmu Tennō, the supposed first emperor of Japan. Elsewhere they displayed the imperial prince Yamato Takeru, Jingū Kōgo (the legendary conquering empress who was supposed to have led military expeditions against the ancient Korean states), and the Tsurugi Sword, one of the imperial regalia. At Ueno Park, the second site for the festival, the special attractions included a new monument commemorating the promulgation of the Meiji Constitution and a huge fireworks display.[11]

But although Tokyo's people jubilantly commemorated the transfer of Japan's capital to their city, several men with firsthand knowledge of Emperor Meiji's move from Kyoto recalled in an interview that contrary to general belief, the new government's leaders immediately after the Restoration had had no intention whatsoever of establishing a single and permanent capital at Tokyo. Inoue Yorikuni, for example, a scholar of National Learning and an ideologue for the early Meiji government, argued that Kyoto continued to be important as an imperial city; in fact, he maintained, the government had never even designated Tokyo as an imperial capital, a *teito*. While admitting that Tokyo had evolved into such a capital naturally over the years, he insisted that this had not undermined Kyoto's ancient standing. As but one proof for Kyoto's continued importance as an imperial capital, Inoue pointed out that the recently established Imperial House Law stipulated that in the future, the two major imperial rites of accession, the *sokui* and *daijōe,* must be conducted there. In Inoue's view, Japan could have multiple imperial capitals, for the present both Tokyo and Kyoto. In the future, should the necessity arise, *teito* could be established in Hokkaido or even Taiwan![12]

Fukuoka Takachika—the powerful Meiji political figure who had been councillor (*sanyo*) in the early government and who had taken part in the drafting of the famous "Charter Oath"—also insisted that while it was certainly appropriate for the citizens of Tokyo to celebrate the transfer of the capital to their city, it had not by any means been thirty years since that move had taken place. Fukuoka claimed that he was in a position to know about the circumstances of the emperor's move to Tokyo because he, along with Tokyo's first governor, Ōki Takatō, Iwakura Tomomi, and Kido Takayoshi, had been closest to the emperor when the issue of a progress to the East had first been broached in 1868. Clearly defining the capital as the location of the permanent Imperial Palace, Fukuoka repeatedly stressed that Tokyo until 1889 had been a mere *anzaisho,* a temporary court for the emperor on progress. "Not once," he noted, "had there been an imperial order designating Tokyo as the location of the Imperial Palace. Only with the move from the temporary Palace at Akasaka to the present Palace (*kōkyo*) in January 1889 was the title Imperial Palace (*kyūjō*) conferred. Therefore, to be precise, the transferal of the capital to Tokyo was not accomplished until then. Prior to this the proper designation must surely be temporary court." Further, in 1868, when Emperor Meiji first journeyed to Tokyo, despite the protests of the Kyoto courtiers,

no one could yet even imagine such a thing as establishing the capital at Tokyo. Rather, it was thought that if necessary, Edo could serve as an *anzaisho* for the purpose of bringing order to the entire country. Moreover, this progress to the East was undertaken with the understanding that it might become necessary to proceed with the Imperial Banner further up to the Tōhoku region, or even as far as Dewa, Mutsu, and Hokkaido. Therefore, even though the decision was made to change the name of Edo to Tokyo [eastern capital], the name meant simply the *kyōto* [lit., capital city] of the East. The Kyoto of old was to remain the true seat of the Imperial Court.[13]

The transfer of the imperial capital was not, however much Fukuoka insisted, a sudden event that was achieved in an instant by the rebuilding and naming of the new Imperial Palace some two decades after Emperor Meiji had come to reside in Tokyo. Nevertheless, Fukuoka's rhetorical suggestion that Tokyo during the first two decades of Emperor Meiji's reign was a mere *anzaisho* does illuminate the ruling elites' fundamental ambivalence about the symbolism of the capital in these years.

To be sure, Tokyo as the de facto administrative center of the national government had inevitably acquired symbolic significance even in the early years. The emperor resided there most of the time, and the government had built a few new impressive public buildings like the General Staff Office (completed 1881) and the castle-like War Museum (Yūshūkan, completed 1882) at Yasukuni Shrine, both of which had been designed by the Italian architect Giovanni Vincenzo Cappelletti. Yet the most important changes in the face of the city that allowed it to become the central arena for the regime's public ceremonies did not occur until the years immediately preceding the unveiling of the new Imperial Palace in 1889. While Fukuoka oversimplified the complex process of creating a capital—and, equally important, a consciousness of that capital—he correctly identified a critical moment in the transformation of the symbolism and ritual significance of Tokyo.

As there are at least two aspects of governing—the administrative and the symbolic—the geographical centers of government also tend to acquire both these dimensions. Thus in considering the Meiji leaders' establishment of the capital at Tokyo, it is important to distinguish between the administrative and symbolic dimensions of the city. If the task of ruling is understood to consist of simply the utilitarian mechanics of administration, the orthodox explanation of the establishment of Japan's capital at Tokyo is quite accurate. According to this interpretation, the move of the capital took place in a rather swift, if piecemeal, fashion during the Meiji government's first few years. It started with the promulgation of an Imperial Edict (*taishō*) in the late summer (3 September) of 1868 that proclaimed that "Edo is henceforth to be called Tokyo" (Eastern Capital) and the arrival later that year (26 November) of Emperor Meiji's first progress to Tokyo. Then in April 1869 the government officially announced the transfer of its highest administrative organ, the high-sounding Grand Council of State (Dajōkan), to the new capital. Soon thereafter Emperor Meiji embarked from Kyoto on a second progress to Tokyo and took up residence in Edo Castle (9 May), which had by then been renamed the "Imperial Palace" (*kōkyo*). Finally, it is held that the transferal of the capital from Kyoto to Tokyo reached its completion with the elimination in October 1871 of a post, the *rusukan,* that had been created in 1869 as a caretaker government in

Kyoto for the emperor and the Grand Council of State. It is thus claimed that a de facto transfer of the government had been accomplished by 1871 and that the absence of any official decree to that effect can perhaps be explained by fears of negative reactions from Kyoto's citizens and other partisans of the ancient capital.[14] Yet this orthodox interpretation conflates the symbolic and the administrative dimensions of politics and capital cities.

Both Inoue Yorikuni and Fukuoka Takachika highlight the fact that however committed the early Meiji government's new leaders may have been to removing the national administrative center to Tokyo, they did not necessarily regard the new capital as a symbolic city. The idea of fashioning Tokyo into the imperial city (*teito*) par excellence—that is, into the nation's symbolic and ritual center—did not become significant until the early 1880s. Few if any of the ruling elites had such visions for Tokyo in the years shortly after the overthrow of the ancien régime in 1868.

As the testimonies of Inoue and Fukuoka suggest, there were two major reasons why the modern idea of Tokyo as the symbolic and ritual center of the nation was slow to develop. The first was the enormous symbolic weight of the ancient capital of Kyoto, accumulated over a millennium in the artifacts of the imperial past found there: the Kyoto Palace (Gosho), the imperial mausoleums, the temples and shrines connected to the imperial family, and, of course, the city as a whole, since it had been built as an imperial city. The second was in fact quite the opposite of the first. It was an image of an itinerant emperor, an emperor in motion who was tied to neither Tokyo nor Kyoto. In this view Tokyo was indeed like an *anzaisho*, a temporary court for Emperor Meiji, because the greatest imperial spectacles of the period until the mid-1880s were the progresses which used Tokyo as a point of departure and return, not as a ceremonial center. Conceiving of Tokyo as little more than an *anzaisho*, the new political leaders were sparing in their efforts to enhance its physical appearance. As a result, Tokyo during approximately the first two decades of the Meiji period offered only pallid reminders of the power of those who had ruled from Edo during the Tokugawa period.

In fact, the leaders of the Meiji regime had inherited a dying city. The tumultuous events of the years just before and after the Restoration had drastically reduced the population of Tokyo and taken a heavy toll on the city's appearance. Of these events the single most important had been the relaxation in 1862 of the *sankin kōtai* system and its subsequent end. Under this system all the *daimyō* throughout the realm had been required to spend alternate years of residence in Edo and their own domains. Not only did the cessation of *sankin kōtai* lead to the sudden disappearance of the *daimyō* and their community of retainers and servants, estimated to have numbered around 360,000 people, but it also contributed to the loss from Tokyo's population of a group of commoners—merchants, craftsmen, entertainers, and other workers— who served this huge class of consumers.[15] The warfare in Edo, culminating in the famous defeat of the *probakufu* unit, the Shōgitai, at Ueno, as well as the departure of Tokugawa Iesato (the new Tokugawa family head) and his retinue to a small estate in Shizuoka, further contributed to the decline in population. As a result, according to the estimates of Ogi Shinzō, one of the leading social historians of Tokyo, the population in the built-up area of Tokyo (*shubikinai*) plummeted from a high of approximately 1,300,000 in the first half of the nineteenth century to just over 500,000 in 1869. The city did not return to its peak level of the Tokugawa period until around 1889.[16]

The departure of the *daimyō* and the shogun, as well as the populations dependent upon them, led inevitably to the rapid dilapidation of many of the samurai estates; and in a desperate measure Tokyo's governor, Ōki Takatō, launched an ill-fated scheme that resulted in almost 9 percent of these lands being planted in mulberry or tea. To be sure, the availability of land had its practical advantages, for the new government was able to put large tracts to use for administrative and military purposes, especially around the palace.[17] Yet, at least in these early years, no one sought to create impressive buildings and grounds that expressed the power of the regime. In fact, at the very beginning the officials of the Meiji government simply moved into the old wooden buildings vacated by the rulers of the ancien régime.[18] While the specific locations and appearances of the new regime's military and official facilities changed over the years, in overall appearance the new government's administrative center was not a visually impressive one.

Perhaps most indicative of the new rulers' attitude toward Tokyo was their almost total disregard for the condition of the very heart of the city. Edo Castle, which became Emperor Meiji's permanent residence, had already deteriorated significantly since its original construction during an age of architectural splendor some two hundred years earlier. That had been a period of political centralization during which, as Herman Ooms has emphasized, the early Tokugawa shoguns attempted to shift the symbolic center of political space, or what he calls the "center of ideological space," away from the cluster of emperor, Kyoto, and Ise, and to the shogun, Nikkō, and Edo.[19]

The large-scale construction projects of the Tokugawas were as extravagant as their ambitions to rule. Thus the first half of the seventeenth century witnessed the erection of not only the Nikkō Tōshōgū, the fabulously ornate mausoleum enshrining Tokugawa Ieyasu, and the Kan'eiji, the temple which became the center of the Ieyasu cult in Edo; it also saw the dramatic and monumental rebuilding of Edo Castle and of the entire city. This ambitious project included the elaboration of a spiraling moat system around Edo Castle and the building of massive gateways (*mitsuke*), which not only protected the approaches leading to the castle but also exuded Tokugawa power. The five-tiered donjon (*tenshukaku*), the most awesome structure in the castle compound, was completed in 1607 and then richly embellished through construction projects in 1622, 1637, and 1653. Soaring to a height of over fifty meters, it was the largest *tenshukaku* in Japan: a fitting centerpiece for a complex which was about twice the size of the next largest castle compound in Osaka.

The Great Fire of 1657 that razed some 60 to 70 percent of Edo and much of the castle consumed the *tenshukaku* and put an end to the early-modern period of monumental building. To be sure, the *bakufu* restored the main structures within the castle compound and continued to do so after the numerous fires that plagued both Edo and Edo Castle through the Tokugawa period; but the *tenshukaku*, a singularly symbolic ornament, was never rebuilt. Then in 1863 two devastating fires destroyed the Nishinomaru, Honmaru, and Ninomaru structures within the castle compound. Because the *bakufu* never replaced the Honmaru, the chief edifice in the complex, the building that Emperor Meiji occupied in 1868 was only a temporary structure which the *bakufu* had hurriedly constructed to replace the Nishinomaru.[20]

The Meiji leaders' lack of concern for the appearance of the palace after their army's takeover of Edo Castle in May 1868 is even more remarkable. The new government did take some minimal measures. Following the surrender of Edo Castle, they removed the treasures and ancestral tablets of the Tokugawa family from Momijiyama within the castle grounds to Ueno; and shortly after Emperor Meiji's first visit in the fall of 1868, they demolished the Tokugawa family mausoleum.[21] In late 1868 the government ordered a new palace built on the site of the former Honmaru. However, no action was ever taken on this order, and in May 1873 a huge fire engulfed the Nishinomaru structure. The emperor and empress were forced to take up residence at what was euphemistically called a "detached palace" (*rikyū*) but which was in fact part of an old *daimyō* estate at Akasaka.[22] They remained there, in the structure newly renamed the Akasaka Temporary Palace, for almost sixteen years. In the meantime, the heart of the city lay empty, "unbearable to look at," as one former Satsuma *han* retainer lamented, as it was "in ashes and going to ruin, becoming the den of foxes and badgers and overgrown with vegetation."[23]

Thus until the late 1880s, the physical appearance of Tokyo, far from connoting that it was the seat of a new government under the direct and divine rule of the emperor, was dismal. And to many contemporaries, Japanese and foreigners alike, Tokyo did not resemble a great capital city. In September 1878 one high official, Senator (*gikan*) Sano Tsunetami, argued that the government should simply abandon altogether the idea of Tokyo as Japan's capital. In what now seems a preposterous idea, this influential figure suggested in an internal petition that is collected among Itō Hirobumi's papers that the government should build a new and permanent capital in the remote town of Honjō-eki, located approximately eighty kilometers north of Tokyo in Saitama Prefecture. Tokyo, in Sano's opinion, could not be easily defended against foreign invasion and was not visually impressive. Furthermore, its people were of such base character that they were unfit to reside in Japan's capital. Displaying an incredible contempt for Tokyo's commoners, he said of them that their "morals are in shambles; they are cold-hearted; [they] completely wallow in their extravagances; they are engrossed in amusements." And even admitting that Tokyo had a large population, he added, the city because of that was "no more than the haunt of indigents" (*hinmin no sōkutsu taru ni sugizu*). On the other hand, he claimed, fanciful as it might at first seem, "in less than twenty to thirty years . . . we can expect that Honjō will become a great and prosperous capital that surpasses Tokyo."[24]

The English traveler Isabella L. Bird recorded her impressions of Tokyo as she saw it in 1878: a city filled with paling reminders of Edo, a burned-out castle conspicuous in its disuse at the center of the city, scattered expanses of greenery, and a few incongruously placed Western and partially Western-style buildings.

Yedo is in fact no more. The moats, walls, and embankments, the long lines of decaying *yashikis,* and the shrines of Shiba and Uyeno, with the glories of their gilded and coloured twilight, alone recall its splendid past. The palace within the castle no longer exists, the last Shogun lives in retirement at Shidzuoka; the *daimiyo* are scattered through the suburbs; not a "two-sworded" man is to be seen; Mutsuhito, the "Spiritual Emperor," the son of the gods, dressed in European clothes, drives through streets of unconcerned spectators in a European carriage. . . .

The first thing a stranger tries to do, is to get a general idea of the town, but the ascent of Atagayama [*sic*] and other elevated places is a failure; there is no one point from which it can be seen, and the only way of grasping it satisfactorily would be from a balloon! From every altitude, however, dark patches of forest, the low elevation crowned by the walls of the Castle topped by dark groves of pine and cryptomeria[,] . . . sweeping, tiled roofs of temples, small oblong buildings glaring with white cement, long lines of low, grey roofs, green slopes, gleams of moats and canals, and Europeanised buildings, conspicuous by their windows and their ugliness, are sure to be seen. . . .

No view of Tokiyo, leaving out the impression produced by size, is striking, indeed there is a monotony of meanness about it. The hills are not heights, and there are no salient objects to detain the eye for an instant. As a city it lacks concentration. Masses of greenery, lined or patched with grey, and an absence of beginning or end, look suburban rather than metropolitan. Far away in the distance are other grey patches; you are told that those are still Tokiyo, and you ask no more. It is a city of "magnificent distances" without magnificence.[25]

Out from behind Jeweled Curtains

Though the Meiji government's leaders virtually neglected the physical appearance of Tokyo, they were not inattentive to the symbolic and ceremonial requirements of politics. Rather than reconstruct the capital as an expression of the power of Emperor Meiji and his government, the new leaders manipulated the monarchical image itself, setting him outside the city on frequent and dramatic tours through the countryside. The dominant image of the ruler was thus the imperial palanquin (*hōren*), not the imperial capital (*teito*), a term that came into widespread use beginning in the late 1880s.[26] In fact, the very idea of transferring the capital (*sento*), which began to be discussed in the weeks immediately following the Restoration, had much less to do with establishing a single and permanent capital in a symbolic sense than with putting the emperor's court into motion. In other words, the idea of the "imperial progress" (*junkō*) and the idea of "transferring the capital" (*sento*) were inseparable.

Such was the position of Ōkubo Toshimichi, Restoration activist and one of the most powerful men in the early Meiji government. In a petition put before the court on 16 February 1868,[27] he argued that the new government needed to take radical measures because it was faced with unprecedented troubles. He warned that while the imperial army had won temporary military victories, the traitorous forces still had not been eradicated. Moreover, the government had no laws establishing procedures for international relations, the *han* of the land had not been completely won over, and the people lived in fear. It was imperative that the government's leaders look far back into the national past and widely throughout the world for political models; only then could they take the bold measures necessary to unify the nation under the emperor.

Reflecting the modern rulers' new desire to include the common people as spiritually committed participants in the national community, he maintained that all without distinction should be made to feel "exceedingly grateful for Him who is called Master of the Realm (*itten no nushi*)" and that "the so-called lowly masses can be greatly relied upon." In the past, the sovereign had been treated as something other than human and had been "kept behind jeweled curtains (*gyokuren*)." With only a few courtiers enabled to look upon him, the sovereign could not fulfill his "natural role as father and mother to the people"; and only by carrying out the "ceremonial act of moving the capital" (*sento no ten*)[28] could he do so. To treat the emperor as one who dwells "above the clouds" and the courtiers as "people above the clouds" carried the danger of making even the emperor himself feel overly noble and lofty, "finally resulting in the estrangement of high and low." He concluded:

To respect those above and to love those below is a general rule of human ethics and is beyond reproach. However, when this is overdone there is a danger of parting from the Way of the Sovereign (*kundō*). The age of Emperor Nintoku will surely be eternally praised throughout the realm. *Now, even in foreign countries, sovereigns taking a few followers walk through the countryside while comforting and nurturing the people. This is certainly in accord with the Way of the Sovereign.* This being so, in this day of renewal and the restoration of Imperial rule, the sacred age of the nation (*honchōno seiji*) should be taken as a model and, overawing the illustrious governments of foreign countries, the bold decision of moving the capital should be made. Making out of this an opportunity for renewal and keeping simplicity and convenience in mind, put into practice the natural Way of the Sovereign as father and mother to the people, and establish a great foundation so that one order sent down will make the realm shudder. If this is not promoted, the Imperial Virtue will not shine across the seas and there can be no contending with foreign countries. (emphasis added)[29]

As to the best site for a new capital, Ōkubo suggested Osaka, primarily because its geographical features made it an ideal location for conducting foreign diplomacy and for building up the military, especially the navy. However, the overall thrust of his petition was less concerned with the advantages of any particular location than with transferring the capital as a means of bringing the emperor "out from behind jeweled curtains" and before the people.

Ōkubo thus envisaged the emperor in a new and peripatetic mode. The governing elites had to bring the emperor down from a godly presence somewhere "above the clouds" in Kyoto to become an active and visible agent in politics. As father and mother to the dependable masses, the emperor could unify the nation in a period beset by domestic turmoil and the threat of the Western powers. It is not altogether clear what Ōkubo had in mind when alluding to the example of Emperor Nintoku. Perhaps he meant only to recall the image of a paragon of imperial rule, a benevolent and active political figure; or perhaps the connection was that Emperor Nintoku's court had been located in Naniwa, the ancient name of the Osaka region. But the remark that follows, "even in foreign countries sovereigns . . . walk through the countryside," suggests that for Ōkubo, Nintoku's reign also signified an age when emperors roamed the land while attending to the needs of the people. This reading of Ōkubo's vision for the emperor is further warranted by the term that he uses to designate the court that would be established in Osaka, namely, *anzai[sho]*, or temporary court.

Ōkubo was not alone in his imaging of an emperor set loose from Kyoto. Ōkuma Shigenobu, another important government leader speaking under the same circumstances as Inoue and Fukuoka, recollected that Ōkubo's ideas were representative of a view that had been dominant at all levels of the government in 1868. According to that consensus, the *bakufu* had purposely treated the emperor "as a sacred thing, not a mortal," and had held him aloof from politics and the people. But with the return of political authority and the affairs of state to the emperor, it was essential that the new leaders treat him differently. "The capital had to be moved," Ōkuma recalled, "in order to remake the hearts of the people of the realm, to make it known that the emperor was not a divine being (*kami*) unconcerned with national politics; that he was, in fact, the government that ruled the people of the country."[30]

Of all the other major petitions that had recommended transferring the capital only one, Maejima Hisoka's, indicated any desire to create a visually impressive, permanent imperial city. Maejima, a former *bakufu* retainer and interpreter for the British Ambassador Sir Harry Smith Parkes, was perhaps the most sensitive to the aesthetic requirements of a new capital. He noted that in contrast to Naniwa, Edo already had expansive avenues and magnificent views of "cloud-covered mountains in the distance" such as befitted a "Great Capital City" (*dai teito*). Moreover, Edo Castle could be used as the Imperial Palace.[31] Yet these were only a few among the many points that, he argued, made Edo a more appropriate location for a new capital than Osaka.

Others who wrote influential petitions urging the transfer of the capital to Tokyo disregarded the city's aesthetics, for like Ōkubo they saw the move away from Kyoto primarily as an opportunity to bring the emperor out in front of the people. Ōki Takatō and Etō Shinpei, former Tosa samurai and officials in the new government, proposed a two-capital plan to Iwakura Tomomi on 22 May 1868. Ōki and Etō suggested that rather than moving the capital from Kyoto to Edo, the government should establish a new capital that would be called the Eastern Capital (Tokyo), as the base for administering the East. Kyoto would remain the capital in the West, and the emperor, perhaps in the future utilizing a railroad, would journey back and forth between the Eastern and Western Capitals. Should the government fail to carry out this proposal, they warned, the possibility of the empire becoming split in two could not be discounted. In closing, they noted that the progress to the East would be a method by which to portray the emperor as a benevolent ruler sweeping away the misrule of the Tokugawa.[32] At about the same time Kido Takayoshi—who, as he indicated in his diary, had been urging the government to allow the emperor "to travel freely to all quarters of the land"—proposed a three-capital plan that would have designated Kyoto as the Imperial Capital (*teito*), Osaka as the Western Capital (*saikyō*), and Edo as the Eastern Capital (*tōkyō*).[33]

The Imperial Edict through which the government's leaders established Edo as the Eastern Capital on 3 September 1868 stressed the need for the emperor's presence at two capitals in order to unify the nation. It announced that Edo would from thenceforth be called the Eastern Capital because the emperor looked upon "the realm as one house, the East and West equally." And the official explanation attached to the edict noted the necessity of "bringing together the strength of the nation" in a time of increased international contact. For this reason the emperor wished to make "frequent progresses (*junkō*) between the East and West while listening to the multitudes."[34]

The archetypes for the two ideas that became so tightly intertwined in the first few Meiji years—that is, the concepts of "transferring the capital" (*sento*) and of the "progress" (*junkō* or *gyōkō*)—were, as one might imagine, quite old. Ōkubo's recommendation that the decision to move the capital should be modeled "on the sacred age of the nation" suggests the idea dominant until at least the mid–seventh century, that capitals need not have permanent locations, and even that multiple courts might exist. In that ancient age, before the impact of Chinese notions of a single and permanent imperial city, rulers had moved their residences upon accession, or sometimes even more frequently; and they often kept other provincial residences as well. Between A.D. 400 and 646, twenty-three Yamato rulers occupied no fewer than thirty-one different principal capitals.[35] Moreover, *gyōkō* and *junkō* were classical expressions that can be found in many ancient works, both Chinese and Japanese.[36] As is suggested by their ideographs, *gyōkō* (blessings of visitation) and *junkō* (blessings of a tour, or of circulating) signified essentially the same type of ceremonial activity, one in which perambulating rulers had tried to present themselves as bestowers of prosperity. In explaining why the character *xing* (Japanese, *saiwai*) meant an imperial progress, Cai Yong (A.D. 133–92), the late Han literary and court figure, noted, "Wherever the Imperial Palanquin proceeds the subjects receive His Grace. Therefore benefits are inestimable. Thus, *xing* is used."[37] And according to a thirteenth-century Japanese source, the *Zoku kojidan,* the Heian courtier Fujiwara Nagakata (1140–91) commented: "It is said that there are blessings (*kō*) wherever the Son of Heaven goes. Therefore the ideograph *kō* is used."[38]

And yet in at least one fundamental way the Emperor Meiji's progresses marked a radical departure from precedent. No emperor had ever attempted to ramble his way to the ends of the four main Japanese islands, Honshu, Kyushu, Shikoku, and Hokkaido; but this was precisely what Emperor Meiji would begin to do. Since the move of the imperial seat to Kyoto in the eighth century, imperial progresses had been limited to places inside or near the capital.[39] And, as Ōkubo and the other Restorationists understood clearly, emperors under the Tokugawa regime had been for the most part confined to the court, "virtually imprisoned," as one historian who has studied the imperial institution of the seventeenth and eighteenth centuries has put it.[40]

While the exact number of imperial provincial outings in any given period is uncertain, all who have studied the activities of Emperor Meiji recognize that he toured the countryside much more frequently during the first two Meiji decades than after.[41] Most important, the long-term and large-scale provincial progresses that are collectively known as the "Six Great Imperial Tours" (*roku daijunkō*) were clustered in these years. The longest progress, the Yamagata-Akita-Hokkaido Tour of 1881 (30 July–11 October) lasted seventy-four days and took the emperor and his retinue of around 350 people as far as the northernmost major island of Japan. Over 700 people made up the largest, the Hokuriku-Tōkaidō Tour of 1878 (30 August–9 November), which lasted some seventy-two days. The four others were the Chūgoku-Saikoku Tour (28 June–15 August 1872), the Tōhoku Tour (2 June–21 July 1876), the Yamanashi-Mie-Kyoto Tour (16 June–23 July 1880), and the Yamaguchi-Hiroshima-Okayama Tour (26 July–12 August 1885).[42]

In his movements throughout the realm the Meiji emperor traversed nearly the entire length and breadth of his territory while attempting to unify the land and the people under himself and the new imperial order. He did so in part by worshipping at what were to become sacred places on the official national landscape. He visited Ise and Atsuta Shrines (Amaterasu, mythical progenitrix of the imperial line, was enshrined in the former and the sacred Kusanagi Sword in the latter), other famous provincial shrines, imperial mausoleums, and memorials to those who had died in the Restoration. At the same time, and again harkening back to archaic models of the benevolent monarch, he also observed the people at their work and distributed gifts and prizes to the aged, the afflicted, victims of disasters, honor students at primary schools, and other individuals of merit. The last, as the Home Ministry informed local officials on the route of the 1876 Tōhoku Tour, included such persons as "dutiful children, devoted servants, and virtuous women."[43] Emperor Meiji and his proxies rewarded individuals such as Kawamura Denbei for his contributions to sericulture and silk-reeling. Kawamura received rolls of red and white crepe. They recognized Tomemori Iyo, skilled in the arts of calligraphy, reading, and sewing, for her diligence as a primary school teacher and especially for her great dedication, even at the advanced age of seventy, to female education. She was honored with a personal audience with the emperor, said to have been arranged by Iwakura Tomomi, as well as an imperial gift. The emperor granted

Takeda Kumashichi an audience, and Kido Takayoshi favored him with a citation. As a dutiful grandchild he had respected his grandfather's wishes and dedicated himself to sericulture and silk-reeling. Moreover, while working to increase production he had also given relief to the poor.[44] The emperor also visited a wide variety of other religious, cultural, industrial, military, and governmental institutions, touching them with his authority and bringing them into the order of which he was to be the center.

Clifford Geertz—building on Edward Shils's argument that sovereigns tend to locate themselves at the "center" and hence sacred part of society—has stressed that royal progresses are a method by which political authority places itself in a "cultural frame" and affirms its "connection with transcendent things." This is true, he argues, of progresses as diverse as those of Queen Elizabeth I, which were framed in the symbols of Protestant virtue; of Hyan Wuruk in fourteenth-century Java, which represented the hierarchical cosmos of medieval Hinduism; and of the old regime kings of Morocco, which were meant to demonstrate "that God had gifted one with the capacity to dominate."[45] Yet in Japan's revolutionary situation following the Restoration—when Emperor Meiji traveled through great multitudes of people who knew little or nothing of either the imperial household or the official myths contained in the regime's most sacred texts, the *Kojiki* and the *Nihongi*—legitimacy did not come so clearly and neatly packaged. It would be too facile an explanation to say that Emperor Meiji's progresses "worked" because they resonated with a cultural framework that was already agreed upon by political elites and the masses alike. In fact there was no consensus about the meanings of the symbols and emblems with which the ritual specialists embellished the emperor's processions; and as a result, semiotic chaos ensued.

The emperor did indeed go about the countryside brandishing such emblems of authority as the Imperial Chrysanthemum Crest and the Imperial Flag. But the rigorous restriction of the chrysanthemum crest's signification to the imperial household dates only from the beginning of the Meiji era, when its use was confined to the imperial household itself and to a number of other specific places, documents, or published materials which either had imperial associations or which, as with a very few shrines and temples, had traditionally used the emblem. While the chrysanthemum had had close associations with the imperial household since the reign of Gotoba (1183–98), the sixteen-petalled Imperial Chrysanthemum Crest was first recognized as the exclusive emblem of the imperial household in April 1868.[46] The Imperial Flag bearing the chrysanthemum emblem was an early Meiji invention as well. The idea of an imperial flag dates from 1870, and in 1871 the prototype for all future imperial flags was unveiled: a gold chrysanthemum on red background.[47] Since in this early period court ritualists themselves were experimenting with imperial emblems, it seems safe to assume that for most people, especially those living in the provinces, the chrysanthemum need not have signified the imperial household.

In fact, during Emperor Meiji's progresses there was sometimes a great deal of confusion in the popular mind about which floral emblem to associate with the emperor. Kishida Ginko, a newspaper reporter for the *Tōkyō nichinichi shinbun* who was then accompanying the 1878 Hokuriku-Tōkaidō Tour, noted that red cherry blossoms had been placed on lanterns hanging from the eaves of houses along the processional route in Niigata Prefecture. When he asked a local if this emblem stood for the province of Echigo, the customary name for the Niigata area, the reply was that the red cherry blossom was the crest of the emperor (*tenchōsama no mon dasuke*).[48]

Emperor Meiji also took with him two of the imperial regalia, the Sacred Sword and Curved Jewel,[49] and he passed through villages and towns that had been ornamented with Rising Sun lanterns (*hinomaru chōchin*) and national flags. But again, the great masses of people were not familiar with any of these symbols. How could they have known that the heavenly gods had conferred the imperial regalia upon Ninigi-no-mikoto, the grandson of the Sun Goddess, with the injunction to rule over the land? The authorities, it must be remembered, had difficulty enough explaining that the emperor was descended from the Sun Goddess.

The Rising Suns gracing Japan's national flag and the *hinomaru* lanterns had an even longer history of association with the imperial household than the chrysanthemums did; but like the floral emblem, the rising sun had no exclusively national or imperial meaning for most commoners until the modern era. Japan had no national flag until 1854, when upon a petition by the lord of Satsuma *han*, Shimazu Nariakira, the *bakufu* determined that Japanese ships should fly a white flag bearing the Rising Sun emblem in order to identify themselves as Japanese. In 1870 the Meiji government, following the late Tokugawa precedent, decreed that Japanese ships ought to use the Rising Sun flag as the national flag. Though in time it became customary for citizens to put out the *hinomaru* on national holidays, the practice was slow in taking root. One early Meiji satirist was even bold enough to chide the government for forcing the people to put out what looked like advertisements for "Red Pill" (*Akamaru*), a common medicine of the day. For most commoners of early Meiji witnessing the imperial progresses, the Rising Sun emblem probably signified, as it had during the Tokugawa period, any auspicious occasion.[50]

Still, even without a consensus about the meanings of the important imperial symbols and emblems, the provincial progresses helped to establish the emperor's legitimacy because they were spectacular and drew attention to the new ruler. Eyewitness testimonies suggest that Emperor Meiji's progresses produced power simply by their pomp and glitter, not because they communicated any particular myth or ideology.

Yanai Nazaemon, at whose house Emperor Meiji had rested during his tour through Fukushima Prefecture in 1876, recalled the splendor of the imperial procession many years after it had come through his village. Even though he had been only eleven years old at the time, he remembered:

Finally, [the procession arrived] through the entrance to the village at Kami-machi headed by imperial honor guards, with triangular flags on staffs which fluttered resplendently; then there was the stately resonation of the clip-clopping sound from the hooves of the horses drawing the emperor's carriage; the coachman's clothes sparkled magnificently. Such were the things that first struck me. The imperial carriage that I saw was a horse-drawn carriage drawn by, I believe, four horses. Now that carriage was black-lacquered and painted on it somewhere was the gilded imperial crest which was radiant and which glittered brilliantly.[51]

Similarly, Kikuchi Minezō—nineteen years old at the time of the 1881 tour that passed through his town of Kuwaori (Date District) in Fukushima Prefecture—recollected that someone accompanying the emperor had "held up a square package wrapped in red brocade which must have been the Sacred Sword and Jewel," and that the emperor's carriage had been "black-lacquered and decorated with the gilded Imperial Crest." Saitō Hiromoto explained that his grandfather had told him of how the family's front gate had been covered with a purple curtain decorated with the Imperial Chrysanthemum Crest and that the sacred objects were placed in a decorative alcove when the emperor rested at their house.

Because people were drawn by the glitter rather than the ideology of rule, the forms rather than the content of ritual, popular perceptions of the emperor and his tours were also informed by folk ideas. Although there is no definitive study of Emperor Meiji's tours, several scholars have noted the festive, *matsuri*-like atmosphere often found in the villages visited by the progresses and the fact that the common folk sometimes viewed the emperor as an *ikigami,* a living deity with magical powers. Such views are supported by contemporary observers. The same Kishida Ginko who later accompanied the 1878 Hokuriku-Tōkaidō Tour described Sukagawa, a post town along the Ōshū Highway in Fukushima Prefecture, as having been in a festive mood during the 1876 tour. He observed that Shinto and Buddhist priests were decked out in their ceremonial vestments and that huge throngs of people filled every available space along the route of the emperor's progress. He concluded that with sellers of festive foods "and warm sake all out and the bustle of activity, it was in general just like a festival for the local shrine (*chinju no sairei*)."[52] In 1878, the commoner in Niigata Prefecture whom Kishida questioned about the red cherry blossom emblem explained that the lanterns with this crest were only to be used for the emperor's festivals (*tenchōsama no omatsuri*).[53]

Perhaps the most famous testimony to the way in which the emperor was seen as an *ikigami* comes from Kinoshita Naoe's *Zange.* According to this novel, based upon the author's own observations of the 1880 tour, the elderly in Matsumoto

clung firmly to the old belief that "the emperor is a living deity with magical powers (*tenshisama wa ikigamisama*)." They believed that if one looked up at the emperor, one's eyes would be crushed. . . .

After the procession had passed and free traffic was again allowed, a great many men and women rushed out from both sides [of the road] competing to get ahead of one another. Pushing and shoving and dirtying their clothes, they began struggling in the mire. Their frantic contest was for the dirt-covered pebbles kicked up by the horses and driven over and sent flying about by the carriage. Among them it was widely believed that possession of a pebble passed over by *tenshisama* brought domestic well-being and abundant crops.[54]

This was not an unusual response. Yanai Nazaemon also remembered that in his village of Fumise "there were not a few people who believed that if one looked up at the emperor one would be cursed, or that one's eyes would be crushed." He also remarked that many people had attributed a magical power to the sand upon which the emperor had walked. Yanai's father had carefully collected several cupfuls of this sand to keep in commemoration of the emperor's visit to their house, only to have relatives and other villagers ask for some of the precious grains. "As for this," Yanai explains, "I learned that in those days people held the belief that having this sand sprinkled on them would cause ague (*okori*) to drop off of them and that it would soften hardened corpses." His father saved the remaining sand in a bag, noting on it " *tenshisama's* sand."[55]

What, then, was the significance of Emperor Meiji's great tours through the realm? Part of it was in the simple fact that these were often the first opportunities to diffuse the symbols and emblems that became common elements in the idiom of modern Japanese public rituals. In accordance with instructions from the central government,[56] Rising Sun flags and lanterns could be found nearly everywhere the emperor went. The occasional confusion about the proper imperial emblem notwithstanding, the Imperial Chrysanthemum Crest was also often the most striking image that people could recall about the tours.

Most important, however, the glitter, color, gold, and magnificence of the progresses demonstrated that the emperor was at the center of societal significance. The progress was above all a ritual of spatial integration wherein the emperor's movements across the land and to the nation's borders signified the spatial coherence of the national territory around the central symbol of the monarch. When these events succeeded, people drawn by the spectacle projected upon him their own deepest meanings, perceiving him as an *ikigami* or creating around him a *matsuri*. Though some unimpressed observers might look on him with little more than idle curiosity,[57] even they could hardly resist altogether the grand processions radiantly ornamented with the imperial flag, the mounted officers, the shiny carriages, the trumpeters, the banners, the splendidly dressed honor guards, some of the highest officials in the land, scores of attendants of various ranks and functions, and, of course, the imperial conveyance. Through these provincial tours the emperor was beginning, as Geertz has put it, "to take symbolic possession of the realm." Yet this "symbolic possession" depended less upon a consensus of meaning, as Geertz might have it, than the very multipolarity of meanings that people ascribed to this new symbol of the national totality.[58]

Furthermore, the imperial progresses provided the first opportunities for the Meiji regime to make real and believable the emperor's ability to see and know the land, the people, and the borders of the nation. Through these pageants and various written and nonwritten representations of them the people could begin to imagine that the emperor was at the apex of a panoptic regime and that he was the Overseer who disciplined the realm and the people with his gaze. In a memorial urging an imperial progress to Hokkaido, probably drawn up in July 1875, Sanjō Sanetomi, then grand minister of state (*dajō daijin*), argued that the people in such remote regions did not even know of the existence of the imperial household and that, conversely, "the emperor does not know the feelings of the people in the remote lands or the conditions there." Thus in addition to explaining that should the emperor undertake such a progress, "all of the people of the nation will turn their eyes (*me o tenjite*) and see the greatness of the emperor's conduct," he also emphasized that there was nothing more urgent than allowing the emperor "to see the extent of the borders and to discern the true conditions of the people."[59]

Official notifications to local officials in the towns and villages along the imperial progresses' routes also fostered the idea that the people, their work, and their land must be made visible to the emperor. Thus the set of instructions sent out to local officials along the route of the Meiji state's largest progress—the Hokuriku-Tōkaidō Tour of 1878—ordered them to compile various reports about the areas under their jurisdiction and to "offer [them] for the emperor's inspection" (*tenran ni kyōsubeshi*) at the prefectural government office. These included reports on what were called "dutiful children, loyal servants (*giboku*), virtuous wives (*seppu*), and any others commendable for their good deeds"; "police stations, substations, and numbers of policemen"; "methods of encouraging [local] industry"; "locations of livestock farming and number of livestock"; "locations of wasteland (*arachi*) and places now being reclaimed"; and "famous products of the area in question." Finally, and most suggestively since these might be thought of as completely objectified representations of the land and the people, "maps and tables (*ichiranhyō*) concerning the area of jurisdiction" were to be made available for the emperor's examination. A similar set of instructions for the Tōhoku Tour of 1876, which bears the name of Home Minister Ōkubo Toshimichi, also instructed local officials to present "a sampling of maps and tables of the area under jurisdiction," and "antiquarian items (*kokibutsu*), paintings and calligraphy, and various [local] products and curios."[60]

As Taki Kōji has already pointed out, written narratives of the progresses also constructed the image of an emperor who watches.[61] According to these descriptions it was he who cast his look upon the peasants harvesting or catching carp. He inspected objects and sites of antiquarian or historical interest. And it was he who subjected schools and schoolchildren, or workers and industrial establishments, to his scrutiny. Consider, for example, the journalist Kishida Ginko's description of the emperor's activities in Morioka on the morning of 7 July 1876. He first inspected the prefectural government office and then

at just before nine o'clock he arrived at the Ningyoku School. There he inspected the physical exercises of about 500 out of the total of approximately 1,500 students from nine schools in Morioka. Some 400 of the students were girls, and they looked absolutely splendid in their waistcoats and skirts, or Western clothes. At about ten o'clock the emperor entered the industrial encouragement grounds and observed women workers engaged in such [tasks] as silk-reeling, raising silkworms, or weaving. Moreover, he also visited the exhibition hall on these grounds and inspected the products from the prefecture that were displayed there.[62]

To be sure, the progress was modeled on an archaic ceremonial style and contained some severe limitations from the perspective of the production of the modern nation-state. In the first place, the progress was not conducive to the production of a sense of national simultaneity—in other words, a feeling among the people that they lived in one national time. Since this is an important point that will be taken up in Part 3, I shall only note here that—especially because of the lack of development of the national communications and transportation network—the people scattered throughout the space of the nation could not share in the time of the emperor's passage through any particular village, town, or city. They saw the emperor at different times and were only incorporated into the nation-state over time, not across or in the same time, through the spatial movement of the emperor's body. This situation was to change with truly national pageants that could be celebrated throughout the country simultaneously. Furthermore, as we shall see in later discussions of the military review as a disciplinary ritual, the progresses marked only the beginning of the construction of the imperial gaze.

There can be no doubt that despite its inadequacies the progressing style of imperial pageantry was not a simple restoration of archaic kingship ritual. Ōkubo, as we have seen, did not think of it as such: writing in 1868, he envisioned it as a means by which to involve the common people in the projects of the nation. Moreover, in observing that "even in foreign countries, sovereigns taking a few followers walk through the countryside while comforting and nurturing the people," he clearly tried to locate the imperial progress as a ritual appropriate for modern regimes throughout the world. It is not clear which "foreign countries" Ōkubo had in mind, but perhaps he knew of the situation in Russia, where around the middle of the century the progresses of the tsar and the tsarevich were still an important form of state ceremonial. Alexander II's greatest tour in 1837, for example, had taken some seven months and covered over 13,000 miles.[63] If Ōkubo had European examples in his thoughts, he was clearly confused, since the great era of royal progresses there had for the most part ended in the early modern age. But the point here is that Ōkubo and the other leaders of the new regime, as with many other policies that they recommended in the name of restoration, attempted to turn archaic precedents toward the new demands of modernity and the construction of the nation-state. Through seeing and being seen—that is, in their mutual recognition through vision—the people and the new ruler began to see (in both meanings of the word) the boundaries of the nation as well as to constitute a new subjectivity for the people as disciplined subject-citizens of Japan.

The Weight of the Imperial Past

While Emperor Meiji spent months away from Tokyo on his great tours through the countryside, during the first two Meiji decades his most extended period of absence from the new capital resulted from a pilgrimage to Kyoto, the ancient capital. On 22 November 1876 the emperor formally announced that he would go to Kyoto the following January in order to worship at two imperial mausoleums: that of his father, Emperor Kōmei, located in Kyoto (Nochi no Tsuki no Wa no Higashi no Yama no Misasagi); and the mausoleum of the founding emperor of the imperial line, Emperor Jimmu, located in nearby Nara (Unebi Yama no Ushitora no Misasagi). The visit to Emperor Kōmei's mausoleum, it was noted, would be for the performance of memorial rites marking the tenth year since Emperor Kōmei's death. Emperor Meiji left on this imperial pilgrimage on 24 January 1877 and did not return to Tokyo until 30 July 1877.[64]

Ten years later the Meiji emperor again embarked on an excursion to Kyoto, mainly to conduct rites commemorating the twentieth anniversary of Emperor Kōmei's death. This stay was considerably shorter, just over a month (25 January–24 February 1887), but longer than the shortest of the "Six Great Imperial Tours," the Yamaguchi-Hiroshima-Okayama Tour.[65] Moreover, Emperor Meiji returned to Kyoto during three of the "Six Great Imperial Tours" (the Osaka-Chūgoku-Saigoku Tour, the Hokuriku-Tōkaidō Tour, and the Yamanashi-Mie-Kyoto Tour), each time worshipping at his father's mausoleum.[66] Clearly, the new government's leaders could not ignore the symbolic weight of the imperial past in Kyoto. Especially prior to the completion of Tokyo's Imperial Palace in the late 1880s, but throughout the era, Kyoto's aura exerted a tremendous pull on the new emperor, drawing him away from Tokyo, and contributed to the ambiguity about the symbolic and ceremonial significance of the new capital.

The official history of Emperor Meiji's reign informs us that the emperor himself, lamenting the disrepair into which Kyoto and the Kyoto Palace had fallen since his move to Tokyo, sent a personal gift of money to the Kyoto prefectural government in February 1877 with instructions to use the funds for the preservation of the city. The history also notes that on passing through Kyoto during the Hokuriku-Tōkaidō Tour in 1878, the emperor reiterated the urgency of preserving Kyoto. In addition, it is said that he suggested a remarkable idea that later gained wide currency among the government's leaders: that just as the Russians held the coronation of their monarch in their old capital, Moscow, the Japanese should conduct their imperial accession rites in Kyoto, the ancient imperial seat. Whether or not Emperor Meiji was personally responsible for this idea, by the late 1870s some of the government's leaders, as well as the emperor himself, were reflecting seriously about Kyoto's physical condition and symbolic importance.[67]

Iwakura Tomomi, once chamberlain in the court of Emperor Kōmei, Restoration activist, and after 1871 minister of the right, was one of the most powerful of such leaders. In a petition (dated March 1878) urging the establishment of an office that would conduct a comprehensive survey of and make recommendations for the imperial household, Iwakura suggested over 130 items such an office should consider.[68] Two of these reveal his great anxiety about Kyoto's decline. In one he raised the issue of whether the government should build two imperial mausoleums for public worship, one in each of the two capitals. This proposal was reminiscent of one discussed in 1869 in Japan's first legislative body, the Kōgisho, to establish a branch of Ise Shrine in each of the two capitals as ritual centers for a national religion.[69] In the other he raised the matter of renaming Kyoto as Western Capital (*saikyō*),

Nara as Southern Capital (*nankyō*), and Sapporo as Northern Capital (*hokkyō*). In both proposals, Iwakura demonstrated his reluctance to afford Tokyo the role of sole capital of Japan.

Iwakura registered his alarm at Kyoto's physical and symbolic deterioration in more explicit terms in a "Petition Concerning the Preservation of Kyoto" of January 1883, only six months before his death. [70] He began his petition with lavish praise for the ancient capital: "Heian-kyō is a place which was established by Emperor Kammu and since then over a millennium has elapsed. It is a region of exquisite mountains and rivers, adorned with great shrines and famous temples. Its people know propriety and esteem frugality and simplicity. The benevolence of the rule of previous emperors remains even today." Yet the ancient capital, Iwakura noted, had been falling into ruin since the emperor's departure. The estates of the former imperial princes, court nobles, and feudal lords had degenerated with disuse and were becoming the "haunts of foxes and rabbits," and the people of Kyoto who had served the palace had been reduced to poverty. He then related how Emperor Meiji on his visit to Kyoto had decried the conditions there and had suggested holding the accession rites in Kyoto to revive the ailing city. Since the emperor's visit, however, little had been done to restore the city. Moreover, almost all local industries were in ruins.

"Perhaps it is inevitable," Iwakura admitted, "that the celebrated thousand-year-old capital should suddenly become desolate," but he also thought it regrettable because of all the ancient capital cities that had been located in Yamato, Kawachi, Settsu, and Ōmi provinces, only Heian-kyō survived. Thus only in Kyoto could the contours of an ancient capital be seen; and preserving the city would be a means of expressing "piety and reverence for the former emperors." As an additional reason for rejuvenating the city, Iwakura observed that Heian-kyō was a city renowned both at home and abroad for its beauty and the goodness of its people's customs.

Iwakura's concrete recommendations for the restoration of Kyoto as a whole, and the palace and folk industries especially, consisted of fourteen points that centered primarily on the revival or creation of various imperial rites. [71] Most important, he proposed that the government conduct what he called the three "greatest rites of state" (*kokka shichō no taiten*) in the Kyoto Palace. These three rites were the *sokui* and *daijōsai* rites, two of the three great movements making up the imperial accession ceremonies, [72] and the empress's rites of investiture (*rikkō*). Second, he suggested the enshrinement of Emperor Kammu's soul in the *kashikodokoro,* the place within the Kyoto Palace that had formerly housed the Sacred Mirror, and the performance of annual rites there that would be open to the public. Such measures were necessary because while the general location of Emperor Kammu's mausoleum in Kyoto (Kashiwabara no Misasaki in Fushimi) was known, the exact site of his remains could not be verified.

Third, he urged the creation of an altar (*yōhaisho*) from which Ise Shrine and Emperor Jimmu's mausoleum could be worshipped at a distance. Ritualists could hold three annual rites that would be open to the public. Fourth and fifth, Iwakura suggested the revival of sumptuous festivals at the Kamo and Iwashimizu shrines. These had been tutelary shrines for the imperial family since ancient times, and Emperor Kōmei had revived the ancient custom of imperial progresses to them on the eve of the Restoration in order to pray for the expulsion of foreigners. He proposed, sixth, the restoration of various court functions and banquets; seventh, the performance of the Great Purification Ceremony (*ōharai shiki*) before the old *kashikodokoro;* eighth, the observance of rites for the Three Great Festivals (*sandaisetsu,* actually recently invented national holidays) before a likeness of Emperor Meiji in the ancient Shishinden ceremonial hall; ninth, indicating an awareness that within the global context of state pageantry imperial cities would have to be able to accommodate foreign dignitaries, the construction of a Western-style hotel next to the palace; tenth, the establishment of a treasury hall within the palace grounds that would be opened up to the public once or twice a year; eleventh, the completion of several different restoration and building projects within the palace grounds; twelfth, attaching the former castle of the Tokugawa, the Nijō Castle, to the Kyoto Palace and putting it under the jurisdiction of the Imperial Household Ministry; thirteenth, appointing caretakers to manage the palace and the palace gardens; and fourteenth, the creation of an office of shrines and temples in Kyoto that would regulate shrines and temples in western Japan.

Iwakura closed his petition by placing the significance of Kyoto's restoration and the revival or creation of imperial rites there within the broader context of the importance of political rituals for the new government. Arguing in Confucian terms, he warned that it was a time when the customs and sentiments of the people were frivolous and unsettled, when the people were failing to follow the Way governing the Five Relationships (between father and son, ruler and ruled, husband and wife, older and younger brother, and friend and friend). He concluded that if in this time of social crisis "the Way of loyalty and filial piety is expressed through the revival of the ancient rites of past emperors, something will naturally be awakened in those seeing and hearing these anew. This will aid in the maintenance of customs and making the sentiments of the people warm and sincere. Therefore, benefits from the standpoint of governance are not few. The so-called Way of the King is made up of rites. Therefore, it is said that their resolute performance is desirable."[73] Thus, Iwakura maintained that his recommendations grew out of more than a former Kyoto court noble's nostalgic attachment to the city of his birth. Articulating a prevailing sentiment among the leaders of the Meiji government, he argued that political rites were essential to politics because through them the government could maintain the stability of the social order.

But why Kyoto and not the new capital? Iwakura and many others both before and after him expressed a profound feeling, whether fully conscious or not, that in Japan's modernity archaic artifacts could hold the power to naturalize and thereby legitimate the imperial regime's rule. The Meiji Restoration had, after all, been carried out in the name of the past, and the leaders of the new regime could hardly jettison from its store of symbolic resources the city that best displayed it. As Iwakura put it, of all the imperial cities that had existed in history only Kyoto remained. The thousand-year-old city and all the mausoleums, shrines, temples, and old palace buildings contained within it gave visible evidence of the antiquity of the imperial house and the nation it claimed to rule.

In contrast, Edo, renamed Tokyo, was a city that the Imperial Army had had to conquer, and the artifacts to be found there represented anything but the depth and centrality of the imperial household in history. By the 1880s the new capital was beginning to be the center of national progress, and through such showcases as the Ginza district, a section of the city built in a Western style with brick buildings and tree-lined avenues, the government's leaders tried to indicate something of the nation's wealth and civilized character. But with regard to the official interpretation of national antiquity, the city was close to mute. To be sure, Tokyo's past was Edo, and its sheer age would later be co-opted when the government built the new Imperial Palace within the walls of the old Edo Castle; but the possibilities of Tokyo's past were highly restricted by the unpleasant fact that Edo also represented the usurpation of direct imperial rule by warrior governments.

Some three months after Iwakura presented this petition, the government through an Imperial Rescript (26 April 1883) announced that future *sokui* and *daijōsai* rites would be conducted in Kyoto, thus overturning a precedent that had been set in 1871. In December of that year Emperor Meiji's *daijōsai* had been held on the palace grounds in Tokyo. Moreover, the government accepted most of Iwakura's proposals and placed the Imperial Household Ministry in charge of the project to preserve Kyoto Palace. In May, State Councillor (*sanji*) Inoue Kaoru and Kagawa Keizō of the Imperial Household Ministry left for Kyoto to begin substantive work on the planning of the undertaking.[74]

The museumification of Kyoto, the purposeful conservation of its buildings and other objects in order to articulate an authoritative history, had thus reached a turning point. This attentiveness to selective historic preservation had not by any means been a priority of government officials when Emperor Meiji abandoned the city in 1869. And it was probably a remote thought indeed when between 1873 and 1880 the Kindairi-gosho (Kyoto Palace compound proper), Sento-gosho (occupied by abdicated emperors), and Ōmiya-gosho (for secondary imperial consorts, dowager empresses, and abdicated emperors) were all at various times used as "exhibition" (*hakurankai*) grounds. The items displayed had ranged from the bizarre, such as exotic animals, to locally manufactured products and foreign-made machines, such as would be common in Western trade fairs and industrial expositions.[75]

But from the early 1880s these palace grounds no longer served such mundane purposes, and by the late 1880s the entire palace enclosure (*gyoen*)—that is, the approximately 220-acre area encompassing the palace compound proper—had taken on its basic modern configuration: an expansive public park in which one could find, after entering through ancient gateways, a scattering of historical artifacts, the most important being the palace compound and the Sento-gosho. The Imperial Park was thus not unlike a public museum in its display of objects that were to be appreciated as the true representations of history, except perhaps insofar as the park was a museum that never closed. As an official guide book to Kyoto described the Imperial Park in 1895:

This is the portion of the city bounded by Imadegawa St. on the north, Teramachi St. on the east, Marutamachi St. on the south, and Karasumaru St. on the west. It is surrounded by walls of stones and earth, and has nine principal gateways. . . . There are a few subordinate entrances opened in recent years for convenience; but the above are the nine Gates to which reference is frequently made in historical works, novels, &c. Within these gates in ancient times were included the Imperial Palace, the Residence of the late Prince Kuni, the Palace of the Ex-Emperor, the Imperial Flower

Garden, the Grass Garden, and the residences of many princes and court nobles. Many of the feudal lords had their Kyoto residences just outside the Enclosure. Most of the buildings inside have been removed so as to make a fine park traversed by roads open to all. The gates remain as memorials to the past; but their doors are always open.[76]

However, in the early 1880s the government's leaders had still not permanently resolved the specific question of where to hold the imperial accession rites; nor had they clarified the official meanings of Kyoto and Tokyo. And in mid-1888 some of the most powerful men in the government met in the Privy Council to settle once and for all the permanent locations for the *sokui* and *daijōsai* rites. During the debate several of the participants cited the practical advantages of Tokyo over Kyoto, asserting that shifting the ceremonial stage to western Japan would simply be a waste of money. This pragmatic perspective, however, was not typical. Nearly everyone who advocated one or the other of the capital cities understood that the question centered on symbolism. Those who favored Kyoto were what I shall call "antiquarians," for they appealed, as Iwakura had, to the importance of honoring Kyoto's thousand-year-old past. On the other hand, Tokyo's supporters, those who might be styled the "civilizationists," invoked Tokyo's representation of national wealth, strength, progress, modernity, and civilization.

The government's leaders established the Privy Council in April 1888 as a body to deliberate and advise the emperor on the Meiji Constitution and several related pieces of legislation—the Imperial House Law, the Law of the Houses of the Diet, the Election Law, and the Imperial Ordinance Concerning the House of Peers—which together formed the legal foundation of prewar Japan. The first concrete matter taken up by the members of the Privy Council when they convened in May 1888 was the Imperial House Law (*kōshitsu tenpan*). This body of law set down in broad if often vague terms the legal basis for the disposition of matters related to the Imperial House. Articles XI and XII in the draft of the law which Itō Hirobumi and Inoue Kowashi had approved for consideration by the Privy Council dealt with the location of the *sokui* and *daijōsai* rites. Article XI read: "The *sokui* rite shall take place in the Western Capital (*saikyō*)." Article XII left the location of the *daijōsai* unclear. It stated: "After the *sokui* rite the performance of the *daijōsai* shall be based upon the precedents of the Imperial Ancestors." These two articles, simply worded but of profound importance from the perspective of political symbolism, were the subjects of the privy councillors' attention on 25 May 1888.[77]

Yoshii Tomozane, privy councillor and also vice-minister of the imperial household, first broached the issue of the two accession rites' location. He asked Inoue Kowashi, acting as chief secretary of the Privy Council and reporter for the Imperial House Law draft, whether there was any reason for holding the *sokui* rite in *saikyō* other than that this had been the practice since the time of Emperor Kammu, who had established Kyoto as the imperial city. Inoue replied in the negative. He added that following this ancient precedent stemmed from the deep "significance attached to the Great Rite, and not forgetting origins (*moto o wasurezaru no i*)." Yoshii then questioned Inoue about the location for the *daijōsai* since it had not been specified in Article XII. Inoue responded that since the article did not stipulate a location "it will be possible to hold it in either the Eastern Capital (*tōkyō*) or the Western Capital (*saikyō*) as is convenient."[78] This was the extent of the discussion over Articles XI and XII at the first reading of the draft. However, the members of the Privy Council continued the debate on 1 June when they split more clearly and contentiously into two groups: one advocating Tokyo and the other *saikyō*, or more accurately Kyoto, since this was the venerable name that the partisans of the ancient capital explained best expressed the significance of the city which they favored.

Emperor Meiji, Itō Hirobumi (president), Terajima Munemori (vice-president), Inoue Kowashi (chief secretary), five imperial princes, five state ministers, ten privy councillors, and two secretaries attended the Privy Council meeting of 1 June. Article XI was the first item on the agenda. After Inoue's reading of the proposed article, Higashikuze Michitomi (privy councillor and Senate [*genrōin*] vice-president) argued that Inoue's reasoning about "not forgetting origins" was faulty since the *sokui* rite had been held in places other than Kyoto in "remote antiquity" (*taiko*). Criticizing Inoue's history, he pointed out that the precedent for choosing Kyoto dated only from Emperor Kammu's reign.[79]

Higashikuze was not, however, an antiquarian advocating a return to an even more ancient precedent. In fact, he was one of the civilizationists who argued against the performance of accession rites in Kyoto because he believed that the ancient city could not provide an appropriate setting for modern state ceremonies. In the future, he pointed out, representatives of foreign countries would attend the *sokui*. Therefore, it was imperative that "the rite be exceedingly imposing." However, Kyoto Palace lacked a sufficiently "grand and lofty appearance."

Higashikuze advised against the Western Capital because in an age of "advancement into the arena of Civilization" (*bummei no iki ni susumi*), as he put it, various practices and institutions were undergoing great change and it was likely that the *sokui* would also be reformed to meet new requirements. Moreover, Higashikuze could not understand the necessity of holding the rite in a "remote place" (*enkaku no chi*), which is what he called the Western Capital, when the imperial seat had already been moved to Tokyo. This would lead to unnecessary inconveniences, both monetary and otherwise, even with the imminent completion of the Tōkaidō railway line, which would link the Western Capital to Tokyo. In concluding, Higashikuze suggested deleting the designation of the Western Capital from Article XI and merging Articles XI and XII to simply read: "The *sokui* rite and the *daijōsai* will be based on the precedents of the Imperial Ancestors."[80]

Privy Councillors Yoshii Tomozane and Kōno Togama followed with arguments against using the Western Capital. Yoshii's reasoning was simple and practical. He maintained that holding the *sokui* in the Western Capital would cost two to three million yen more than conducting it in Tokyo. Using the Western Capital in spite of the huge added expense would elicit a great outcry from the people; for they would wonder, "Why go to all the trouble of having [the *sokui* rite] in the Western Capital when the Great Capital of Tokyo exists?"

In contrast to the pragmatically minded Yoshii, Kōno sounded very much like Higashikuze. He emphasized Tokyo's overall suitability based on what he believed were the modern requirements of setting for the *sokui* rite. Since the *sokui* rite was the greatest rite mentioned in the Imperial House Law, he argued, "the place chosen for its enactment should also be the most flourishing in the nation and should have the greatest concentration of people." Therefore, he concluded that the argument about "not forgetting origins" was really irrelevant to the choice of location. For, "Tokyo is the Imperial Capital and has become the locus of Civilization (*bummei no chi*). It is the crown of the entire flourishing nation. If this capital is rejected I know of no other appropriate location. Even granting that the Western Capital is the emperor's birthplace, this is hardly a reason for holding this Great Rite there." Then, perhaps sensing that he and the other Tokyo partisans were in the minority, Kōno concluded with the suggestion that if the Western Capital advocates could not be dissuaded, the location should not be specified in the Imperial House Law so that changes could be made as necessary in the future.[81]

Enomoto Takeaki (minister of communications and also of agriculture and commerce) countered with a short statement in which he expressed his preference for the Western Capital. Nevertheless, he agreed that it might be a good idea to leave the location of the rite unclear. Privy Councillor Hijikata Hisamoto (also vice-minister of the imperial household) endorsed Higashikuze's advocacy of Tokyo but not, he emphasized, for financial reasons. Rather, he believed that with the East prospering every year it might not be appropriate to hold the rite in the Western Capital.[82]

Thus the Tokyo advocates spoke first, maintaining that Tokyo was simply the more convenient and less costly choice. More important, however, they pointed to the contrasting ritual settings of Tokyo and the Western Capital. Higashikuze and Kōno, especially, rejected the Western Capital because its setting seemed to them inappropriate for an age of civilization. From their perspective the Western Capital was no more than a "remote place," whereas Tokyo represented national vigor, progress, and civilization. However, the Privy Council members who advocated the Western Capital did so for almost exactly the same reason that Higashikuze and Kōno rejected it: its age.

The primary spokesman for the Kyoto advocates was Imperial Prince Arisugawa Taruhito. He reiterated the argument about precedents and maintained that the *sokui* should be held in the ancient capital because that "magnificent ceremony" had been held in the "ancient capital through the successive imperial reigns." Like Iwakura and others, he asserted that the location could be justified in an international context because the Russians also continued to hold their coronations in Moscow, the former capital. That it was primarily the pastness of the practice that commended the performance of the *sokui* in the ancient capital is likewise highlighted by the fact that Prince Taruhito began to shift the focus of the discussion from the location of the rite to the selection of a name that would best express the former capital's age. Since "Western Capital (*saikyō*) is the new name," Prince Taruhito reasoned, "the [wording of] the draft should be revised to Kyoto."[83]

Prince Komatsu Akihito, Prince Arisugawa Takehito, and Privy Councillor Sano Tsunetami (also imperial household councillor) all agreed that the rite should be performed in the ancient capital and that the city should be called by its venerable old name. As Sano put it: "Though Western Capital is the name that corresponds to Tokyo, the ancient name should by all means be retained. Kyoto should be used instead."[84]

The debate over Articles XI and XII closed with final arguments by Inoue Kowashi and Privy Councillor Soejima Taneomi (also imperial household councillor).[85] Inoue occupied a position between the civilizationists and the antiquarians. While he supported the decision to hold the *sokui* in the Western Capital, he did not feel that it was appropriate to change the former capital's name back to Kyoto. He opposed such a revision because doing so, he contended, would be tantamount to changing the name of Tokyo back to Edo, presumably because as Tokyo corresponded to *saikyō*, Edo corresponded to Kyoto. The name Kyoto, literally "capital city," would also give the impression that the Western Capital was in fact the Imperial Capital (*teito*) because the character "tō" (eastern) of Tokyo would then appear to make Tokyo a secondary capital in the East. Inoue's main point was that insofar as Tokyo was home to the Imperial Palace, it was definitely the capital of the country. For the Privy Council to change the wording of Article XI from Western Capital to Kyoto would make it appear that Kyoto was the location of the Imperial Palace, while Tokyo was only the site of a detached palace. In short, while Inoue joined the Western Capital partisans in advocating the ancient capital as the place for the *sokui*, he opposed their motion to change the former capital's name back to Kyoto because such a move might imply that Tokyo was not Japan's capital.

Soejima had no such qualms about undercutting Tokyo's position as national capital. He maintained that as the court had originally intended only to move the emperor to the East temporarily in order to save the dying city of Edo,[86] he had no reservations about supporting Prince Taruhito's motion to revive the ancient capital's old name. Soejima thus appeared to suggest that Kyoto was still Japan's only true imperial capital.

In the final vote on Article XI on 1 June 1888, eleven of the Privy Council members, a bare majority, approved changing the name of the ancient capital in Article XI to Kyoto and designating it as the site for the *sokui*. The Privy Council members did not indicate the place of the *daijōsai*.[87] Then on 18 January 1889 the Privy Council demonstrated even more strongly its favoritism for Kyoto by approving a recommendation to combine Articles XI and XII and to specify Kyoto as the location for both the *sokui* and *daijōsai* rites. In doing so—that is, in designating Kyoto as the locus for two of the regime's most public and spectacular ceremonies—the government's leaders secured Kyoto's position within the modern nation-state's symbolic and ritual topography.[88] Moreover, as we shall see in Part 2, the ritual makers continued to involve Kyoto in the performance of equally ostentatious imperial death rites.

In a broader sense, the debate over the site of the accession ceremonies had been a discussion about the relative importance that those concerned with state rituals would place upon the two major sources of the modern Japanese regime's legitimacy. One of these was the past, the depth and particularity of the national experience centering on the imperial history; the other was the present and the future, much of which, under the rubric of Civilization, was inspired by examples from the Western powers. When the governing elites planned any public ritual, these two sources of legitimacy pulled them in contradictory directions and compelled them to give Japan's modern rituals and ritual settings a bifurcated image: one of which seemed ancient and singularly Japanese, the other of which seemed modern and often Westernized. I will describe the dualism in Japan's modern ceremonies in more detail in the chapters that follow. Here I need only note that the two sources of the regime's legitimacy left Japan's modern symbolic or ritual topography with two capitals. Kyoto was to be the dominant sign of Japan's past; Tokyo, of its present and its future.

Throughout the modern era, from the second half of the Meiji period onward, Japan's rulers would utilize the ritual settings of both cities. But while Kyoto would continue to serve as an important symbolic and ritual center, especially during imperial accession and death rites, Tokyo would become the dominant ritual center for the great majority of state ceremonies. This was a development in marked contrast to the situation in the first two Meiji decades when Tokyo had been almost insignificant as a ritual center; and it can only be explained by a radical transformation, beginning in the early 1880s, in the governing elites' perception of Tokyo's Imperial Palace and the city of which it was the center.

From Temporary Court to Imperial Capital (*teito*)

In the very early hours of 5 May 1873 a fire broke out in the Momijiyama section of the Imperial Palace grounds in Tokyo. It spread quickly into the palace proper, destroying the emperor's private quarters (*tsunegoden*) and the other structures within the palace compound. Within a matter of three hours the conflagration had destroyed the entire palace and consumed the offices of the Grand Council of State and the Imperial Household Ministry. The emperor and empress escaped harm, however, as did the imperial regalia and other objects representing the gods of heaven and earth (*tenshinchigi*) and the souls of the imperial ancestors. That same morning the government transferred the Imperial Household Ministry to the Akasaka Detached Palace and the Grand Council of State to a building in front of the former palace. The emperor and empress also moved into the Akasaka Detached Palace[89] located beyond the old outer moat of the city at a considerable distance west of the shogun's former castle. They did not return to the heart of the city for nearly sixteen years.

The government did not even begin construction on a new palace until 1884. Ostensibly, these delays resulted from concerns about the Meiji government's straitened finances, conflicting opinions on the style in which a new palace should be built, and the government's primitive technological resources. Less than two weeks after the fire the emperor, through an imperial announcement (*chokuyu*), informed Sanjō Sanetomi, the head of the Grand Council of State, that he should not begin reconstruction of the palace because of the strain that such a project would place on the national treasury and on the people. In the following year the Grand Council of State announced a plan to rebuild the palace within the former palace compound. This plan also called for new government ministry offices at the old Honmaru site. However, in January 1877 the emperor ordered another postponement, again citing financial difficulties and this time referring to the government's recent reduction of the land tax. Finally, in September 1879 the Grand Council of State ordered the Ministry of Industry (*kōbushō*) to begin taking construction surveys; but conflicts over whether to build in a Western style with stone, or in a Japanese style with wood, coupled with the length of time that it took just to determine if the palace grounds could even support the weight of a stone building led to further delays. The ground-breaking ceremony (*jichinsai*) finally took place on 17 April 1884.[90]

Yet these financial and technical reasons alone cannot account for the eleven-year hiatus between the great fire and the official start of the rebuilding. If the reason for delaying the palace's construction had been only financial, it seems unlikely that the government would have launched such a massive rebuilding project during the height of Finance Minister Matsukata Masayoshi's deflationary retrenchment policy.

Moreover, the government's leaders would surely have taken less than five years to settle their differences over the new palace's style and to resolve any engineering problems had they considered the project to be a high priority. Rather, the extremely long delay in even beginning the building project, followed by a rush to build an extravagant palace and surrounding area, can only be explained by a radical change in the governing elites' perception of the palace. During approximately the first decade and a half of the era—that is, the period coinciding with the height of the great progresses—they conceived of the palace as little more than the emperor's residence. This view is indicated by the wording of the imperial announcement, dated 18 May 1873, that urged Sanjō Sanetomi to be deliberate in his reconstruction efforts: "The other day We experienced a disastrous fire that completely destroyed the Palace. However, since this is a time of great national expenditures, We certainly do not desire its immediate reconstruction. Our *living quarters* (*kyoshitsu*) ought not to be a cause for damaging folk industries and the suffering of the common people. You, Sanetomi, should comply with this wish" (emphasis added).[91] However, by the early 1880s the government's leaders' views began to change. As late as September 1880 Iwakura Tomomi (minister of the right) and Yoshii Tomozane (senator [*genrōin gikan*] and vice-minister of the Ministry of Industry [*kōbu tayu*]) still urged postponement of rebuilding efforts so that scarce government funds could be allocated elsewhere.[92] But others both within and outside the government soon began to insist that in the modern age the importance of palace reconstruction far outweighed the government's fiscal limitations. They maintained that the palace, much more than simply being the residence of the emperor, was a representation of imperial authority and national honor; and they stressed that it was the central location for the nation's public rites as well. They thus urged completion of a magnificent new palace despite the fiscal problems that remained.

Kawaji Kandō, whose grandfather Kawaji Toshiakira had supervised the Kyoto Palace's reconstruction in the 1850s, explained to Prince Arisugawa Taruhito, who was also minister of the left, that the government should spare no expense in order to build a great palace for the modern age. He maintained, in this petition dated June 1883,[93] that in antiquity material culture (*bunbutsu*) had been undeveloped and transferals of the capital had been commonplace. Consequently, the palace did not have to be a great edifice (*taika*). However, since the Restoration great strides had been made in material culture and institutions and the emperor had established Tokyo as the "eternal and immutable imperial capital." Therefore, it was absolutely necessary to have an "eternal and immutable palace in Tokyo." After all, the emperor ruled the people from the palace and he received Japanese officials and subjects as well as foreign emperors and nobility there. Thus Kawaji felt that the palace's reconstruction bore "greatly upon the majesty of the emperor and Japan's national honor."

Shishido Tamaki—vice-president of the Office of Palace Construction (*kōkyo gozōei jimu fukusōsai*) and the holder of a number of other high official positions during his career—summed up the new perception of the palace in extremely explicit terms in a petition that he presented to the Grand Council of State on 12 February 1883.[94] He began by pointing out that though repairs on the Akasaka Temporary Palace had been made, the structure was nonetheless totally inadequate—whether as the emperor's residence, as the location for conducting national and international political affairs, or as a ceremonial site. After all, it had only been part of a *han* lord's dilapidating estate when the emperor first occupied it after the fire of 1873. He conceded that in the past there had perhaps been financial and political barriers to the palace's rebuilding, but these must now be overcome. He then explained exactly why a new and very lavish palace was necessary. "All things," he maintained, "have an inherent essence." The emperor's essence is to perform national rites for domestic and international audiences, but without a central location in which to perform them he would lose this essence. As Shishido put it: "The emperor occupies an intermediate position. He reigns over the people below. Outwardly, he faces the foreign countries. When court ceremonies, banquets, and rites, both major and minor, are not conducted, the public order (*chitsujo*) becomes disarrayed. This would not be the so-called Way of ruling the country through rites and music." Shishido further emphasized that an imperial palace should not by any means be considered only the emperor's living quarters, and using the classical reference to a "thatched-roof hut" he suggested that the domestic and global situation of his age was far different from the simpler times of that paragon of imperial virtue and frugality, Emperor Yao.

Therefore, the Imperial Palace does not by any means have solely the function of housing the sacred body of the emperor (*seikyū*). It is the place for the great affairs of ruling the nation, and people here and abroad look up to it with reverence and adoration. It is the place where national rites for the realm are conducted. In recent years, royalty and gentlemen from

Europe and America increasingly journey to our country and relations are becoming more and more intimate every day. World affairs ebb and flow through rites. With regard to governing the country this is not an age [like that of the Chinese emperor Yao] when the emperor can rule the realm from a thatched-roof hut with earthen stairs.

Shishido also proposed a specific timetable and budget for the construction project, prefacing his plan with a final statement about how urgent it was for a great empire to possess a magnificent symbolic and ritual site: "As we are an independent empire (*waga dokuritsu teikoku ni arite*) it is truly necessary to secure an appropriate grandeur for the palace. The emperor's mind is set. The leaders have already committed themselves. With regard to foreign relations and domestic governance this is not, of course, an ordinary construction project." Moreover, he maintained that because the construction effort was of the highest priority generous funds should be appropriated in order to complete the task quickly: "If by any chance the matter of this construction goes for naught, the immediate problem will be that there will be no place for great national ceremonies and intercourse with foreigners; and there will be a great blemish on the Empire's dignity. Thus, this is an urgent task that must be accomplished, even at the sacrifice of other matters."

Shishido recommended that construction begin immediately and that it be completed by 1889, before the opening of the Diet in 1890. It was important to complete the task by that date because the great ceremonies that would attend the opening of the Diet, including presumably the promulgation of the Meiji Constitution, required the new palace. The ceremonies would be a means of "joining the majesty of the imperial household with the reverence and adoration of the people. This is the reason for setting the deadline for that year."

Many of Shishido's colleagues in the construction effort also urged the palace's completion before the opening of the Diet. While his plan differed in some details from Shishido's, Kagawa Keizō, assistant vice-minister of the Imperial Household Ministry, also recommended in April 1883 that great haste be made to complete the palace by the opening of the Diet. Like others, Kagawa insisted that the Akasaka Temporary Palace was really no more than a deteriorating *daimyō* estate.[95] And many years after the completion of the palace, Nakamura Tatsutarō, an architect employed by the Office of Palace Construction from 1882 to 1887, also recounted that there had been great pressure to complete the job by the opening of the Diet.[96]

As for the budget, Shishido suggested the figure of 10 million yen, an enormous and in retrospect totally unrealistic amount when one considers that the entire yearly national revenues during the first half of the 1880s averaged just over 60 million yen.[97] While the government completed the palace at about half the amount of Shishido's original budget request,[98] this was still a tremendous outlay. Shishido thus presented an extremely costly proposal that ran directly counter to the current of Matsukata Masayoshi's deflationary policies. Clearly, the necessity of economizing in governmental expenditures had seemed an adequate reason for delaying the palace's reconstruction only to the extent that the government's leaders imagined it to be the emperor's mere "living quarters." As the new perception of the palace in Tokyo began to emerge in the early 1880s, when it became typical among the government's leaders and advisors to think that it should be the national ceremonial center, governmental retrenchment was no longer sufficient reason to allow the heart of Japan's capital to remain the "den of foxes and badgers."

Officials directly involved in formulating concrete plans for the capital's renovation and critics concerned with the overall planning of Tokyo also began to view the palace differently. This fundamental shift in thinking about the palace affected their perceptions of the city and resulted in the long run in dramatic changes in Tokyo's physical configuration. The most remarkable fact about official plans for the renovation of Tokyo prior to late 1884 is that none of them had even considered an imperial palace.[99]

The government had, of course, carried out a major rebuilding project in the Ginza area at a very early date. Through the Tokyo government the national leaders began this famous "brick town" project in August 1872 for the ostensible purpose of fireproofing a very flammable wooden city. However, as the Ginza section edged up against the Foreign Concession to the east and was bounded to the south by Shinbashi Station, the terminus of Tokyo's artery to the international port of Yokohama, these leaders also obviously meant to give Japan's major gateway to the world a modern appearance. When completed in May 1877 this "showcase," to use Henry D. Smith II's apt phrase, included two-storied brick buildings built in a uniform Georgian style, a tree-lined boulevard with gas lamps and arcades, streets straightened out in a grid pattern, and the first sidewalks in Japan.[100]

Several years after the completion of the Ginza project, Matsuda Michiyuki, a bureaucrat and then governor of Tokyo, offered a comprehensive plan for the capital's renovation.[101] While Matsuda's scheme included measures to improve streets and canals, a sewer and waterworks system, and the construction of a port, he especially stressed the necessity of marking off a core area of the city for immediate attention. Put differently, like his predecessor as Tokyo governor, Kusumoto Masataka, he proposed that any areas lying outside of the core should be given only minor attention.

Yet Matsuda and those who had earlier directed the Ginza project had completely ignored the idea that the regime's power should be represented on the face of the city, either by an imperial palace or other government buildings. To be sure, the Ginza project had created a modern shopping district at the city's gateway; but it stopped there. And the core area in Matsuda's plan—made up of Kanda, Nihonbashi, Kyōbashi, and Shiba Wards along with a section of Asakusa Ward—was the center of the city's economy, not of the national polity.

Clearly, Matsuda's plan had been influenced by the liberal economist Taguchi Ukichi's commerce-centered vision for the city. Taguchi had been even less attentive to questions regarding the capital's representation of political power. Whereas Matsuda simply ignored the problem of the burned-out palace grounds, Taguchi had suggested in his "Tōkyōron" (1880) that this space and some of the former *daimyō* estates should be made available to what he called the new "merchant gentlemen" (*gōshō shinshi*) as part of a venture to remake Tokyo into an international port city. As Taguchi put it quite bluntly, "Ah! Once commerce flourishes all things progress."[102]

However, Matsuda's plan and the commercially oriented view that it represented quickly came under criticism. Fukuzawa Yukichi, for example, the important and highly influential social and political critic, argued in June 1883 that Tokyo urgently needed a comprehensive city plan that would revolve around a magnificent palace's construction.[103] Citing Euro-American examples of monumental building efforts such as the Washington Monument and the Köln Cathedral, Fukuzawa began by noting that while the capital's planning required immediate attention, the actual rebuilding would probably be carried out over generations or even hundreds of years. Nevertheless, officials of Tokyo's prefectural government acted as if they were unaware of how urgent the city's reconstruction was; and they still had no concrete designs. Instead, they set about constructing waterways, gas lines, railways, and bridges in a piecemeal fashion with no overall plan.

Fukuzawa insisted that while such people as Matsuda Michiyuki had argued for the construction of Tokyo harbor, and others had suggested erecting a structure like the Capitol building in Washington or any number of other edifices, the most urgent, large-scale, and long-term task should be to build the imperial palace. The capital could then be fashioned around it. Since the palace would be a permanent structure for the "Japanese emperors whose successive reigns are coeval with Heaven and Earth," and since such a palace is "the place where the emperor of our divine country (*waga shinshū*) conducts ceremonies of intercourse with monarchs and presidents of the myriad nations," he stressed that every effort should be made to make the palace "splendid and beautiful to accord with our national power." With regard to the surrounding capital city, he reminded his readers that "if there is any desire at all to make the palace splendid and beautiful to accord with our national power, it is insufficient to make the interior of the palace splendid and beautiful. The area outside the palace, outside the gates, must also be made splendid and beautiful." And in what was for Fukuzawa a typically disparaging remark about the life of commoners, he insisted that the customs of their everyday lives should be kept out of view. To allow "the purveyors of stews (*nikomiya*) to exist side by side with wealthy gentlemen on Nihonbashi Avenue and to allow fluttering loincloths (*fundoshi*) out on drying racks above the 'Brick Avenue,'" he mocked, would be just like "sweeping heaps of rubbish in front of the main entrance to the palace."[104]

The manufacturers of national monuments and the inventors of national rituals generally sought to impress both domestic and foreign audiences with their creations. Fukuzawa, however, was primarily concerned to demonstrate national power and the level of Japan's civilized character to the official and unofficial representatives of the foreign powers. He urged, in other words, the Japanese state's full-blown entry into what David Cannadine has described as a kind of international ceremonial rivalry during the late nineteenth and early twentieth centuries.[105] I want to take up the significance of this global ceremonial competition in more detail in Part 2, but suffice it to note here that Fukuzawa passionately believed that in an age in which the entire world was linked as if "one house" and many foreigners came directly to Tokyo through Kobe and Yokohama, these foreigners' impressions of Japan would be determined by the capital and the imperial palace at its core. Thus the construction of both the palace and the capital were matters that directly affected "national prestige and the intimacy of foreign relations."¹⁰⁶

Fukuzawa specifically criticized those who hesitated to build a great capital city with a splendid imperial palace because of concerns about the government's straitened financial circumstances. He chastised those who praised the virtues of monarchical self-sacrifice for the people and said that they simply did not understand the necessities imposed by international politics and progress. He rejected the claims of those who reasoned that

both [the case of the emperor Yao who] "did not trim the grasses with which he thatched his roof and had three earthen stairs" and the [case of Emperor Nintoku] who did not repair his crumbling palace but gave the people three years for recuperation, are examples of imperial virtue [i.e., they had lived in simplicity out of concern for the people]. It is said that the ancients only treasured goodness. Thus how can one justify embellishing the city and making the palace absolutely beautiful in order to boast to the people of the world?

Fukuzawa rejected such reasoning as anachronistic.

This is an argument ignorant of contemporary relations and the progress of Civilization. It goes without saying that the society of the renowned Yao was primitive and uncivilized and knew nothing of cultural things. The rule of Emperor Nintoku notwithstanding, the times under his reign were undeniably uncivilized. Moreover, Empress Jingū's Korean expedition had only recently taken place, and the people's resources had been exhausted as a result. It was necessary to undertake a course of great frugality and recuperation. However, this is not a primitive and uncivilized age like that of Yao; and the people's resources are not exhausted as they were during the reign of Nintoku. Rather, this is an age of mutually intimate relations with the monarchs and presidents of the myriad nations. Thus, our empire of 36 million people must fully endeavor to build a palace of absolute beauty equal to itself. Why should we learn from a primitive age when we are not primitive, and act as if impoverished when we are not impoverished? For in so doing we shall bring about the loss of our imperial household's rites of equal intercourse with the myriad nations.¹⁰⁷

The views of such persons as Fukuzawa concerning the importance of including the imperial palace in an overall design for the renovation of Tokyo soon appeared in official plans for the rebuilding of the capital. In the plan that he presented to Home Minister Yamagata Aritomo in November 1884, Tokyo's governor Yoshikawa Akimasa deemed it necessary to include four great avenues radiating out from the imperial palace. As Yoshikawa himself indicated, these would be used for the comings and goings of the imperial family as well as by visiting dignitaries. While Yoshikawa underlined the importance of opening up the entire city through a sweeping improvement of its transportation network—including its streets, railways, canals, and bridges—his plan marks an important moment in rethinking the capital's structure in that it was the first official city plan to make explicit provisions for the imperial palace.[108]

Yamazaki Naotane—a Home Ministry official selected as a member of the investigatory committee established (7 December 1884) to consider the Yoshikawa plan—articulated the imperial palace's centrality to the capital in a far more ambitious way and from an international perspective. He suggested that the creation of a majestic capital city should be modeled on Paris as it had been rebuilt under the direction of Napoleon III. His concrete proposals included the construction of expansive boulevards, parks, a central market, a theater, a hotel, and monuments positioned throughout Tokyo. However, of most interest here was his proposal to cluster the various government buildings scattered throughout the capital around the imperial palace.[109]

While officials connected with the Home Ministry looked to the great capital cities of Europe and the United States during the 1880s for suggestions on remodeling their capital, those affiliated with the Foreign Ministry went further and commissioned Western architects to submit designs for the rebuilding of Tokyo. These planners, the most important of them German, reflected the contemporary trends in capital city construction and emphasized the expression of political power in urban architecture and space. When applying their conceptions of capital city planning to Tokyo they envisioned this city with its public buildings centralized around the imperial palace and expansive avenues that would provide grand vistas of strategically placed buildings and monuments.

The most influential and best known of such designs was that drawn up initially by Wilhelm Böckmann and then elaborated upon by his architectural firm partner, Hermann Ende. Their plan featured two broad avenues named for the emperor and his consort, the Mikado Avenue and the Empress Avenue. These avenues began at the north and south ends of a central station and converged on a monument to the west. Another expansive avenue, the Japan Avenue, started at this monument and extended further east past an exhibition grounds and a military parade field, before breaking off into two more diverging avenues. One, the Parliament Avenue, terminated at the Parliament while the other terminated at the Imperial Palace. Important monumental buildings would also be placed along the Mikado Avenue and east of the exhibition grounds.[110]

The planning of and debates over Tokyo's rebuilding culminated in the cabinet's promulgation of the Municipal Improvement Act (*shiku kaisei jōrei*) in August 1888 and the Municipal Improvement Committee's (*shiku kaisei iinkai*) subsequent proposal of specific recommendations. The government had by then rejected the German plans, primarily because their primary proponent, Inoue Kaoru, had lost influence following his failure to revise the unequal treaties with the Western powers. Moreover, those with commercial interests who still held a commerce-centered vision of the capital forced a considerable dilution of Yamazaki's scheme for a spectacular city in the mode of modern Paris. Yet by the time the Municipal Improvement Committee made their plan public in May 1889, the idea of representing the regime's power through a lavish Imperial Palace and other impressive public buildings in the core of the city had become a matter of common sense. In fact, the palace and its fronting Palace Plaza were already near completion.

The committee's proposals ranged widely over streets, waterways, railways, parks, markets, crematoriums, and cemeteries and provided for a composite core area that would represent both public authority and rising commercial interests. The committee's plan included the Imperial Palace with an adjoining Palace Plaza at the very heart of the city. The committee members suggested clustering governmental buildings just south of the palace in the Kasumigaseki and Hibiya sections and opening up the Marunouchi and Ōtemachi sections east of the palace to commercial development.[111] Over the years, the Tokyo government carried through the committee's basic design for the core of the capital, although additions were made and then the plans considerably reduced as a result of fiscal limitations. The result of this design for the capital can still be seen in its structure today: the Imperial Palace with a fronting Palace Plaza, all of the central government's ministry buildings gathered together at Kasumigaseki, and one of the major centers of Japanese capitalism located in the Marunouchi area.

The momentous transformation in the governing elites' view of the Imperial Palace and Tokyo that took place during the 1880s resulted in concrete changes in the capital's appearance. Most obviously and significantly, the Imperial Household Ministry, through its Office of Palace Construction, rebuilt a new and permanent palace over the ruins of the burned-out Edo Castle. The palace that was finally completed in October 1888, less than four months before the promulgation of the Meiji Constitution, consisted of thirty-six buildings linked together by a common corridor. These buildings were said to be primarily Japanese in inspiration, built of wood and with roofs fashioned in the classical *irimoya* style. However, the interiors of the private and public rooms differed in style. The architects employed by the Office of Palace Construction designed the rooms in the section of the palace used as the private residence of the emperor and empress, the *oku kyūden*, in what was considered an entirely Japanese style. In contrast, they built the rooms in the section of the palace used for public purposes, the *omote kyūden*, in a mixed style, with most of the interior decorations and furniture selected from Germany by Katayama Tōkuma, the well-known architect who would later design the new Akasaka Detached Palace.[112]

In other words, the Office of Palace Construction built the publicly visible sections in the palace's interior with the intention of creating a ceremonial setting similar to those of the most powerful and "civilized" nations. This was nowhere more true than in the Throne Room (*seiden*), a ceremonial space that one British writer for the *Japan Weekly Mail* described in the following way:

The Throne Room in the Imperial Palace is a noble chamber, Japanese in conception, but not without features imported from the West. The ceiling is a tessellation of pictures, representing conventionalized forms of the chrysanthemum, the paullownia, and the peony, in rich but subdued colours, each picture set in a deep frame of lacquered ribs, the angles of which are wrapped in elaborately carved plates of gilded copper. Descending by a curved cornice similarly panelled but having peony designs on an Indian-red ground, . . . the ceiling reaches a second plane where the same fashion of decoration is repeated in colours slightly more subdued. The upper section of the walls is in light buff, chastely decorated, and the arras are of dark ruby brocade, pleated and ruffled. The Throne, which is in gold and red, stands on a slightly raised dais and overhead, supported by two sloped lances, hangs a silk canopy having the Imperial arms, the chrysanthemum and paullownia, beautifully embroidered in purple on a straw-yellow ground.[113]

Dr. Erwin Baelz, the well-known German doctor employed by the Japanese government, also praised the palace and noted in his diary: "Certainly I cannot remember having ever seen in Europe a finer hall than the throne-room in this palace"[114] (see Figure 2).

When asked many years after the Meiji Palace's completion why those who had designed the rooms had imported so many of the interior

Figure 2. Woodblock print of the Meiji Constitution's promulgation in the new Throne Room. "Shin kōkyo ni oite seiden kenpō happushiki no zu," 1889. Courtesy of Asai Collection.

decorations from Germany and few from other countries such as France or England, Nakamura Tatsutarō, an architect employed by the Office of Palace Construction, replied quite simply that it had had to do with the relative power of those nations. As he admitted quite frankly, "Well, I believe [Itō Hirobumi] had, how would you say it, to curry Germany's favor (*gokigen o totte okanai to ikenai*)." Nakamura felt that the respect for German palace decor had been directly related to the rise of German military power, for he also remembered this as the period when the Japanese army had been refashioned after the German model. Moreover, he recalled that there had been a more widespread German architectural influence, and he gave the example of the Foreign Ministry having also invited German architects (probably referring to Ende and Böckmann) to Japan around that time. Thus in Nakamura's mind, as well as in the minds of several prominent architects questioning him, Japanese national architecture had been decisively influenced by European and particularly German styles, not for purely aesthetic reasons but because aesthetic choices were predicated upon perceptions of relative national power.[115] In this connection, it may also be noted that the Nijū Bridge linking the palace grounds to the Palace Plaza, one of the most prominent national symbols in modern Japan, was built in what was described as a German Renaissance rather than Japanese style.

At the same time, the Imperial Household Ministry took over jurisdiction of the space in front of the main entrance to the palace and began to prepare it as an open plaza that could be used for public rituals. Known today as the Outer Garden of the Imperial Palace (*kōkyo gaien*), or the Imperial Palace Frontal Plaza (*kōkyo mae hiroba*), during the Tokugawa period this area had been called Nishinomaru Shita and high-ranking *bakufu* officials maintained their official residences there. After the Restoration the new government housed various military and governmental facilities on this space with apparently no desire to utilize it as a ceremonial theater or to fill it with impressive buildings.

As late as 1883, for example, the area appears on the General Staff's very detailed map of Tokyo as a site cluttered with an assortment of miscellaneous buildings, enclosed compounds, and only limited open space. Starting from the northeastern corner at the Wadakura Gate and moving southward, we see first the Home Ministry's library and then installations for horse training and the Tokyo Garrison (*Tōkyō eiju shuei*). Below that compound and to the west is a small field used by the police, to its east the Peers' Club, and next to that the estate occupied by Iwakura Tomomi, complete with areas marked as *hatake*, cultivated

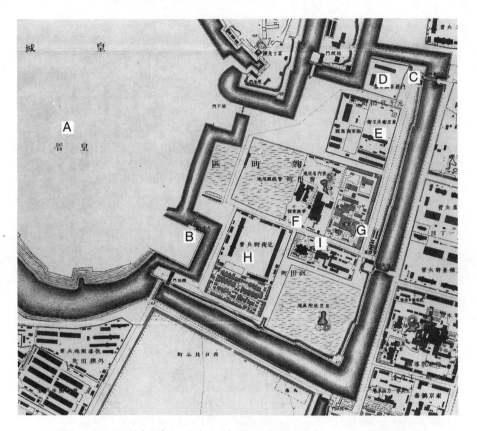

Map 1. Imperial Palace, Palace Plaza, and environs in 1883. From Sanbō
Honbu Rikugunbu Sokuryōkyoku, *Gosenbun no ichi Tōkyō-zu sokuryō genzu*
(Tokyo, 1886). Courtesy of East Asian Library, University of California,
Berkeley. A: Imperial Palace. B: Nijūbashi. C: Wadakura Gateway. D: Home
Ministry Library. E: Tokyo Garrison. F: Peers' Club. G: Iwakura Tomomi
Estate. H: Imperial Guards' Barracks. I: Senate (*genrōin*).

plots. On the southwesternmost extremity of this area are the barracks
of the Imperial Guards and to their east is the Senate (*genrōin*) and
another small field (see Map 1).[116]

Since segmented compounds or small unfilled spaces created fragmented compartments over the area, it was not in any way like a ceremonial arena. But shortly before and after the palace's completion in
1888 the Imperial Household Ministry removed almost all these structures and left a huge and sprawling open plaza. In terms of public ritual

making, the decision to fashion an expansive open plaza in front of the palace was extremely important for several reasons. First, with the magnificent grandeur of the palace walls, gates, and turrets and the restrained elegance of Nijūbashi forming a backdrop, the area could provide a sublime stage for the regime's most sumptuous public ceremonials. Just as noteworthy, however, was the fact that such an enormous tract allowed great masses of people to be gathered together in front of the palace. This was a new and necessary sort of public space, one that allowed crowds to both see and be seen by the emperor.

In a related way, the plaza constituted a space on which to actually see the people of the nation, "We the Japanese People," in their relation to the monarch and each other. Particularly after the late 1880s, few visual representations (for example, woodblock prints and postcards) of the emperor in public spaces such as the plaza show him in the absence of crowds. Seeing the crowds, in fact themselves, and the emperor in their mutual recognition allowed subject-citizens throughout the nation to imagine themselves as one community under the symbol, rule, and gaze of the emperor. Put differently, the Palace Plaza provided a location on which to diagram the Nation.

Two other places outside the capital's symbolic and ritual center became important points in Tokyo's ritual topography beginning in the late 1880s: Aoyama Military Parade Field and Ueno Park. The former, along with Yasukuni Shrine, became one of the two most significant locations for a variety of public military rites. The military completed construction of the Aoyama Military Parade Field in April 1886 as part of a more general dispersal of military facilities. The parade field at Aoyama replaced the older one at Hibiya, near the core of Tokyo.[117] Emperor Meiji first visited Aoyama Military Parade Field in October 1887 in order to view a discharge ceremony for the Imperial Guards, and between 1887 and 1911 he visited the parade field a total of thirty-two times. While the majority of these visits were for military reviews held in observance of the annual commencement ceremony for the army (8 January) and the emperor's birthday (3 November),[118] a number of them were for military reviews held as part of the one-time imperial pageants that will be discussed in greater detail in the following chapters. Moreover, the first few public rites making up the 1897 and 1912 imperial funerals also took place on the parade field.

Throughout the modern era Ueno Park has been a site of enormous national importance, both because of its institutions of civic education— the National Museum, the Imperial Academy, the Tokyo Music

Academy, the Japan Art Association, the Tokyo Art Academy, and the Imperial Library, to name only the best known of such institutions established in Ueno during the Meiji period[119]—and because many national ceremonial events sponsored by either the government or Tokyo's citizens have utilized that space. Already in 1879, prior to Tokyo's emergence as the central arena for Japan's national ceremonies, the national government and the people of Tokyo held a welcoming celebration in Ueno Park for former U.S. President Ulysses S. Grant. In addition, between 1877 and 1890 the government sponsored three national industrial exhibitions at Ueno that drew millions of spectators from all over Japan and the world. In 1886 the park came under the direct jurisdiction of the Imperial Household Ministry,[120] thus ensuring that the ministry most directly responsible for the nation's rites would also have full control over the nation's foremost civic park. From then on governmental, military, and civic groups wishing to use the park—and many did for ceremonial purposes—required the Imperial Household Ministry's prior permission. Beginning in 1889, when Emperor Meiji visited Ueno Park as part of the national celebration for the Meiji Constitution's promulgation, it became regularly utilized in conjunction with commemorations of notable political and military national accomplishments.

In sum, by 1889 the new perception of Tokyo as a symbolic and ritual center had led to massive transformations in the capital's core. The regime's leaders had equipped it with a magnificent palace that demonstrated through its architecture not only the particularity and sublimity of the national past but, even more important in terms of Tokyo's symbolism and public pageantry, the nation's ability to stand at the forefront of civilization. They had also attached to the palace an expansive open area, the Palace Plaza, that could be used for public ritual. Adjacent to this plaza and sometimes also mobilized for ritual purposes was another open space, the Hibiya Field. Crowds gathering in front of the palace would often overflow onto this field, which in 1903 became a public park. Outside of the capital's political core, the Aoyama Military Parade Field and Ueno Park were set in constant and creative tension with the Imperial Palace and the Palace Plaza. Through numerous and spectacular imperial and civic processions between the political core and its outlying civic and military regions, Tokyo's center began to exert a strong symbolic centripetal pull on the whole of the city and, in time, upon the entire nation.

National Landscape and National Narrative

Historians have often explained the rise and fall of the Meiji emperor's great progresses throughout the land in terms of the emergence and decline of the antigovernmental "Freedom and Popular Rights Movement." It is claimed that the large-scale and lengthy progresses tended to cluster together in the second decade of the Meiji era because that was precisely the period of the movement's height. Through the imperial tours the government sought to capture the people's support—especially the backing of the village economic and social elite (*gōnō*) most likely to join in the movement—when its leaders faced their greatest domestic challenge. Thus, the progresses ground to a halt precisely when the movement no longer posed a serious threat.[121]

This argument is partly correct, but it is also somewhat misleading. The "Freedom and Popular Rights Movement," and especially the "incidents of intensified violence" (*gekka jiken*), about a dozen of which occurred between 1881 and 1886,[122] certainly exacerbated the governing elites' general sense of crisis and contributed to their mobilization of the imperial progress as a means of controlling the populace. But the tours neither began nor ended as a simple reaction to the emergence and decline of the popular protest movement. They were part of a much more sweeping enterprise that constructed the emperor as the active, visible, and actively seeing center of societal significance. The explanation that links the progresses too closely to the "Freedom and Popular Rights Movement" ignores the fact that the first of the "Six Great Imperial Tours" took place in 1872, before the period associated with that movement.

More important, when the government's leaders began in 1868 to seriously consider "transferring the capital (*sento*)," this concept was already suggesting that the emperor would be fashioned into a dynamic Ruler in motion. The progresses between Kyoto and Tokyo in 1868 and 1869 were, in fact, the Meiji emperor's first, largest, and most brilliant progresses and they became prototypes for the emperor's later tours. Over 3,300 men accompanied the first procession to Tokyo when it took over three weeks (4–26 November) to cover the distance between Kyoto and Tokyo. And 3,500 men were massed together to form the emperor's second progress, which lasted about the same length of time (10 April–9 May).[123] During the first progress Emperor Meiji stopped near Ise Shrine to "worship from afar" (*yōhai*) and then visited Atsuta Shrine personally. On his second trip he made the journey all the way to Ise, the first monarch to do so since the seventh-century visit of Empress Jitō.[124]

The decline of the "Freedom and Popular Rights Movement" also cannot explain the end of the great progresses. Though there can be no simple explanation for this sudden termination of the state's most extravagant public ceremonials of the first two Meiji decades, at least two factors must be considered. First, the governing elites had begun the task of creating imperial symbols and national rituals that did not require the physical presence of the emperor in the provinces. Most important, they had begun to place imperial portraits in the nation's schools and to implement a standardized and mandatory system of national rituals to be held there. The Ministry of Education began to send photographs of Emperor Meiji to schools in the early 1880s, and it is thought that by 1897 all lower elementary schools had imperial portraits. The language used in the ceremonial delivery of the imperial portraits dramatically underscores the relation between the end of the progresses and the diffusion of imperial symbols and rituals in schools: the dispatching of the portraits was called the "departure of the imperial conveyance" (*gohatsuren*), while their reception by schools was called the "imperial arrival" (*chakugyo*).[125] In 1890, the Ministry of Education also began to deliver official copies of the Imperial Rescript on Education to schools.

As Yamamoto Nobuyoshi and Konno Toshihiko have shown in their detailed study of school ceremonial events during the Meiji period, national rites for schoolchildren also began to take hold in the late 1880s.[126] The most important of these were observances of national holidays. A few schools had acknowledged these holidays from an earlier date, but they did so based on local initiative and usually did no more than allow their pupils to take a day off from school. Only in the late 1880s, especially after the Ministry of Education established ceremonial guidelines in 1891, did a nationwide and standardized system of national holiday ceremonies begin to take root. Various other ceremonies for important imperial events, as well as for war celebrations, also became commonplace.

Second, the gaudy but cumbersome progresses through the countryside drew to a close because the governing elites had prepared Tokyo and Kyoto to become the symbolic and ritual centers of the nation. These permanent ceremonial arenas precluded the necessity of a perambulating emperor. The emperor did not simply disappear from public view to a place "behind jeweled curtains" in the manner of Kyoto's previous emperors. For the modern regime was one based upon the idea of "direct imperial rule," *shinsei,* and its leaders sought to unify the people under the illusion that the emperor was as deeply immersed in politics as he was aloof and untainted by it. Therefore, he had to be seen actually engaging in such activities as bestowing the Meiji Constitution on the people, opening the Diet, or triumphantly returning to the Imperial Palace from victory in war. Moreover, as the Japanese regime became enmeshed in a new kind of international ceremonial rivalry, the emperor was presented as the main performer in a variety of spectacular rituals. In order to be seen the emperor needed a front stage, splendid and open to the world. The primary stage was Tokyo.

Tokyo, however, was not Japan's only capital. Actually, Japan's modern symbolic and ritual topography very much resembled Russia's, and the meanings that the Russian ruling elites found in Moscow and St. Petersburg were remarkably similar to those that Japan's ruling elites attached to Kyoto and Tokyo. In fact, as we have seen above, the example of Russia's two capitals appears to have exerted a considerable influence upon those who chose to retain Kyoto, along with Tokyo, as one of Japan's capital cities. Just as Slavophiles from the mid- to late nineteenth century might defend Moscow as Russia's true capital, the "heart of Russia" and the national past, even while St. Petersburg had become the imperial residence and the preeminent city for Westernizers, Japan's ruling elites would involve the ancient capital in the nation's ceremonies even as Tokyo became the imperial seat, was equipped with a new imperial palace, and was the favorite of the civilizationists.

However, the relation between Japan's two capitals was less conflictive, as that of Russia's two major cities seems often to have been, than complementary.[127] Kyoto rather successfully became the representation of the imperial family's and by extension the nation's past, even as Tokyo became the theater for the majority of public state rituals and the symbol of its present and future. Furthermore, as we shall see, the government's leaders would rather unproblematically evoke the symbolism of the ancient capital for state ceremonies, especially when the need to affirm the regime's continuity with a sublime and deep past was felt most acutely—that is, during imperial death and accession rites. By way of contrast, in Russia after the assassination of Alexander II (during the reigns of Alexander III and Nicholas II), the nation's Muscovite heritage received renewed emphasis through the performance of such ceremonials as the coronation rite that was held in the old capital, but at the expense of St. Petersburg's aura. Put differently, Japan's ruling elites succeeded in harmonizing the relation between their two capital cities—in fact, between representations of the past and of the present and future—while in Russia St. Petersburg and Moscow, present and past clashed and could not be successfully narrativized together on the national landscape.

Even after the Privy Council debate described earlier, Kyoto continued its evolution into the official representation of the national past. Nowhere is this better seen than in the construction of Heian Shrine in 1895, and the invention of what was called the "Period Festival" (*jidai matsuri*). Heian Shrine, housing the spirit of Emperor Kammu and unveiled in the year marking the 1,100th anniversary of his founding of Heian, was a model within a model, a reproduction of an imperial court within Japan's exemplary imperial city. The imposing shrine complex, anointed by the government with its highest shrine ranking, *kanpei taisha*, replicated the eighth-century Heian Court's Official Compound (Chōdōin). This had been the core area of a larger "Great Palace Enclosure" (*daidairi*). The new shrine's large, two-storied front gate copied the ancient Ōtenmon, the towers attached to two long corridors reproduced the Sōryūrō and the Byakkorō, and the main oratory was a model of the Daigokuden, the Great Audience Hall. The red paint on the exposed wood portions of the structures and the green tiles on the roofs also followed the Enryaku palace style.[128]

The invention of what was called the "Period Festival" accompanied this remanufacturing of a part of the Heian Court. The highlight of this dramatic festival, held annually on 22 October, the day on which Kammu is said to have moved his court from Nagaoka to Heian, is a procession of people dressed in costumes representing the various periods between the founding of Heian and the Meiji Restoration. As the designers of the *jidai matsuri* explained about their festival and presumably the entire moving tableau, they had decided to perform it in order to "exalt history from Enryaku down to the present day."[129]

Thus the buildings of Heian Shrine and its most famous festival, both of which can still be seen today, were crafted so as to reinforce the sense of Kyoto's centrality in Japan's history. This is not to deny, of course, that the city's infrastructure and economy had in fact experienced dramatic modernization in the late nineteenth and twentieth centuries. Electric lights, the transformation of traditional industries (such as the introduction of French looms for Nishijin weaving), and a railway—

Kyoto's people had become familiar with all of these by the 1880s. And in 1890 the people witnessed the completion of the first stage of the city's crowning technological achievement, the Lake Biwa Waterways project. This system began to draw Lake Biwa's water by canal and aqueduct through mountains to Kyoto some eleven kilometers away. The feat not only earned for its young designer, Tanabe Sakurō, the sobriquet the "Lesseps of Japan" after the Suez Canal's builder, it also introduced Japan's first hydroelectrical power plant and aided in the modernization of Kyoto's transportation system, drinking water supply, irrigation facilities, sanitation, fire fighting, and more. Kyoto even held a festive paean to progress in the form of a great industrial exhibition that also took place in celebration of the 1,100th anniversary of the capital's founding.[130] But the Fourth National Industrial Exhibition might best be described as a festival of progress within a city of history. It demonstrated how Japanese history had developed unilinearly through time into the modern age. The examples of material progress notwithstanding, Kyoto's primary official symbolism was to be of its past, a fact that was underscored each time one of the great imperial ceremonies took place there.

While Part 1 has dealt primarily with the symbolic and ceremonial dimensions of Kyoto and Tokyo, it is also important to note that these were not the only places that Japan's modern rulers had molded or refashioned into official loci of meaning and memory. Very soon after the Restoration the Meiji governing elites began to fill the physical landscape, both within and outside the capital cities, with new or re-furbished shrines. These shrines tended to be placed on historically significant sites such as castle ruins, near dilapidated grave sites, on ancient battlegrounds, or at places mentioned in the *Kojiki* and the *Nihongi*, the modern regime's two most sacred texts. The sitings and simple style of the shrines gave them a kind of aura that in modern times has come with the look of the archaic, an almost-naturalness that bestowed truthfulness or unquestionability upon what they represented. But among the myriad deities of popular and elite culture and out of an infinite variety of people who had lived in the past, these sacred sites celebrated only those gods and men who could be incorporated into the dominant national narrative of direct imperial rule.

By the late 1880s an enormous number of such shrines exalting national gods, past emperors, and national heroes dotted the countryside. At the apex of this constellation of shrines, and the most significant symbolic site for the modern regime aside from Kyoto and Tokyo, was

the Grand Shrine at Ise. During the Tokugawa period, as other re-
searchers have shown, this shrine had been the object of a widespread
worship of Amaterasu Ōmikami and Toyouke Ōkami as deities of bountiful harvests and prosperity, not necessarily of Amaterasu as the progenitrix of the imperial family. Itinerant priests attached to Ise Shrine,
onshi or *oshi*, made annual rounds to believers throughout the country
while distributing such gifts as Ise amulets and Ise almanacs and collecting cash offerings. The *onshi* also gave sermons and conducted
prayers or purification rites. However, soon after the Restoration the
new government reinvoked the shrine's ancient connections with the
state while making great efforts to sever many of its connections to folk
beliefs and practices. The latter was accomplished by, among other
measures, abolishing the *onshi* who had spread and helped sustain popular Ise beliefs during the Tokugawa period.[131] At the same time,
numerous local shrines to Amaterasu and "sanctuaries for worshipping
Ise Shrine from afar" (*yōhaisho*) that reinforced the official narrative of
an imperial past that reached back to the Sun Goddess sprang up nationwide, in places as varied as newly settled villages, the principal cities
of Japan, and the recently opened international port cities of Yokohama,
Kobe, and Nagasaki.[132]

Since the modern regime's dominant historical narrative was that of
the imperial household's centrality in the past—indeed, the near identity
between imperial history and the significant past—it also promoted the
fabrication of shrines to exemplary emperors in history-myth. The most
exemplary was of course the first, Jimmu, who had allegedly founded
Japan through the act of imperial accession. He had initiated into history
the idea of the unity of the imperial household and the national community. Among the numerous shrines to him that had been built by the
late 1880s, those that would become the most famous were Miyazaki and
Kashiwara Shrines. The former had been erected in an area of Kyushu
known in earlier times as Hyūga, where, according to the *Kojiki* and the
Nihongi, Ninigi-no-mikoto, the grandson of Amaterasu, had descended
from the heavens with a divine mandate to rule and where in the third
succeeding generation of divine descendants Jimmu had been born.
Kashiwara Shrine, positioned in the area of the ancient Yamato courts,
testified to the claim that Jimmu's accession had taken place there.[133]

Many other historical emperors also acquired representation on the
modern symbolic topography. New shrines spoke, for example, of
the virtue of Sutoku Tennō, the tragic hero of the Hōgen disturbance
in the twelfth century; the three imperial heroes of the thirteenth

century's Jōkyū disturbance, Go-Toba, Juntoku, and Tsuchimikado;[134] and, most important, the leader of the fourteenth-century imperial restoration, Go-Daigo. In the official history, all of these emperors acquired significance insofar as they sought to reverse the historical tide of the usurpation of imperial rule by the rising warrior class.

For the Meiji Restorationists, Go-Daigo's Kemmu Restoration had in fact been the epochal, paradigmatic event in Japanese history, for they found in that complex political drama, which included an attempt to overthrow the *bakufu*, a model for direct imperial rule. Supporters of Go-Daigo's southern court in Yoshino thus became national heroes, and shrines exalting their virtues materialized within years after the Meiji Restoration. The Grand Council of State (*dajōkan*) formally suggested the building of a shrine for Kusunoki Masashige, that ill-fated paragon of loyalty to the imperial cause, as early as 13 May 1868—in other words, only ten days after the imperial army had captured Edo Castle. Minatogawa Shrine, when completed in 1872, marked the site of the battle at Minatogawa where Kusunoki had reputedly fought valiantly to the end against the forces led by the story's antiheroes, Ashikaga Takauji and Tadayoshi. Moreover, this was only one of several sanctuaries signifying Kusunoki's valor. Many other shrines celebrated the numerous other exemplary figures of the Kemmu Restoration: most important, Imperial Princes Morinaga, Munenaga, and Kanenaga; the loyalist warriors Nitta Yoshisada, Nawa Nagatoshi, Kikuchi Taketoki, Yūki Munehiro, and Kusunoki Masatsura, Masashige's son; and court noble Kitabatake Chikafusa, who had been adviser to five emperors and written a history of Japan centered on the reigns of emperors, and his son Akiie.[135]

The cavalcade of men whom the ruling elites elevated to the status of national heroes stretched forward and backward in time from the period of the Kemmu Restoration; and each of them acquired concrete expression in one or more shrines. The Buddhist sanctuaries to Nakatomi Kamatari, interpreted as having prevented the usurpation of imperial rule by the Soga family in the seventh century, as well as one to Wake no Kiyomaro, who was rendered significant as the monarchy's defender against the machinations of the Buddhist priest Dōkyō in the eighth century, were both transformed into national shrines, the former being renamed Danzan Jinja and the latter Goō Jinja (Defender of the Monarch Shrine).[136] Sixteenth-century warlords, particularly Oda Nobunaga and Toyotomi Hideyoshi, also found their way into the official pantheon of heroes and onto the national terrain. It was said that they had reunified the war-torn country while defending the imperial institution against the *bakufu*. According to the early Meiji Shinto ideologue Kamei Koremi, Emperor Meiji himself had broached the issue of erecting shrines to Oda Nobunaga and Toyotomi Hideyoshi in 1868, at the same time that he had suggested a shrine to Kusunoki Masashige. Oda's shrine in Kyoto, Kenkun Jinja, Toyotomi's shrine in the same city, Toyokuni Jinja, and a branch shrine to Hideyoshi in Osaka were all completed in 1880.[137]

The most recent of modern national heroes were those who had either given their lives for the loyalist cause leading up to the Meiji Restoration or subsequently died in defense of the country. As early as June of 1868 the new government's Grand Council of State ordered the construction of a sanctuary for the war dead in the eastern hills of Kyoto. The shrine that went up on Mt. Ryōzen came to be known as Ryōzen Gokoku Shrine, or Defender of the Nation Shrine at Ryōzen. Then in the following year, with the nation's administrative seat moved to the Eastern Capital, another *shōkonsha*, or "shrine to beckon the souls [of the war dead]," was erected on Kudan Hill in Tokyo. This shrine, later renamed Yasukuni Shrine, or Protecting the Nation Shrine, became modern Japan's central war memorial. These two principal sanctuaries in the two capital cities, however, were only the most conspicuous monuments to the war dead; for provincial *shōkonsha* existed even in the years immediately preceding the Restoration, and then proliferated throughout the country just after the regime's establishment. One early chronicler of shrines to the war dead has noted that some 105 officially supported shrines sprang up in the short span between 1865 and 1870 alone, and at least 150 *shōkonsha* are extant today.[138]

In short, by 1889 the Meiji regime had worked out what was to become the basic configuration of modern Japan's symbolic and ritual topography. Ise Shrine was to represent the political order's continuity with a part of the putative past that blended into a timeless time, before the imperial line's eruption into history. And in a symbolic sense there was not one but rather two capital cities. Kyoto embodied the authentic history, that single and thin strand out of the past that the regime certified as significant. Tokyo, on the other hand, represented the official version of the present and the possibilities of the future, of the nation's and the regime's present and projected power, wealth, and degree of Civilization. Finally, scores of recently remanufactured or newly invented shrines, sanctuaries of meaning and memory, filled out and completed the regime's symbolic topography.

In other words, a narrative expressing the shared time of the nation, seen by many recent theorists of nationalism as central to the constitution of the nation itself,[139] had been written onto the everyday world of the built environment. Together, this network of inscriptions on the landscape narrativized the national community's relationship to the past, present, and future—it told a story about the national community in time that was difficult for the nation's new subject-citizens to ignore, contest, or disremember.

To be sure, this was not a seamless or unproblematic narrative, but one that into the twentieth century contained within it the potential for its own unraveling. The temporalities represented by Kyoto and Tokyo were in fact incommensurable, conjoined only by the artifice supplied by the new regime. Exposure of the arbitrariness of the seam that had woven together Kyoto as the past to Tokyo as the present and future could allow a questioning of the entire national narrative. For example, the question could be asked: why was the past confined to the imperial line and Kyoto rather than Edo or the larger Kanto region, even though Tokyo, the representation of the present and the future, had its own past, Edo? Such an alternative as remembering Edo as the past carried with it all sorts of dangers, including opening up the possibility of considering the ancien régime as legitimate or of remembering the imperial household as irrelevant. That is why the new regime needed to be vigilant about occluding and constantly restitching the seam to produce a forgetting both of the dominant narrative's origins and of alternative pasts. That is why Taira no Masakado, the previously mentioned tenth-century rebel against imperial authority who became a popular deity in Edo folklore, was moved to a peripheral shrine within Kanda Shrine. That is also why the articulation of Toyotomi Hideyoshi as the defender of the imperial line against past *bakufu* found expression in the Meiji period shrines, while Tokugawa Ieyasu was absent from them.[140]

The space of the exposed seam could also open up a different kind of challenge, that of contesting the idea that the current regime represented the interests of the people. An example of an attempt to foreclose imagining this possibility is the positioning of Saigo Takamori's bronze statue at Ueno Park. For rather than face toward Kagoshima—the stronghold of the rebels from Satsuma that he led against the new government in 1877—and reinvoke the memory of Saigo's belief that he had been betrayed by the Meiji government, the statue was made to look toward Edo Palace. This signified him as the hero of the

Restoration who led the imperial army in its takeover of Edo Castle, not as the disgruntled leader of samurai interests who had been forsaken by the Tokyo regime.

But these faultlines notwithstanding, there can be no doubt that the dominant national narrative proffered a powerful suggestion about the nation and its people in time. It proposed that the people of the nation shared one history centering on the imperial household—or, put differently, it tried to discipline memory[141]—and it suggested that there was a unified will of the national community represented by the emperor and his regime that could be projected into the future.

Yet the modern symbolic landscape ought not to be thought of in its static condition alone, as a part of everyday life through which national subjects became daily subjected to, or interpellated by, the significances represented there. For soon after the great progresses of the Meiji emperor wound to a close in the mid-1880s, new spaces, especially in Tokyo and Kyoto, became the sites of spectacular state pageants that periodically interrupted quotidian rhythms to exclaim, in ritual form, a host of social and political ideas supportive of the regime and of modern nationalism. These not only elaborated through performance a range of official ideas, they also helped to cover up the major seams holding together the national narrative. As we shall see more fully in Part 2, through the construction and representation of a set of associations or homologies that replicated the meanings of Kyoto and Tokyo, those who invented the emperor's pageants sought, whether consciously or not, to render this system of representations unproblematic.

PART 2

Modern Imperial Pageantry

Overview

The closing of the era of the great imperial progresses did not lead to the Meiji emperor's return to a world hidden "above the clouds." Even as those spectacular imperial treks through the countryside ground to a halt, the Japanese governing elite and their bureaucracies were busily fabricating a new assortment of imperial pageants. Just as in the period's first two decades, the government's leaders in the second half of Meiji continued to utilize public ritual as a means of effecting or exercising power, not simply reflecting it. Yet the models for the regime's new ceremonials were no longer only those out of a reclaimed native past. Even more important were contemporary blueprints provided by the rival courts and governments of the Western powers, so that the pomp and pageantry that was such an important component of the Meiji state began to take on a new and cosmopolitan style.

Before proceeding with my analyses of these newly fabricated state rituals, however, I want to clarify where I stand with regard to some recent theoretical, comparative, and historical approaches to the study of political ritual. Above all, it is *not* my objective to construct universally valid generalizations about political rituals—to argue, for example, that all polities need them at all times, or that rituals always have certain identifiable effects, such as the ability to induce a sense of political solidarity. Nothing could be further from my objective than the humanistic goal of an anthropologist who recently wrote that he had searched throughout the world, "from mountain tribesmen in New Guinea to construction workers in Ohio, from the rites of chiefs in

precolonial Chad to the rites of modern presidents and prime ministers," in order to "make out the common threads that unite us,"
meaning all of humanity.[1]

Instead, my purpose is to historicize the political rituals which are the
subject of this study, using the insights of others who have studied
ritual, but not with the assumption that rituals are everywhere and
always basically the same because we are all human. I have no particular
stake in establishing a privileged place for ritual in the analysis of political
power, and I find it refreshing to learn from another author, in a more
historically oriented collection of essays on ritual and power, that sometimes rulers seem to have cared very little about ritual making, that they
expressed "their power in the crudest and ultimate manifestation of
individual power: in personal acts of violence." In making this statement, Teofilo F. Ruiz is maintaining that while the Castilian kings of the
late Middle Ages did not dismiss ritual altogether, power was more
often than not tied to sheer physical force.[2] Moreover, I would argue
that in our current historical moment television has so altered the nature
of ritual that for many of its viewers electronic pageantry succeeds at
least as often in collapsing as in constructing meaningful frameworks for
politics.[3]

These reservations about the study of political rituals notwithstanding, it is possible to demonstrate that pomp and pageantry were important to the ruling elites' perception of governance in Japan during
the late nineteenth and early twentieth centuries, just as they seem to
have been for governments in many other places at that time. The need
to create a ceremonial style of governance, even for a modern bureaucratic state under a constitutional monarchy, was well understood by
many political figures familiar with constitutional monarchies in Europe. Yano Fumio, for example, wrote in a petition presented in March
1891 to Imperial Household Minister Hijikata Hisamoto that the establishment of various court forms (*shiki*)—by which he meant a variety
of rules, regulations, and guidelines for the imperial household, especially prescriptions for the performance of the court's most important
ceremonies—was the "key to success" (*yōketsu*) for a regime under a
constitutional monarchy. Such a political system required the cultivation of the majesty (*songen*) of the imperial household and this "majesty" could "only be made real before the eyes of the people through
shiki."[4]

Yano was no stranger to the workings of constitutional monarchies
in the West. He had studied in England as a young man, had been one

of the leading intellectuals in the movement to establish a constitutional form of government during the 1880s, and had journeyed again to Europe in the middle of that decade.[5] Yet his familiarity with European politics led him to the conclusion not that ceremony had become obsolete for modern governments, but that it was an integral part of governance. Far from suggesting that the symbolic or ceremonial dimension of the state be abandoned, he argued that the government's leaders should compile a modern equivalent of the *Engishiki*, the tenth-century state's compilation of rules, forms, and practices that included guidelines for state ceremonies. In creating a Western-influenced constitutional monarchy, then, the Japanese governing elites understood that in addition to adopting institutional frameworks, they would have to fashion a ceremonial style appropriate to the form of government predominant in Europe.

Yet few scholars—whether historians, anthropologists, ethnographers, or anyone else—have taken these new Japanese ceremonials very seriously. For most, the ceremonial and festivities accompanying the promulgation of a constitution, an emperor's wedding anniversary, a crown prince's wedding, and victory parades through a city filled with triumphal arches and captured weapons have apparently seemed like just so much fluff. Imagine, for example, the imperial carriage used in the most majestic of state ceremonies: a modern English coach, but one curiously topped with a golden and very ancient-looking phoenix— "with its wings spread out, looking as if about to take off in flight."[6] Think again of court ritualists in archaic-looking robes solemnizing before the Sun Goddess an event of clearly Western inspiration: a silver wedding anniversary for a Japanese monarch who was not even monogamous. Try to envision Tokyo, with its skyline much closer to the ground than it is today, festooned with a dazzling array of monumental triumphal arches, mostly Western in inspiration. Through this city the emperor paraded in triumph, rejoicing over victories that he had neither planned nor commanded, but that official propaganda as well as newspapers and magazines attributed to him. Furthermore, what significance could there be to national pageants which the masses greeted with seemingly nonsensical popular revelry, complete with *sumō* wrestlers, festive displays, giant floats, wild dancing, festival clothes, gluttonous eating, and masqueraders in transvestite dress, accompanied by the sort of frenetic music which sounded to at least one European observer like "the most heathenish clamour."[7] All of this ceremony and festivity has generally been passed off as of little historical importance. These ritual events have been ignored, dismissed as "only ceremonial," or re-told in the form of colorful and exotic anecdotes.[8] There has been little awareness that they may be connected with the real workings of power.

These ceremonial occasions were not trivial to the powerful men in government who created them, most notably Itō Hirobumi. They ordered surveys to determine how such ceremonies were conducted by Western royalty, and they formed commissions to work out the details of the Japanese rites. They invited as many as two thousand Japanese and foreign dignitaries to the new Imperial Palace in Tokyo to observe the ceremonies. They spent enormous amounts of money to ensure sufficient pomp, magnificence, and authenticity in detail. And they flooded the world with visual and written accounts of the occasions. Moreover, hundreds of thousands of the nation's local elites, also moved by the gravity of the events, often mobilized whole communities to take part in local celebrations that mimicked the rites at the ritual centers. But why should such men have been so obsessed with ceremony? And why did a contemporary like the journalist Ubukata Toshirō count several of these ceremonial occasions among what he called, using the English expression, the "epoch-making" events of the late Meiji to Taishō period?[9]

In our continuing examination of the ties of power to visibility, it is possible to identify at least three dimensions to the relationship between these new pageants and political power. First we must consider a viewing audience normally forgotten in the study of political ritual, namely the world community. While military might and national wealth were the most obvious means by which nations jostled for position in the late nineteenth- and early twentieth-century world order, international politics also had a significant symbolic or ceremonial aspect that should not be minimized. The new imperial pageants were performed at least as much for a global as a domestic audience, and they helped construct an internationally comprehensible framework for understanding and carrying out diplomacy. In an age of imperialism Japanese political elites hoped to carve out a privileged position in the world order equal to those of the great Western powers through the performance of impressive national pageants.

David Cannadine has argued that the period from about 1870 to 1914 was marked by an efflorescence of national rituals in the Western world, especially of ceremonies centering on royalty and other heads of state. He also maintains, even while recognizing that the new ceremonies served a domestic need, that the state rituals did not emerge independently of one another but developed within the context of an international ceremonial rivalry. Thus the Austrians held grand celebrations for the six hundredth anniversary of the Habsburg monarchy, for the millennium of the Kingdom of Hungary, and for Francis Joseph's Golden and Diamond Jubilees, as well as for his eightieth birthday. The Italians observed a funeral for Victor Emmanuel II and the unveiling of a monument dedicated to him which coincided with the jubilee celebrating Italian Unification. The Russians witnessed a funeral for Alexander III and the tercentenary celebration of the Romanov dynasty. The Germans solemnized Kaiser Wilhelm I's funeral and the Silver Jubilee of his grandson. The French invented Bastille Day in 1880 and observed the funeral of Victor Hugo and the centennial of the revolution.

Americans joined in the making of rituals as well. They held tremendous celebrations commemorating the centennial of their Revolution and the four hundredth anniversary of Columbus's "discovery" of their country. The British, the focus of Cannadine's study, took part in Queen Victoria's Golden and Diamond Jubilees and her funeral, Edward VII's coronation and funeral, George V's coronation, and a number of other events.[10]

As the Japanese state and people became increasingly drawn into the world order during the late nineteenth century, the government's leaders became enmeshed in this ritualistic rivalry, and many of them came to believe that state ceremonials could be a genuine force in international politics. The dozens of surveys of Western courts, mostly dating from the 1880s and now deposited in the archives of the imperial household, the letters of important figures in Japanese ritual making, and the modern Japanese pageants themselves, some obviously direct copies of Western national ceremonies and every one filled with borrowed ritual forms—these all reveal the Japanese ritual makers' concern that their state ceremonies equal those of their Western counterparts. And we have already seen the impassioned and influential testimony of such men as Shishido Tamaki and Fukuzawa Yukichi, who maintained that a great empire such as that of Japan required a magnificent setting for its state rites—that the imperial palace and, for Fukuzawa, the capital itself should be able to impress not only the Japanese people but foreign dignitaries as well.

Cannadine has argued that the tense international situation in the late nineteenth and early twentieth centuries contributed to these developments because in such an era, "national rivalry was both expressed and sublimated in ceremonial competition."[11] This statement is suggestive in pointing out that international relations have had something to do with the invention and performance of modern national ceremonies, but it is too vague. While I cannot attempt to improve upon Cannadine's analysis of ceremonial rivalry among Western powers, a bit more can be said about Japan's entrance into this international ceremonial contest.

The purpose of Japan's active engagement in ritualistic rivalry among nations contrasted sharply with that of another form of international rite being performed in other countries of the non-Western world during the same period, namely, colonial ritual. As Bernard Cohn has argued, the British in India, especially after the Great Rebellion of 1857–58, fashioned a "ritual idiom" in order "to express, make manifest and compelling" their colonial authority.[12] Focusing especially on the durbar, Cohn showed how ceremonials could be a means by which Western rulers articulated and constructed their domination. The Japanese political elite, on the other hand, seized upon the international visibility of their national ceremonies to demonstrate the regime's modernity, its power, the loyalty of its population, and the depth and majesty of its "Tradition" to the aggressive imperialist powers of the West. The Japanese rulers developed an internationally comprehensible ceremonial idiom through which they expressed their nation's sovereignty. Moreover, beginning in the late 1890s the Japanese ceremonies dramatized Japan's political, cultural, and military superiority over Korea and China and thereby helped construct Japan's prerogatives as a colonial power in its own right.

The Meiji government's leaders, however, also put pageantry to domestic uses as they transformed these ceremonials into the most spectacular ideological performances that the masses who were becoming the nation's new citizens would ever see. Thus while Japan's modern national pageants were constructed within the context of the invention of a transnational ceremonial language, the particulars of the rites evolved with an eye turned toward the special requirements of the Japanese political order. While the details of these performances will become clearer in the ethnographic descriptions that follow, the objects, images, gestures, values, and meanings discernible in these ritual events were not random and disparate, but rather formed a system of interconnected and mutually referential signs and meanings.

In the dominant symbolic order constructed by the ruling elite, the imperial pageantry diagrammed, objectified, and attempted to make real and unproblematic two sets of homologies that were particularly congenial to the maintenance of the emperor and nation-centered order of meaning. On the one hand, there was a chain of analogies that centers on the place of Kyoto as I have described it in Part I—the site of history-myth and Tradition. It includes the idea of emperor as divine and above politics, or of the emperorship, as opposed to the mortal emperor. And it contains the category of sexual ambiguity: the flowing robes of court dress, the smooth face of the youthful emperor, and the invisible body of the emperor, one and the same as all other descendants of Amaterasu, the Sun Goddess. On the other hand, a contrasting set of homologies converges on the physical location of Tokyo—the place of progress, prosperity, and Civilization. It includes the idea of emperor as mortal and head of government, military uniforms, the bearded visage of the monarch, the ruler and the domain of government and public politics as unambiguously masculine, and the visible emperor as a ruler unique in history—the Meiji emperor, for example, rather than his father, Kōmei, or his son the Taishō emperor, and so on.[13]

These two series are in fact connected to each other in an oppositional relationship. Thus we find in the pageants analyzed below the following homologous oppositions:

Kyoto	Tokyo
past	present
history	future
Tradition	Civilization
gendered ambiguity	masculinity
emperor as god (emperorship)	emperor as mortal
emperor as above politics	emperor as head of state
spirituality	mundane prosperity
court robes	military uniform
beardless face	bearded face
invisibility	visibility

While every imperial pageant took elements from both sets of homologies, some drew more heavily from the former, others from the latter.

The ceremonials described and analyzed in the segment "Civilization, Prosperity, and Power" tended more emphatically to repeat elements in the series that included Tokyo, masculinity (except for women in the imperial family in opposition to whom the meaning of the masculine was constructed), Civilization, the military, mundane prosperity, and so on. The other set of homologies became much more prominent during moments of crisis in this dominant symbolic order, most especially in the period between the monarch's physical death and the accession of his successor. While I will not take up the grand public accession of Emperor Taishō in 1915, the section "Spectacles of Antiques" examines the death rites of both Empress Dowager Eishō and Emperor Meiji. Physical death posed the most serious threat to the fiction of imperial and national permanence and transcendence because such immutabilities were represented by the imperial body. It was thus in this liminal phase between the demise of the old emperor and the accession of the new that the Meiji leaders constructed spectacles out of the chain of associations linked to Kyoto.

This is not an exercise in decoding ritual that looks for the deep structures in Japanese kingship that transcend history;[14] it is rather an interrogation of the processes by which power has worked through the historical construction of binaries in culture, the monarchy, and the national landscape since the late nineteenth century. The success or failure of the imperial regime in creating modern subjects who would willfully participate in the national political community, *despite benefiting differentially from it,* rested in large part on producing the believability of key and frequently conflicting ideas, many of which commoners in the Tokugawa era would have found odd or nonsensical. Such beliefs as the permanence of the nation and the imperial line, the unity of the Japanese people despite their diversity, the ability of the emperor to be both divine and mortal, the position of the emperor as above politics and yet intimately immersed in it, and the naturalness of excluding women from government and political activities—these were hardly self-evident ideas.

Following Pierre Bourdieu, I find it unlikely that the "sheer power of discourse" could ever have produced beliefs about the national community that had not previously been held.[15] There is no inherent reason why those peasants in the provinces who saw notices in early Meiji explaining that "in this land called Japan there is one called the emperor [*tenshisama*] who is descended from the Sun Deity [*tenshō kōtai jingūsama*]" [16] should have felt anything but bewilderment. No simple and straightforward explanation would have been convincing. Yet I cannot agree with Bourdieu that you have to be born into it, that is, into the conditions of existence that reproduce the same sets of mental dispositions, the *habitus,* and the objective structures that seem always to have existed. Another process must have been at work that allowed for the acceptance of recently minted beliefs; and we must ask how it is that people can adopt beliefs that are imposed from the outside or, to put it differently, are a historical intervention.

If we again take a suggestion from Bourdieu,[17] but open up a wider space for the possibility of acquiring belief in cultural fabrications, it seems possible that believability can be engineered by dominant groups, though not necessarily always consciously, through the strategic manipulation of oppositional series of analogies that dissuade us from recognizing the arbitrariness of any particular element. More specifically, by producing the two mutually and multiply referential chains of homologies noted above, the ruling elite constructed a system of representations that was difficult to critique. Belief, then, depended less upon explanation than upon the production and dissemination of a mystifying swirl of analogous signs, meanings, and values, as well as their opposites. To make the claim of imperial divinity convincing, for example, required not simply explanation through official texts, but the making visible of an appropriate mode of dress, supplying references to Kyoto, Ise, and many other physical places in the nation's symbolic topography, as well as cultivating the ambiguously gendered monarch. Similarly, the strategy for inducing the belief that government should be the domain of men repeatedly invoked the set of homologies that centered on Tokyo and the masculine. There is a system in this mode of thought which was not precisely logical, but not entirely illogical either. An example of this sort of reasoning can be seen in a French survey of 1975 cited by Bourdieu, in which 29 percent of the people being polled associated Giscard d'Estaing with the ant rather than with any of five other animals, and 31 percent linked him to the oak tree rather than five other types of trees.[18]

Unlike Bourdieu, whose contribution is to elucidate the question of believability from the point of view of the actor's "logic of practice," here I am reasoning more from the point of view of the orchestrators of state pageantry in order to expose the strategies they used in their attempts to impose believability. I do not assume that they always succeeded, a point that I shall discuss in Part 3 and my conclusion. Yet it seems worthwhile to investigate the logic of their efforts to create belief, since history makes clear that they were not wholly unsuccessful either.

We come now to the third way in which imperial pageantry helped to produce a relationship of power. While these new imperial pageants occupied an important place within a system of representations that was made visible to international and domestic audiences, they were also occasions that made the people visible to the emperor. Like the earlier imperial progresses, these new public ceremonials helped fashion an image of the monarch as Overseer. Though he no longer rambled across the countryside directly subjecting the people and the land to his inspection, he regularly emerged from the palace in full pomp demonstrating that he could discipline with his gaze all those who gathered around him. And in the end, this new and internationalized style of public pageantry was even more effective than the progresses in creating the suspicion that the people might be the constant targets of the emperor's sight. While this ocular dimension of the monarch can be located in nearly all the pageants described below, I will especially focus on the imperial military reviews because they most clearly diagrammed for the people then, and for the historian today, this relationship of visual domination.

Part 2 is divided into two chapters. What follows immediately, "Fabricating Imperial Ceremonies," is a fairly straightforward description of the imperial pageants that especially emphasizes their newness and the logic of their constructions. The interplay of the two sets of homologies, the one centering on Tokyo and the other on Kyoto and other important sites in western Japan, should be fairly obvious. So also should the construction of the visionary monarch. The second chapter, "The Monarchy in Japan's Modernity," places the pageants and the imagery found there within a more rigorous and comprehensive analysis of Japan's modern monarchy.

CHAPTER THREE

Fabricating Imperial Ceremonies

Civilization, Prosperity, and Power

Although they remain impoverished, the poor greet the New Year with a fresh sense of hope. Similarly, as the twentieth century approached, it really did seem as though Japan was somehow advancing toward Civilization and that we [as individuals] were becoming, to some degree, more important. In fact, it was an age in which we did grow richer in all things, day by day, month by month. Japan, too, moved ever forward, month by month, year by year. In the twentieth century, we definitely became greater.

We moved into the twentieth century, first one year and then another, filled with great hopes of a dawning age. In 1900, that is, the thirty-third year of Meiji, the wedding ceremony of our present emperor, then the crown prince, took place. The date was the Tenth of May....

We got ourselves ready in the morning and made arrangements among our friends. About ten of the most intimate of us departed from the boardinghouse, entered [the Palace Plaza] through Sakuradamon, and stood just in front of the wooden barricade at Nijūbashi. We waited in order to see the carriages of the crown prince and princess pass by. A considerable crowd had already gathered by the time we got there and it grew as people with the same objective as us came in unending succession. Mounted policemen went here and there, while regular policemen

*controlled the crowd which moved recklessly forward. There
were people who climbed up to sit on the wooden barricade;
and even some who scrambled up the willow trees in front.
When one climbed up a tree, several others climbed up in
imitation. Policemen came around and brought the people
down from the barricade. Those in the trees were pulled
down by their feet. Yet, no sooner had the policemen gone
than the people once again scurried up the trees or seated
themselves on the barricade. I was reminded of the Bible
wherein it is written that Zacchaeus, a man of short
stature, climbed up a sycamore tree in order to see Jesus'
procession. I looked over the crowd that day. They also
seemed to share the feelings of the multitudes of Jerusalem
who saying, "Hosanna, oh Hosanna. Blessed is He who
comes in the name of the Lord," laid their garments down
on the road and welcomed the King who had come as the
Son of Man.*
                    Ubukata Toshirō, *Meiji Taishō kenbunshi* (1926)

Aside from imperial funerals the most spectacular pageants of the Meiji era demonstrated the imperial regime's ability to ensure national prosperity or well-being. They took place primarily in Tokyo, the city representing the nation's modernity, progress, wealth, military power, and ability to join in world civilization; and through them the governing elites legitimated their rule, both to foreigners and the Japanese people, by demonstrating their ability to produce prosperity in a world of intense international rivalries.

All these ceremonial events certainly included ancient-looking rites performed within the innermost sanctuary of the Imperial Palace; and imperial messengers reported on the occasions to the imperial ancestors and the supposed primordial gods at sites sacred to the national memory throughout the nation, especially in western Japan. However, the archaic-looking elements of ceremony were shed as the pageantry moved out into public view. In public the central actor, Emperor Meiji, rode in carriages modeled on those used by European monarchs, always wearing his modern, Western-style military garb. Civil and military officials, dressed in the latest European fashions, packed the emperor's processions. And huge numbers of soldiers, sailors, and weapons displayed the scale of the nation's military might. Through these public displays the emperor's regime asserted that its government brought national well-being, that it was at the forefront of the modern world, and that it was thus justified in its rule. In short, these ceremonies gave the impression, as Ubukata put it, of Japan "advancing toward Civilization" and of becoming "richer in all things, day by day, month by month."

THE CONSTITUTION'S PROMULGATION

It would be difficult to overemphasize the significance of the Meiji Constitution's promulgation on 11 February 1889. The Constitution not only established the legal basis for Japan's constitutional monarchy; the ceremonies and festive activities held in conjunction with the promulgation inaugurated a new style of imperial ceremonial event. Furthermore, this event set the standards for all future national pageants held to celebrate auspicious occasions of the imperial household. With the recently reconstructed palace and imperial city used as the nation's central ceremonial complex, the flooding of people into and information out of the city, and innumerable local observances timed to coincide with activities in the ritual center, this was Japan's first modern national ceremony.

Itō Hirobumi, then president of the Privy Council, initiated the planning of the promulgation ceremonies. While the particulars of the planning are not clear, the Board of Ceremonies' (*shikibushoku*) official record of the event notes that on 8 November 1888, the president presented his suggestions on the order of the ceremonies to the emperor. On that day the cabinet and the Imperial Household Ministry appointed a committee to work out the details. Ten days later, the official plan, endorsed by Prime Minister Kuroda Kiyotaka, Itō, and Imperial Household Minister Hijikata Hisamoto, was presented to the emperor for approval.[1]

The rites began by emphasizing the divine aspect of the emperor and rendering sacred the political act of establishing the Constitution. The ceremonies took place in sacred and national time, on *kigensetsu,* the holiday created in 1873 to commemorate the accession of the first emperor, Jimmu, and hence the founding of the nation. The core rites were held in the most sacred space of the palace, the Palace Sanctuary, a space unseen by any but the rites' performers. There, as the print media reported in minute detail based upon official schedules, the emperor, dressed in the ceremonial vestments of his ancestors, first offered a sacred sprig at the *kashikodokoro,* literally, "the place of awe," and made a solemn vow to the first ancestress of the imperial line. He pledged both to preserve the ancient form of monarchical government and to uphold the new laws, that is, the Imperial House Law and the Constitution. The emperor repeated this oath before the imperial ancestors in the *kōreiden* and then worshipped the myriad deities of the *shinden*. Imperial messengers had been dispatched to report the accomplishment to the nation's gods at Ise Shrine, the mausoleums of Emperors Jimmu and Kōmei (Meiji's father), and Yasukuni Shrine. Other messengers informed the dead heroes of the Restoration—men such as Iwakura Tomomi, Ōkubo Toshimichi, and Kido Takayoshi. Prefectural governors also delivered news of the Constitution and the Imperial House Law to the gods enshrined in all of the central government shrines (*kankokuheisha*) throughout the land.[2]

Having thus sacralized the establishment of the Constitution and the Imperial House Law and given these laws a suprahistorical foundation, the emperor stepped out of his priestly robes and donned his military uniform for the formal and visible granting of the Constitution in the new Throne Room. The emperor's reading of the "Imperial Speech on the Promulgation of the Constitution" and his handing of the Constitution to Prime Minister Kuroda highlighted this ceremony. The emperor declared that he promulgated the Constitution "in virtue of the supreme power" that the imperial ancestors had invested in him; and he urged the cooperation of the nation's subjects in "making manifest the glory of Our country, both at home and abroad, and of securing forever the stability of the work bequeathed to Us by Our Imperial Ancestors."[3] The actual passing of the Constitution to Kuroda was the physical enactment of the idea that the Constitution was a gift of the emperor and his one line of ancestors to the Japanese people.

Princes and princesses, the state ministers, members of the peerage, prefectural governors, presidents of prefectural assemblies, other high-ranking civil and military officials, the foreign diplomatic corps and other foreign guests—these dignitaries, representing the people of Japan and of the Western world, had all witnessed the "dignified and brilliant" ceremony.[4] But even more important, the event had been opened to the editors of ten Tokyo newspapers, five provincial newspapers, and three English language papers.[5]

In fact, the advertising of the ceremony had begun days before, with the newspapers describing the schedule of ceremonies and even printing a plan showing how the various personages would be ranged around the Throne Room.[6] This plan showed the emperor's throne—marked by a circle and the characters for *gyokuza* (imperial seat) in the largest print—on a dais at the head of the room. To his right and left were the

Sacred Jewel and the Sacred Sword. The high officials of the imperial household could be seen surrounding the dais. Just off to the right in front of the dais was the empress's seat, dignified in print almost as large as the emperor's. She was surrounded by princesses of the blood and important members of her entourage. Just in front of the empress as well as across the open space in front of the throne were the princes of the blood. All of the people positioned toward the front of the room were part of the imperial household. They would in theory be governed by their own body of law, the Imperial House Law—not by the Constitution. Members of the foreign diplomatic corps stood close to the front of the room, but far off to the left. Although distinguished spectators, they were not participants in the ceremony. The recipients of the Constitution, the ministers of state and other high officials, stood facing the emperor. As Ikeda Terusuke, president of the Chiba Prefectural Assembly, put it in his eyewitness description of the ceremony, since the presidents of the prefectural assemblies represented the people of their prefectures, the attendance of all the presidents was tantamount to the attendance of the people of the nation.[7]

The formal morning ceremonies were reserved for the eyes of the notables and reporters arrayed within the palace, but the governing elites felt it necessary to push the emperor and his entourage out of the palace and before the people. In the afternoon the ceremonial flowed out of the palace in the form of a stately procession that crossed the newly renovated Nijūbashi and the recently cleared Palace Plaza and moved through the capital's avenues, finally stopping at the Aoyama Military Parade Field.

The pageantry outside the palace was nearly as carefully orchestrated as the ceremonies within. Around five thousand students from schools under the direct control of the Ministry of Education—schools such as the Imperial University, the Upper Middle School, the Upper Normal School, the Upper Commercial School, the Upper Girls' School, the Industrial School, and the Fine Arts School—waited for the imperial procession in the area of the Palace Plaza between Nijūbashi and the south entrance to the Plaza, Sakuradamon. They had received their instructions from the Ministry of Education. Primary school children from the fifteen wards and six districts of Tokyo Prefecture were stretched out along the entire route from Sakuradamon to the Aoyama Military Parade Field. Their roles had been arranged through the Education Section of the Tokyo Metropolitan Government.[8] When the imperial procession appeared, all the students performed their tasks perfectly, the students of the Imperial University shouting *banzai,* the girls of the Upper Girls' School singing the recently composed *ki-gensetsu* song, and the primary school children singing an endless chorus of *kimi ga yo,* the de facto national anthem, as the imperial procession passed before them.

The imperial procession, newly devised and called the state ceremonial cortege (*kokugishiki robo*), represented the structure of the new constitutional monarchy. Authority was heavily weighted toward the procession's center, for the imperial cluster was to be found here; authority diminished with distance from the core. The princes and princesses of the blood immediately preceded the imperial coach. They were in turn led by the high officials of the Imperial Household Ministry, beginning with the highest, Minister Hijikata Hisamoto and Lord Keeper of the Privy Seal Sanjō Sanetomi. Prime Minister Kuroda and Privy Council President Itō rode together in the carriage immediately behind the imperial center. They were followed by the other cabinet ministers. This arrangement, with the highest members and officials of the imperial household preceding the emperor and the highest officials in the government following, duplicated the legal separation of the court and the new government.

The imperial coach, "its gold-tasseled draping glittering in the sunlight,"[9] was a stunning if curious centerpiece for the procession, which signified the modernity and international prestige of the Japanese monarch: an English carriage driven by six perfectly matched bays and attended by grooms in full livery. The architects of the modern imperial image claimed it and its associations for the emperor by its decorations: chrysanthemum crests and a crown of the same gilded phoenix that had formerly adorned the ancient imperial palanquins. Clearly visible within rode the emperor and the empress. The innovation of the imperial couple riding together, widely publicized as never having been seen in all of Japanese history, signaled the empress's new prominence in the process of manufacturing a public image for the imperial family.

After about a two-hour ride through the immense crowd that had gathered on the Palace Plaza and along the route, the cortege arrived at the parade field. Officials of the *chokunin* (second highest) and *sōnin* (third highest) ranks, chairmen of prefectural assemblies, members of the foreign diplomatic corps, and other invited guests sat in grandstands underneath tents pitched in the northern part of the field. These dignitaries first greeted the emperor and empress and then watched as the imperial couple inspected over 11,000 soldiers and sailors lined up on the field. The emperor, as usual, rode on horseback. In the second part of the ceremony the soldiers and sailors, led by the Imperial Guards and the Tokyo Garrison, marched past the imperial couple as they stood in front of the tents. The imperial procession then returned to the palace, again through cheering crowds, to await a state banquet that would be held in the evening for the Japanese and foreign dignitaries.

For the people of Tokyo, the celebrating continued into the next day as the emperor, responding to the request of Tokyo's governor, agreed to parade through the city a second time. On 12 February the imperial procession, less formal than that of the previous day, again exited through Sakuradamon but then proceeded to Shinbashi. From there the emperor, empress, and their entourage of princes, princesses, high officials, and escorts of various types paraded up the nearly straight eight-kilometer boulevard that stretched from Shinbashi to Ueno Park (see Figure 3). At key locations along the route, private companies or local associations had built enormous arches. From these hung lanterns, electric lights, streamers, and national flags. The gigantic *torii* (shrine gateway) built by the Tokyo Tramway Company at Shinbashi featured a covering of green leaves and was decorated with numerous flags and lanterns. A pair of crossed national flags topped the highest beam of the *torii*, and below them was a plaque that read, "The Imperial Throne Is Eternal" (*hōsō mukyū*). The great arch at Kyōbashi, built by the Tokyo Kōronsha, a newspaper company, reached a height perhaps twice that of the surrounding two-story buildings and was remarkable for the use of mandarin oranges to form the imperial chrysanthemum emblem. Electric lights illuminated the arch in the evening. But perhaps the most stunning of the monumental creations for the festival was a huge greenery-covered facsimile of a suspension bridge built on Nihonbashi by the Japan Railway Company. Huge characters made of sacred bamboo stated, "Long Live the Throne" (*hōsō banzai*). As during the previous day, great crowds, schoolchildren singing *kimi ga yo,* and floats of all sorts filled the city, especially along the procession's route.[10]

THE GREAT IMPERIAL
WEDDING ANNIVERSARY

Those who fashioned Japan's modern monarchy borrowed the idea of celebrating the twenty-fifth wedding anniversary of the emperor and empress directly from the practice of Western royalty. As early as 1882, Yanagihara Sakimitsu, then envoy extraordinary and

Figure 3. Woodblock print of the 12 February 1889 imperial procession along the boulevard from Shinbashi to Ueno. Inoue Tankei, "Kenpō happu gotsūren no zu," 1889. Courtesy of Kanagawa Prefectural Museum of Cultural History.

minister plenipotentiary in Russia, sent a report on the silver wedding anniversary of the Swedish monarch to Foreign Minister Inoue Kaoru. Inoue in turn forwarded this report to Nabeshima Naohiro, grand master of ceremonies (*shikibuchō*) within the Imperial Household Ministry.[11]

In 1893 the Foreign Ministry conducted a more systematic survey of silver and golden anniversaries in Western courts through Japanese ministers residing in Europe. One of them, Nakashima Nobuyuki, wrote on imperial wedding anniversaries in Italy. He indicated that the celebrations in Italy for the silver anniversary of Emperor Humbert I and Empress Margherita Teresa Giovanna had been held over thirteen days, from late April to early May 1893, in the three cities of Rome, Naples, and La Spezia. He described the visit to Italy of the German emperor and empress, William II and Augusta Victoria, the Italian imperial couple's greeting of Italian and foreign dignitaries, the banqueting, the theater, the music within the palace, and the imperial military review held on 24 April. Nakashima indicated that both the Italian and German emperors had worn the uniforms of military commanders and had ridden on horseback as they reviewed about 20,000 troops. The empresses had accompanied the emperors, but by carriage. Most important, the Japanese minister in Italy indicated that the celebration had been significant politically. It had not been simply a private affair of the imperial family. With the German emperor and empress journeying to Italy, the event had served as an opportunity to "strengthen ever more the Triple Alliance of Italy, Germany, and Austria."[12]

The Japanese government's leaders, intent on mastering the ceremonial style of the Western monarchies and cognizant of the political importance of such national celebrations, began to make concrete plans for Emperor Meiji's twenty-fifth wedding anniversary celebration. On 17 January 1894, Emperor Meiji, at the urging of Prime Minister Itō, ordered the formation of a committee within the Imperial Household Ministry that would conduct yet another survey of the silver wedding anniversary celebrations of foreign monarchies. On 26 January the decision to have the ceremony on 9 March was made public, and the foreign diplomats in Japan were duly informed. The official gazette (*Kanpō*) reported the full schedule of events on 15 February.[13]

The core ceremonies followed closely the pattern established at the Constitution's promulgation. They began within the sacred and invisible confines of the Palace Sanctuary, continued into the public rooms of the palace where Japanese and foreign dignitaries observed them, and culminated with an imperial military review at the Aoyama Military Parade Field. At the palace, the most sacred rites took place within the mysterious confines of the inner sanctuary. These rites, hidden from the general public, were so mysterious that newspapers and magazines reported them incorrectly. While according to the official history of the Meiji emperor's reign the chief ritualist (*shōtenchō*), Kujō Michitaka, worshipped as proxy for the emperor and the empress did not worship at all, the media reported that the imperial couple, dressed in their ancient ceremonial robes, had personally worshipped before the three shrines of the palace's inner sanctuary. Be that as it may, clearly what mattered to those addressing the people of the nation was the fabrication of an image of the emperor and empress worshipping the national gods rather than accuracy about what had "really" happened.[14]

A proxy for the empress dowager, the crown prince, seven princes of the blood, Prime Minister Itō Hirobumi, and other high officials followed the example of Emperor Meiji's proxy. Later, in the afternoon, dignitaries below the level of count also went before the national gods in the Palace Sanctuary. In the meantime, as in the previous national ceremony, rites were held at Ise Shrine, all of the central government shrines, and the mausoleums of Emperors Jimmu and Kōmei.

Before noon, the emperor, dressed in his formal military uniform (*seisō*), and the empress, dressed in a white Western gown, received the felicitations of Japanese and foreign dignitaries. These included over two hundred Japanese princes, peers, and high officials, both civil and military. In most cases they were accompanied by their wives. Next, the imperial couple granted audiences to the foreign ministers. First, French Minister Sienkiewicz, doyen of the foreign diplomatic corps, read a letter of congratulations from the French president. The message seemed to indicate that the government had succeeded in impressing the foreign powers of Japan's civilized stature and progress: "Because the president of France has the most cordial and sincere feelings for His Majesty, he is honored to be given the opportunity to declare that the past twenty-five years providing this opportunity to celebrate the Silver Anniversary Ceremony today has been a period of extraordinary progress for Japan." The president also expressed his best wishes to the empress and the people of Japan. Ministers of other foreign powers— England, Germany, Russia, the United States, Belgium, Korea, and Austria—all followed with similar messages from the monarchs or presidents of their countries.[15]

Following the pattern established at the time of the Constitution's promulgation, the emperor and empress rode together out of the palace in a state ceremonial carriage and proceeded through the city for an imperial military review at Aoyama. Again led by students of the Imperial University, a huge crowd of people filled the Palace Plaza and greeted the imperial couple with cheers of *banzai*. While the newspapers reported that due to the inclement weather the crowds in the city as a whole were not nearly as large as during the Constitution's promulgation, spectators thoroughly packed the processional route from the palace, past Toranomon, along the moat, and up Aoyama Avenue to the Parade Field.[16] After arriving at the Parade Field, the emperor and empress entered a specially constructed Imperial Pavilion where they granted audiences to their most important guests: primarily members of the imperial clan (*kōzoku*), high officials, and foreign diplomats. The imperial review commenced with the couple riding together in an open carriage, accompanied by a train of princes and princesses of the blood. After the review the emperor and empress watched the march-past ceremony from their carriage in front of the Imperial Pavilion. The ceremony at the Parade Field lasted about two hours.

The celebration continued into the night at the palace with a banquet and performance of *bugaku,* the ancient court music and dancing. Many of the guests, echoing the matrimonial theme, came as couples, starting with Itō Hirobumi and his wife, and the foreign representatives accompanied by their wives. The emperor and empress entered both the banquet hall and the Throne Room for the *bugaku* arm in arm, further demonstrating their modern and civilized conjugal relationship. At the conclusion of the banquet they shook hands with their guests and conversed with the most important of them, including the foreign representatives and their wives. For the *bugaku* performance the emperor and empress sat side by side on their thrones upon a dais that had been specially erected for the occasion.

The government used the opportunity provided by the Great Imperial Wedding Anniversary to inaugurate what would become an extremely popular visual medium through which to circulate some of the key symbols and images of the modern regime: it issued Japan's first commemorative postage stamps. Such stamps have become such a common everyday object that surely most people today give them little thought. But it is important to recall that they did not exist in Japan until the end of nineteenth century, and their production, as well as the custom of collecting them, must be understood in the context of modern nationalism. For the imperial wedding anniversary the Ministry of Communications printed over fourteen million two-sen stamps and a million five-sen stamps. Of the five commemorative postal stamps issued during the Meiji period, three were designed for ceremonial events I discuss in this section: namely, the imperial wedding anniversary, the wedding of the crown prince, and the Triumphal Military Review of April 1906. Moreover, stamps honoring the imperial family's and the nation's auspicious events have continued to be produced throughout the twentieth century.[17] As tiny as they are and as insignificant as they might seem, stamps were and continue to be widely disseminated repositories of national meaning and memory.

JAPAN'S FIRST IMPERIAL WEDDING

Early on the morning of 10 May 1900 Crown Prince Yoshihito, the future Taishō emperor, departed with his entourage from his residence in Aoyama. He was bound for the Imperial Palace. Just a little earlier Kujō Sadako, the daughter of Kujō Michitaka, who was the patriarch of one of the "five regent families" (*gosekke*), also set out for the palace with her attendants from the Kujō estate at Akasaka.[18] Their ultimate destination was the Palace Sanctuary, where they were to be married.

The formal rites had actually begun some three months previously. On National Foundation Day (*kigensetsu*) imperial messengers announced the couple's engagement to the imperial ancestors at Ise Shrine, the mausoleum of Emperor Jimmu, and the mausoleums of Emperor Kōmei and his recently deceased consort, Empress Dowager Eishō. Court ritualists also performed rites within the Palace Sanctuary and announced the engagement to the national gods. On the same day the Imperial Household Ministry informed the nation's citizens of the engagement through a public notice (*kokuji*).

For the wedding, court ritualists prepared all three shrines of the Palace Sanctuary with decorations, offerings of food, and sacred music, and Chief Ritualist (*shōtenchō*) Iwakura read a Shinto prayer. When the crown prince and future princess arrived at the *kashikodokoro*—both dressed in ancient court robes—they first purified themselves with water (*temizu*) and then offered the sacred sprig. The crown prince personally reported the marriage to the Sun Goddess. He and the princess then received sacred wine. This concluded the Shinto-style wedding ceremony. The crown prince and princess moved on to worship at the two other shrines within the Palace Sanctuary.

The rites making up this Shinto-style wedding in front of the *kashikodokoro*, though ancient-looking, were yet another conscious invention of the Meiji regime's leaders. Throughout all of Japanese history no religious ceremonies, let alone ceremonies before the Sun Goddess, had ever accompanied the marriage of any member of the imperial household. The ceremony most closely approximating the marriage was the *judai*, the formal entry into court of the principal imperial consort (*nyōgo*) before her installation as empress (*kōgo*). This ceremony, which had dated at least from the reign of Emperor Daigo (885–930), declined after the fourteenth century but was revived during the early Tokugawa period and lasted until the *judai* of Emperor Meiji's principal consort.[19] Thus Ichijō Haruko, later known as Empress Dowager Shōken, entered Emperor Meiji's court on 9 February 1869 with no invocation of the gods at any stage.[20]

The notion of a formal religious marriage ceremony, like the celebration of wedding anniversaries, was inspired by Western courts. Sometime in the 1880s, Fujinami Kototada, an influential bureaucrat within the Imperial Household Ministry and in 1900 a consultant for the wedding of Crown Prince Yoshihito (*tōgu gokongi goyōgakari*), wrote a report entitled "A Survey of the English Monarchy's Practices" ("Eikoku teishitsu shorei torishirabesho"). In one section of this commentary, included among the papers that Itō Hirobumi collected during the drafting of the Meiji Constitution, Fujinami noted the following:

In Europe, marriage is a religious matter. Thus marriage ceremonies are conducted in churches. They are performed by priests. Civil marriage ceremonies are modern and there are not many who have these. Even in France, a country that requires civil marriage ceremonies, there are still many who have religious marriage ceremonies. Therefore, it should be realized that the marriage ceremonies of the royal houses and families are also usually religious marriages. The most prominent features of the religious marriage ceremony are the following. The priest who performs the ceremony stands in front of the altar, accompanied by his assisting priests. Facing the two newlyweds, he asks the ceremonial questions. The newlyweds reply to this; and when they answer in the affirmative, the attending priest announces the conclusion of the marriage and prays, facing God. With regard to this part [of the ceremony], there is no difference between the high and the low, among ceremonies generally. However, in the case of the marriages of the royal houses and families it is desirable to have a stately escort (*gijō*). Therefore, a number of dignitaries (*kōki no hitobito*) are summoned for a grand procession to the place of the marriage. . . . Of course, much concern is given to the monarch's marriage ceremony and it is carried out with pomp. The crown prince's wedding ceremony is next in importance. Such things are clear.[21]

In this period, with the Meiji government's leaders still striving to create a modern monarchy that they believed would represent a level of civility equal to that of the West, such reports as Fujinami's appear to have had a great impact. Itō Hirobumi was again the key figure in adapting the Western ceremony to the Japanese monarchy. On 24 August 1899—only three days after Grand Chamberlain Tokudaiji Sanenori formally notified Kujō Michitaka that his daughter had been designated as the crown prince's future bride—Itō assumed presidency of a new Imperial Institutions Investigatory Bureau (*teishitsu seido chōsa kyoku*). The drafting of a law pertaining to marriages of the imperial household was one of the first concrete tasks that fell to this bureau. Itō personally wrote a draft of the law and designed the marriage ceremony for the crown prince and Princess Sadako in December 1899. The Imperial Household Ministry announced the law on 25 April 1900. The most outstanding feature of the twenty-six articles making up the "Imperial Household Marriages Law" was the stipulation that marriages of the imperial household would take place before the *kashikodokoro*,[22] a "tradition" that continues to this day.

An interesting document in the Imperial Household Agency's archives testifies to the great confusion that the invention of this ritual could produce even for those it most directly involved. The document is collected among typed copies of Itō's "miscellaneous writings" of 1907, when deliberations on supplements to the Imperial House Law of 1889 were taking place. From its labeling as "Drafts Responding to Imperial Questions" ("Gokamon hōtōan"), it is clear that Itō had written these various explanations about the imperial household's organization, practices, and regulations as answers to the emperor's questions. It reveals even the emperor's confusion about the meaning of the imperial wedding ceremony and suggests an uncertainty about the new attempt to construct the imperial family as a nuclear family bound together by a singular and lifelong marriage tie. In one explanation Itō wrote, "The crown prince does not have a marriage ceremony after the enthronement because he is already married." And he elaborated:

I respectfully offer that since the princess as a matter of course becomes the empress upon the imperial accession of [her husband]—the crown prince or the eldest grandson in the direct imperial line—it is unnecessary to have another imperial marriage ceremony. Article 11 of the Regulations Governing Accession to the Throne states that "prior to the enthronement ceremony's appointed day the emperor bearing the imperial regalia and accompanied by the *empress* moves to the imperial palace in Kyoto." Article 16 states that "after the conclusion of the enthronement ceremony and the *daijōsai* the emperor worships with the *empress* at Ise Shrine, Atsuta Shrine, Jimmu Tenno's mausoleum, as well as at the mausoleums of the four previous emperors," and it is said in Article 17 that "when the emperor and the *empress* return to the palace in Tokyo following the enthronement ceremony and *daijōsai* they worship at the *kōreiden* [enshrining the imperial ancestors] and the *shinden* [enshrining the innumerable deities of heaven and earth]." Thus it goes without saying that this empress is the same empress that was formerly crown princess or princess of the eldest grandson in the direct imperial line. (emphasis on the word "empress" in original)[23]

Apparently the idea of a marriage ceremony for imperial family members and perhaps the notion of one monogamous marriage bond was so unfamiliar that even the Meiji emperor himself did not understand that a single marriage ceremony should suffice for an heir to the throne, or that the wife of the heir would automatically become the empress.

Itō could be extremely candid about the Meiji leaders' rather ruthless manipulation of the crown prince in nearly every way, as on the occasion of his marriage. The German doctor Erwin Baelz, who not only taught at the Imperial University but also served as a court physician, participated in making arrangements for the crown prince's wedding. He noted Itō's attitude toward the royal heir: "Yesterday (8 May 1900) we had another meeting at Prince Arisugawa's about the crown prince's wedding. Itō made a remark which struck me by its extraordinary frankness. Addressing himself to Prince Arisugawa, he said: 'It is really very hard luck to be born a crown prince. Directly he comes into the world he is swaddled in etiquette, and when he gets a little bigger he has to dance to the fiddling of his tutors and advisers.' Thereupon Itō made a movement with his fingers as if he were pulling the strings of a marionette."[24]

Many elements of this ceremonial event followed precedents set by the previous two imperial ceremonies, with the obvious exception that the crown prince played the central role. Like the emperor, the crown prince suggested both the human and the divine aspects of the monarchy by the clothes he wore. Whenever he appeared outside the Palace Sanctuary he dressed in the uniform of an army major, while within that most sacred place he assumed the ancient vestments. Even commercial advertisements of the period associated particular clothes with such images. "And the crown prince's formal clothes," says one party to a conversation within the advertisement, "these are called his *sokutai*. He is certainly splendid (*rippa*) in his Western clothes, but clothes from ancient times such as these sure are noble. It makes one naturally clap one's hands together in worship." "Of course," replies an acquaintance, "he's a living god who's directly descended through generations from the Sun Goddess. I tell ya, somehow tears of gratitude overflow. *Banzai, banzai.*"[25]

After the rites in the Palace Sanctuary, the emperor and empress greeted the crown prince, dressed now in his army major's uniform, and Princess Sadako, who wore a *manteau de cour*. The senior imperial couple offered their felicitations and cups of congratulatory wine. The morning ceremonies thus concluded, the new imperial couple boarded a state ceremonial carriage, "a glittering structure of rich lacquer, glowing gold and bright glass," for the procession that would take them to the crown prince's palace at Aoyama. The coach had been designed by Fujinami Kototada, the court official who had earlier written a report on the English monarchy.[26]

The scene outside the palace, with tens of thousands of people gathered on the Palace Plaza, was a result of both official planning and unanticipated enthusiasm. Viewing areas had been reserved for people with special affiliations. The most important of them were members of the Association for the Celebration of the Crown Prince's Wedding (*tōgū denka gokeiji hōshukukai*); students from the Peers' School, the Imperial University, and other schools under the direct jurisdiction of the Ministry of Education; and various officials. Again, as in the previous national events, schoolchildren lined up along the route of the imperial procession. However, onlookers began spilling into the specially reserved areas, disrupting the arrangements before the departure of the new couple from the palace. The confusion out on the plaza delayed the departure of the procession by about twenty minutes. Nevertheless, the crown prince and Princess Sadako finally managed to exit from the palace and to return to Aoyama through huge crowds of *banzai*-shouting onlookers. All along the way, the imperial couple waved through the carriage windows in acknowledgment to the crowds.[27]

In the afternoon, the couple again proceeded to the palace for a grand reception and banquet. The emperor, empress, crown prince, and Princess Sadako received the congratulations of the highest dignitaries, both Japanese and foreign, and their wives in the Phoenix Room (*hōōno ma*). Next came a grand banquet that utilized three sprawling rooms of the palace in order to accommodate the two thousand guests.[28]

The banquet concluded the events of the tenth. The crown prince and Princess Sadako departed from Tokyo on 23 May for Ise Shrine, the mausoleum of Emperor Jimmu in Nara, and the mausoleums of Emperor Kōmei and Empress Dowager Eishō, in Kyoto. The pilgrimage to these sites of national and imperial memory dramatized the frequently stressed legitimating idea that the imperial family stood at the end of a "line unbroken since time immemorial" (*bansei ikkei*). Students, officials, Red Cross members, military reservists, religious leaders, and other spectators came out all along the lengths of the Tōkaidō Line and the routes to these mnemonic sites to greet the imperial couple. In Okazaki, citizens echoed the theme of continuity with the sublime past. They put out two huge signs which together read, "Oh! How Great, the Power and Virtue of the Imperial Ancestors" (*Ah, dai naru ka na—kōso itoku*), and between them was placed a painting depicting a scene from the "age of the gods" (*kamiyo*). On 2 June, having dutifully reported their marriage to the imperial ancestors in western Japan, the future emperor and empress began their return journey from Kyoto to Tokyo.[29]

WAR RITES AND VISUAL DOMINATION

Around the turn of the twentieth century Tokyo became the center of the Japanese people's celebrations of war. These large-scale ceremonial events began during the Sino-Japanese War, proliferated in number and magnitude through the Russo-Japanese War, and reached their Meiji period climax in the week or so around the Meiji era's greatest military spectacle, the Triumphal Military Review of 30 April 1906. With these celebrations the governing elites displayed the enormous military might of the regime, placed the emperor and his city at the center of that power, and also constructed the image of the monarch as the Overseer to a greater possible degree than in any other form of public ritual. Moreover, in large part because of the great pathos of a nation in which nearly every village and town produced war dead,[30] the rites that followed the Russo-Japanese war drew the Japanese people together as no other previous event had done.

The regime's military character had, of course, affected the appearance of the city prior to the Sino-Japanese War. The Yasukuni Shrine complex, Japan's central and most visible war commemorative site, had

Figure 4. Glass photographic plate of the bronze gateway at Yasukuni Shrine. "Yasukuni jinja." Courtesy of Yokohama Archives of History.

already acquired its most famous embellishments of the modern era, and the War Museum had opened in 1882. Then in 1887 the army erected one of modern Japan's most famous new shrine gateways (*torii*), un-precedented in its scale and in its construction of bronze instead of wood. As they explained it, the planners of the enterprise, a group of high army officials headed by Army Minister Ōyama Iwao, decided to build the *torii* on such a "grand scale and of such a construction that it would be imperishable for all time," so that the nation would venerate eternally the shrine dedicated to the "divine souls of those who had assisted in the restoration of imperial rule and established the great peace of today." The imperishability of the gateway "represented (*daihyō suru*) the intention of never allowing the meritorious service of the divine souls at the Shrine to be forgotten"[31] (see Figure 4).

For many of us today who are less appreciative of human-made heights, it may be hard to imagine the impressiveness of this *torii* still standing on the shrine grounds at just over fifteen meters. However, for the Japanese of the Meiji period the *torii* was unlike anything that had ever existed, and Tayama Katai would later remember having been struck by the "fabulously enormous" (*bakagete ōkiku*) size of what he called the "iron *torii*."[32]

What we might call a monumentalism in *torii* building is, on the whole, a phenomenon of the modern era. According to a survey conducted in 1974, of the ten tallest *torii* in Japan at that time, nine were built after 1875. The tallest, at twenty-five meters, was the new Yasukuni *torii*, built in 1974, which now towers over the Kudan Hill. There are also several other well-known *torii* nearly equal in size to the older of the two Yasukuni *torii*, and a few that dwarf this mid-Meiji relic. The gateway to Heian Shrine built in 1929, for example, measures twenty-four meters; that to Izumo Taisha built in 1915, twenty-two meters; and across the city at Meiji Shrine, there is a *torii* erected in 1920 that, at twelve meters, is almost as large as the older Yasukuni *torii*. Moreover, the one *torii* among the ten that predates Meiji—that at Yasaka Shrine in Kyoto—is only the ninth tallest. Thus those massive and soaring shrine gateways that often dominate the landscape in some of Japan's most famous "traditional" tourist spots were built in relatively recent times, and it does not seem far-fetched to conjecture that the growing size of such stunning examples of public architecture has corresponded in a general way with the rise of nationalism.[33]

"Political power," the historian and ethnographer Maurice Agulhon has written, "expresses itself with the historical characters it chooses to honor." Therefore, "the old French monarchy erected statues of kings and saints almost exclusively. The idea of bestowing this honor on other 'great men'—on servants of the state or on national heroes—came only with the Enlightenment."[34] In pre-Restoration Japan public statuary depicting rulers must have been rare, if it existed at all. Indeed, a 1908 article in the architectural journal *Kenchiku zasshi* noted that the only bronzes prior to the Meiji era were Buddhist images. In Japan, it explained, the casting and display of bronzes to honor "historical persons of merit" (*rekishijō no kōsekisha*) began with a statue of Yamato Takeru, the heroic imperial prince, that was put up in Kanazawa's famous Kenroku Park in 1877.[35]

Ishii Kendō, the great chronicler of *The Origins of Meiji Things* (*Meiji jibutsu kigen*), not only noted the newness of the phenomenon of bronze statuary in Japan in a section titled, "The Beginnings of Commemorative Bronze Statuary"; he also identified the erection of public statuary in general and stone monuments as "Western customs" (*seiyō fūzoku*) that were tied to the question of memory and the danger of forgetfulness. He found first mention in print of these customs in the *Kenbunroku,* a work published in 1869. There it was said that "benevolent lords and meritorious retainers build roadside images or stone monuments and record the virtues of their governance on them. In praising their loyalty and merits and making these widely known, they see to it that the [loyalty and merits] are recollected and not forgotten by later peoples." Moreover, quoting from an 1881 article in an art newspaper, *Geijutsu shinbun,* Ishii noted that in Japan the custom of putting up bronze statues was "a form of commemoration that was learned from the West" and was unheard of in Japan until recent times.[36] Nonetheless, much as happened in modern France, public representations of national heroes proliferated with the rise of the modern Japanese nation-state. Later, around the turn of the century the journalist Ubukata Toshirō was so impressed by what might be called the "statumania" of that period that he noted, with no small bit of sarcasm, that "bronze statues became so fashionable that even cats and ladles (*neko demo shakushi demo*) had bronze statues erected for them."[37]

Most of the bronze statues ornamenting Tokyo's public spaces celebrated national military heroes. The first, built in Yasukuni Shrine in 1893 with the aid of an imperial grant, was that of Ōmura Masujirō, a hero of the Meiji Restoration and one of the primary architects of the modern Japanese military system (see Figure 5).[38] Two of Japan's most famous modern public statues appeared between the two major foreign wars of the Meiji era. The unveiling ceremony for the statue of Saigō Takamori took place in Ueno Park in 1898.[39] As part of the state's hegemonic movements to incorporate potentially oppositional signs into the dominant system of representations, the statue helped mute the memory of Saigo as the leader of the 1877 rebellion against the new Meiji state as it reconstituted him into a military hero of the imperial forces. His statue, as I have noted earlier, faces the former Edo Castle whose capture from the anti-imperial forces he had led. Then in 1900 artists of the Tokyo Art School, headed by the renowned Okakura Tenshin and funded by the Sumitomo family, completed an enormous figure of Kusunoki Masashige on the Palace Plaza. Kusunoki, of course, was the famous fourteenth-century loyal imperial retainer who had fought to defend the Emperor Godaigo, and who became in modern Japan the paragon of loyalty to the imperial line.[40] Many more public statues depicting national heroes went up in Tokyo in the prewar and wartime years, but as proof of their entanglement in the symbol system

Figure 5. Postcard of the first bronze statue in Tokyo: Ōmura Masujirō's at Yasukuni Shrine. The shrine is labeled as one of Tokyo's "scenic sites."

of the pre-1945 regime, many of those that survived the war were taken down on orders of the Occupation authorities.[41]

The war celebrations held in Tokyo were of several types. The wealthy class of Tokyo's citizens organized some of them. The first civic victory celebration took place on 9 December 1894,[42] and it was planned by prominent men in Tokyo's business community—men like Sonoda Kokichi, Ōkura Kihachirō, and Umeura Seiichi. The First Tokyo City Victory Celebration (*daiichi Tōkyō-shi shukushō taikai*) began with a parade of citizens which assembled across from the Palace Plaza on Hibiya Field. After regrouping in front of Nijūbashi, the procession exited the plaza through Wadakurabashi, crossed over Gofukubashi, and went on to Nihonbashi before turning up the main boulevard to Ueno Park. A number of ritualized events took place at the park. These included the viewing of spoils of war by Tokyo's citizens and the crown prince, victory rites performed by Shinto priests, Buddhist memorial services for the war dead, and war theater performed in Kawakami Otojirō's new theater style.[43]

As a result of the explosive increase in the numbers of war dead from non-samurai backgrounds, Yasukuni Shrine's annual festivals and enshrinement rites also came to have a widespread significance for the nation's citizens. In the entire twenty-six year period between the establishment of Yasukuni Shrine (or Shōkon Shrine, as it was called then) in 1869 and the first enshrinement ceremony for those who had died in the Sino-Japanese War, only 14,520 souls of the war dead had been enshrined. While no precise figures can be given, a great number of these must have come from the samurai class, since about half of the total number of deceased had died fighting in the predominantly samurai armies active around the time of the Restoration. In the two major enshrinement festivals following the Sino-Japanese War, 12,877 souls were deified, or nearly as many as had been enshrined in all the years until then. However, this figure pales in comparison to the 85,500 national heroes laid to rest at Yasukuni in the three major enshrinement festivals that followed the Russo-Japanese War. Moreover, as a result of universal manhood conscription, deification as well as death involved a more representative cross-section of Japanese society after the wars with China and Russia.[44]

When Emperor Meiji wrote in a poem following the Russo-Japanese War, "The souls of heroes whose bones lie bleaching, / On foreign strands, / Have even now returned to the capital,"[45] he might also have written that the living would also journey to the city en masse. People generally, but especially survivors of the war dead, came in great numbers to worship at Yasukuni Shrine after the Sino-Japanese War. The highly resourceful and imaginative historian Ōhama Tetsuya has pointed out that it is possible to get a rough sense of the tremendous increase in numbers of worshippers to the Yasukuni Shrine complex by examining the increase in money offerings (saisen) collected and in numbers of people admitted to the war museum. Following his lead we may note that while money offerings increased steadily in the first half of the 1890s, they skyrocketed in the years of and immediately following the Sino-Japanese and Russo-Japanese Wars.[46] Collections, which had been just under 232,000 yen in 1893, grew to about 342,000 yen in 1894, and over 526,000 yen in 1895: an increase of more than 220 percent in two years. The increases were even more significant in the years around the Russo-Japanese War. In 1904, money offerings almost doubled the previous year's total of about 678,000 yen to about 1.24 million yen. In 1905 the collections nearly doubled again to about 2.18 million yen and then in the next two years stabilized at over 2 million yen. Similarly phenomenal increases can be seen in the number of visitors admitted to the Yūshūkan. In 1894, the year in which war broke out against China, attendance at the war museum exceeded the previous year's total almost sevenfold, from just over 1 million to over 7 million visitors. Attendance rose again in the years of the Russo-Japanese War and immediately after, reaching a peak in 1905 when over 11 million people trekked through Japan's central war museum.

Tokyo also became the center of national celebrations for the triumphal returns of military commanders at the head of their armies and naval forces. The triumphal entries followed a pattern: the commanders returned to the ritual center of the nation via Shinbashi Station, and then paraded through the city *en fête* before reporting on their military victories to the emperor. The peak of such victory celebrations came after the war with Russia, from late 1905 to early 1906. Among these, the greatest of such occasions were the triumphal returns of Admiral Tōgō Heihachirō, commander of the Combined Fleet, and of the army commanders beginning with that of Field Marshal Ōyama Iwao, commander of the Manchurian Army, on 7 December 1905.

Admiral Tōgō began his triumphal pilgrimage across Japan's modern ritual landscape by worshipping at Ise Shrine on 18 October 1905. There, invoking the sacred and mythical past, he thanked the imperial ancestors for victory in war and prayed for future military successes. Tōgō's ultimate destination was Tokyo; and he arrived at Shinbashi Station in the capital on the twenty-second. He then paraded through a city filled with triumphal arches, troops, and huge crowds of schoolchildren and other spectators—before finally entering the Palace Plaza through the triumphal arch set up at Sakuradamon (see Figures 6 and 7). Then crossing over Nijūbashi he reported on the war victory to the emperor within the palace. Tōgō emphasized in his report that the victories in battle as well as the opportunity for the "emperor's servants to return triumphantly to the capital were solely due to the illustrious virtues of His Majesty, the Generalissimo of the Army and Navy." In welcoming the commander of the Combined Fleet, the emperor, for the first time in his reign, wore a naval uniform.[47]

Like the commander of the Combined Fleet, the commanders of the armies returned to the nation's center through Shinbashi Station and then paraded through the city before crossing over the Palace Plaza and reporting on their troops' victories to the emperor. And like Tōgō, they usually attributed their successes to the emperor. As General Kuroki Tamemoto, commander of the First Army, put it in his report to the emperor on 9 December 1905, "it is owing to the Imperial Virtues and to the guardianship of the Sacred Ancestors, that we have now the honour and the unspeakable happiness of returning victorious to bow before the Throne."[48]

Figure 6. This postcard carries the title, "The Welcoming Arch at Shin-bashi," and shows one of the well-known triumphal arches of the post–Russo-Japanese War period. The emperor left for Ise Shrine on 14 November 1905 and worshipped there on the seventeenth to report the restoration of peace. The collector of this postcard has written, "The scene on the day prior to the emperor's departure to worship at the Great Ise Shrine," and he has signed it with the character *kokorozashi*.

Yet the most spectacular and well-remembered war pageants of the age were those in which the emperor himself paraded through the imperial city in triumph, demonstrating the enormity of national and imperial military might while also representing himself as the monarch who subjected all to his disciplinary gaze. These military rites were magnificent displays of national power, prosperity, and modernity that were meant to impress both the nation's people and the representatives of the foreign powers. The imperial regime deserved to rule, it could be seen, because it ensured national prosperity in an age of intense inter-national rivalries. At the same time these were "disciplinary ceremoni-als," fantastic spectacles in which previously unheard of numbers of soldiers, sailors, weapons, ships, and crowds were brought together in the nation's capital and made visible to the emperor's disciplinary ex-amination. The first of such imperial triumphals took place on 30 May 1895, about six weeks after the signing of the Shimonoseki Treaty

第一番に
海の親父が
御凱旋
御門

志

櫻田門前ニ於ケル凱旋奉迎門

Figure 7. This postcard is titled, "The Triumphal
Arch at Sakuradamon." The inscription, handwritten
by the previous postcard's (Figure 6) collector, carries
multiple honorifics and reads, "The Triumphal Arch
first passed through by the Father of the Sea
[Admiral Tōgō]."

formally ended the war against China. On that day "His Majesty the
Emperor, so long absent from his Imperial city, returned to the me-
tropolis, crowned with the laurels of a victorious war."[49] Shortly after
the outbreak of hostilities the Japanese Supreme Command (*daihon'ei*),
headed by the emperor, had been moved to Hiroshima in order to be
closer to the battle front. Thus the conclusion of war afforded a grand
opportunity for the war leader's triumphal entry into the capital.[50]

He arrived at Shinbashi Station on the thirtieth, in military dress as usual, and paraded through a garishly decorated city that was packed with huge throngs of people. Tokyo's citizens put out national flags and decorative lanterns in front of their houses and filled the streets with banners, streamers, and arches of many kinds. The most striking temporary monument for the city was a huge "triumphal arcade," widely touted as having no equal in any country, which was constructed at Hibiya between the official residences of the presidents of the two Diet houses. So large was this arcade—110 meters long and 18 meters in height, with a main tower over 30 meters high and 8 meters wide—that the city government reportedly put one thousand laborers to work to widen Saiwaichō Avenue on which it was constructed. The Tokyo City Assembly also built two other great triumphal arches, one each at Shinbashi and Sakuradamon, both of which were thirty-three meters high and over three meters thick.[51]

Not only was national power expressed in the colossal triumphal arches, but the war leader was displayed in plain view at the center of a huge procession of the nation's highest civil and military officials. "Learning from the triumphal ceremonies of the Western countries,"[52] the fashioners of this celebration had the top of the state ceremonial carriage taken down so that the emperor could acknowledge his subjects. The people reacted enthusiastically, for as he moved out of Shinbashi Station "the whole great concourse was rending the air with cheer upon cheer, the stirring cries of Tennō Heika Banzai! [Long Live His Majesty the Emperor] Teikoku Banzai! [Long Live the Empire] coming from tens of thousands of patriotic throats with a thunderous roar such as Tokyo has never heard before."[53] His course took him through the triumphal arcade at Hibiya, across the Palace Plaza, and finally into the palace, where once again he disappeared from public view.

The most spectacular imperial military pageants, however, came with the conclusion of the war against Russia. On 23 October 1905, the day after Admiral Tōgō's triumphal entry into the capital, the emperor conducted a personal review of the nearly two hundred warships making up almost the entire Japanese navy. The event began with the emperor's procession from the palace to Shinbashi Station, a train ride to Yokohama, the emperor's boarding of the battleship *Asama*, and then his examination of the entire fleet anchored in Tokyo Bay. The review itself, which took the emperor past such renowned battleships as the *Asahi*, *Fuji*, and Tōgō's flagship, the *Shikishima*, lasted for nearly four hours. Also among the ships were several which had been captured from

Japan's enemies. These were ships such as the *Chinyen*, taken from the Chinese at Weihaiwei ten years previously, and newly seized spoils of war such as the battleships *Nicolai* and *Poltava*. After concluding the ceremony by inspecting the maneuvers of five submarines (submarines having been introduced into the Japanese navy during the war), the Emperor Meiji returned to Tokyo through Shinbashi and once again proceeded through enormous crowds of onlookers to the palace.[54]

The media described the celebration centering on the triumphal return of the Combined Fleet to Tokyo Bay, and the emperor's Naval Review, as an event quite without precedent. A writer for the *Fūzoku gahō*, for example, commented on the "tremendous size and magnificence" of the fleet (*yūdai sōgon naru koto*), adding that in it he had seen the "glory of the Empire, unmatched from remote antiquity." The crowds too had far surpassed any within recent memory, for he estimated that several tens of thousands of spectators had watched the Naval Review from boats and that the number of those viewing from shore "must have reached a million." Tokyo's appearance had also impressed the writer, for triumphal arches, each unique, had been put up all along the main avenue stretching from Shinbashi to Ueno. Finally, he observed that not even Tokyo's two most splendid events of the past—the celebration of the Meiji Constitution's promulgation and the thirtieth anniversary of the capital's transfer to Tokyo—could compare to the present celebration, for lavish electrical illumination, previously not possible, had been used to light up both the city and the naval fleet, creating a scene of "hitherto unparalleled beauty."[55] But we must keep in mind that the effect of such a review was not so much to enable the people to see the emperor (how could they see his tiny body on board the *Asama*?) but rather to display the enormous spectacle of men and ships, an incredible mass of volatile military power, transformed into completely docile objects of the emperor's gaze.

The string of national victory celebrations reached a grand climax with the Triumphal Military Review of 30 April 1906. Preparations for this event began considerably in advance of the appointed day with a major renovation project on the Palace Plaza that the Tokyo city government, under the direction of the central government and assisted by a large imperial grant, completed just before the thirtieth. The construction consisted of the building or renovation of entranceways and the creation of triumphal avenues. The Tokyo government built a new entrance on the south side of the plaza opposite Hibiya Park, while laborers removed the old Babasaki Gate and replaced it with an unobstructed 72-meter- (40-*ken*-) wide entry on the plaza's eastern side. Both the new passageways were created by partially filling in the plaza's surrounding moat. At the same time, the Tokyo government laid down two broad triumphal avenues (*gaisen dōro*) that intersected near the center of the plaza. The wider of the two began at Nijūbashi and extended to the newly renovated Babasaki entrance. The other stretched from the new Hibiya entrance to the northern extremity of the plaza (see Map 2).[56]

While the city government timed the completion of this construction project on 26 April to coincide with and to commemorate a specific event, the Triumphal Military Review, this undertaking was just one part of Tokyo's transformation into a massive state theater during the late nineteenth and early twentieth centuries. Examined from a long-term historical perspective on urban planning, the structure of Edo clearly had been ill-suited to public pageants at the city's core and to allow enormous number of spectators easy access to the city center to witness them. In fact, Edo's architects had hoped to obstruct movements into the middle of the city. With a spiraling moat system complemented by the strategic placing of thirty-six large enclosure-type (*masugata*) gates, wooden gates (*kido*) separating every neighborhood from its adjoining neighborhoods, and narrow, convoluted streets, an intricate set of obstructions protected the city core from outside intrusion as effectively as any European or Chinese walled city. To be sure, the removal of barriers to free traffic within Edo had begun very shortly after the Restoration. The new government ordered removal of the neighborhood wooden gates, construction of streets and bridges, and destruction of the *masugata* gates.[57] However, until just prior to the Triumphal Military Review, the obstructive *masugata* gates at the entrances to the Palace Plaza still had not been removed; and there were only three public entranceways through these gates to the plaza.

The problem of crowd control during state ceremonials highlighted the inadequacy of this urban structure. During festivities for the Meiji Constitution's promulgation a surging crowd at the Sakurada Gate had caused the injury of a number of spectators. A similar mishap occurred at the Babasaki Gate during a victory parade held in May 1905, this time with loss of life.[58] A logical solution was to enhance the openness of the plaza so that the immense numbers of citizen-subjects who gathered in front of the palace on any national occasion could move easily to and from the city's ceremonial center. At the same time, the increased accessibility of the plaza with its new triumphal avenues and

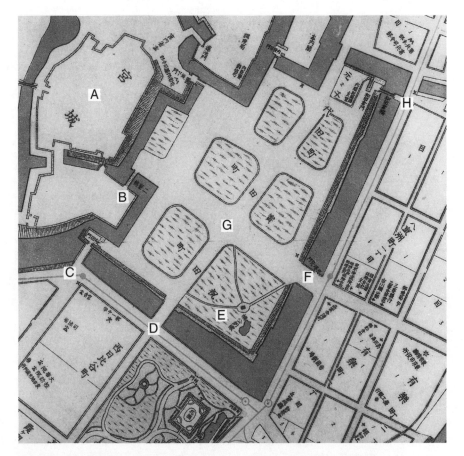

Map 2. Imperial Palace, Palace Plaza, and environs in about 1909. From Kimura Ryōichi, *Saishin banchiiri Tōkyō-shi jūgo kubun chizu* (Tokyo: Heirinkan, 1909). Courtesy of East Asian Library, University of California, Berkeley. A: Imperial Palace. B: Nijūbashi. C: Sakurada Entrance. D: Hibiya Entrance. E: Kusunoki Bronze Statue. F: Babasaki Entrance. G: Intersection of two triumphal avenues. H: Wakadura Entrance.

its entrances would facilitate the movements of the state's public ceremonies, for these generally started in front of the palace and then spilled out of the plaza and into the city's boulevards, or culminated with a procession that moved from the city streets onto the plaza, or began and ended on the plaza after a procession through the city.

In addition to making these permanent improvements, those involved in the planning of the Triumphal Military Review staged an

Figure 8. Postcard of the triumphal arch at Babasaki. The postcard bears a seal commemorating the May 1906 enshrinement rites at Yasukuni Shrine and postage stamps in the "Chrysanthemum" series.

incredible show of national power on the plaza. The Tokyo City Welcoming Committee built two monumental arches wrapped in evergreen branches, one at each of the two newly constructed entrances at Hibiya and Babasaki. The larger of the two, towering over the triumphal avenue at Babasaki, rose to a height of some 18.5 meters and had three separate corridors, each topped with pinnacles (see Figure 8).Though smaller, about 15 meters tall, the triumphal arch at Hibiya was still impressive. Both arches were illuminated for six nights starting on the evening of the review.[59]

Even more striking was the enormous and mind-boggling display of captured weapons that the Army Ministry, by arrangement with the Imperial Household Ministry, placed in front of the palace. In March, the preparations committee (*junbi iin*) within the Army Ministry ordered its artillery department to bring all captured weapons stored in the arsenals at Moji, Hiroshima, Kokura, and Osaka to Tokyo. As a result, weapons that had been seized from Yalu to Mukden, and at Nanshan and Port Arthur, came pouring into the capital. When completed on 26 April, the spectacle filling the open spaces of the plaza included 281 pieces of field artillery, 178 pieces of garrison artillery, 1,235 swords and lances, 70,000 rifles, over 2,000 wagons, and a huge hoard of ammu-

Figure 9. Postcard showing weapons display on the Palace Plaza.

nition.[60] One impressed British correspondent surmised that the show was "unquestionably a spectacle altogether without precedent in the history of the world . . . nor is anything of equal magnitude and interest likely to be ever seen again." He described the arrangement of weapons on the plaza: "Roughly speaking, it may be said that as many weapon [*sic*] are massed in this space between the inner and the outer moats as the wide area can accommodate without such crowding as would impede vision. The guns and waggons are ranged along the margins of every section of the enclosure, and in many instances the spaces within these formidable borders are filled with thousands of piled small arms, stacks of ammunition and phalanxes of swords and lances"[61] (see Figure 9).The review itself began in the morning with the emperor's procession from Nijūbashi to Aoyama Military Parade Field. Wearing the generalissimo's new khaki uniform, he paraded in an open carriage down the triumphal avenue leading from Nijūbashi to Babasaki past the sea of captured weapons. At Babasaki the procession passed under the triumphal arch in full state (*dai ichi kōshiki*) before proceeding to Aoyama past huge throngs of students, soldiers, families of the war dead, and other spectators. At the parade field an unprecedented 31,203 troops, mostly soldiers and officers representing the seventeen divisions that had fought in the war, had been assembled for the emperor's inspection.

They stood facing north in three long and motionless rows while the emperor, riding in his scarlet and gold coach, moved slowly down the lines, taking about an hour for his inspection. The total length of the rows of troops was some 15.7 kilometers.

During the tour of inspection, Emperor Meiji's carriage was followed by those of the crown prince, the Korean Prince Ŭihwa riding with Prince Fushimi no miya Sadanaru, and the other princes and princesses of the blood. Senior staff officers on horseback also followed the emperor, the most conspicuous being Colonel Hume, British military attaché.[62] The inclusion of foreigners into the ceremonial event allowed Japan's political elite to dramatize the nation's position within the new world order—both to the Japanese people and the world—thereby rendering these international relations of power more real. The Japanese government had just recently, in 1905, formally made Korea a protectorate, with Itō Hirobumi as resident general, and during the ceremonial the media described Prince Ŭihwa as the representative of Japan's "intimate neighboring Protectorate (*shinrin hogokoku*)." Moreover, the new Anglo-Japanese alliance of 1902 found its expression in the fact that, as an official record put it, Hume "alone was treated as equal to our officers, attending upon (*baijū*) the emperor and given a place in the inspection and review of troops."[63]

Immediately following this inspection the emperor took up a stationary position in front of the troops and for an hour watched them as they marched past. At the review's conclusion the emperor handed Field Marshal Ōyama an Imperial Rescript in which he praised the "martial spirit" of the troops and expressed his desire that Ōyama and the army "work enthusiastically for the development and progress of the Imperial Army." The monarch also reminded Ōyama that the troops had been gathered together in Tokyo to present their disciplined bodies for his visual examination. "I have assembled my triumphal troops here and reviewed them personally," the rescript began, "I have seen the fine display of martial discipline and the good order of the formations; and I am greatly pleased."[64] Almost 40,000 people who had been given tickets to sit in the grandstands set up around the field watched these proceedings, as did approximately 10,000 students. Included among those in the stands were the members of the foreign diplomatic corps and several hundred other foreigners.[65] The emperor returned to the palace via the new passageway at Hibiya and on the new triumphal avenue that started there. Inside the plaza the emperor inspected the hoard of weapons before crossing over Nijūbashi.

The display of Japanese military might did not end with the emperor's withdrawal into the palace, for at 1 P.M. the troops that had taken part in the review started marching out of the field at Aoyama and began a parade that would have them loop around the entire palace before entering the Palace Plaza through Wadakura. On the plaza the troops marched down the triumphal avenue before exiting at the Hibiya entrance and disbanding. The tail end of the procession, however, did not even leave Aoyama until 6 P.M., meaning that the whole line took five hours to pass any one point. The last section did not reach Hibiya until past 7 P.M.[66] After this unprecedented military march through the city, the war display on the Palace Plaza was opened to public viewing. The festivities spilled over to the next few days as Yasukuni Shrine held a series of rites for the war dead, including an enshrinement ceremony for 29,960 souls the day after the review.[67]

Among the pageants that helped construct an image of the monarch as one who could dominate with his vision, such military reviews as the triumphal review of April 1906 most clearly diagrammed for the people then, and for the historian today, this particular relationship of sight. Imperial military reviews actually predate Tokyo's physical transformation into a new ceremonial theater in the 1880s, to the period when the dominant style of imperial pageantry was still the progress. In 1872 the emperor conducted his first review of soldiers. On 8 January, the day of the annual Army Commencement ceremony, he inspected some 10,000 troops on the Hibiya Field just east of the Imperial Palace. The Naval Review also began in the early Meiji years, the first taking place just offshore from where the Tempōzan Park in Osaka is today.[68] Nevertheless, it is most likely that the military review only became a highly visible and widely recognized event in late Meiji after the tremendous development of the national communications and transportation network.

In the twenty-three years following his move into the new Meiji Palace in 1889, Emperor Meiji conducted twenty-two military reviews at Aoyama Military Parade Field on either Army Commencement Day (*rikugun hajime,* usually 8 January) or *tenchōsetsu* (3 November), the national holiday in honor of the emperor's birthday. Bad weather, the emperor's ill health, or difficulties in assembling the troops because of war or demobilization sometimes forced the cancellation of these reviews, but whenever possible the monarch came out of the palace dressed as supreme commander. Riding by carriage to the Aoyama Military Parade Field, he then mounted his horse (until 1907, when age forced him to stay in his carriage), first to inspect the troops and then to watch them march past. The dramatics for these annual reviews peaked on the emperor's birthday in 1904, when, with Japan at war with Russia, the emperor came out in full battle dress.[69]

As we have already seen, however, these annual reviews were not the only occasions on which the emperor inspected the military. The ceremonial for the Meiji Constitution's Promulgation in 1889 and the public fete for the emperor's Silver Wedding Anniversary in 1894 also included grand imperial reviews. And even more spectacular were the triumphal imperial reviews that followed Japan's victory in the Russo-Japanese War.

To develop this argument about the emperor as the all-seeing, disciplinary monarch, I want now to adopt a slightly different strategy— that of analyzing in some detail three pictorial representations of these "ceremonials of discipline." The first is a lithograph that appeared in the illustrated magazine *Fūzoku gahō* shortly after the Triumphal Review of 1906. The others are commemorative postcards issued by the Japanese Ministry of Communications around the same time.

The lithograph (Figure 10) is found near the front of a special commemorative edition of *Fūzoku gahō*, the fifth and final volume in a series of "illustrated triumphal editions" (*gaisen zue*).[70] Titled "Scene of the Emperor's Procession to the Great Military Review" ("Daikanpeishiki gyōkō no kōkei"), it shows the emperor's coach passing through a crowd of onlookers on the Imperial Plaza. The emperor's seat is toward the right of the whole scene, and the procession is moving to the left. The imperial carriage, marked in several places with the gold chrysanthemum crest, is drawn by two perfectly matched horses and preceded by an escort of uniformed men on horseback who carry banners. Far in front—that is, to the left—we can see the scarlet and gold imperial flag. In the right foreground three elderly people are crouched on the ground, and two of them have their hands together (perhaps indicating an enduring folk belief in magical deities, *ikigami*) as they face toward the imperial coach and away from us. They appear to be from the provinces, since they are wearing traveling coats and two small cloth-wrapped bundles (*furoshiki*) lie next to them on the ground. That these are what the newspapers would have called *inakamono* (country bumpkins) or *akagetto* ("red blankets," after what many of these travelers supposedly wore as shawls) is also suggested by the straw sandals of two of the travelers and by the top end of a rolled-up umbrella (the sky shows that it is a bright, clear day) sticking out from under one of the

Figure 10. Lithograph showing the Meiji emperor parading toward Aoyama for the Triumphal Military Review of 30 April 1906. "Daikanpeishiki gyōkō no kōkei." From *Gaisen zue—daigohen,* a special issue of *Fūzoku gahō,* no. 340 (May 1906).

overcoats. In the center foreground is a young mother kneeling on the ground with her two young children; one is waving a small *hinomaru* flag, and she carries the other on her back. The people in the left foreground are standing, and several of them are dressed in black. Perhaps the mother wearing black and holding the small child in a sailor's uniform is one of the many war widows who made the journey to Tokyo. Beyond the imperial cortege, in the background, a sizable crowd of onlookers stands several rows deep. Two policemen salute in the emperor's direction. Several people are taking off their hats. All of the spectators, save for one old woman, are cheering and looking to our right, in the direction of the emperor. Sitting in a fully open carriage, the emperor appears to be completely visible to the crowd.

But he is not visible to us. The extended branch of a willow tree hangs over the emperor's location so that we can only see his silhouette. We can discern the back of his head and the outline of his uniform, but we do not see his face or his eyes. On the other hand, Grand Chamberlain Tokudaiji Sanenori, who rides opposite the emperor, is in full view. He marks the site of power by bowing his head down toward the seat of the invisible emperor. The representation diagrams a power whose presence is verified by the crowd and the imperial entourage, but it also prohibits us from knowing where the emperor looks and thereby prevents us from imagining the finitude of the monarch's gaze.

The commemorative postcards that the Communications Ministry issued a few days after the Triumphal Military Review of 30 April 1906 are part of a three-postcard set, the Communications Ministry's final set of commemoratives following the war with Russia. The two discussed here feature photographs of the Triumphal Military Review and the 23 October 1905 Naval Review. The third carries photographs of Ise and Yasukuni Shrines.[71] Altogether, the Communications Ministry issued some 100,000 of these commemorative sets, and newspapers and magazines described them in meticulous detail. Incidentally, it was the Russo-Japanese War that inaugurated the large-scale official use in Japan of pictorial postcards as a means for circulating images of heroes, places, and events of national significance. The Communications Ministry issued its first set of commemorative postcards in 1902; included among these was a postcard showing the palace and the new bronze of Kusunoki. However, with the outbreak of war, official commemorative postcards as well as privately printed cards began flooding into the visual world. Battle scenes, battleships, weaponry, war leaders (such as Ōyama, Tōgō, Nogi Maresuke, and Kodama Gentarō), and sacred places on the nation's symbolic landscape (like Nijūbashi, Yasukuni, and Ise)—all became more familiar throughout the country.[72]

The postcard commemorating the Triumphal Military Review centers on a shot of the review at Aoyama and is framed by a chrysanthemum floral design. The photograph used in the postcard (Figure 11) shows a side view of the imperial carriage just after it has passed one line of troops and turned the corner in a southerly direction. But the camera is at quite a distance from the carriage, and we can just barely make out the diminutive figures of Tokudaiji and the emperor sitting across from him. The emperor's cortege follows, most of it still facing west. Beyond the imperial carriage is the object of the review, a sea of soldiers that appears to be perfectly immobile. The formation extends to the borders of the photograph, and toward the upper left and right corners they are no more than tiny dots. At first glance, one might be struck by the almost ridiculous smallness of the emperor's form and puzzled by the apparent disjunction between the monarch's enormous claims to power and the unimpressiveness, the near-anonymity, of his tiny body seated

Figure 11. Photograph used in the postcard issued by the Communications Ministry to commemorate the Triumphal Military Review of 30 April 1906. "Sanjūshichi hachinen sen'eki gaisen kanpeishiki." Courtesy of Tokyo Metropolitan Central Library.

in the carriage. But the point of this photograph is not to impress the viewer with the brilliance of the sovereign's body. Rather, it is to make his absolute power known through its effects. Though we can barely see the emperor, we can imagine his power in the presence of his gaze, which has become inscribed and objectified in the perfect order of the soldiers' bodies.

The photograph on the postcard (Figure 12) commemorating the Grand Naval Review is likewise an idealized figure of the emperor's visual domination. The place of power is marked only by the Imperial Flag (*tennōki*) flying high above the ship that has been placed closest to the viewer, in the left foreground. This ship, the *Asama*, is turned toward the Combined Fleet, and the ships, apparently in perfect formation, become smaller and smaller before they disappear into the horizon. The body of the monarch on board the *Asama* cannot be seen. His presence has been reduced to an almost anonymous gaze as we see it in its compelling effects upon the spectacle of orderly ships.

Although my framework for understanding this relationship between visibility and power owes a great deal to Michel Foucault, there are some considerable differences between his description of the formation of

Figure 12. Postcard issued by the Communications Ministry on 6 May 1906 to commemorate the Grand Naval Review of 23 October 1905. "Kaigun gaisen kankanshiki." From Hibata Sekko, *Nihon ehagaki shichō* (Tokyo: Nihon Yūken Kurabu, 1936).

what he calls the "disciplinary society" or the "society of surveillance" in Europe and the emergence of what might be called Japan's emperor-centered society of surveillance as I have charted it here. Most important, while his analysis is predicated upon the Western historical narrative that sees the rise of modernity as coincident with the decline of the monarchy, such an understanding is completely inappropriate to Japan. In general, Foucault has treated disciplinary power as the polar opposite of monarchical power: he even refers to the former as "non-sovereign power."[73] The question of visibility is central to his understanding of the difference between the mechanisms employed by monarchical and disciplinary power.

According to Foucault, under the old regime it was the king, the source of power and justice, who was made visible to the people. He was the luminous center of power whose magnificence became apparent to the people during various and irregular public spectacles, including royal ceremonials. This was a system of what Foucault calls "'ascending' individualization," in which those in the higher reaches of power were most striking in their individuality. In his words, "the more one possesses power or privilege the more one is marked as an individual, by rituals, written accounts or visual reproductions."[74] Thus the sovereign was most distinct, and the objects of his rule were an invisible, anonymous mass. The power of the monarch was also made visible through architecture. Therefore, prior to the late eighteenth century, "the art of building corresponded to the need to make power, divinity and might manifest. The palace and the church were the great architectural forms, along with the stronghold. Architecture manifested might, the Sovereign, God."[75]

In the disciplinary regime of power, visibility is completely reversed. Power becomes invisible and anonymous, impossible to locate, while those who are the objects of power become completely illuminated. This is a system where "'individualization' is descending," where those furthest from power become in fact the most conspicuously individualized. Thus, "in a system of discipline, the child is more individualized than the adult, the patient more than the healthy man, the madman and the delinquent more than the normal and the non-delinquent."[76]

While monarchical power sought to display itself through architecture, disciplinary power aspires to render power invisible while ensuring the complete and constant visibility of those upon whom power is exercised. Thus Foucault claims that Jeremy Bentham's Panopticon, more than being simply a design for a penitentiary, is "a diagram of a mechanism of power reduced to its ideal form. . . . [I]t is in fact a figure of political technology that may and must be detached from any specific use."[77] The design of the Panopticon impressed upon its inmates the belief that they might always be visible to the Overseer in a central observational tower. Two cell windows ensured the visibility of the prisoners. One window facing the outside of the building allowed light to travel through the cell. The other, facing the center of the building and the tower, allowed the inspector to look in. The cells were thus like "so many small theatres, in which each actor is alone, perfectly individualized and constantly visible." But the prisoner can never know whether or not he is actually being observed because the inmates are prevented from seeing into the tower. This leaves the prisoners unable ever to relax because they can never know whether or not they are being observed. In the end, this arrangement forces those upon whom power is exercised to interiorize their own surveillance.[78]

On the whole then, Foucault has argued that the disciplinary regime's power is exercised through the anonymous gaze of the unidentifiable, invisible overseer—not the spectacle or the gaze of the king. And the decline of monarchical power coincides exactly with the rise of its opposite, disciplinary power. However, he does note two historical moments in which the monarchical and the disciplinary modes of power came together: first with the military reviews of Louis XIV and second in the figure of Napoleon.

The military review, according to Foucault, was quite different from such royal spectacles as the coronation, the return from victory, and the funeral. In these conventional ceremonials, power worked through the spectacular display of itself; but Foucault observes that in Louis XIV's military review, and in the commemorative medal which depicted the first review of 1666, the king himself was becoming less visible. As in Japan's modern imperial reviews, the focus of the ceremonial had shifted from the monarch's body to the objects of his gaze, that is, the men making up the parade. This was a new type of ceremony, one suited to the disciplinary society; for those upon whom power is exercised have become perfectly visible to the disciplinary gaze. As Foucault says of the commemorative medal, "The scarcely sustainable visibility of the monarch is turned into the unavoidable visibility of the subjects. And it is this inversion of visibility in the functioning of the disciplines that was to assure the exercise of power even in its lowest manifestations."[79]

However, the closest historical parallel to the rise of Japan's emperor-centered society of surveillance is to be found in the instant of Napoleon's ascendancy, as described by Foucault. According to Foucault, the Napoleonic character was

at the point of junction of the monarchical, ritual exercise of sovereignty and the hierarchical, permanent exercise of indefinite discipline. He is the individual who looms over everything with a single gaze which no detail, however minute, can escape: "You may consider that no part of the Empire is without surveillance, no crime, no offence, no contravention that remains unpunished, and that the eye of the genius who can enlighten all embraces the whole of this vast machine, without, however, the slightest detail escaping his attention" (Treilhard, 14). At the moment of its full blossoming, the disciplinary society still assumes with the Emperor the old aspect of the power of spectacle. As a monarch who is at one and the same time a usurper of the ancient throne and the organizer of the new state, he combined into a single symbolic, ultimate figure the whole of the long process by which the pomp of sovereignty, the necessarily spectacular manifestations of power, were extinguished one by one in the daily exercise of surveillance, in a panopticism in which the vigilance of intersecting gazes was soon to render useless both the eagle and the sun.[80]

The reinvention and dominance of the monarchy in Japan's political and cultural history from the late nineteenth century onward coincided precisely with the production of Japan's disciplinary society. In other words, in Japan what Foucault called "monarchical power" and "disciplinary power" came together in the same historical moment. Power was not anonymous but centered on the figure of the Meiji emperor. The construction of the emperor as the Observer and the unprecedented visibility of the people to power coincided exactly with the new visibility of the modern monarch.

Spectacles of Antiques

In national pageantry of the sorts described above, the regime displayed its military power, modernity, progress, and its "civilized" character as a demonstration of the national collectivity's prosperity and mundane well-being in the modern world. To be sure, there were many ritual gestures made toward western Japan and the memories of past imperial and national greatness that found their expression there. These included dispatches of imperial messengers to these memory sites as well as pilgrimages of imperial family members and national heroes. We can also note the performance of archaic-looking rites within the palace's innermost sanctuary that invoked memories of a time ages before the capital had been moved to Tokyo. Yet all of the late Meiji national pageants discussed thus far—whether through their use of such locations as Tokyo, the throne room inspired by European models, the modernity and "civilized" character of the emperor and his family, the splendid new processions centering on English coaches, or the celebrations of military glory—resounded with affirmations of the reality of present accomplishments and the possibilities of the future. Only in the severest crises of the regime's symbolic order—that is, between the death of an emperor (or to a much lesser extent other members of the imperial family) and the public accession of a new one—would the public aspect of national pageantry evoke the past over progress and the modern. Only in imperial funerals did the imagery of the archaic connected to Kyoto and western Japan overwhelm.

In July 1912 the state's symbol of the well-being and immutability of the national community fell ill; and the makers of the modern imperial image commenced the protracted ritual separation of the now feeble and dying emperor from the immortal emperorship. Only by clearly disjoining the two aspects or "bodies" of the Meiji emperor could the newly fabricated political center be given a sense of permanency beyond his lifetime. This process began on the twentieth with the Imperial Household Ministry's announcement in *Kanpō*, the official gazette, that the emperor was gravely ill. From the twentieth until his death on the thirtieth, the Imperial Household Ministry released several medical bulletins each day describing in pathetically graphic detail the emperor's physical condition. These reports, available for all to read in the newspapers and at public bulletin boards, expressed the emperor's corporeality as never before. Thus the people learned of fluctuations in the emperor's temperature, respirations, and his pulse. They became acquainted with the history of his gastrointestinal problems, his diabetes, his chronic nephritis, and his uremia. They could even know how many grams of urine the emperor produced, the quality and weight of his stool, and whether or not he released gas. As he lay near death on the twenty-ninth it was reported that the tips of his arms and legs began to turn a dark purple. Finally, on the following day, his heart failed and he succumbed.[81]

The dramatization of Emperor Meiji's gradual approach toward death did not conclude with his physical demise. Nearly a month and a half of ritual activity, both hidden within the palace's confines and public, preceded his interment in the Fushimi Momoyama Mausoleum in southeastern Kyoto. From 31 July to 13 August, the emperor remained mysteriously alive even after the public announcement of his death. It was reported that his "godly countenance remained in every respect unchanged from when he was alive",[82] and inside a palace hall, temporarily called the *shinden*, high-ranking court ladies continued to treat him as if he were still living, serving him his customary three meals a day. From 13 August until his funeral and his interment the corpse remained in the Throne Room, now temporarily called the *hinkyū* (or *mogarinomiya*). There court ritualists made ritual offerings of imperial meals.[83] Thus during this period the emperor was neither completely dead nor wholly alive; he passed through an ambiguous stage.

Most people probably understood little of this elaborate fiction, even as they read about it. Yet many were clearly shaken by the same crisis of the national imaginary that the court rites attempted to control—namely, the fear that the national collectivity might be as impermanent as the imperial body that represented it. Some people at first refused to believe that the emperor's natural end was approaching. Some thought that the press's extra editions reporting on the emperor's illness were no more than "bogus extras."[84] The stock market crashed, but a writer for the *Chūgai shōgyō shinbun* advised his readers that they must be calm, not only for the sake of nation and the economy but also because "the emperor's recovery cannot be precluded."[85] When the announcement of his death finally came, many people of the nation appear to have been affected by what has been called "a sense of ending."[86] The malaise and the general feeling of personal displacement among intellectuals that followed the emperor's death and lasted at least until his funeral has been so often described that it is hardly necessary to belabor the point. Suffice it to note the response of writers like Natsume Sōseki, who had the protagonist of his novel express it as a feeling of "being left behind to live as anachronisms," or Tokutomi Sohō, who wrote of how he felt that his "life had been broken off."[87]

It is impossible to determine the feelings of people less famous since they did not leave written accounts of the event. Yet not everyone seems to have been affected in the same way. On 23 July a writer for the *Tōkyō asahi shinbun* wrote in disgust that while many people had assembled in front of Nijūbashi to pray for the emperor's recovery, someone accompanied by a geisha had been riding around the Palace Plaza in a car, apparently practicing his new driving skills.[88] If the wearing of mourning badges can be taken as a rough indication of individuals' sense of loss over the emperor's death, a limited survey of those who wore them on 9 August suggests that individual reactions differed by social background. Apparently, those who appeared to be bureaucrats, company employees, and students almost all wore badges, while craftsmen and small shopowners were less likely to do so. Indeed, almost none of the people the surveyor identified as small shopowners were badge-wearers. And older people were much less apt to wear badges than youth, which again indicates that the emperor-centered national community was in fact a new idea and not one dating back to pre-Meiji times.[89] Nevertheless, the outpouring of emotion was widespread. Tens of thousands of people ranging from schoolchildren to *yamabushi* (mountain ascetics)[90] came to Nijūbashi daily in hopes of aiding in the emperor's recovery. And millions of people throughout the nation prayed at shrines, temples, schools, and other public places.[91]

As the mortality of the emperor became ever more obvious, the highest men in the government and in the Imperial Household Ministry prepared for the spectacular funeral that would be necessary to overcome the regime's greatest symbolic crisis. All of the national pageants that I have previously described centered on the living emperor, a visibly strong and virile man who was also a god. But now the emperor, the embodiment of national well-being, was dead and a celebration of his accomplishments alone could not sustain the idea of the nation's immutability. Instead, the governing elites believed that an imperial funeral required the public demonstration of the greatness and depth of the imperial and hence the Japanese past. Eventually, this belief necessitated taking the ceremonies back to Kyoto, the point on the national landscape that best represented the current regime's link to remote antiquity and ultimately to an invisible place before time.

Those involved in the fashioning of Japan's modern imperial pageants understood that it was of utmost importance to show the great antiquity of the imperial line and the nation through ceremony. They had wanted to create a progressive-looking monarchy, to be sure; but their surveys of the royal rituals of European states had confirmed their view that part of modern ritualmaking required the preservation or even invention of archaic ceremonial forms. Such was the position of Yanagihara Sakimitsu, perhaps the most politically influential observer of European courts and royal ceremonies during the 1880s. "In now establishing the Imperial Household's ceremonies," he had emphatically argued in a lengthy memorial written from Russia and dated May 1882, "old precedents ought to be preserved, insofar as is possible, in order to express the age of the Imperial Household. This is the most important principle."[92] He admitted that certain exceptions would have to be made: it would sometimes be necessary to follow Western examples in such matters as formal court dress. But he used his knowledge of European ceremonies to argue that prestigious European countries under strong monarchies maintained their own archaic-looking ceremonies and that the Japanese should do the same.

The Austrians "in keeping with the ancient origins of their Imperial Household," he noted, "even now adhere to old practices (*kosei*)." He wrote of the purposeful archaism they retained in their pageants, illuminating them with bonfires in addition to gas and electric street lighting. They also performed archaic accession rites involving the nobility and the clergy. Yanagihara also made the argument that we have already encountered in our discussions of Kyoto's selection as the site of the accession rites—namely, that the Russians held their coronations in the ancient capital. Additionally, the Russians continued to celebrate their traditional river festival at the beginning of the year. Finally, in Prussia, Chancellor Bismarck himself sometimes took the role of torchbearer in important ceremonies. Yanagihara concluded of these examples: "In this way, these three great nations all follow ancient precedents closely.

Any assessment that would disparage this as clinging to the hackneyed and outmoded (*chinpu no koto*) is shallow. Therefore, in order to express the over two-thousand-year age of our Imperial Household, an effort should be made to preserve those rites for which there are ancient forms. . . . It is my humble opinion that this is an essential means for expressing the majesty and glory of the Imperial Household." While Yanagihara acknowledged that it would be necessary to borrow many ritual styles from Western courts, he "desired to nurture within the public mind the sense of the Imperial Household's solemnity" through the use of ancient Japanese forms.

The death rites of 13 September began in the morning with the installation of Meiji's spirit in the palace's Kiri Hall, now renamed the Karitono. There his spirit would rest until a year later, when it would finally be enshrined along with the other imperial ancestors within the Kōreiden of the Palace Sanctuary.[93] The public ceremony commenced at eight in the evening when the massive funeral train, composed of over 20,000 persons, began to roll slowly out of the palace, across Nijūbashi, and through Babasaki Gate en route to its destination at the Funeral Pavilion on the Aoyama Military Parade Field. The overwhelming atmosphere created by both the funeral procession and the funeral pavilion at Aoyama was of the regime's tie to the sacred and weighty past.[94]

The funeral procession, like those of other national pageants, contained the usual honor guards, princes, and high military and civil officials. The extraordinary number of honor guards within the procession, 10,000 of them, as well as the nearly 24,000 soldiers lined up along the processional route, certainly gave visible testimony to the regime's continuing power. But the funeral cortege was most distinguished from the imperial processions during other national pageants by the large number of men in courtly robes, both high-ranking and lowly, who dramatized the great age of the imperial household, both by their dress and the ancient objects that they carried. Thus the court attendants designated as *tsukōdo*, *udoneri*, and *toneri* carried torches, ancient court drums and gongs, white or yellow banners, quivers, bows, shields, halberds, moon or sun banners, cuttings of the sacred *sakaki* plant, and chests for arrows, bows, and offerings. Few people, of course, could have been familiar with most of the names of these men and objects, and still fewer with what these may have signified in remote times; but the age that they represented was certainly obvious. The funeral commission's assistants, ritualists, musicians, and even the Imperial Household

〔行錢合組業知書繪業本日〕　寫謹籌函葬大御皇天治明　〔日三十月九年元正大〕

Figure 13. Postcard of ox-drawn hearse in the Meiji emperor's funeral procession.

Minister also came out in ancient court dress. Authority, as in all previous imperial processions, was located at the center of the cortege. Previously, however, the imperial conveyances had been shiny Western carriages, representing the monarchy's modernity and equality with Western royalty. Now the funeral hearse at the center was an ancient ox-driven cart built by a Kyoto craftsman. Finally, musicians playing the solemn funeral dirge on classical reed mouth organs (*hichiriki*), gongs, and drums enveloped the entire spectacle with their ancient strains (see Figure 13).

The main funeral rites took place at the *sōjōden*, a specially constructed funeral pavilion built in a stark wooden Shinto style with fronting shrine gateways (see Figure 14). The rites too took Shinto forms and began with the reading of a *norito* prayer by the chief ritualist, Takatsukasa Hiromichi, followed by offerings of sacred *tamagushi* sprigs. Though apparently reflecting traditions reaching back to remote origins, the obsequies owed a great deal to modern cultural artifice. According to experts on the history of imperial funeral rites, since at least the seventh century Buddhist priests had dominated the performance of

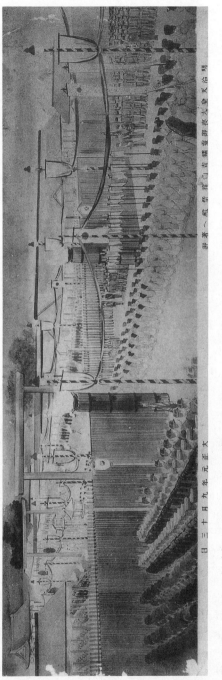

大正元年九月三十日　明治天皇大喪御轜車奉遷し尓伊予屋橋下御通輦ノ光景

Figure 14. Postcard of funeral pavilion used for the Meiji emperor's death rites, with fronting gateways.

imperial death rites—even those of Emperor Kōmei, Meiji's father, who died only about a year before the Restoration. At that time priests from Sennyūji, a temple with strong historical ties to the imperial household, performed Buddhist rites centering on the chanting of sutras within the Kyoto Palace. They then conducted the interment rites at the mausoleum located adjacent to the Sennyūji.[95] However, as part of the radical post-Restoration elimination of anything that smacked of Buddhism from the imperial household and the modern propensity to construct sharply distinct religious traditions, death rites also took on renovated Shinto forms.[96]

The modern regime's first public imperial funeral was actually not that held for Emperor Meiji but rather for Emperor Kōmei's chief consort, Empress Dowager Eishō, in 1897. In those rites court ritualists had taken the place of Buddhist priests and the obsequies themselves had been Shinto in style, complete with offerings of sacred *tamagushi* sprigs and the reading of Shinto *norito* prayers. The only Buddhist trace was the location, the Sennyūji.[97] The rites for Emperor Meiji followed the precedents set by Empress Dowager Eishō's funeral, with the exception that a complete break with the Buddhist past had been made in building the *sōjōden*. Thus, the modern imperial funeral rites, gradually stripped of their Buddhist elements and providing an aura of an age even before Buddhism, were modern creations that ignored conventions which had been followed for almost all of recorded Japanese history.

Following the ceremony at Aoyama—which had included eulogies praising Meiji's accomplishments by the new emperor, Prime Minister Saionji, and Imperial Household Minister Watanabe—the imperial casket was put on the funeral train and sent to Kyoto. From 2 A.M. on the fourteenth the funeral train steamed down the Tōkaidō Line, drawing worshippers to the stations all along the way.[98] It arrived at the Momoyama railway station in the ancient capital just past 5 P.M. the same day and was placed in an archaic palanquin, known as the *sōkaren*, which, according to custom, was carried on the shoulders of fifty-two men from Yase village at the foot of Mt. Hiei. The procession from the train station to the mausoleum site was smaller than the earlier procession in Tokyo, but similar in its adherence to ancient forms. Again, court servants in antique robes carried drums, gongs, quivers, bows, shields, halberds, chests for arrows, bows, and offerings, and the same banners that had been displayed earlier. Finally, the procession arrived at Fushimi-Momoyama for the interment rites that were completed early on the

Figure 15. Photograph of ox-drawn hearse on public display in the Meiji emperor's funeral pavilion. From *Meiji tennō gotaisōgi,* 1912. Courtesy of Tokyo Metropolitan Central Library.

morning of the fifteenth. It was a place described by one journalist as "rich in history but poor in material things."[99]

The spectacle of antiques did not end with the interment. The funeral commissioners placed the ox-cart funeral hearse in the *sōjōden* at Aoyama, and opened the pavilion up for public viewing between 18 September and 6 November (see Figure 15). In pavilions to the left and right of the main funeral site they set out the ancient ritual paraphernalia that had been carried in the funeral cortege—halberds, shields, banners, bells, drums, and boxes. Similarly, the commissioners allowed mass viewing of the interment site at Momoyama from 18 September to 3 November. There the main attraction was the *sōkaren* palanquin.[100] From the official point of view, in this age of mass nationalism, when all the nation's citizens should identify with the imperial and national tradition, it was imperative that the material objects of that tradition be seen by as many people as possible.

In fact millions of Japanese subjects journeyed to Kyoto or Tokyo to see the funeral processions as well as to take in the displays at Aoyama and Momoyama, and in so doing they could imagine the greatness and central significance of the imperial past. The emperor's funerary rites and all of its associated objects had been above all mnemonic sites that were meant to recall, or more aptly to construct a memory of, a past that was only recently becoming known in some way to most commoners. The symbolic crisis brought on by the emperor's death had produced a display thoroughly modern in its immense scale and its openness to public view, but just as purposefully antiquarian looking in its forms. For this ceremony some of the most powerful men in the government at that time—the *genrō*, or state elders, Yamagata Aritomo, Inoue Kaoru, Ōyama Iwao, Matsukata Masayoshi, and Saionji Kinmochi—as well as high officials within the imperial household[101] understood that it was necessary to invoke the weight of the imperial past. And thus at enormous added expense to the government, they agreed to send the body of the emperor back to Kyoto, drawing the attention of the nation's people to the center of the glorious imperial tradition.

CHAPTER FOUR

The Monarchy in Japan's Modernity

The Emperor's Two Bodies

In early 1881 a young man named Suematsu Kenchō, then studying at Cambridge University, began sending a series of reports on the English monarchy to the imperial household minister, Tokudaiji Sanenori. Suematsu had been taken under Itō Hirobumi's wing in 1875 and had been serving on the staff of the Japanese Legation in England since 1878. Suematsu became an influential member of the ruling circles in the 1880s, becoming not only Itō's son-in-law in 1889 but also a prominent politician who sat in the Diet for many years and who also served in different capacities in several of Itō's cabinets; eventually, he became a member of the Privy Council in 1906.[1] In the first of these reports, Suematsu arrived at some observations that are striking both in articulating the idea of a dualism in the official British idea of kingship and in suggesting the relevance of this dualism for understanding the Japanese monarchy.

In England, as with ancient practices in Japan, the new monarch's great ceremonial of enthronement does not take place on the same day as the accession. . . . To begin with, according to the spirit of the royal line's transmission, the king is said to be one who never dies. In the legal idiom this is the so-called immortal king. This does not mean that the life of the king is in reality undying but that when the sovereign dies his power and majesty as king are immediately conveyed to the royal heir. Because it is deemed that not a moment intervenes, it is said that while there is a replacement of the old king's physical body (*shintai*) by the new, it is as if there has never been a change in the king's spirit (*seishin*). (In France under the monarchy when the time of the king's death arrived it was the practice to hurriedly come to the side of the bed and to shout "Le roi est mort. Vive le roi." It seems that this practice also stems from the same idea. It is said that in England, as well, at the time of George III's death a shout of "the king is dead, long live the king" came through the latticed windows of the palace in unison with the sound of trumpets.) . . .

Legally, the end of the king's life is called his "demise" [English in original]. It is as in the East where rather than speak of *shi* (death) we say *hō* (demise).[2] In all likelihood the original meaning of "demise" indicated nothing more than the conveyance of an estate. And the usage of this [term] to refer to a king's death arises from the interpretation—based upon the [idea] of the immortal king described above—that when a monarch dies he conveys the kingdom to his heir. [3]

Suematsu may have been the first in Japan to explain the idea of the "king's two bodies" that the historians Ernst H. Kantorowicz and Ralph Giesey would explore in their much later studies of the political theology of kingship in England and France, respectively,[4] and he may also have been the first to theorize the Japanese monarchy in terms of a similar dualism. In *The King's Two Bodies* (1957), Kantorowicz wrote on the late medieval origins of the idea that the king had not one body but rather two. This fiction, he claimed, became dominant in the age of Elizabeth and the early Stuarts and then continued with some transformations into the twentieth century. On the one hand, this theory held that the king had a "body natural," a body "subject to all Infirmities that come by Nature or Accident, to the Imbecility of Infancy or old Age, and to the like Defects that happen to the natural Bodies of other People." On the other hand, the king had a "body politic," a body that transcended the king's physical body, was invisible, and represented the immutability of the political order. This "Body politic is a Body that cannot be seen or handled, consisting of Policy and Government, and constituted for the Direction of the People, and the Management of the public weal, and this Body is utterly void of Infancy, and old Age, and other natural Defects and Imbecilities, which the Body natural is subject to, and for this Cause, what the King does in his Body politics, cannot be invalidated or frustrated by any Disability in his natural Body."[5]

Furthermore, as Suematsu had astutely observed, the death of the English king's natural body was called his "demise" because this term suggested the transferal of the body politic to a new king, not its extinction. Again as Kantorowicz explained through Elizabethan jurists, "for as to this Body [politic] the King never dies, and his natural Death is not called in our Law (as Harper said), the Death of the King, but the Demise of the King, not signifying by the Word (*Demise*) that the Body politic of the King is dead, but that there is a Separation of the two Bodies, and that the Body politic is transferred and conveyed over from the Body natural now dead, or now removed from the Dignity royal, to another Body natural. So that it signifies a Removal of the Body politic of the King of this Realm from one Body natural to another" (emphasis in original).[6]

It is not my purpose to simply accept Suematsu's argument that there is a duality in Japanese kingship comparable to the fiction of the English "king's two bodies." Nor do I wish to claim a place for Japan's monarchy within a universal theory that posits such a duality within kingships nearly everywhere. It would certainly be possible to do so; ever since E. E. Evans-Pritchard's famous essay on "The Divine Kingship of the Shilluk of the Nilotic Sudan" (1948), in which he argued that for the Shilluk the kingship or Nyikang never dies though individual kings do, much writing on kingship has worked through the idea of this duality in particular cultural settings throughout the world.[7]

On the Japanese side one could also point to Origuchi Shinobu's classic argument that in archaic Japan people had understood the emperor's body to be but a "receptacle" (*iremono*) for the immutable "imperial spirit" (*tennōrei*) that attached itself to each new emperor and was the source of the emperor's extraordinary authority. According to Origuchi, while the early Japanese had thought that there might at any moment be a number of *potential* imperial successors (*hitsugi no miko*)—a matter determined by blood lineage—the sole successor of each reign was determined only through the enactment of the *daijōsai,* the "great food tasting festival." This latter belief was a matter of faith rather than of blood lineage: it was imagined that during this pivotal rite the "imperial spirit" entered the new emperor after he had undergone a period of confinement and abstention while wrapped in a type of bedding that Origuchi traced back to the *madoko obusuma* that had covered the imperial ancestor Ninigi no Mikoto when he descended from the Plain of High Heaven (Takamagahara) with the mandate to rule over the land. The *daijōsai* was thus part of an elaborate theology in which it was posited that while the emperor's "fleshly body lived and died, the spirit (*tamashii*) that filled this fleshly body never changed from beginning to end." Therefore, all the successors of the Sun

Goddess, while different in the flesh, were in fact the same in spirit and every emperor was in essence the same emperor.[8]

These analyses of both Japanese and non-Japanese kingship are useful metaphorically in that they suggest ways of understanding the Japanese emperor as multiply and complexly imaged, as having not one but at least two "bodies." But rather than contribute to a universal theory of kingship outside history, or to the Meiji Restoration's myth of a return to Japan's originary model of emperorship and governance, I choose rather to situate this idea of the emperor's duality historically, to demonstrate what particular binaries were constructed in the specifically modern era in Japan, and why. Whether or not an abstract and ahistorical thing that one might call "Japanese kingship" was or was not dualistic is not part of my concern. Moreover, I am not suggesting that Kantorowicz's discussion of the European political theology of the "king's two bodies" can be applied mechanically and unproblematically to understand modern Japanese kingship. Instead, I am arguing that Japanese thinkers in the late nineteenth and twentieth centuries wrote *as if* European and Japanese ideas about kingship were similar, and in so doing participated in the construction of the modern emperor's dualism.

In other words, men such as Suematsu, writing in the 1880s, and Origuchi, speaking and writing on the "imperial spirit" just before the *daijōsai* of 1928, were not simply describing Japanese "kingship" as an objective reality; they were in fact contributing to its production in modern times. Most important, they helped to create an image of the modern emperor as participating in one mystical "body" or spirit linked in an unbroken chain stretching back to the Sun Goddess and a fleshly body that changed with each imperial reign. Interestingly, not only does the Imperial House Law of 1889 contain this idea in its statement that the imperial institution, "enjoying the Grace of Heaven and everlasting from ages eternal in an unbroken line of succession, has been transmitted to Us through successive reigns," but the official English language translation of the section on "Ascension and Coronation" used the term "demise," as employed in English political theology, to refer to the emperor's death. Moreover, as Origuchi plainly stated in "Daijōsai no hongi," his purpose in risking the disclosure of the hidden affairs of the ancestors and the imperial court was precisely to produce a memory of the archaic: in other words, to "recall the age of the nation and the age of the household (*ie*)." His endeavors, he assured his listeners, stemmed from an unsurpassed "love of nation and respect for the imperial court."[9]

My motives are quite different. I want to remember and problematize the fabrication of the particularly modern binaries that centered on the monarchy as part of a critique of the modern imperial institution and the modern nation-state. The modern emperor's duality, as I have already suggested in the previous chapter and as I will try to make more explicit in this one, centered on the construction of images of him as being as intimately involved in the affairs of governance and military planning as he was aloof from them. As it was constructed in the late nineteenth and early twentieth centuries the modern Japanese "kingship" could be imagined to have at least two "bodies," one that represented the mundane and mutable prosperity of the national community and another that represented its transcendence and perpetuity.

From the late 1880s the Japanese governing elites increasingly confined their modern monarch to his new palace in the heart of the capital city. They thereby kept him apart from society and emphasized his divinity. They promoted the mystery of the emperor by wrapping him in his archaic- and ethereal-looking priestly robes. Dressed in this way he performed seemingly timeless rites before the national gods in the innermost sanctuary of the palace. The most important of these gods were said to be the emperor's ancestors. Through his transcendence of existing society in space and time, the emperor, as the embodiment of the imperial institution, represented the sacredness, permanence, and unity of the entire national community.

Yet these same elites also cultivated the human dimension of Emperor Meiji. Whenever the emperor appeared in public, he wore not the flowing court garbs of his ancestors—which seemed to hold him above the mundane affairs of society, politics, and warfare—but modern military uniforms, covered with medals, which suggested his direct involvement in the critical matters bearing on the life of the national community. Through the creation of the illusion of his immersion in society, the emperor as man became a palpable presence legitimating the constituted sociopolitical order. Emperor Meiji was thus emperorship as well as emperor, mystical but palpable, transcending and yet directing, divine but human, and exempt from all human failings but responsible for all national accomplishments. The emperor's dual nature, logically difficult to sustain, became real in dramatizations such as those described in the previous chapter.

That Japan's governing elites promoted the divine aspect of the emperor and his heir during the national celebrations dating from 1889 needs only a little further elaboration. As the description of the events has shown, each of the ceremonial occasions included rites performed within the most sacred, mystical, and invisible area of the palace; and imperial messengers went to the other sacred sites that made up the nation's symbolic topography.

Moreover, those who have studied the prewar Japanese imperial institution have already often noted that the late Meiji period witnessed the "partial withdrawal of the monarch into the palace or, to change the metaphor, above the clouds"; and they have understood that this was a "part of enhancing his mystery and effectiveness."[10] One scholar, for example, has suggested that the ability of the emperor to confer legitimacy upon the government was in great part a result of the emperor's ritual activities within the Palace Sanctuary, coupled with isolation. The emperor's transcendence, in this explanation, was maintained by keeping him physically confined, or we might say invisible, even while ritually active. Thus the number of outings from the palace decreased markedly after the promulgation of the Meiji Constitution: while there had been an average of 90.2 and 69.2 outings per year in the decades of 1871–80 and 1881–90, respectively, the corresponding figures for the following two decades dropped to 17.4 and 14.6.[11]

The ritual space in which the makers of the modern monarch fostered this mystical aspect of the emperor, and of the other members of the imperial family to a lesser extent, was made up of the three main shrines of the Imperial Palace, the *kyūchū sanden*. In the preceding descriptions of the imperial pageants I have referred to this space as the Palace Sanctuary. On 9 January 1889, two days before the move of the emperor and empress to the new Imperial Palace, the emperor directed the transfer of the national gods to these three shrines—the *kashikodokoro,* the *kōreiden,* and the *shinden.* Of these shrines only the *kashikodokoro,* in which the replica mirror representing the Sun Goddess was enshrined, had existed in the Kyoto Palace during the Tokugawa period. The *kōreiden,* created in 1871, housed the divine spirits of over 2,200 imperial ancestors—emperors, empresses, imperial consorts (*kōhi*), and other members of the imperial family (*kōshin*). The *shinden,* originally invented in 1869 and called the *hasshinden,* was dedicated to the myriad deities of heaven and earth (*tenshin chigi*). Within these shrines the emperor and his ritualists performed the sacred imperial rites. It mattered less that the *kōreiden* and *shinden* were actually new shrines—and that the majority of rites performed there were also recently invented— than that both the shrines and the rites appeared to be archaic and created a world mysteriously removed from everyday affairs.[12] In describing some of these rites shortly after the transfer of the emperor to the new palace, one journalist noted the difficulty of his task, for "with due reverence, the matters above the ninefold clouds are remote and difficult for the ruled (*shimosama*) to know."[13]

However, it would not have been possible for the emperor to become the unifying symbol of the national community and the legitimator of the existing regime had the governing elites kept him a remote figure detached from the human concerns of everyday life. While most scholarly and popular writings emphasize the divine and mystical dimension of the emperor in pre-1945 Japan, during the period of our concern it was just as necessary to construct an image of him as a human being. In the 1880s, as the leaders within the government sought in earnest to work out the configurations of their future constitutional monarchy, some warned about the dangers of re-isolating the Japanese monarch. They worried, in short, about returning to the situation preceding the Restoration, when the emperor had been a figure so mystical and removed from the lives of the common people that his centrality to the national community had been lost.

In his fourth report on the English monarchy, for example, Suematsu Kenchō reminded Imperial Household Minister Tokudaiji Sanenori of the necessity of creating a public and human face for the Japanese emperor. And he suggested that this point had been made long ago in Ōkubo Toshimichi's famous petition of 1868. Paraphrasing from that petition, which called for the transfer of Japan's capital to Osaka, Suematsu noted that the emperor had once been kept too far "beyond the ninefold [clouds]" and treated as "something other than human." Reverence, taken to an extreme, would result in "the estrangement of the high and low." Suematsu felt that the meaning of Ōkubo's argument was that "the secret (*hikei*) to harmony between ruler and subjects is mutual acquaintance and mutual love." He proposed that "there are several Ways for the ruler. One is to dwell deeply and sit quietly—the people precluded from knowing of matters within his gates and walls. One, using authority and power, is to make the people submit from fear. Nevertheless, looking on several millennia of historical experience, there is nothing better for the well-being of the state than to make the people love the ruler. Through this, keep up a constant intimacy and make it unbearable to part from the ruler."[14] Basing his suggestion on the practice of the English court, Suematsu encouraged the Imperial Household Ministry to advertise the mundane daily activities of the emperor and the crown prince through the capital's newspapers. He felt that the dissemination of such information to the people would foster a feeling of intimacy and love (*shin'ai no kokoro*) for the monarch.

While advisors such as Suematsu warned that a totally transcendent monarch would be unable to unify the people, others within the government feared an even greater danger—namely, that such a monarch would be able to unify the opposition. As simply a transcendent symbol representing the people and not the government, this imperial symbol could possibly be turned into a critical lever against the existing regime in the name of the people. Irokawa Daikichi has pointed out that the Popular Rights activists of the 1870s and 1880s offered precisely this mode of criticism. They did not reject the idea of a unique and mystical Japanese political community distinguished especially by the rule of an unbroken succession of emperors. Instead, even the most radical critics of the Meiji government incorporated this notion of *kokutai* into their thought. Moreover, in the private draft constitutions that they wrote in opposition to the constitution being prepared by the government's leaders, they generally stressed the unity of the nation under the rule of the eternal imperial line. Irokawa has argued, however, that the Popular Rights activists did not emphasize the centrality of the imperial household to the national community in order to legitimate the regime. Rather, they hoped to drive a wedge between the emperor and the government, thus rendering the government of the Meiji oligarchs vulnerable. The government's leaders—most notably Ōkubo Toshimichi, Iwakura Tomomi, and Itō Hirobumi—responded by asserting the reality of direct imperial rule, that is, by identifying the government's policies with the emperor.[15] Put differently and returning to the notion of incommensurable temporalities within the national narrative, it is possible to think of this mode of critique as one that was aimed at exposing the seam between the emperor-centered past, on the one hand, and the present and future, on the other.

Thus, through the 1880s the government's leaders felt it necessary to foster both the human and societally involved image of the emperor and the reality of direct imperial rule. These two efforts were related in that direct rule by a human figure was far more conceivable than that by an absolutely transcendent god. Certainly, the oligarchs could to some degree enhance the societally involved aspect of the emperor through the expanding medium of the newspaper, as Suematsu suggested. However, the mere diffusion of information was insufficient. Publicly dramatizing national ceremonial occasions as well as producing more general imperial imagery, aided by the news media, served to create and sustain an image of the emperor as a man directly involved in governmental and military affairs.

The manner in which public ceremonials fostered the human and societally involved image of the emperor was often expressed as the cultivation of intimacy (*shin'ai, shinmitsu, shinsetsu seshimeru*) between the people and the imperial family. Clearly, such celebrations as imperial weddings and imperial wedding anniversaries contributed to the sense of nearness between the ruler and the ruled. The very notion of an emperor's family, to borrow from Walter Bagehot's remarks on the English monarchy, "brings down the pride of sovereignty to the level of petty life." Through depictions of his participation in such a mundane matter as the conjugal relation, the emperor could become a more comprehensible figure for the great masses of the Japanese people. Bagehot's observations on the sovereign under the English constitutional system are just as relevant to the modern Japanese monarchy:

No feeling could seem more childish than the enthusiasm of the English at the marriage of the Prince of Wales. They treated as a great political event, what, looked at as a matter of pure business, was very small indeed. But no feeling could be more like common human nature as it is, and as it is likely to be. . . . A princely marriage is the brilliant edition of a universal fact, and, as such, it rivets mankind. . . . Just so a royal family sweetens politics by the seasonable addition of nice and pretty events. It introduces irrelevant facts into the business of government, but they are facts which speak to "men's bosoms" and employ their thoughts.[16]

Reflecting on the wedding of the crown prince, one writer for the *Chūō shinbun* remarked that "the essence (*taiyō*) of the restoration of imperial rule [had] consisted of making the Imperial Household and the subjects intimate and eliminating the smallest distance between them."[17] Prior to the Restoration, he continued, the governments of regents or of warriors had intruded between the imperial household and the people, but with the eradication of such obstructions the people had shown their love for the imperial household by a great outpouring of congratulatory messages and gifts on the occasion of the crown prince's wedding. The degree of intimacy between a monarch and a people that could be found in Japan was rare, even in Europe. In concluding his editorial, however, the writer, who wished that the crown prince's wedding celebration had taken place over three days rather than only one, recommended more parading through the city. This would allow greater opportunities for the crown prince and princess personally to receive the felicitations of the people and further increase the loyalty of the people to the imperial household.

In fact, in staging these imperial celebrations, a wide variety of means had been utilized to foster the people's sense of intimacy with the imperial household. Some of these methods predated the Restoration and the late Meiji period and were only new in their scale. For example, imperial gifts of money went out to the elderly. When such gifts had been made during the emperor's early Meiji progresses, however, only those living along the routes had benefited. But from the time of the Meiji Constitution's promulgation, as the governing elites attempted to involve all the people of the nation in one imperial ceremony, all the elderly in the nation received such gifts simultaneously. In celebration of the Constitution's promulgation the Imperial Household Ministry used the prefectural offices to make gifts of one and a half yen to 167 centenarians, one yen to 14,013 persons over ninety, and fifty sen to 277,597 persons over eighty.[18] Thus over 290,000 of Japan's elderly received imperial gifts in celebration of one event. Even prison inmates might feel the emperor's direct concern for them, since in many jails the authorities fed beef or other treats to the prisoners and wardens explained the importance of the day's ceremony.[19] For the national celebration of the imperial couple's twenty-fifth wedding anniversary, 289,000 Japanese citizens over the age of eighty again learned of the imperial event and, more important, of the imperial benevolence through direct gifts of money from the emperor.[20]

The imperial pardon constituted another method of demonstrating the emperor's concern for the common people. At the promulgation of the Constitution the emperor ordered the release of hundreds of political prisoners.[21] In granting the pardons, the authorities reminded those who had erred in the past of the greatness of the imperial benevolence and of their responsibility to become good subjects.

Miyakawa Tsumori was one such recipient of imperial benevolence. Formerly a Shinto priest and secretary of the Poor People's Party (Konmintō), he had been jailed for his role in the huge antigovernment rebellion known as the Chichibu Incident, an uprising in which perhaps 10,000 people had taken part.[22] Shortly after his release, he received a letter and an "admonitory notice" (kunyusho) from the warden of Saitama Penitentiary. The notice indicated that while Miyakawa had been convicted for the crime of organizing a mob, he was being pardoned because "with the Meiji Constitution's promulgation, the people had been showered with the emperor's benevolence." Not only had

Miyakawa received his freedom, he had also "immediately regained the honor of having his rights restored, and been enabled to take his place among the good subjects of the realm." The warden advised, "Into the distant future, while never forgetting this great benevolence, repent deeply; ever loyal in speech and action, devote yourself solely to diligence in the occupation followed by your house. In this way, you should endeavor wholeheartedly to repay the infinite imperial benevolence."[23]

Most important, the governing elites had fashioned public ceremonial practices conducive to the creation of a sense of nearness between the imperial household and the people. The *banzai* cheer, for example, expressing the people's love and respect for the monarch, was also developed in conjunction with imperial pageants. Prior to 1889, as a writer for the *Tōkyō nichinichi shinbun* explained, the people did not know how to greet the emperor in public. They often failed to remove their hats and scarves or neglected to fold up their parasols. But above all, the Japanese had no practice for hailing their monarch respectfully. "As regards the countries of Europe," he noted,

in examining the way in which the people greet their monarchs and presidents, when they see [the monarchs and presidents] approach, all wave their hats, wave their handkerchiefs and shout a congratulatory "hooray" [English in original] in unison. In such places as ceremonial halls they shout "Long live the king," "Long live the queen" [English in original] (*kō banzai, jokō banzai*). In France they shout "Vive la Republique" or "Vive la France" [French in original] (*kyōwa banzai, bukkoku banzai*). In these countries people join together to sing their national anthems as we sing *kimi ga yo*.[24]

Suematsu Kenchō had also pointed out the marked contrast between the Japanese people's often fearful greeting of their emperor and the European people's expression of love and respect for their monarchs:

Throughout the West, when monarchs pass by, crowds cheer and wave their hats and scarves. Expressing love and respect in this way is a regular occurrence, and on a day when there is an occasion such as a birthday, the people form a crowd in front of the palace and cheer. It is often the case that they wait for the monarch himself to come out onto the veranda (*ranto*) to greet them. . . . These customs differ greatly from those for the tours (*gyōkō*) of monarchs in the East, where, for example, dignity alone is the rule and the people's fear is all that is expected; where in the extreme case even looking upon the imperial procession is not allowed.[25]

While I am skeptical about the argument that the Japanese *banzai* cheer was a complete late Meiji invention,[26] there can be little doubt that its widespread popular use dates from the promulgation of the Meiji Constitution, and many Meiji contemporaries believed that their generation had invented the term in emulation of various Western cheers. In 1905, a controversy even broke out between some members of Tokyo's Imperial University and the Upper Normal School as to which school had been responsible for creating the cheer.[27] In any case, from the time of the Constitution's promulgation, as one English observer put it, "The spirit of the Anglo-Saxon cheer seemed to have descended on the heads of the Tokyo citizens, for such shouts of *Banzai! Banzai! Ryōheika Banzai!* (Long live Their Majesties) made the streets ring that one might well have imagined oneself listening to the lusty cheering of a London crowd."[28]

Finally, the construction of the human emperor required the fashioning of strategies to display the emperor's and the other imperial family members' human bodies. To put these new strategies of visualization into perspective we may note that while Tokugawa and pre-Tokugawa imperial portraits certainly did exist,[29] they were not produced for broad public consumption and, as I have already explained, commoners knew little about emperors and how they might look. Instead, the bodies of the emperors had been shrouded in mystery; there were no techniques for representing the imperial body before a wide public. Moreover, even as late as the time of the first imperial progress to Tokyo, a palanquin completely concealed the young emperor.

To be sure, the imperial progress to the East was precisely intended to mark the emperor's physical presence and movement before the people. Yet there was apparently still neither the desire nor the means to reveal him in the flesh. Woodblock prints, the primary visual medium linking the state to the people in the early Meiji decades, both reflected and fulfilled the aims of this campaign. For example, Sakigakesai Yoshitoshi's "Bushū Rokugō funawatashi no zu" (Figure 16)[30] shows the imperial progress's crossing of the section of the Tama River known as Rokugō River, on the day before the procession's entry into Tokyo on 26 November 1868. The use of perspective, with the long and seemingly unending procession crossing over the long curving pontoon bridge, as well as the intimation of legs in motion, the fluttering imperial flag and banners, and the weighty imperial palanquin, all convey the dynamism, power, and scale of the new regime. By illustrating the procession's confident and apparently effortless passage over the river, the print demonstrates that the imperial power is impervious to natural or topographical boundaries. In short, the print is a representation of

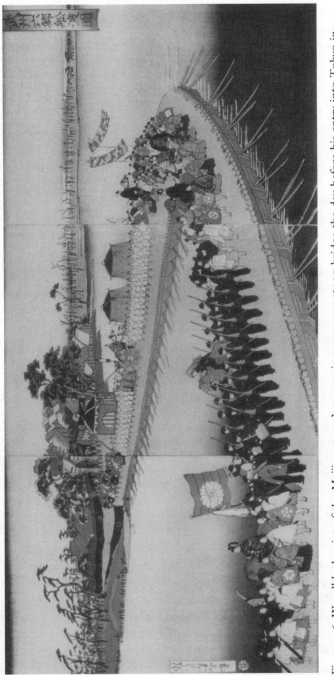

Figure 16. Woodblock print of the Meiji emperor's procession over a pontoon bridge the day before his entry into Tokyo in November 1868. Sakigakesai Yoshitoshi, "Bushū Rokugō funawatashi no zu," 1868. Courtesy of Kanagawa Prefectural Museum of Cultural History.

the imperial procession in motion ritually marking the physically fragmented landscape as a unified political territory under one ruler.

In keeping with the emperor's actual invisibility in the procession,
however, this print and others depicting the Eastern Progress (Tōkō),
such as Ichiyokusai Kuniteru's "Tōkyō-fu Kyōbashi yori Gofukubashi
no enkei" (Figure 17),[31] did not display the emperor's physical body.
Instead, they suggest the presence of a powerful but visually absent
body by focusing on the magnificent imperial palanquin with its blinds
pulled down. This is especially true of Kuniteru's print: the imposing
imperial palanquin, carried by a mass of men, is placed prominently in
the scene's foreground, imperial body unseen, while in the background
we can see the former Edo Castle, just recently renamed Tokyo-jō, to
which the imperial body will presumably be carried and hidden away
again. The emphasis on the palanquin over the body is particularly
remarkable if we are to accept the British diplomat Ernest Satow's word
that the emperor himself was carried in a smaller and far less conspicuous
enclosed chair, an *itagoshi*, and not the *hōren*.[32]

But as William Elliot Griffis, who had resided in Meiji Japan and
observed the modern transformation of the emperor, reflected:

gradually, the mystery play of medieval and musty Mikadoism gave way to
modern reality. The new god now descended to the earth and came out of
his box shrine into the air. When Mutsuhito visited the Strand Palace he
rode not in a screened bullock cart but in an open carriage drawn by four
horses. . . . On His Majesty's way back the people stood as usual, gazing at
their sovereign, just as civilized people do in other parts of the world. This
became the rule, the Emperor and Empress going about freely like other
rulers, and after their silver wedding [*sic;* actually after the Constitution's
promulgation], riding side by side in the same carriage. What had once been
a mysterious idol seemed now to have a human soul.[33]

While the unveiling of the emperor and his family began shortly after
the Restoration—it is generally agreed, for example, that the first visual
representation of the imperial body to appear in a woodblock print
which was not of a completely imaginary kind dates from 1876[34]—the
process continued through the late Meiji period. At the time of the
Constitution's promulgation, the newspapers, obviously still unaccus-
tomed to the practice, emphasized that with the imperial coach's window curtains drawn, spectators had a clear view of the imperial couple,
and prints such as Inoue Tankei's "Aoyama kanpeishiki shinzu" (Figure
18)[35] once again participated in the unveiling. For some, however,

東京
京橋ゟ
呉服橋ゟ
堤之景

Figure 17. Woodblock print of the Meiji emperor's entry into Tokyo in November 1868. The imperial palanquin is crossing over the bridge at Kyōbashi. Ichiyokusai Kuniteru, "Tōkyō-fu Kyōbashi yori Gofukubashi no enkei," 1868. Courtesy of Kanagawa Prefectural Museum of Cultural History.

Figure 18. Woodblock print showing the emperor and empress at the Aoyama Military Parade Field just after the Meiji Constitution's promulgation and prior to the review. Inoue Tankei, "Aoyama kanpeishiki shinzu," 1889. Courtesy of Kanagawa Prefectural Museum of Cultural History.

nothing but an open coach would suffice. One writer for the *Tōkyō nichinichi* recommended, just prior to the Constitution's promulgation, that the imperial couple should ride in an open coach "so that the people are enabled to look directly upon their fine countenances." In the West, weather permitting, "monarchs always ride in open coaches, receive the salutations of the people, and even politely look around to acknowledge the people."[36] For the imperial review held in conjunction with their twenty-fifth wedding anniversary celebration, the imperial couple did ride in an open carriage, and while not always the rule, this practice has continued throughout the modern era.

The Politics of Gendering and the Gendering of Politics

As I suggested earlier, the modern imperial binary was a gendered one. I want to elaborate here on the complex of factors that necessitated the construction of a masculinized emperor and to consider the contexts for and repercussions of such a gendering. In her enormously suggestive essay on the gendering (though she does not use the term) of the modern Japanese emperor,[37] the feminist activist and writer Kanō Mikiyo has argued that for the Japanese people, especially during the period of the Fifteen Year War, the allure of the monarch lay in its "motherly" dimension. She maintains that the general willingness of men to sacrifice themselves, and of mothers to send their sons and husbands to their deaths, can be explained by the loving, forgiving, all-embracing, and comforting aspect of the imperial image. In short, the active participation of the people in the prewar and wartime emperor system came not from the symbol of the emperor as patriarch, as it might as first seem, but rather through the mutual identification of the "imperial heart" (*ōmigokoro*) and the "motherly" (*haha naru mono*).

One of the great contributions of Kanō's essay is its radical break with the idea that the gendering of the emperor need necessarily be limited by our assumptions about biological sex. Rather, she explains that even the Meiji leaders who sometimes constructed the "fatherly" emperor in order to justify their own rule typically deployed the "motherly" dimension of the monarchy in order to appeal to the masses. Thus rather than harken back to Emperor Jimmu, for example, they stressed the monarchy's relationship to Amaterasu, the Sun Goddess.

There is much explanatory power in Kanō's description of the modern emperor's "feminized" dimension, most especially in her observations on the overlapping of the monarchy and "maternity" in the wartime years—an analysis that seems to demand comparisons with what has been described as the mother-bound or feminized dimension of the European fascism that could mobilize a new type of fascist subject.[38] Nevertheless, it is necessary to do more with her passing suggestion that the Meiji rulers also promoted the patriarchal emperor to legitimize their own positions. In fact, I would argue that during the Meiji era the emperor's physical "body," what Kantorowicz might have called the emperor's "body natural," became masculinized and that this masculinization was central to making believable the dominant national narrative—one that articulated the emperor as not only standing for national continuity and the past but also as the Ruler who was at the center of a powerful nation-state.

As recent works on the intersection of nationalism and sexuality/ gender have shown, in modern times there has been a tendency in Europe, if not so much in the United States, for feminized symbols such as Marianne in France, Britannia in England, or Germania in Germany to represent the nation. George L. Mosse has written that these femininized representations "stood for immutability rather than progress, providing the backdrop against which men determined the fate of nations." Maurice Agulhon has similarly conjectured that one of the reasons why the feminine allegory came to represent the French Republic was that such a figure could be distinguished from all those real-life male leaders of the French Revolution that eventually "turned into renegades, dictators or monarchs. The French Republic, immunised by so many disillusionments against the cult of great men, thus strove always to diminish the power of the presidency, to keep a close check on its statesmen and to deify nothing but itself." [39] In other words, since men dominated the modern world of politics, in the narrow sense of government, only a feminized symbol could represent the perpetuity, respectability, and beauty of the nation that transcended the mundane and usually sullied affairs of state.

Yet in modern Japan the imperial figure—though also the symbol of the nation's past and its perpetuity—needed to be gendered as male in at least one of his "bodies." There were at least two reasons for this. In the first place, the Meiji emperor was masculinized with military uniforms, medals, and facial hair simply because his image was modeled on that of the male monarchs then reigning in Europe. This mimicry was a matter of great importance in the field of international symbolic rivalry. Through the image of their monarch Japan's leaders represented their nation, state, and people not as childlike, weak, dependent, or womanly, but rather as virile and mature. Through allegory they asserted Japan's right to independence from subordination by the Western powers and even the legitimacy of their own domination of Asia.

A second pressing matter that helped fashion the emperor's masculinized image was the ideology particular to Japan in the late nineteenth and twentieth centuries—the ideology of "direct imperial rule." It is conceivable that had the emperor remained simply a symbol of the nation's continuity above the fray of everyday political struggles, he could have stayed an ambiguously gendered, or perhaps by modern norms an even somewhat feminine, figure in his Kyoto courtly robes. But according to the official discourse of "direct imperial rule," he was the central actor in the actually existing contemporary state. And because it was an age when the world of politics was becoming a clearly masculinized arena, the suggestion of the emperor's deep immersion in it could only be believed insofar as he was imaged as a man. Thus putting aside for now the question of how "maternalized" the emperor might have been in Meiji, a question that Kanō has raised but that is too complex to be considered here, we can surmise that he could not be only the feminized sign of the nation, because the concept of "direct imperial rule" connoted not only reign but also rule.

During the earlier Tokugawa period, when emperors had been kept "above the clouds," dissociated from direct political action in both form and fact, they had neither a military function nor a masculine image by modern norms. Rather, living largely within a secluded world dominated by court ladies, even male emperors had been what might now be considered effete figures, their hairless faces softened with white powder and their long hair tied back in the genteel style of the court nobility. In general, Tokugawa-period men did not display facial hair; as Kuroda Hideo has pointed out in his study of imperial and shogunal portraits, whereas during the medieval (*chūsei*) period representations of emperors depicted them with beards and moustaches. This practice ended after the reign of Emperor Goyōzei (1586–1611).[40] When the British diplomat Ernest Satow first saw the Meiji emperor in May 1868, he was apparently struck by the paleness of the young monarch's face and the passivity of his demeanor. Perhaps revealing much about his own

European expectations that modern rulers be masculine and dynamic, he remarked:

As the Mikado stood up, the upper part of his face, including the eyes, became hidden from view, but I saw the whole of it whenever he moved. His complexion was white, perhaps artificially so rendered, his mouth badly formed, what a doctor would call prognathous, but the general contour was good. His eyebrows were shaven off, and painted in an inch higher up. His costume consisted of a long black loose cape hanging backwards, a white upper garment or mantle and voluminous purple trousers. . . . Sir Harry [Parkes] stepping forward put the Queen's letter into the hand of the Mikado, who evidently felt bashful or timid, and had to be assisted by Yamashina no Miya.[41]

However, Emperor Meiji's physical appearance changed dramatically as he quickly became "dressed" to be the principal in politics, the Ruler. As the active agent in politics the old image—passive, nonmartial, and whitened—gave way to a new one—masculinized, active, and militaristic. Thus in 1871 the emperor declared through an internal rescript that he would reform the existing style of court dress because these clothes, originally from Tang models, "gave the impression of weakness" (*nanjaku no fū o nasu*). He reminded those close to him that the nation had originally been ruled militarily, that the emperor had been the commander-in-chief, and that he had appeared before the people as such. His new image was further enhanced by the adoption in 1873 of a short haircut, a moustache, and a beard. Within the next few years, as the historian Sasaki Suguru has pointed out, when the emperor appeared before the people, he almost invariably did so in military uniform. Thus Sasaki notes that of the fifty-one different woodblock print depictions of the emperor between 1877 and 1888 that he has seen, forty-seven show him in military dress.[42]

Moreover, as earlier descriptions of the emperor's military ceremonials and the militarization of the emperor's capital suggest, the militarization and hence masculinization of the emperor and his city continued through the late Meiji years. In his role as the generalissimo of the army and navy, the nation's leader in war, he demonstrated his absolute involvement in the critical affairs of the national community. He was, of course, the lawgiver, who created internal order in the national community through his Constitution. But in the late nineteenth and early twentieth centuries, when no greater threat to the integrity of the nation existed than the foreign powers, he dramatized

Figure 19. Uchida Kuichi's 1872 portrait of the Meiji emperor. From Sudō Mitsuaki, *Meiji tennō gyoden* (Tokyo: Kaneo Bun'endō, 1912).

his protection of the nation both through his military persona and through the military embellishment of the capital.

There is perhaps no better way to illustrate the rapidity and decisiveness with which the new Meiji political elite refashioned the imperial body than by comparing the Meiji government's three official photographic portraits of the emperor.[43] While the first two were both taken by the professional photographer Uchida Kuichi, the first photograph, taken in 1872, captures the emperor before his spectacular transformation (Figure 19).He is dressed in the *sokutai* formal court style, with flowing robes loosely enveloping his body. His hair is tied back and on

Figure 20. Uchida Kuichi's 1873 portrait of the Meiji emperor. From Sudō Mitsuaki, *Meiji tennō gyoden* (Tokyo: Kaneo Bun'endō, 1912).

top of it is a tall, spindly headpiece. He is seated on a low chair, wearing high clogs, and his face is youthful, with no facial hair. The second photograph, taken in the following year, is quite different (Figure 20). Though he still has a youthful visage, he now wears a tight-fitting Western military uniform. His hair has been cut short and parted, and he displays a moustache and beard. He sits on a Western-style chair, wears Western shoes, and holds a saber prominently in front of him. Thus already in the early Meiji years and very closely coinciding with the emperor's move to the Eastern Capital, the governing elite created for him a masculinized, active, and militaristic image. This was the look appropriate for an emperor who supposedly ruled personally, and it contrasted sharply with the appearance of the Kyoto courtiers, whom Ōkubo Toshimichi in a letter of May 1868 once disparagingly likened to "women in a harem."[44]

However, the photographic portrait crafted by the Italian artist Edoardo Chiossone in 1888, which became the official portrait distributed throughout Japan in the second half of Meiji, did even more to construct the emperor as a dignified man. Interestingly, this portrait was not a photograph of the emperor himself, but rather a copy of a copy of a representation of the emperor. Chiossone, who was employed by Japan's Mint Bureau, first sketched the emperor. He then drew a seated portrait of the emperor based on his sketches. The Japanese photographer Maruki Toshiaki then photographed Chiossone's drawing. Yet, for most people in Japan in the late nineteenth and early twentieth centuries, this simulacrum three steps removed was the emperor's real presence (Figure 21).

Following and building upon Taki Kōji's numerous insights, we can note that this real emperor of the portrait was a considerably more dignified, militarized, and masculinized man than even the emperor of Uchida's 1873 photograph. To be sure, the emperor who had been sketched in 1888 had matured physically from the youth of the earlier photograph, but there were many more subtle matters of composition that enhanced the later imperial image. The emperor of the 1873 portrait is almost slouching in his chair, whereas the emperor of the 1888 portrait sits forward stiffly with his back straightened. The latter, more disciplined and more militarized posture gives the emperor a far more majestic bearing and suggests his greater capacity as a political actor. The earlier portrait, even though it portrays the full length of the emperor's body, contains a considerable amount of empty space so that the imperial body relative to the entire frame seems much smaller and has a less imposing presence than the body in the later photograph. In the later portrait the body is not depicted in its entirety but nevertheless fills up most of the picture. Finally, while the later emperor places his right arm away from the front of his body to reveal a large and heavily decorated chest, the earlier emperor has his arms crossed rather weakly in front of his body in order to grasp the saber.

Woodblock prints also provided an important site for the construction of a masculinized emperor. As an example, let us here examine Yōshū Chikanobu's print, "Hokkaidō gojunkō no zu," that depicts the Meiji emperor's departure from Tokyo on 30 July 1881, for his tour through

Figure 21. Edoardo Chiossone's 1888 portrait of the
Meiji emperor. From Watanabe Gintarō, *Gotaisō go-
shashin chō*, vol. 1 (Tokyo: Shinbashidō Shoten, 1912).

Yamagata, Akita, and Hokkaido (Figure 22).[45] The emperor is now
clearly visible, and the uncovered window of the imperial carriage invites
us to look in on the emperor's physical body. The curtains which might
potentially conceal the carriage's interior are tied back so that the window
creates a frame rather than an obstruction for viewing the body of a
moustached man with his hair cut short and wearing tight-fitting, mil-
itary-style Western clothes. Here we have not only an emperor in physical
motion, an image enhanced by the militarized body; we also see him
marked with what had been becoming a sign of masculinity, facial hair.

Woodblock prints continued to promote this militarized and masculinized image of the emperor for the period under consideration,

Figure 22. Woodblock print depicting the Meiji emperor's departure from Tokyo on his tour of the Yamagata, Akita, and Hokkaidō region. Yōshū Chikanobu, "Hokkaidō gojunkō no zu," 1881. Courtesy of Kanagawa Prefectural Museum of Cultural History.

reaching a climax with Japan's victory over China in 1895. Baidō Kokunimasa's "Daigensui heika gochaku hōgeimon no zu" (Figure 23)[46] depicts the emperor's triumphal return to Tokyo on 30 May 1895 after his spending nearly the entire war period at the Japanese Supreme Command (*daihon'ei*) located in Hiroshima. The emperor is shown almost full face, moustached, bearded, and wearing his military uniform, and in the background is the enormous "triumphal arcade" (*gaisen aakeido*) that had been built for the occasion and that suggests the immensity of national and imperial power, as well as, once again, the idea of the emperor in motion, even as the age of the great imperial tours had already come to an end.

While inventing a masculinized, militarized, and dynamic figure for the emperor as political actor, the makers of the modern monarchy also fashioned a new public image for the women of the imperial household as serving and nurturing, as representations of the *ryōsai kenbo* (good wife, wise mother) ideal. This took place within the context of the production of the Meiji fiction of an imperial family, and it was part of the construction of an intricate web of officialized meanings that placed men and women, both inside and outside the imperial household, in a neat binary opposition, wherein the one was implicated in the definition, clarification, and exclusion of the other. Thus even as the leaders of the Meiji government eliminated the possibility of women inheriting the emperorship, a possibility that had been rare but not unknown in the Tokugawa period and earlier, by declaring in Article II of their new Constitution that "The succession to the throne shall devolve upon male descendants of the imperial House"—in other words, legally defining the emperor as male—they created a new public image for women of the imperial family. The subordination of these women within the imperial family took place, then, not through their withdrawal from public view, but rather by their becoming more visible than any imperial consorts had ever been in all of previous Japanese history.

As the descriptions of the individual imperial celebrations have shown, the women of the imperial family—most notably the empress and, to a slightly lesser extent, Princess Sadako—were important and visible performers in Japan's first modern imperial ceremonies. Moreover, two of the greatest imperial pageants of the late Meiji era celebrated the imperial marriage and created unprecedented opportunities to construct domesticated images of the imperial consorts. The empress also began to accompany the emperor publicly, riding in the same coach for the first time for the military review held in conjunction with the

Figure 23. Woodblock print of the Meiji emperor's triumphal return to Tokyo from Hiroshima following the Sino-Japanese War. Baidō Kokunimasa, "Daigensuiheika gochaku hōgeimon no zu," 1895.

Constitution's promulgation. For the promulgation ceremony held in the new Throne Room, she sat on a specially prepared throne, just off to the emperor's side. To watch the *bugaku* performance held on their twenty-fifth wedding anniversary, the emperor and empress sat together. Moreover, on all of these public occasions the empress accompanied the emperor as he greeted Japanese and foreign dignitaries. Later, for Emperor Taishō's *sokui* accession ceremony held in 1915, the court's ritual specialists fashioned a throne, called the *michōdai,* for the new empress's participation in that rite. Though appearing to date from remote antiquity, no such throne had existed until then because imperial consorts had not taken part in the *sokui* ceremony.[47]

In addition to noting that woodblocks of various imperial ceremonials represented and hence helped to produce and circulate an image of a militarized and masculinized emperor, it is important to recognize that such media were also involved in the production and circulation of images of the imperial women as subordinated to and less dynamic than the imperial men. Take, for example, Chikanobu's print cited earlier (see Figure 22). Here we see very clearly the empress and then the empress dowager in the two carriages following that of the emperor. Yet as newspapers indicated, the women had only gone as far as Senjū to send the emperor off on his long and arduous journey. In fact, with the second of the Six Great Imperial Tours, the Tōhoku Tour of 2 June–21 July 1876, this practice of the two most prominent women of the imperial household sending off the emperor but not accompanying him became a custom; it was repeated with every one of the great tours.

In 1915 the Englishman William Elliot Griffis observed that a great transformation in the empress's image had taken place since his arrival in Japan during the early 1870s. Reflecting as much about his own Victorian ideal of womanhood as the new Japanese empress's image, he wrote:

As man advances so also must woman. The first lady of the land was now to win fresh honors with her husband. The time was ripe for the Empress to be more of a wife and a woman and participate in the new and broader life of the nation. . . . The Mikado's wife, in Kyoto days, had never been considered his equal. She was never addressed with the corresponding title, nor awarded the same honors as a woman of like rank and name in Europe. Such equality of wifehood is logically impossible in any country where a harem, or seraglio, or, legalized concubinage exists. By the new privileges accorded to his consort Mutsuhito recognized that the freedom enjoyed by women in Western countries was "in accordance with the right Way between Heaven and earth," and here again his example has been powerful with his people. . . .

So far as Haruko, the wife of Mutsuhito, being an "Empress," in the European sense of the word, the Japanese of the early seventies, as I can testify, strenuously objected to speaking of the gracious lady as "Her Majesty." But now Japanese would be indignant if one did not address or speak of the Emperor's wife as "Empress," for they see things more clearly.[48]

The women of the imperial family, like the men, did not withdraw into the private quarters of the palace during the late Meiji period; rather, they emerged as public figures, subordinate to but actively supporting their husbands and families. How can this sudden emergence of the imperial family's women be explained?

Part of the explanation may again be sought in the Meiji leaders' emulation of Western monarchies. In Europe, as some Japanese observers noted, sovereigns generally appeared in public with their spouses. The court bureaucrat Fujinami Kototada wrote of the English monarchy, for example, that the widespread European practice of husbands and wives accompanying one another extended to royal families. Furthermore, Fujinami observed that emperors and empresses always appeared in public together for military reviews. "Though it is said that this is a man's world," concluded Fujinami about European countries, "the empress generally accompanies. The consort of France's Napoleon III, for example, always rides along on horseback."[49]

The image of Louis Napoleon's spouse accompanying the emperor on horseback caught the attention of Suematsu Kenchō as well, for in one of his reports on the English monarchy he also described this French practice while more broadly considering the proper public display of monarchs and their spouses.[50] The main subject of this report was Queen Victoria's visit to France in 1855, when with England and France allied in the Crimean War it was necessary to "represent the increasing friendship and harmony between the two countries." But Suematsu used this retrospective account of Victoria's foreign visit of some sixteen years before to reflect in some detail upon how the Japanese imperial household might emulate European practices. He noted that "throughout the West sovereigns and their consorts always accompany one another (except when there are unusual circumstances), whether it be on pleasure outings or ceremonials for official functions and they thereby demonstrate the virtue of marital harmony." The members of an envoy sent by the old Tokugawa *bakufu* had witnessed a dramatic demonstration of an empress assisting an emperor when they visited Paris and saw Napoleon III's consort not only ride behind him during a great military review but even come to the aid of a cavalryman who had fallen off his horse.

Yet in making his concrete suggestions of what the Japanese imperial household might learn from the West, Suematsu emphasized that this practice of appearing in public as a married couple had an impact far beyond the kings and queens or emperors and empresses themselves. They provided an example that helped to sway the minds of all the people. This was an example, he went on, that would also be useful to have in Japan. As even the practices found in a text like the *Tale of Genji* demonstrated, while women in the past sometimes sat with men at functions within the court confines, they did not accompany men in the outside world. Moreover, this custom had not undergone a complete change in the present. "Isn't there room for some thought?" he asked, "for times have changed, human sentiments have been transformed, and we are now in a world where it is believed that a nation's progress lies in the mutual assistance of men and women." He concluded that perhaps the Japanese empress should accompany the emperor on functions such as the opening of exhibitions and that she and even the empress dowager might join him in viewing the items displayed on such occasions.

Thus imitation of the behavior of European royalty can only partly explain the imperial women's new prominence in public life. Instead, as Suematsu understood as early as 1881, the imperial family could become a model for social practices at large, and by late Meiji it was widely believed that the emperor and his family members had become such a model—"the source of social morals," as the influential writer Tokutomi Sohō put it.[51] The *Fūzoku gahō*, a magazine that took pride in reporting on "customs of the nation-state, both old and new" (*kokka fūzoku no kokin*), told its readers that "because the multitudes look up to the Imperial Household for its standards, this [the crown prince's wedding] is not simply a ceremony of the Imperial Household; it provides a model for the subjects of the Empire."[52]

During the 1890s and through the turn of the century—that is, precisely the period of the rise of imperial pageantry—the official policy on education for girls turned toward *ryōsai kenbo shugi*, the "good wife, wise mother doctrine." As one educator put it in 1895, a woman had three great roles in life: daughter, wife, and mother. As a daughter, she ought to be gentle and ladylike (*shukujo*); as a wife, she ought to be "completely dutiful in obeying her husband"; and as a mother, she should be "completely devoted to the proper upbringing of the child whom she has borne." By fulfilling these three roles, wrote Samusawa Shinsaku, a woman's purpose in life could be accomplished.[53]

The *ryōsai kenbo* policy became entrenched in girls' education after the Sino-Japanese War (1894–95). The Girls' Upper School Edict of 1899 (*kōtō jogakkō rei*) emphasized the teaching of skills likely to be beneficial for managing the household—sewing, homemaking, etiquette, and the arts—at the expense of a more general education. And girls learned that they should be "gentle, modest, and ladylike."[54] Moreover, one authority on the Japanese family has written that "by around 1899 the debate on women had been completely stifled due to the dominance of *ryōsai kenbo shugi*."[55]

The modern image for the women of the imperial family was formed during the production of this discourse on women. As in many other cases, emulation of the images and practices of Western courts met a domestic need; for the women of the imperial family not only became respectable around the world, they also became the paragons of womanly virtues for the Japanese citizens. They were portrayed as ideal mothers and wives, trained in the feminine arts and possessed of the proper ladylike and nurturing qualities. Even when seen or represented in nondomestic activities, they displayed the "womanly" and "motherly" qualities of nurturing or service, most conspicuously in war relief efforts, nursing, and charity work.[56] Their supportive and nurturing role was, of course, displayed in the widely publicized imperial pageants. However, lest the message of the images be too oblique, the official image found its way into news media.

Typically, at the time of the imperial couple's twenty-fifth wedding anniversary, the *Fūzoku gahō* described the empress as having from a young age "far excel[led] other young ladies in the virtues of modesty and grace (*seishuku*), and even admirably distinguishing herself in such accomplishments as reading and calligraphy."[57] Princess Sadako's virtues, not surprisingly, were nearly the same as those of her mother-in-law, except perhaps that because she would be the mother of the future emperor, much was made of her physical health. Thus one newspaper noted that Princess Sadako "had been healthy in mind and body from an early age; and with an outstanding reputation for brightness, and possessing chaste and gentle feminine virtues (*teishuku*), she lacks none of the qualifications to be the future 'national mother' (*kokumo*)."[58]

Social commentators also took the opportunity of the imperial celebrations to explain ways in which Japanese women could, in following the example of the imperial family, become good wives and wise mothers. An anonymous writer for the *Miyako shinbun* suggested one method by which a tradition in the popular folklore could be refashioned to become a part of what I have been calling the folklore of the Meiji regime. The writer believed that people should revive the traditional doll festival (*hinamatsuri*), but with a new national and didactic significance. First of all, the date of the festival should be moved to 9 March in order to coincide with the wedding anniversary of the imperial couple. Also, when a couple married, they should make a doll for this annual festival fashioned to resemble the emperor. It would be the duty of the new bride and children to care for and make offerings to the doll. Reconstituting the festival in this way would have several benefits. It would transform a formerly private festival into a national observance in which "loyalty to the monarch" could be shown. It would also "nurture the Way of Man and Wife" (a subject to which I shall return below). And finally, the main point to be made here, such a festival would be highly educational for women. Apparently because women would be primarily responsible for caring for the dolls, "in becoming wives, [women] would be moral and tender in their social relations; and in becoming mothers they would with their beautiful hearts manage the household."[59]

Even advertising made the connection between these imperial celebrations and the fostering of "good wives and wise mothers." A one-half page advertisement in the *Miyako shinbun* on the day of the crown prince's wedding went to great lengths to claim that the use of its product, "Anzanto" (safe childbirth water), would make patriotic women—meaning mothers. In what is presented as a discussion about the crown prince's wedding, several speakers agree that the preservation of the mental and physical health of oneself and one's children and descendants is the first step in serving the nation. "Even today, on this auspicious occasion," exhorts the primary speaker, "it is precisely due to our physical health that we are enabled to see the crown prince's procession." Furthermore,

the necessity of preserving one's health does not apply to men alone. Women must also do the same. Women have the duty to bear children, the glory of the nation. However, if their bodies are not healthy they will not be able to promote the growth of the fetus. Moreover, if they are sickly they will be unable to raise the child that is born. The ill health or sickliness of a mother is a great misfortune for a child. Naturally, this will also bring misfortune upon the nation. Therefore, on a small scale the ill health or sickliness of a woman leads to the detriment of oneself and one's family; on a large scale it leads to the detriment of the realm, the nation. On the occasion of this splendid ceremony, blessed with the opportunity of living in this great reign, I hope that our compatriots will build strong bodies and will be inspired to render service to the nation.

Another speaker agrees and adds that it is precisely because of the patriotic necessity of maintaining the health of women that he makes his wife and daughter take a good medicine. The potion turns out to be none other than "Anzanto," a concoction that apparently leads to the birth of healthy children such as the one shown in the advertisement. The picture is of a robust-looking boy riding on the backs of two turtles with storks flying in the background—turtles and storks, of course, signifying long life. The child is holding up a streamer of carp, identified with vigor; and behind him rises the majestic Mt. Fuji. "Anzanto," the advertisement claims, is a cure-all for women's maladies and is even guaranteed to make "barren women pregnant."[60]

Not only did the celebrations of imperial marriages provide opportunities to display ideal women, they also helped redefine the qualities of imperial men and the families in which women would fulfill the roles of wife and mother. The restructuring of the imperial family, with a single and permanent marital bond between emperor and empress (or crown prince and princess), sanctified by a wedding performed in the Shinto style, can only be fully appreciated by noting its relation to the new official emphasis on marriage as a sacred institution, which also dates from the 1890s.

The relationship between husband and wife had, of course, been one of the Five Relations. The maintenance of these relations, according to the Confucian tradition, was the foundation upon which a well-ordered society rested. However, both hard statistics and the observations of contemporaries indicate that most Japanese treated marriage with considerable laxity in the first half of the Meiji period and through most of the 1890s. Men of *bushi* origin openly kept mistresses, while commoners entered rather casually into marriage and then dissolved them with great frequency—most likely because of the absence of legal restrictions, and perhaps more important, of moral sanction (such as Christian condemnation) against divorce.[61]

In the years between 1881 (the first year for which complete data are available) and 1897 (the year before the new Meiji Civil Code went into effect), the national rate of marriages to divorces ranged from 2.28 (1885) to 4.34 (1876), and averaged 3.08.[62] Put differently, statistically one out of every three marriages ended in divorce. Tokyo had an even lower marriage to divorce ratio in these years: the lowest figure was 1.90 (1880), the highest 4.50 (1896), and the average 2.74.[63] In the years of highest divorce, then, around one in every two marriages was dissolved.

Remarking sarcastically on the discord between the ideal marriage exemplified in the celebration of the emperor's twenty-fifth wedding anniversary and the great frequency of divorces among the Japanese people, one writer noted that while many people ought to be celebrating silver wedding anniversaries, few were entitled to: "While many have passed twenty-five to thirty years in marriage, this means ten years with one's first wife and fifteen years with one's second wife; it means fifteen years with one's first husband, and ten years with one's second husband. In the extreme case, some people are married five or six times without ever achieving twenty-five years of marriage."[64]

The family and inheritance provisions of the Meiji Civil Code, which went into effect in 1898, helped put an end to the rather lax popular perception of marriage and divorce. First, it required the official registration of all marriages and divorces. In the past, although some marriages had been registered, filing was far from universal, and unregistered marriages as well as divorces were recognized in law. More important, the new provisions stipulated that divorces would be allowed only for a limited number of very specific reasons. This also contrasted with past legal practices that had acknowledged divorces without grounds (*muin rikon*).[65] Thus marriages, once entered into, became legally fixed and, from the point of view of the governing elites, protected from the whims of popular practice.

Indeed, the statistics might lead one to assume that these legal changes alone led immediately to a precipitous decline in divorces. In the year between 1897 and 1898 the national ratio of marriages to divorces jumped from 2.94 to 4.74. Then, in what appears to have been a unique development among modern nations, the Japanese divorce rate, with only a few brief periods of exception, continued to decline steadily throughout the twentieth century until the mid-sixties. At that time marriages outnumbered divorces by over 13 to 1.[66] Legal changes alone, however, cannot explain the constant drop in the divorce rate through most of the century. The creation of a moral atmosphere sanctifying lifelong marriage must also be considered. As the most visible family, the imperial family provided a national model, especially on occasions such as weddings and wedding anniversaries.

This fact was not lost on newspaper writers, who explained to their readers the exemplary role of the imperial family. A writer for the *Miyako shinbun,* for example, correctly pointed out that both international and domestic concerns had led to the imperial family's adoption of the twenty-fifth wedding anniversary celebration. On the one hand, because of Japan's increasing contact with foreign countries, "adoption of such matters as the ceremonies of foreign countries is natural." On the other hand, the author believed that the emperor wished to make the celebration of wedding anniversaries a regular custom so that "the people, without distinction between the noble and the mean, would value the *sanctity of marriage and uphold public morality* (*fūkyō*); and in so doing increase their happiness" (emphasis added).[67] The *Kokumin shinbun* noted that "the Way of Man and Wife is the Great Foundation of human ethics"; and it added rhetorically: "Doesn't the celebration of the emperor's twenty-fifth wedding anniversary have the magnanimous intention of teaching the Great Foundation of human ethics to the people of the nation?"[68] Another writer—while he did not think it a good idea to make dolls of the emperor that could be worshipped as "the god of matrimonial harmony" (*fūfu wagō no kami*)—enjoined the Japanese people to follow the example of the emperor in celebrating their own wedding anniversaries: "There can be no more auspicious sign than for the great numbers of subjects to learn from the emperor's wedding anniversary ceremony. From their weddings through their silver, golden, and diamond wedding anniversaries, they should also value marriage eternally and realize the beauty of the relation between Man and Wife by practicing matrimonial harmony."[69]

Writers made the same point in conjunction with the crown prince's wedding, stressing the beauty of the projected monogamous relation between the crown prince and Princess Sadako. While evading the discomfiting fact that the reigning emperor was not monogamous and that the crown prince was the biological son not of Empress Haruko but of the court lady Yanagiwara Naruko, the newspapers condemned the practice of polygamy and praised the younger imperial couple for providing "the most beautiful and finest model for social customs."[70]

One commentator accurately explained that until the crown prince's wedding, imperial marriage rites had not existed. Rather, the consorts of emperors and crown princes had simply been installed as empresses and princesses. Therefore, the crown prince's wedding was an innovation that "forthwith made the Way of monogamy clear." He concluded, "We subjects, in keeping with the emperor's wish, should understand that the great foundation for governing one's family is the Way of Man and Wife; and in practicing this [Way], we must by all means strive not to err."[71] Similarly, a journalist for the *Chūō shinbun* declared that the crown prince's wedding was "a great ceremony, shining brilliantly for all time as a model for the relation between the men and women of the nation. To put it frankly, it abolishes the pernicious old custom of polygamy. The imperial family enlightens society by being first in taking monogamy as the proper principle." Furthermore, the writer rejected the opinion that since the imperial wedding was not as important as an accession ceremony, it should not be celebrated on an overly grand scale. "This [erroneous opinion]," he concluded, "stems ultimately from the mistaken view that the great imperial wedding is merely a normal, everyday wedding. This is an opinion of ignorant people who do not know that this great imperial wedding will revolutionize (*isshin*) the moral character of our citizens."[72]

While it is doubtful that two imperial ceremonies alone could have revolutionized popular attitudes toward marriage, from the late Meiji period the Japanese people witnessed numerous imperial weddings and wedding anniversaries as they became accepted occasions for national celebrations. In these imperial ceremonies the people saw a single and lifelong marriage bond, sanctified by Shinto rites conducted in the most sacred space of the nation's capital. In pre-Meiji Japan the marriage rites of the common people throughout the country, like those of the imperial family members, had not been conducted before sacred beings.[73] But to a great extent because of the precedent set by the imperial family, the Shinto-style wedding had by the 1940s come to be recognized as a "traditional" custom for the Japanese people.[74] Along with the force of law, the exemplary role of the imperial family must be recognized as having played an important part in making the modern Japanese marriage inviolable.

Ultimately the *ryōsai kenbo* doctrine, the insistence upon marriage as a lifelong commitment, and the dramatization of these ideas by members of the imperial family were all complicit in the construction of modern and stable families made up of disciplined individuals. With women secure in their marriages as the stabilizing influence, such normalized families might serve as the primary units of the national community. At the same time, since by the 1890s the nation was coming to be represented in the dominant discourse of the time as a family writ large, as a "nation-state family" (*kazoku kokka*), in which the imperial household and the people were mystically bound together as a family and where "the righteousness (*gi*) between the ruler and his subjects and the intimacy between father and child are absolutely the same,"[75] it was imperative that the family itself be a properly ordered model for the nation. In other words, for the metonymic relationship between the family and the nation to work as an effective mechanism of control, it was necessary that the part, the family, be understood as the stable and properly hierarchized social unit that would correspond to the stable and properly hierarchized whole, the nation. In fact, we might also note that only the emperor's children could unproblematically enact the equation made in the *kazoku kokka* discourse between "loyalty" (*chū*) and "filial piety" (*kō*). For even if it was said that all the nation's citizen-subjects should equate "loyalty" with "filial piety" (*chūkō ipponron*),[76] only the imperial children were positioned to do so with no slippage between the two concepts.

In any case, through education, law, imagery, and drama the official model of the family spread through society, attaining during the twentieth century the dominant place in social practice. Moreover, the invention of the imperial family—where women represented what men were not, and vice versa—provided the context for the masculinization of the emperor in his "body natural," a man in both senses of the term, who could be imagined as directly and actively involved in society and politics.

At the same time, the politics of gendering the imperial household's members resonated with—that is to say, was both implicated in and reflective of—the masculinization of politics in its conventional and limited sense of governance. In this regard it is possible to conceive of the bodies of the imperial household's members and the space of modern politics as mutually engendering (in both meanings of the word) cultural sites. While men marked themselves as men with facial hair and short haircuts in the fashion for the Meiji political elite (and as we have seen, the emperor), and while they also ran the national and local governments and then from 1890 began to vote, the state systematically excluded women from political activities and prescribed guidelines for their physical appearance. A series of legal measures, including the 1890 Law on Associations and Meetings (*shūkai oyobi kessha hō*) and the Security Police Law (*chian keisatsu hō*) of 1900 explicitly prohibited women's participation in political meetings or political organizations.[77] Somewhat earlier, an 1872 law had already banned women from cutting their hair short, as men did, and in 1873 the empress demonstrated the proper look.[78]

Hence it would be improper to naively maintain that the body of the emperor that represented his immersion in politics became "masculinized" in some universal or ahistorical sense during the Meiji era. I am arguing from the position of many recent theorists of gender and sexuality that there are no timeless and universal categories of "femininity" or "masculinity" and that not just women and men proper but that all phenomena, including forms of social organization, tend to be understood, differentiated, and hierarchized according to gendered categories.[79] What must be understood here is that the Meiji emperor became "masculinized" only to the extent that he was refashioned according to the modern norms of masculinity that were being produced at precisely the same moment that the ruling elites created him. The corresponding claim could be made for the women of the imperial family. At the same time, the men and women of the imperial family acted out what it meant to be men and women—the former were dynamic and actively involved in political affairs—and were marked as such as they participated in the construction of dominant expectations of manhood and womanhood. In the end, in modern Japan politics in its narrow sense of involvement in government became a masculinized arena and closed to women at the same time that the emperor in his "body natural" became the paradigmatic man and the women of the imperial household became respectable models of womanhood.

＋Ｉ＋

During the Meiji era the governing elites constructed an emperor who could be imagined to have not one but at least two bodies. Homologous to the relationship of the two capital cities on the nation's symbolic and ritual landscape, the one imperial body was a human and masculinized body that represented the mundane and changing prosperity of the national community in history, while the other body, often invisible or described as wrapped in ancient courtly robes, represented the emperor's godliness or transcendence and the immutability of the nation. Thus while the metaphor of the palace as a place "above the ninefold clouds" continued to be used, on occasions such as the celebratory imperial pageants the emperor descended down into the streets and other places of the capital in new imperial conveyances designed to make him open to public view. Through such public displays and other visual representations of him in the flesh, the emperor became a palpable figure—not only a god, but a man involved in the critical affairs of society and government.

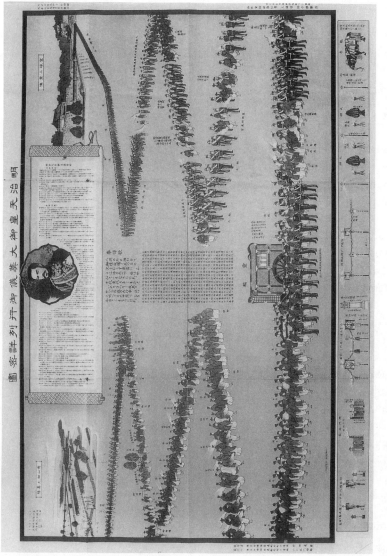

Figure 24. Lithograph of the Meiji emperor's funeral procession. Shibata Ryōun, "Meiji tennō gotaisōgi on gyōretsu shōmitsu zu," 1912.

This bodily and symbolic duality is neatly diagrammed in a lithographic representation of the Meiji emperor's funeral that has as its title "Detail of the Meiji Emperor's Grand Funeral Procession" ("Meiji tennō gotaisōgi on gyōretsu shōmitsu zu"; Figure 24).[80] First, it is important to notice the presence of not one imperial body, but rather two. The figure of the Meiji emperor that has been taken from Chiossone's official portrait of 1888 occupies the top center of the scene. This is the masculinized, militarized, politically engaged, unique, historically located, and ultimately human emperor[81] that is homological to the entire right half of the lithograph as we view it. This right side is dominated by the spectacle of a scene of military men and civilian officials—that is to say, by a representation of military activity and governance—who are dressed mostly in various tight-fitting and Western-style uniforms. They are pouring out of Tokyo's Imperial Palace through the Nijūbashi passageway. The great events of the Meiji emperor's lifetime and reign are inscribed on an opened scroll that frames the emperor's portrait. Between the dates of his birth and death we can read the arrival of U.S. warships in 1853, the Restoration, the renaming of Edo as Tokyo, the imperial progresses and the major imperial pageants of the late Meiji era, including the military ones, the establishment of the new educational system and military conscription, the promulgation of the Constitution, and many other great moments in the establishment of the modern bureaucratic state and constitutional monarchy, as well as military campaigns in Taiwan and Korea and their annexations. The chronology and the scroll—the latter looking as if ready to be rolled up—suggest a closure to the emperor's life and reign.

There is, however, another body at the bottom of the picture and at the center of the funeral cortege. This is a body whose presence is indicated by the imperial hearse, but which remains invisible. To be sure, in an uncomplicated sense one could simply say that this is the Meiji emperor's corpse, but the presentation of the body is not one that suggests his natural infirmities and limitations. Rather, it is one that glorifies the deceased emperor's return to an ever-present past, a living tradition. This body, in other words, is homologous to the scene on the lithograph's left half where we see the spectacle of antiques and men in loose-fitting court robes bound for the Aoyama Funeral Grounds. This space is framed by clouds and stamped with signs of pastness and the traditional, such as shrine gateways and the "Shinto"-style funeral hall, and it is the site from which the body will depart for its journey to Kyoto.

PART 3

The People

CHAPTER FIVE

Crowds and Imperial Pageantry

"The Great Silver Anniversary Ceremony"

Ah! A day for celebration,
And the world of commoners,
is also a silvery one.

From the 9 March 1894 diary entry of Tanaka Sen'ya

Imperial Pageants as National Communions

In writing this short poem Tanaka Sen'ya, a Shinto priest from a village in the Chichibu region of Saitama Prefecture, registered his belief that the imperial wedding anniversary ceremony was not simply the private affair of the imperial household but was the occasion of a national communion in which the entire "world of commoners" was involved.[1] But from the official point of view, not all people in the emerging nation participated with equal enthusiasm or the appropriate frame of mind in the imperial pageants that have been described earlier and, more broadly, in what I have called the folklore of the new regime. For example, the journalist Ubukata Toshirō remarked that in his hometown of Numata (Gunma Prefecture), the people celebrated the ceremony of the Constitution's promulgation with "less than one-tenth the gaiety of the annual summer festival."[2] A writer for the *Miyako shinbun* noted in December 1895 that though tens of thousands of worshippers had gone to a national festival at Yasukuni Shrine following the Sino-Japanese War, few had shown the proper military spirit and respect. None had bowed in front of the regimental banners on display, and he had even seen some laughing at their war-worn condition.[3] Even in 1906 a journalist for the *Kokumin shinbun* scornfully noted that some families of the war dead residing in Tokyo were giving their special tickets to worship at Yasukuni as presents for their neighbors, or even secretly selling them.[4] Aizawa Kikutarō—who had by 1900 become an official of Aihara village and who had sent a congratulatory letter to the imperial household on the occasion of the crown prince's wedding— recorded that his village assembly held a special meeting on 8 May 1900 in large part to discuss the question of villagers putting out national flags and taking a holiday from work on the tenth. However, on the day of the wedding, Aizawa merely completed his duties at the village office, went home at three, and then went *ayu* fishing at Okawa River.[5]

The pageants themselves could sometimes even be objects of political satire, such as Miyatake Gaikotsu's famous lampoon of the Meiji Constitution's promulgation ceremony. The 28 February 1889 issue of his outrageous "journal," the *Journal of the Society of Ready Wit (Tonchi kyōkai zasshi)*, carried a print by Adachi Ginkō entitled "Tonchi kenpō happushiki" (Figure 25). By the clever substitution of a few characters in what should have been entitled the "Meiji Constitution Promulgation Ceremony" ("Meiji kenpō happushiki"), Miyatake and Adachi had changed the meaning to "Promulgation Ceremony for the Sharpening of the Ready Wit Law." And where the emperor would have stood on a raised dais in the palace Throne Room handing Prime Minister Kuroda the Constitution, Adachi put a skeleton—the Japanese word for which, *gaikotsu*, is homophonous with Miyatake's own adopted name. Along with the cartoon Miyatake printed a set of laws for the Society of Ready Wit, mimicking the official language and form of the Constitution. As an example, while Article II of the Meiji Constitution stated that "The Imperial Throne shall be succeeded to by Imperial male descendants, according to the provisions of the Imperial House Law," Miyatake's Article II read, "The headship of the Society shall be succeeded to by Gaikotsu's descendants, as established by Dr. Scatterbrain (*tonkyō hakase*)." For their good humor Adachi and Miyatake were imprisoned for one and three years, respectively. Ironically, in reflecting many years later on his punishment for lese majesty, Miyatake wrote that through this incident the Meiji state actually pushed him to become a consistent and committed critic of the establishment.[6]

Figure 25. Miyatake Gaikotsu's lampoon of the Meiji
Constitution's promulgation. The print "Tonchi kenpō
happushiki," is by Adachi Ginkō. From Miyatake
Gaikotsu, *Tonchi kyōkai zasshi* (28 February 1889).
Courtesy of Meiji Shinbun Zasshi Bunko, Tokyo
University.

There were also alternative mappings of the national landscape that
competed with what I have called the modern regime's ritual or symbolic topography. Most conspicuously, popular leaders of the so-called
new religions that were founded in the late Tokugawa and Meiji years
sometimes conceptualized the new regime's symbolic center, Tokyo,
not as the center of the national community's prosperity but rather as

a hell or a place of disease, the location of an oppressive regime whose "civilization and enlightenment" policies and whose prioritizing of the development of capitalism and the interests of the economic elite brought severe hardship upon the people.[7] Furthermore, most "new religions" developed their own centers of meaning and memory that often challenged the dominant ones located in Kyoto, Ise, Tokyo, and many other places throughout Japan. For Nakayama Miki and her followers in the Tenri religion, especially prior to its recognition as one of the officially recognized Shinto sects in 1908, the center of the world was not any of the Meiji regime's official sites but rather a sacred location called the *jiba* in what is now Tenri City, where a sweet heavenly dew was expected to fall onto a pillar and usher in an age of perfect happiness.[8]

The charismatic foundress of the Ōmoto religion, Deguchi Nao, spoke of her world under the Meiji regime as a place of "money, beasts, and egoism" ruled over by evil deities, of Ise as polluted, and of Tokyo as a place that the deity Ushitora no Konjin would destroy prior to his establishment of a divine paradise on earth. Indeed, she claimed that a new "capital city" (*miyako*) centering on the Ōmoto religion's headquarters in Ayabe—not Kyoto or Tokyo—would flourish after the cataclysm inaugurating the millennium and that even the emperor would be free to seek refuge there if he so desired. So disturbing was this alternative mapping of the world that in 1921 state authorities destroyed the main sanctuary of the Ōmoto religion in Ayabe. They also forced the followers to rebuild Nao's mausoleum because they claimed that it bore too much of a resemblance to the Meiji emperor's mausoleum in Momoyama. The second and even more destructive attack upon the Ōmoto religion took place in 1935, and at that time Nao's coffin was disinterred and removed to a less conspicuous place.[9]

Finally, if soldiers' letters during the Russo-Japanese War are in any way representative of commoner consciousness around the turn of the century, it would appear—as Ōe Shinobu's analysis has suggested—that even men situated in an institutional setting which was saturated with official propaganda rarely revealed any consciousness about either the nation or the emperor in their letters home.[10]

It will do us no good, however, to wish away the nation, the imperial symbols, or the entire "folklore of the regime," including its symbolic topography and disciplinary practices, that began to take hold over the people who were starting to recognize themselves as the Japanese. Instead, we need to steer between two poles. On the one hand, we must avoid a Durkheimian tendency to assume that national symbols and ceremonials necessarily reflect and reproduce a sense of national unity,[11] or that invented traditions and beliefs are necessarily and unproblematically accepted. On the other hand, we must guard against a desire to deny the impact and hold over the Japanese people of a whole host of symbols, beliefs, and practices that were clearly fabrications of the late nineteenth and early twentieth centuries.

It is not enough to say that much of what the Japanese people today take for granted is of recent vintage. We also need to gauge, if only in a suggestive way, how and to what degree these inventions were received by the people. That is the purpose of this chapter. Its focus continues to be the imperial pageantry, the symbols and the disciplinary practices that have already been described. However, my strategy here will be to look at these fabrications from the "bottom up," so to speak—from the perspective of those in local communities.

In his influential book on modern nationalism, Benedict Anderson has argued that an important precondition for the ability of people to imagine themselves as belonging to a common national community is a shared sense of time. Such a "homogenous empty time" that could cut transversely across vast geographical spaces allowed the members of a national community, unable to have face-to-face contact, to imagine themselves as sharing in a simultaneity in time and hence made the belief in a shared community possible, if not necessarily inevitable. This is a type of time in which simultaneity is imagined as "transverse, cross-time, marked not by prefiguring and fulfillment, but by temporary coincidence, and measured by clock and calendar." Anderson emphasizes the development of print capitalism and the role of such media as the novel and newspapers in constructing this sense of simultaneity.[12]

It is difficult to believe that during the period of the imperial progresses citizens throughout the nation felt themselves to be participating in a single ritual simultaneously. Rather, the progress as a ritual of territorial domination worked primarily through a logic of spatial integration whereby the numerous places along the routes of the emperor's progresses were constructed into a spatial continuum *over* time—not in the same time—by the movement of the emperor's body. That is to say, the people in the different villages and towns that the progress passed through did not share in the time of the emperor's passing through— the emperor arrived in different villages in different times. Thus while the people in these local communities might be able to share in the numerous practices and symbols of the new regime, this style of state ritual was not conducive to the idea of temporal coincidence—the idea that all the people of the nation lived in the same time. In this regard, the imperial progress could not be an adequate focus of national communion. And for a modern nation-state, it was an anachronistic ceremonial style.

In contrast, the imperial pageants beginning in 1889 that took place in the reconstructed Tokyo, as well as in Kyoto, enabled the people of the nation to imagine a simultaneous link: regardless of where they lived, they could believe themselves to be joined at exactly the same moment in history that was marked by the ceremonial event. These occasions could thus be true national communions in which, as descriptions of popular involvement often put it, the "noble and mean" and "men and women of all ages" (*rōnyaku nanjo*) in every "corner of the land" (*tsutsu uraura ni*) participated. Through the collective act of cotemporaneously recognizing such national symbols as the emperor, the imperial family, the Constitution, the imperial capitals, the national anthem, the national flag, Rising Sun lanterns (*hinomaru chōchin*), and places such as Ise, Kyoto, Tokyo, the Imperial Palace, Nijūbashi, and Yasukuni Shrine, it became possible for individuals to experience their continuity with one another across space, in and through time. In this sense, that the nation's people might see a variety of meanings in any national ceremonial, that many people's imaginings might even differ wildly from the official intentions, was not as important as their participation in these national communions synchronically.

Yet the production of a sense of simultaneity throughout the nation during the national ceremonials would not have been possible without the rapid development of the national transportation and communications network during the late Meiji period. The new pageants that used Japan's capital cities as state theaters only became visible to the great numbers of people who were becoming Japan's citizens because technological developments facilitated the rapid circulation of signs, images, and people. For example, the railways, in just the ten-year period between 1885 and 1895, expanded from about 350 to over 2,000 miles of track. In 1889, less than half a year after the Meiji Constitution's promulgation, the last section of the Tōkaidō line connecting Tokyo and Kōbe was completed. In 1891, with the completion of the 450-mile Ueno–Aomori segment, the main line along the Pacific coast stretched from Aomori to Kōbe; and in another ten years this line was further extended to Shimonoseki, where it linked up with the Kyūshū railway system. A spur from Tokyo to Naoetsu connected the capital to the

Japan Sea coast. By 1907 there were about 5,000 miles of track, augmented by an improved system of roads, transporting some 140 million passengers per year.[13]

In stressing the importance of the transportation and communications network in the production of nationalism, I hope that I do not appear to be agreeing with one theorist of nationalism who has claimed that the ideas transmitted through the media do not matter. Ernest Gellner has argued:

It matters precious little what has been fed into them [the media]: it is the media themselves, the pervasiveness and importance of abstract, centralized, standardized, one to many communication, which itself automatically engenders the core idea of nationalism, quite irrespective of what in particular is being put into the specific messages transmitted. The most important and persistent message is generated by the medium itself. That core message is that the language and style of the transmissions is important, that only he who can understand them, or can acquire such comprehension, is included in a moral and economic community, and that he who does not and cannot, is excluded. All this is crystal clear, and follows from the pervasiveness and crucial role of mass communication in this kind of society. What is actually *said* matters little. (emphasis in original)[14]

I, on the other hand, have been concerned throughout this book to describe and assess the politics of various dominant representations of the nation, the emperor, and the imperial household. Ideas matter a great deal.[15] And it is the media and the transportation system that made these discursive and visual representations available to the people, with some important effects. My specific argument here is simply that the shared sense of national simultaneity that was facilitated by the media and the transportation network was a necessary but not sufficient condition for the production of the subjective belief that one belonged to a single national community; and that this is indeed true regardless of how individuals might have consumed the messages.

Largely as a result of such developments in the national transportation system, provincials, or "red blankets" (*akagetto*), could be seen throughout the ceremonial cities during all of the imperial pageants discussed earlier. Newspapers commented frequently on the number of people who were clearly not from the capital cities. The *Jiji shinpō*, for example, reported that the majority of people standing just outside the Sakurada entrance to the Palace Plaza during the Constitution's promulgation were in fact provincials (*inaka no hitobito*) who could be distinguished by their traveling clothes.[16] Another estimated that between 11 and 13 February the trains coming into Tokyo carried five times the normal number of passengers.[17] Similarly, at the time of the emperor's twenty-fifth wedding anniversary, newspapers and magazines again noted the huge numbers of people thronging to the capital from the provinces.[18] Passenger cars owned by the Japan Railway Company were so overcrowded that the company was forced to convert freight cars into makeshift passenger cars. Because of the unusually large number of users, two days before the event trains along the Tōkaidō Line were delayed some thirty to forty minutes, a delay that increased to between one and two hours on the day preceding the celebration. The Ueno Railway Company, which had reduced its fares by 20 percent, was reported to be carrying three times its normal number of riders. The *Jiji shinpō* summed up the situation in the capital:

Tourists wishing to behold the imperial cortege began arriving in the capital in huge numbers from a day or two ago. They had heard that an unprecedented ceremony was to be held yesterday [9 March 1894] and that the emperor and empress would be riding together in a procession to the parade field at Aoyama. It has been reported that, as a result, all the inns around Bakuro-machi [an area of Tokyo noted for its large number of inns] were filled with people. In fact, yesterday there was an extremely large number of groups of five to ten people, wrapped in their red or green blankets who were saying *"gansu"* or *"danbe"* [i.e., using regional dialects]. They could be found not only along the main route of the imperial procession but also from the main [Ginza] boulevard to such places as Ueno and Asakusa Parks.[19]

Similar movements of people to the capitals typified all of the events treated above—whether Emperor Meiji's triumphal return following the Sino-Japanese War, the crown prince's wedding, or any of the national celebrations following the Russo-Japanese War.[20]

Nishigata Tamezō, an active participant in party politics from the 1880s until around 1906 or so, recorded his very hectic schedule of activities in the days just before and after the 30 April 1906 Triumphal Military Review in Tokyo. His diary entries between 28 April and 6 May 1906 not only suggest the intensity of his experience of a national simultaneity in those heady days, they also demonstrate the role of the transportation system, the rapid circulation of such new mnemonic sites as commemorative postcards and stamps, and the significance in the national imaginary of such new physical sites as the Yasukuni Shrine complex.[21] On the twenty-eighth he traveled by train from his village in Niigata Prefecture to Tokyo. Seven or eight acquaintances who had lost relatives in the Russo-Japanese War boarded the train with him at Sanjō city. However, they were forced to get off at Karuizawa because the train became overly crowded with people traveling to Tokyo. Nishigata managed to stay on board and arrived in the capital later that day. On the twenty-ninth Nishigata visited the Army Ministry in order to acquire tickets to view the Triumphal Military Review, which was scheduled to take place on the following day. He also located his traveling companions, gave them tickets for the review, and bought commemorative postage stamps and postcards. On the thirtieth he went to Aoyama Military Parade Field to witness "His Majesty the Generalissimo of the Army and Navy" (*daigensui heika*) conduct "a grand ceremony, unprecedented since remote antiquity."

On 1 May Nishigata went to a post office to have his postcards rubber-stamped with a special commemorative stamp. In the evening he visited Yasukuni Shrine for the enshrinement rites held there. On the following day he went to the Palace Plaza in order to see the triumphal arch set up at Babasakimon and the captured weapons that had been placed in front of Nijūbashi. He then proceeded to Yasukuni Shrine for the second day of observances. The shrine was so packed with surviving family members of the war dead, himself included, that it took over four hours before he could worship at the main sanctuary. People commented that the raindrops which began to fall in the afternoon were "the tears of those who had died of illnesses while serving in the war"; for those who died of illnesses were thought to be less heroic than those who had died as a direct result of combat, and they were not enshrined until 1907.[22] On the third Nishigata again went to Yasukuni, this time to view the emperor's personal visit. He went yet again on the fourth to observe the worship of the crown prince, as well as four princesses of the blood. On the fifth he visited the war museum at Yasukuni, the Yūshūkan. On the sixth Nishigata attended a victory celebration in Tokyo for Niigata military men returning from war. Before doing so, he attempted to purchase more commemorative postcards at the Tokyo post office. Having no luck, however, he gave up and went to the Kioi-chō branch where he managed to buy commemorative stamps. Those in the crowd at the Kioi-chō postal office were so unruly, apparently in their excitement to buy commemorative issues, that some people were injured.

While the nation's citizens streamed into the ceremonial centers, information and images traveled swiftly out to the provinces through the evolving forms of print, visual, and to a lesser extent electronic media. Inexpensive newspapers published in the provinces as well as in the major cities provided fast and realistic descriptions of the events in the ritual centers. The *Osaka asahi*, which had printed just over 3 million copies in 1881, printed over 18 million in 1891, and around 40 million at the turn of the century.[23] Tokyo's newspapers combined to print a total of 42 million copies in 1887, including almost 14 million destined for areas outside Tokyo Prefecture (*fu*). By 1889, in only two years, the numbers had jumped to about 65 and 19 million copies, respectively. The phenomenal increase continued throughout the 1890s; in 1899, the Tokyo newspapers printed over 200 million copies with almost 40 percent of these sent out of the capital.[24] This coincided with a steep drop in the price of newspapers. In 1886 the *Yūbin hōchi* cut the price of a month's subscription from 83 to 33 sen . Other papers quickly followed suit.[25] Not all the Japanese people could read, of course. But the great proliferation of newspapers that began in the 1880s surely made any event in Tokyo much more visible to the people in the provinces than had previously been possible.

National ceremonials were not simply mediated by existing and proven technology. An event as important as the promulgation of the Meiji Constitution could even stimulate experiments with new media forms. On 11 February 1889 the *Jiji shinpō* announced that in an attempt to increase the speed and geographical extent of its news reportage, it would use the telephone to send the text of the Meiji Constitution to Atami immediately after its being made public. In this way, it explained, "it should be possible to send news of a grand event which comes just once in a millennium, widely and quickly, to Izusan-mura and the areas nearby." The following day the *Jiji* reported that this plan had in fact been accomplished: the texts of the Constitution and several related pieces of legislation had been sent, and the recipient of the information had reported briefly on the celebrations taking place in Atami. "It had been," the writer remarked, "no different from talking directly while sitting knee to knee, shoulder to shoulder."[26] The promulgation also touched off the use of extra editions by the Japanese press. The *Osaka asahi*, which wired the over 11,300 characters making up the Constitution to Osaka, was so fast in getting out its extra edition that the authorities launched an investigation to determine if the text had been leaked prior to its official promulgation.[27]

The development of print capitalism and the media in general was conducive to the widespread experience of national simultaneity, even for those who did not witness the pageants in person. For example, in an extraordinary diary that he kept between 1885 and 1962, Aizawa

Kikutarō—a wealthy farmer and member of the local elite in a village in Kanagawa Prefecture—wrote an extremely detailed description of the ceremonies held in Tokyo on 11 February for the Meiji Constitution's promulgation. In doing so he remarked that his family had begun subscribing to the *Chūgai shōgyō shinpō* in the previous year. "Because of this," he noted, "on the thirteenth it was possible for me to examine the illustration showing the distribution of the Constitution and such things as the Imperial Rescript [promulgating the Constitution] and the rules." On the fourteenth he copied the "Preamble to the Constitution" and the "Imperial Rescript on the Constitution" into his diary directly from the newspaper.[28] The media, in short, allowed Aizawa to experience the coincidence of events in his daily life with the pageantry taking place quite far away.

At the same time, a far greater number of the nation's subjects experienced the national communions by participating in local observances that coincided with and mimicked those at the nation's centers. At the time of the Constitution's promulgation, people throughout the country celebrated what they often called the national festival (*kokusai*) or the Constitution festival (*kenpōsai*) at local shrines, temples, parks, schools, and other sites. Some local gatherings seem to have been limited primarily to politically active elites. In one assemblage at Himeji, for example, prefectural assemblymen, members of a youth organization and a "club" held a party (*enkai*) and athletic meet.[29] There were also many activities in which only students took part. Thus in the city of Saga students lined up in military formations on school athletic grounds and fired salutes.[30] Nevertheless, many communities did take part in large numbers and with great enthusiasm. "The scene in Kyoto," one newspaper reported, "was like that of the Gion festival." And even in Ubukata Toshirō's "small town in the mountain country" of Gunma Prefecture, the townspeople put out various festive displays and his family ate *kowa meshi*, the steamed rice eaten on festival days.[31]

Such mass participation in Japan's first national communion at cities, towns, and villages throughout the country marked only the beginning of a practice which would continue and grow throughout the modern era. Thus Aizawa, who had earlier recorded in his diary the details of the Constitution's promulgation ceremony, noted that on the day of the emperor's twenty-fifth wedding anniversary, "from Tokyo Prefecture to the villages outside the city, all took part in the celebrating. An official order was also sent down to my village and on this day [we] put out flags and took a holiday from work."[32] In the provincial city of Saga, as one journalist put it, "it goes without saying that on this day everyone—young and old, men and women—were caught up in the great excitement; and the size of the crowds was unparalleled from ancient times to the present."[33]

The *Saga shinbun* reported that at the time of the crown prince's wedding the enthusiasm in one village, Ashikari (Ogi District, Saga Prefecture), was so great that the whole community took a holiday from work, all households put out national flags, and over 2,000 people took part in a ceremony conducted on a school field. While the story may be somewhat embellished, the reporter also noted that an itinerant paper peddler making his rounds through Ashikari was sent packing with the words, "aren't you a subject of the Great Japanese Empire? Why are you peddling on this holiday?"[34] Similarly, all fifty of the households in one hamlet in the administrative village, Asahi (Saga Prefecture), took part in a celebration held at a local shrine. As part of the festivities, those over sixty years of age danced and performed comical antics (*dōkemono*).[35] Coincidentally, a great number of villagers in Komikado (Katori District, Chiba Prefecture)—village officials, village assemblymen, ward headmen, military reservists, other "like-minded elites" (*yūshisha*), and schoolchildren—gathered together at Komikado Shrine, which had been designated by the central government as a "special government shrine" (*bekkaku kanpeisha*). They participated in rites held there and listened to speeches given by the higher elementary school's principal, the village headman, and a representative for the military reservists. The village headman then led a chorus of *banzai*s to the emperor, empress, crown prince, and Princess Sadako; and the schoolchildren sang "*Kimi ga Yo*."[36]

Often crowds recognized Tokyo as Japan's symbolic center by facing in the direction of the capital. Thus at Osaka's Nakanoshima Park an immense crowd stood facing east, in front of an altar which had been built so that the worshippers could gaze toward the Imperial Palace. While a band played "Kimi ga Yo," the congregation bowed as one toward the palace. Then Mayor Tamura led a hail of *banzai*s to the emperor, empress, crown prince, and Princess Sadako.[37]

Many provincial functions were also timed to coincide with the war rites held in the nation's capital. Thus Aizawa Kikutarō, the assiduous diary keeper of a village in Kanagawa Prefecture, noted that his brother joined the heads of nearby towns and villages at Fujisawa in order to welcome the passing trains of the emperor and empress as they returned in triumph to Tokyo after the Sino-Japanese War. Moreover, Kikutarō himself "put out a national flag in order to honor the event." His entire village had received a notice to do so.[38] The residents of Aomori city also put out national flags and lanterns while schoolchildren took an afternoon holiday. Simultaneously, in nearby Maiko village (Nishi-tsugaru District) one group calling itself the "Peace with China Celebration Association" occupied a local primary school and set up pictures of the emperor and empress. Schoolchildren and association members bowed before these pictures and shouted *banzais* to the emperor and empress, the empire, and the army and navy.[39]

It should be noted, however, that on the whole there was less concern with timing local celebrations of military victories to coincide exactly with those at the ritual center than was shown when the auspicious occasion for the imperial family was nonmilitary. Just as often, rather than bother to synchronize local celebrations with those in Tokyo, provincials imitated the central ceremonials according to their own schedules. Thus they set up their own triumphal arches and decorations as they welcomed not the highest-ranking war leaders of the nation, but fellow villagers, townsmen, and city dwellers making their victorious returns from war. Seventy villagers and thirty schoolchildren from Aizawa's village, for example, went out to the train station at Hachiōji, about two weeks after the emperor's triumphal return, in order to greet their local hero, one Matsuura Aisaburō. The villagers escorted Matsuura back to the village shrine where they drank congratulatory sake and then returned him to his house.[40] Later, in September, Aizawa became a member of a committee formed for the purpose of planning a joint "victory ceremony" for four villages, including his own. The ceremony took place on 29 September 1895 at the Kōfuku Temple. In front of the ceremonial grounds the committee placed a great triumphal arch with a plaque which declared, "In Celebration of the Triumphal Return." The main ceremony consisted of the handing of silver cups to six soldiers and the representatives of four others who had served in the war. The planning committee was enabled to meet nearly the entire cost of the ceremony by collecting a total of sixty-five yen from the 569 households making up the four villages. The amount that each individual household paid was calculated according to the proportions of the total cost each normally bore for such village activities as festivals.[41]

The same tendency toward local imitations of Tokyo's rites of war can be seen in the development of rites for the war dead held at local shrines, memorials, and even Buddhist temples. Provincial monuments to the nation's war heroes had already existed prior to Japan's major foreign wars. These had honored the fallen men of the Restoration. However, the building of local shrines (*shōkonsha*) and, to an even greater extent, memorials (*chūkonbi*) to the war dead proliferated following the Sino-Japanese War and, to a much greater degree, the Russo-Japanese War.[42] Sometimes rites held at these provincial places took place at the same time, at least roughly, as those held at Yasukuni Shrine in Tokyo. Thus the shrine to the war dead in Hirosaki (Aomori Prefecture) held its annual festivals in conjunction with those at Yasukuni, and an enshrinement festival held on 5 and 6 May 1905 came only two days after a national enshrinement festival in Tokyo.[43] Elsewhere, rites for the war dead simply followed local, rather than Tokyo, schedules. In Nagano city, to take just one example, prefectural authorities sponsored rites to the war dead (*shōkonsai*) at the Zenkōji Temple on 16 May 1906, about two weeks after central enshrinement rites took place in Tokyo.[44]

While the national celebrations held throughout the country came and went, commemorative objects, produced by individuals and communities, served as permanent reminders of these collective experiences and later enabled the emplotment of a history of collective simultaneity. Through these objects, whether large and imposing or small and seemingly insignificant, the nation's subjects were enabled to reimagine or remember having once shared a simultaneous experience. The production of these mnemonic sites in conjunction with national pageants began at the time of the Constitution's promulgation. Some, like the confectioner Fūgetsudō's "Constitution Cakes" (*kenpō okoshi*), or the five-meter temporary monument in Asakusa Park, made of plaster on which "Long Live the Empire" was written,[45] probably contributed minimally to the creation of a collective memory. Other commemorative articles, however, had a more lasting effect. Volunteers from Shiba Ward, "seeking a more enduring record of the great occasion than the memory of an ephemeral festival could furnish," planted about 150 cherry trees along the bank of the moat outside Toranomon.[46] Numerous woodblock prints, one of Tokyo's most famous souvenir items (*miyage*), captured different views of the ceremonial event in the capital. These included depictions of the emperor's granting of the Constitution within the Throne Room, the scene outside Nijūbashi, the crowds and the imperial procession, the military review at Aoyama, and the procession to Ueno Park on 12 February 1889.[47] Commemorative literature also began to be published. One book, written in the popular style of an illustrated novel (*eiri shōsetsu*), was entitled *The Gaiety of the*

Great Ceremony for the Promulgation of the Constitution. It described the festivities and decorations throughout Tokyo and concluded: "How blessed are we that the emperor has given happiness to us, the people! Indeed, tears of joy overflow!"[48]

Commemoration through the production of material objects continued with the wedding anniversary celebration of 1894. Again woodblock prints, silver anniversary combs, and commemorative badges, cups, and literature appeared.[49] The literature achieved a new degree of detail. *The Glad Tidings on the Great Celebration of the Twenty-Fifth Imperial Wedding Anniversary,* for example, began by noting that the purpose of the book was to commemorate the occasion and to serve as a reference source for future celebrations of the imperial household. It included sixty-five pages of newspaper articles dealing with the event, a description of the Italian emperor's silver wedding anniversary celebration, and a brief review of other commemorative books then available. Then clearly recognizing and helping construct the idea that such celebrations as the Constitution's promulgation and the wedding anniversary should be thought of as national ceremonials that could be emplotted on a singular history, the book described the ceremonies that had been held in conjunction with Japan's first national ceremonial. Another book, *The Auspicious Event of the Twenty-Fifth Wedding Anniversary Grand Ceremony,* provided eighty-one pages of detail including an explanation of the Western practice of celebrating wedding anniversaries and an exhaustive description of Umberto I's silver wedding anniversary celebration.[50]

Objects commemorating the crown prince's wedding proliferated in unprecedented quantity and variety. Here I will mention just a few. Tokyo's citizens and visitors from the provinces crowded Tokyo's print shops (*ezōshiya*) once again to buy commemorative woodblock prints and lithographs. One Katō Sukesaburō, who had been making commemorative cups since the Constitution's promulgation, produced imperial wedding cups.[51] And over 1,500 students from throughout the country joined "The Sincerity Association of the Empire's Youth" (Teikoku Shōnen Shiseikai) in order to put together a book commemorating the wedding. As the members of the association explained in their bylaws, they wished to "commemorate forever the great ceremony."[52] The headman of Jusan village (Nishi District, Aomori Prefecture), "a place so remote that even on important holidays only schools and prominent persons put out Rising Sun flags," commemorated the occasion by using village funds to distribute national flags to every household in the village.[53]

But the people left their most lasting memorials on the nation's landscape. Tokyo's Shiba Ward residents, for example, built a giant electric lamp for Shiba Park. New stands of commemorative trees appeared in villages, towns, and cities throughout the country. In addition to holding a "celebration festival," the people of Nawa village (Ako District, Hyōgo Prefecture), planted pine trees and erected a stone plaque engraved with the words, "Imperial Wedding Commemorative Pine Trees" (*godaikon kinen matsu*). The people of Mitsuke-machi (Shizuoka Prefecture) planted paulownia and wisteria trees in a local shrine and placed a commemorative hanging within the main sanctuary.[54] Fifty commemorative trees were planted at the Higashi District Office in Aomori Prefecture. The Aburakawa village assembly in the same district directed the planting of trees at two local shrines.[55]

Many communities went further than planting trees, opening entire parks instead. At Yokosuka, for example, "like-minded elites" opened an "Imperial Wedding Commemorative Park" (*gokeiji kinen no kōen*) on the grounds of Suwa Shrine.[56] In Kuroishi town (Minami District, Aomori Prefecture) local leaders, anticipating a project which would take two to three years, began to build a commemorative park on the site of an old castle. Of the cost, estimated at 5,000 yen, the Town Assembly contributed 250 yen, while the rest was to be made up in private donations. One Katō Ubei donated 200 yen and 150 cherry trees.[57]

Commemorative buildings—ranging in size, cost, and fame from such local structures as the Kizukuri Village Office (Nishi-tsuguru District, Aomori Prefecture), projected to cost 1,500 yen,[58] to the massive Hyōkeikan at Tokyo's Ueno Park—left the most impressive and indelible imprints on the land. The single most ambitious building effort had resulted in the erection of the Hyōkeikan, an art museum built adjacent to what was then called the Imperial Museum, now the National Museum. The leading figures in Tokyo's "Association for the Celebration of the Crown Prince's wedding"—founded by the wealthy businessman Shibusawa Eiichi, Tokyo Governor Senge Takatomi, and Tokyo Mayor Matsuda Hideo—launched the project in March 1900. They commissioned the renowned architect for the imperial household, Katayama Tōkuma, to design the museum and enlisted 7,310 members and 15,890 other contributors to fund their wedding gift to the crown prince. The two-story stone edifice, still standing today, was finally completed after eight years at a cost of just over 540,100 yen.[59]

This obsession with commemorating national ceremonial events through the production of material sites of memory should be understood within the more general context of the spreading modern idea that objects and ceremonials could serve a memory function. I have already remarked on the Meiji beginnings of what Ishii Kendō called "commemorative bronze statuary" (*kinen dōzō*), but the general custom of attaching the prefix *kinen* to ceremonials and objects to indicate their mnemonic purpose seems to have begun in the late 1870s, and the development of the idea of commemoration appears to have been very closely tied to anchoring heroes and events in the dominant national memory.

Thus Ishii observed in his discussions of the "Beginnings of Commemorative Medals (*kinen-shō*)" and the "Beginnings of Memorials (*kinen-hi*)" that the practice of prefixing this word meaning "to commemorate" to ritual occasions, as in *kinen-sai*, began in 1881. Further, although Fukuzawa Yukichi as early as 1869 had referred to "stone memorials erected for the purpose of commemoration" while describing their legal protection in France, the first such "memorial" (*kinen-hi*) in Japan had been built on the grounds of the famous temple, the Miidera, in 1879. It recalled those of the Ninth Regiment who had lost their lives in the Seinan War. Then from around 1882 memorial construction became "something of a fad." Finally, Ishii maintained that the government first became involved in the work of *kinen* when it issued the medals commemorating the Meiji Constitution's promulgation and that "from then on the characters for *kinen* came to be frequently used in such [words] as commemorative forestation, commemorative library, memorial, commemorative postcard, and so on."[60] In short, the idea of commemoration took hold during the period of modern nationalism, and it does not seem unreasonable to conjecture that the practice flourished because it fit well with the need to produce a sense of national simultaneity through time.

To sum up this section, the imperial pageants enabled the people scattered through the country to experience their communion with the monarchy and with one another. They did so by journeying to the nation's capital cities, by participating in local observances, or simply by recognizing the coincidence of their everyday lives with events in the ceremonial centers. Moreover, for themselves and for later generations commemorative objects, ranging from cups to massive buildings, were material sites that gave a temporal depth to that feeling of simultaneity, for through them they might later remember their having been a community through different moments in the past.

Mobilizing the Masses

It should not be assumed that mass participation in these new national ceremonials was the simple result of spontaneous patriotic enthusiasm. Rather, mobilization of the masses was initiated from above, through both official and unofficial channels. Official notices to put out national flags, to take a holiday from work, to accept imperial gifts of money, or to hold local observances came down through local governments. In schools, perhaps the foremost agency of the central government in local communities, children participated in rites planned by their teachers and school principals. And local elites—local officials, politicians, industrialists, businessmen, journalists, landowners, teachers, and religious leaders—formed ad hoc committees to plan ceremonial events and to encourage widespread involvement. For the great majority of the people who were becoming the Japanese, then, participation in these modern mass national ceremonies was a part of the process of acquiring a sense of national community, not an outcome of it. Their participation was made possible by the workings of a vast network of governmental institutions and nationalizing local elites.

One example from the village of Shichinohe (Kamigata District, Aomori Prefecture) illustrates the general method by which local elites encouraged the participation of the rest of the population. A few days prior to the promulgation of the Meiji Constitution, the planners of Shichinohe's celebration posted notices at various places informing the local populace of the upcoming festival. They also prepared the site for the rites, the Zuiryū Temple, by putting up decorations and hanging a set of pictures of the emperor and empress. In front of the pictures they constructed a place of worship (*sanpaisho*). On the day of the promulgation, singing schoolchildren lined up on one side of the altar while musicians playing Shinto music stood on the other. Over 250 community leaders, both official and nonofficial, formed the nucleus of those who attended. Some of these core members read *norito* prayers while others delivered speeches. The mobilization of the local populace, however, was also impressive, for "the young and old, men and women, who gathered together from neighboring hamlets and places grew to number over 3,000 people. It is said that they received oranges, candies, and other things donated by the 'like-minded elite.'"[61]

Because of their attendance at schools, children could be most effectively mobilized for the national events. We have already seen that a system of ceremonies for nationally significant occasions, especially national holidays, took hold in schools during the late 1880s. In addition to the ritualized observation of annual national holidays, schoolchildren during late Meiji took part in ceremonies commemorating important "one-time" national events, including the national ceremonials described above.

As Yamamoto Nobuyoshi and Konno Toshihiko have observed, school celebrations of the Meiji Constitution's promulgation often served as models for future national rites held in schools. In Kanagawa Prefecture, for example, on 11 February over 3,000 students and teachers from thirteen schools marched in formation to Hachiman Shrine. They carried with them banners bearing the names of their schools or the words, "Long Live the Basis of Imperial Rule—Peace and Prosperity to the Nation" (*kōki banzai kokka an'ei*). Prefectural officials joined the students at the shrine. The central rites consisted of singing "Kimi ga Yo" and "Kigensetsu no Uta," reading Shinto prayers, firing gun salutes, and shouting "Long Live the Basis of Imperial Rule." Amusements followed the formal ceremonies, as those in charge released balloons and distributed treats. Students took part in athletic matches and sang military and school songs. According to Yamamoto and Konno this school ceremonial was prototypical in the following ways. First, it celebrated the emperor and the nation. Second, the ceremonial took place at a local shrine. Third, music and balloons imparted an extraordinary atmosphere to the occasion. Fourth, the ceremonial included military-inspired exercises such as falling into formation. Finally, officials attended the event and children received treats.[62]

Schoolchildren continued in similar ways to celebrate the imperial family and the nation during most of the late Meiji mass national ceremonials. Between March 1894 and December 1895, one school, the Nagasaki Primary School (Nagasaki Prefecture), held thirteen ceremonies for imperial or military events, not including those for national holidays. These included a rite for the emperor's twenty-fifth wedding anniversary and a "worshipping from afar" (*yōhaishiki*) ceremony at the local shrine to the war dead, Sako Shōkonsha. The "worshipping from afar" ceremony was held to coincide with enshrinement rites held at Tokyo's Yasukuni Shrine.[63] Sometimes, as in the town of Imari's (Saga

Prefecture) celebration of the emperor's twenty-fifth wedding anniversary, schools and schoolchildren provided the local focus of general merrymaking. For that event, the main ceremonial took place on the Imari Primary School grounds and over a thousand students, officials, and other citizens attended. The central rite consisted of worshipping the pictures of the imperial couple. Later, over four hundred community leaders held a banquet at the school, though their party was interrupted by a group of "drifters" (*furyū*) and "rowdy dancers" (*araodori*) who made their way onto the school athletic field. National flags, festive decorations, and parading schoolchildren filled the rest of the town. One of the most impressive sights was a demonstration of over a thousand students and teachers, all dressed as sailors and completely outfitted with rifles and swords. Throngs of people from neighboring villages came to Imari to view the town's festivities.[64]

Local governments often collaborated with local notables in order to mobilize the masses. The residential neighborhoods of Tokyo Prefecture, though of course affected by their nearness to the central symbols of the capital, were discrete communities nonetheless. An examination of the way in which governmental authorities utilized local Tokyo elites in order to achieve mass involvement may serve to illustrate a more general pattern.

The most important established patrons in Tokyo's neighborhoods were landlords (*jinushi* or *yanushi*) and managers for these landlords (*sahainin*). According to Hirade Kōjirō's ethnographic account of Tokyo, written around the turn of the century, both landlords and their managers had held local power during the Tokugawa period. Those who were not absentee landlords derived much of their power from their responsibility for the physical upkeep of neighborhoods—for example, the repair of gates and neighborhood watch stations (*jishinban*)—and, perhaps more important, for the collection of funds used for festivals and other neighborhood activities. In their capacity as neighborhood officials (*machi toshiyori, jinushi,* and *nanushi*) they also served as local agents of the Tokugawa authorities. Hirade informs us that at the time of his writing, these notables still remained men of wealth who held great political power "both in front of and behind the scenes," though they had no official title under the Meiji system of local administration and no longer completely possessed the responsibilities named above.[65]

In preparing for the celebration of the Constitution's promulgation, the governor of Tokyo notified the heads of Tokyo's districts (*gun*) and wards (*ku*) to participate in the event "with enthusiasm." The district and ward heads in turn arranged meetings of local notables, who in many cases were the landlords and their managers. The head of Kanda Ward, for example, called together over thirty landlords and consulted with them concerning the hanging of Rising Sun lanterns from the eaves of neighborhood buildings. They also discussed the preparation of *dashi* (festival floats) and agreed that as Kanda's floats were "the number one pride of Tokyo" (*Tokyo ichi no homare*), a number of them should be displayed on 11 February.[66] In another ward, Nihonbashi, the ward head met with a similar group of leaders on the sixth in order to discuss Nihonbashi's contribution to the festivities. They decided to build great arches at the ward boundaries and to set out festive bamboo (*aodake*) shaped into gates. At the same time they established a festival committee.[67]

The network of landlords and their managers continued to be vital to the mobilization of Tokyo's neighborhoods at least through the turn of the century. A notice sent down from the Tokyo Prefectural Office reached the city's *jinushi* and *sahainin* just prior to the emperor's triumphal entry into the capital after the Sino-Japanese War; and the *Miyako shinbun* noted that largely as a result of this, the people of the city renewed their enthusiasm in preparing to welcome the emperor.[68] Again, in preparation for the crown prince's wedding, Tokyo's first mayor[69] sent notices to district and ward heads, who in turn encouraged landlords and managers to make preparations in their neighborhoods. One of the most widespread activities of the landlords and managers was organizing neighborhoods to decorate the city with lanterns and flags. The most common type of lantern, in accordance with the directives sent from the ward offices, carried the Rising Sun emblem and the word "Felicitations" (*hōshuku*).[70]

As the frequent use of shrines and temples as locations for local ceremonies suggests, religious leaders were also an established elite that assisted the central authorities in rallying the masses. The diary of Tanaka Sen'ya, the head priest of Muku Shrine in the Chichibu District of Saitama Prefecture with whose poem this chapter begins, provides a glimpse at one such leader's mediating position between the central authorities and common villagers. Tanaka notes that on a personal level he and his two assisting priests sent a letter of congratulations to the emperor and empress on their twenty-fifth wedding anniversary. Not content with this limited demonstration of loyalty, however, the three priests brought together their parishioners (*ujiko*) for a festival at their shrine, distributed sacred sake , and thereby involved members of the community in this national celebration. Several days after the event, Tanaka visited the Shimo-yoshida village office in order to accept an imperial gift of twenty-five sen. The imperial household had given money to local elites throughout the entire nation in order to help defray the costs of providing food and drink for local festivities.[71]

Newly emerging elites also joined old ones in planning local ceremonies. In a large city such as Kyoto, new government officials (Diet members, prefectural and city officials, prefectural and city assemblymen, and prefectural and city councilors [*sanjikaiin*]), businessmen constituting the Chamber of Commerce (*shōgyō kaigisho*), and teachers joined long-standing religious leaders in order to form an ad hoc committee called the Association for the Celebration of the Crown Prince's Wedding (*tōgū gokeiji hōshuku kai*). Such associations could be found in many cities throughout the nation. Kyoto's group of about 10,000 people planned a celebration at Heian Shrine. Perhaps as many as 50,000 people gathered there before pictures of the emperor, empress, crown prince, and Princess Sadako in order to commemorate the imperial wedding.[72]

Journalists, through their writings, contributed to the pervasive sense among the literate elites that the mobilization of all the subjects of the empire in local observances was no less than a moral imperative. To take just one example, the *Yūbin hōchi* ran a lead article less than a week before the Constitution's promulgation entitled, "The Day of the Constitution's Promulgation Set—All the People of the Capital Should Celebrate That Day with Great Fervor." The writer argued that as the establishment of a constitutional system benefited the common people of the nation (*ippan jinmin*), they should by all means take part in the celebrating. He suggested that the appropriate method of popular celebration might be to begin by taking a holiday from work and then allowing one's employees to do the same. Other activities could include pulling festival floats and carts with dancers, setting off firecrackers, and preparing festival displays.[73]

Finally, the contribution of semiofficial patriotic associations around the turn of the century, and especially after the Russo-Japanese War, must be mentioned. Groups such as the Japan Red Cross and the Women's Patriotic Association remained to a great degree elite organizations.[74] Yet they were important because with a nationwide organizational network it was possible for them to mobilize effectively at least the upper elements of local society, as is evidenced by the attendance of their members in many local activities even when other members of the community did not take part. In addition, the Women's Patriotic Association played a key role in bringing survivors of the war dead to Tokyo for Yasukuni enshrinement rites.[75]

In the long run, however, the two most important types of patriotic organizations were young men's associations (*seinendan*) and military reservists' associations (*zaigō gunjinkai*). Until around 1906 these grassroots organizations had only a small impact on local society. The number of local groups was still limited, and formal umbrella organizations linking together these regional associations on a national scale did not yet exist. Tremendous growth came after 1906, as the number of military reservists' associations increased from 4,367 in 1906 to 11,364 in 1910, when formation of the Imperial Military Reserve Association brought the regional groups under one national organization. While no comparable national growth figures for young men's associations are available, in Hiroshima Prefecture the number of youth belonging to such associations increased from 5,652 in 1904, to 89,634 in 1910.[76] The first national meeting of the young men's associations took place in 1910, and a national organization, the Great Japan Youth Association, was established in 1913.[77]

The leadership of these organizations in assembling the masses for national ceremonials had become commonplace by the time of Emperor Meiji's 1912 funeral. By then a young men's association existed even in Fujisaki, a remote hamlet in Aomori Prefecture made up of a mere thirty-seven households. Fujisaki's association had been established in 1909 by one Kimura Ken'ichi. Just before the funeral Kimura directed members of his association to instruct every household in his hamlet to send one representative to the funeral ceremony being conducted in a neighboring village, with preference given to young men's association members and military reservists. On the day after the national funeral Kimura organized yet another observance for Fujisaki in the young men's association's meeting room. A Shinto priest officiated at the rite and over a hundred people attended.[78]

Even before the Russo-Japanese War some young men's associations rallied their local communities to participate in national ceremonies. In Tara village (Fujitsu District, Saga Prefecture) members of young men's associations took the initiative in planning a local festival for the crown prince's wedding. Three young men's associations, their founders especially concerned with "reforming local customs" (*fūzoku kairyō*), agreed to make joint arrangements for the festival. They first acquired the cooperation of local "like-minded elites" and then proceeded to solicit donations. The members of the young men's associations, along with the "like-minded elites," set up their headquarters at a temple, the Enkyōji, and established various preparation committees. Tara Shrine, fronted by a splendid arch and decorated with flags of various types and mini-lanterns (*kyūto*), became the site for the festival. The ceremony began with a speech explaining the purpose of the gathering and ended with *banzais* to the members of the imperial family. So successful had the young men's associations been in mobilizing the populace that a provincial newspaper reported that the celebrants had consumed eighty-five kegs of sake and the catch of twenty village fishing boats on that day.[79] The activities of these young men's associations anticipated the way in which such groups with national ties that cut across hamlets and reached down through all levels of society would succeed, by the end of Meiji, in the nearly total mobilization of society for national observances.

Popular Folklore and the Folklore of the Regime

Though the vast, intricate, and overlapping web of government officials, schools, local elites and members of semiofficial patriotic associations assisted in the dissemination of the new regime's symbols, rituals, images, beliefs, and practices and thereby helped create a sense of national community—a shared spatiality and temporality within the confines of the nation—they could ensure neither a seamless uniformity of belief nor the easy acceptance of the new and disciplinary practices of the regime. Instead, the old and the recently invented commingled. The familiar folklore of everyday life blended into the new "folklore of the regime." This mixing left an ambiguous legacy for the modern nation-state. While the customary folklore frequently provided the vehicle for the surprisingly enthusiastic reception of the new—as when the nation's citizens observed national ceremonials through local festive forms and meanings or when they began journeying to the imperial capitals, acting as if they were on a pilgrimage or a tour to any other famous site or religious center that had no national meaning whatsoever—it also opened up the possibility of transforming or even contesting the regime's folklore.

We have already seen that in the first half of Meiji the people often treated the emperor's progresses as occasions for festivals and that in doing so they made these unfamiliar state pageants intelligible. The same tendency for the common folk to project local meanings onto state pageantry can be seen when these became national communions that were observed throughout the country, beginning with the Constitution's promulgation ceremonies. The new types of ceremonials, national in scale and centering on the emperor or members of his family, had never before been heard of, let alone seen, by either the people or their ancestors, and they often only became sensible insofar as people imagined them as similar to the festivals (*matsuri*) customarily celebrated in countless city neighborhoods, towns, and villages throughout Japan. When commoners joined in these national festivals they were likely to behave as if participating in the local festivals to which they were accustomed. They gathered at sacred places to partake of sacred sake and festival foods. They dressed themselves in festive clothes (*haregi*) and decorated their communities with lanterns, bamboo, pine branches, and other auspicious displays. Entertainment, too, was of the sort that could be found in any popular festival: floats, festive music, *sumo* wrestlers, and dancing.

Hirade Kōjirō, the turn-of-the-century ethnographer of Tokyo, wrote that when Tokyoites held their usual neighborhood festivals, preparation of temporary shopfront shrines (*mikisho*) constituted one central activity. In making these, Hirade explained, "the shopfront area of a house is swept clean, curtains (*manmaku*) are hung out on the eaves, screens are lined up, a hanging designating the name of a deity is suspended out in front, such objects as lion's masks are placed nearby, and a high altar is built with many offerings, beginning with sacred sake and rice cakes (*kagami mochi*)."[80] Such *mikisho* could be found throughout the city during the crown prince's wedding celebration. However, instead of popular deities Tokyo's citizens enshrined pictures of the crown prince and Princess Sadako, or the emperor and empress, or both imperial couples. Landlords in both Omote-machi and Daimon-machi of Koishikawa Ward, for example, built *mikisho*. Around these they placed folding gold screens and within them they enshrined pictures of the crown prince and princess.[81]

The festive atmosphere in Tokyo before and on the day of the earlier Meiji Constitution's promulgation has been much remarked upon.[82] The prices of foods and paraphernalia used in *matsuri* —such as sake, oranges, candles, and lanterns of various sorts—skyrocketed, or worse yet for those staging the festivities, the items sold out. The demand for lanterns was so great that prices increased six- to sevenfold by the day before the promulgation, and one company, the Japan Shipping Company (Nihon Yūsen Kaisha), bought up tens of thousands of lanterns destined for export in order to meet the domestic demand.[83] At least one shrine, Asakusa Shrine, even decided to hold its annual festival in conjunction with the promulgation.[84] The headquarters of a new religious group in Tokyo, the Jinshūkyō, also planned a *kigensetsu* festival and a "great celebration festival" (*daishukusai*) for the same day.[85] Not to be left out of the excitement, all the parishioners of Kotohira Shrine agreed to dress up in matching festive clothes.[86] Finally, when 11 February arrived, *sumo* wrestlers, dancers, carts with dancers, great arches, floats, lanterns, and flags of all sorts filled the streets.

But historians who have commented on the festival-like atmosphere in the capital have tended to overlook the significance of such popular participation. They have gone no further than contemporary observers at the time of the Constitution's promulgation, both foreign and Japanese, who ridiculed the masses for their seemingly ludicrous ability wholeheartedly to celebrate an event—the establishment of a constitutional form of government—for which they had no understanding. One such foreigner was Erwin Baelz. On the day of the promulgation he wrote in his diary:

I had never seen so many pretty girls in Tokyo as today. Their fresh colouring, their radiant health, their pretty dresses, their excellent behaviour, were all delightful. The streets were full of "dashi," the processional cars which on festal occasions are drawn through the streets by men or oxen. They are wheeled platforms with complicated buildings on them, usually of several stories, or with great figures or groups of figures, and a sort of band in front making the most heathenish clamour. In front of some of these cars walked geishas in various sorts of fancy dress. The prettiest was a group of geishas masquerading as ninsoku (handicraftsmen).

But two days earlier he had also written, in what is now quite a well-known passage, that while Tokyo was "in a state of indescribable excitement over the preparations for the promulgation[,] . . . [t]he great joke is that no one has the least idea of what the constitution will contain!"[87]

Japanese journalists also complained about the ignorance of the people. A writer for the *Jiji shinpō*, for example, maintained that "those of the lower class (*katō shakai*) wonder what the citywide festival planned for the eleventh is for. Moreover, they do not understand its significance. There are many who simply get excited thinking that it is one festival or another." A different article in the same issue claimed that there were "some among the ignorant and uncivilized of the lower orders" (*muchi mōmai naru kamin*) who believed that the emperor, who worshipped a certain Jizō deity who called himself "Kenpōsama" (Constitution Deity), planned to hold a festival for that god. Others, the article alleged, supposedly misled by the words for promulgation of a constitution, *kenpō happu,* thought that the emperor intended to give the prime minister a silken coat, a *kenpu happi.* [88] Another journalist wrote that he felt impelled to explain what the Constitution was because, in addition to other popular misconceptions, many people believed that the "Constitution Festival" (*kenpōsai*) was simply an "enlightened and civilized [version of the] Sannō festival" (*bummei kaika sareta Sannōsai*).[89]

There can be no doubt that the great majority of the people comprehended little of the Constitution's contents or the political concepts associated with it. But simply following elite contemporaries in their derision of popular consciousness blinds us to the significance of the fact that the masses had taken part for the first time in history in a national communion. From this perspective, while we might note the rather unsurprising fact that the common people possessed an incomplete knowledge about the new Constitution, it is at least as important to point out that the forms of the familiar community festival facilitated mass participation in new celebrations of the emerging national community. New national symbols—such as national flags, portraits of imperial family members, the "Kimi ga Yo" anthem, and Rising Sun lanterns—began to combine with customary festival objects and music. In time, people would begin to forget the newness of most of these symbols and ceremonials and they would come to think of them as an unproblematic part of received Tradition.

As we have seen, one of the most remarkable aspects of mass participation was the tremendous movement of people from the provinces to the capital on all of these occasions. Actually, the flow of people did not always lead to Tokyo. Many stopped at the larger provincial cities in order to take in urban festivities located nearer to their own communities, while others sometimes chose to make pilgrimages to Ise Shrine instead.[90] Moreover, during the imperial funerals, when much of the national pageantry took place in Kyoto instead of Tokyo, provincials streamed into the old capital. But regardless of where provincials went, they displayed an untiring enthusiasm and curiosity about events that led them beyond their local communities.

This habit of traveling for the purpose of observing national ceremonials was no doubt linked to the common folk custom of tourism and pilgrimage that predated the Meiji regime's establishment. It is generally agreed that ever since the beginning of the Tokugawa period, pilgrimage and tourism (usually with a tenuous distinction between the two) have composed an important part of popular religion. At least four religious centers or regional clusters of sacred sites—Kumano, Ise, the thirty-three stations of Saikoku, and the eighty-eight stations of Shikoku—all drew pilgrims from throughout the country; many other less famous but regionally important sacred places and circuits also existed in the provinces.[91] By all accounts, the numbers of common people who went on pilgrimages after the late seventeenth century reached prodigious proportions. Every year perhaps as many as four million pilgrims set out for Ise; and in the years when the greatest numbers of people went, ten million may have made what were known as "pilgrimages of grace" (okage mairi). Though no precise figures can be given, specialists agree that the estimate of over three million, or over one-tenth the population of the country, for the number of Ise-bound pilgrims during a less than two-month period in 1705 is not unreasonable.[92] Tokugawa local communities, then, were far from culturally isolated, and travel to even distant places was an accepted part of popular folk practice.

That travelers during the new national ceremonies often understood their journeys to modern Tokyo and other important national centers from within the folk custom of pilgrimage and tourism is revealed by their behavior. On every occasion in which provincials came to Tokyo, they came primarily, of course, to see the central national pageants. At the same time, however, they made their rounds to other famous scenic and religious sites within the city, as would have been the habit during the Tokugawa period. Thus viewing the national pageantry was simply the spectacular climax to a tour which would have been, in many respects, intelligible to the provincials' Tokugawa period ancestors. Sometimes tourists seemed as enthusiastic about festivals at well-known shrines as they were about the central pageants. Thus during the crown prince's wedding celebration many provincials stopped to take in the annual festival at Shiba Ward's Konpira Shrine in addition to the imperial ceremony.[93] When enshrinement rites at Yasukuni coincided with the great Tokyo "Cock Fair" (tori no ichi)—that is, the fair at which people would buy good luck charms such as rakes (to rake in good luck)—throngs of people could be seen going to and from Yasukuni and the sites for the fair, such as Ōtori Shrine in Shitaya, Hanazono Shrine in Shinjuku, and Suga Shrine in Yotsuya.[94]

The continuities with the tourism of the Edo period were also evident at the time of the Triumphal Military Review of April 1906. When huge crowds watched the imperial procession and the Triumphal Military Review on the morning of the thirtieth, Ueno and Asakusa Parks, two of Tokyo's most popular religious-entertainment areas since the Edo period, stood nearly empty. But in the afternoon the spectators continued touring the city, stopping not only to see the show of weapons on the Palace Plaza and Nijūbashi but also to visit such places as the Zōjō Temple in Shiba Park, and of course Ueno and Asakusa Parks.[95] One of the war bereaved, having come to Tokyo for the Yasukuni enshrinement rites held in conjunction with the review, also toured Tokyo as if on a pilgrimage, collecting tickets for Tokyo attractions in an amulet pouch (*mamori bukuro*).[96] The sights in Tokyo were not limited to those that had existed since pre-Restoration times. Some were products of the capital's modernization: the zoo in Ueno Park was one of the most popular new attractions. There, according to the same reporter, people from the "snow country" were heard to say that while bears were nothing special, they had never before seen the likes of elephants and lions. At the zoo "people forgot their age" and hoped to return home with "good stories as souvenirs" (*miyage banashi*). Again, reminiscent of Edo-period tourists, provincials bought souvenirs. But by 1906, souvenirs of the capital were not limited to those that had been available in the Edo period. Lithographs and postcards were replacing woodblock prints, and as provincials returned home from the Triumphal Military Review they took with them other remembrances of their modern and now nationalized pilgrimages: portraits of imperial family members and such war toys as play soldiers, bugles, sabers, and rifles.[97]

Kyoto's *Hinode shinbun* reported that during a ten-day period, the police estimated that 950,000 people worshipped at the Fushimi-Momoyama Mausoleum, where the Meiji emperor had just been interred; groups of quite jovial worshippers stopped there but then continued touring such popular religious sites as Inari Shrine and Otokoyama Hachimangū.[98] People unexpectedly left money offerings (*saisen*), as they would be likely to do at any shrine or temple, and two surprised Imperial Household Ministry officials queried their superiors about what they should do with the almost 300 yen that had been left by visitors during the public viewing period.[99] As one writer for the *Fūzoku Gahō* also disapprovingly observed about these people from the provinces who came to worship at the Meiji emperor's mausoleum, "There were those who prostrated themselves on the gravel and chanted sutras. And there were many ignorant country bumpkins who offered *saisen*."[100]

In large part because they carried such familiar customs and beliefs with them into the age of nationalism, the thoughts and behavior of crowds could not easily be brought under control. This was particularly true in the period of the progresses that lasted into the 1880s, but this resistance to the official point of view persisted even during the later imperial pageants of the remaining Meiji years. We might take as an important example the rather unorthodox perceptions of the emperor that continued to be mediated by the popular folklore. For many, the modern monarch at the center of the nation's greatest pageants, though dressed in the style of European royalty and officially presented as the dynamic and manly ruler of the national political community, might still be conceived, in part, as a beneficent and magical deity. We have already seen evidence of this folk perception during the early Meiji period. For the late Meiji period, clear evidence of this enduring attitude is rare, and it appears to have operated at a deep level of consciousness as newer official representations of the ruler competed with customary beliefs. Nevertheless, in some instances the older folk belief erupted to the surface of popular consciousness and resulted in what, from the governing elites' point of view, appeared as bizarre behavior.

One such instance occurred when a sixty-year-old worker from a horse ranch in the town of Kitakata (Iwase District, Fukushima Prefecture) came to Tokyo in May 1895 in order to witness the Meiji emperor's triumphal return from Hiroshima. Early on the morning of the thirtieth, Nosaki Sokejūrō prepared himself to greet the emperor by seating himself in the formal style (*seiza*) on the Palace Plaza lawn. As the emperor passed, "Sokejūrō dropped his head to the ground and shouted *banzai*. However, he was so overcome with elation that he proceeded to take a money offering (*saisen*) wrapped in white paper from his pocket and threw it in the direction of the imperial carriage. He then repeatedly clapped his hands together and bowed." The police concluded that an act of lese majesty had taken place and took Sokejūrō into custody for questioning. But upon interrogation Sokejūrō explained, "with the utmost sincerity, that he had completely believed that the emperor was a deity (*kamisama*). And he had felt so grateful that he could not help but make a money offering." Then, as the newspaper article reporting this incident concluded, "The police explained to him his error and released him from custody."[101]

The official discourse and representations of the emperor certainly constructed him as divine, but in the sense that he was one in a line of emperors that stretched back to the time of the gods and who now ruled the government and directed the military as both man and god. He was not supposed to be among any number of magical deities who granted this-worldly benefits to individuals and to whom one might toss money offerings. Sokejūrō's perception, however, remained rooted in just such customary and nonnationalized folk beliefs.

With respect to discipline, the authorities demanded disciplined bodies, as exemplified by schoolchildren who could be induced to dress properly, stand at attention, march, or perform other physical exercises. But the people themselves sometimes came out completely naked or even in transvestite dress to watch the emperor; and they might opt for the wild, unstructured, and often farcical dancing of the *niwaka odori* or the *araodori* (literally, "rough dancing"). The authorities promoted singing in the practiced and reverent tones of what was becoming Japan's de facto national anthem, *kimi ga yo*, but the people often performed the spontaneous and frenetic music of revelry, the *hayashi*. The authorities promoted the respectful worship of the emperor or his portrait; but the people often chose the nonsensical or even the scandalous.

This tendency of the people toward the undisciplined, unselfconscious, and disorderly troubled many representatives of the state. Though in some instances local elites might advertise a festival in order to entice the people into joining in these imperial ceremonials, the authorities consistently worked to impose a new kind of self-consciousness and physical discipline. In this normalization of behavior within a crowd, individuals learned to subject themselves to a viewers' code of behavior. One commemorative publication on the Meiji emperor's funeral also contained photographs of the funeral for General Nogi, the loyal imperial subject who had committed ritual suicide following the emperor's death. And under one such photograph that showed crowds observing Nogi's funeral procession, the caption directed readers to "Look at the solemn deportment of the crowd watching the passing casket."[102] In other words, while ostensibly the watchers of spectacles, onlookers were at the same time compelled to become cognizant of themselves and other spectators as objects of observation. In fact, the caption forced the people to see themselves as models of their own discipline.

A document produced for the emperor's 1876 tour called "General Instructions for Those Viewing [the emperor]" included a warning about improper dress: "since it is inappropriate to appear indecently (*migurushiki sugata*), whether naked or bare to the waist, it is imperative that [onlookers] be informed about this." Improper noise was also noted. People should also be informed, the "General Instructions" stated, "not to make a big clamor by talking to each other in loud tones or to shout out in booming voices. All should be completely quiet." The General Affairs Section of the Home Ministry subsequently sent out a notice to all village, town, and ward heads that described the proper way to greet an imperial progress for those who happened to be traveling along a progress's route. "They should get down from their horses or carriages," it indicated, "hats or caps should be removed, and they should wait for the imperial conveyance by standing at attention on the roadside. Then, they should bow down, putting both hands down on the thighs, and greet the emperor. They should not sit down on the road."[103]

The emperor's silver wedding anniversary and the crown prince's wedding, it will be recalled, were in large part events that displayed the imperial family as a model for society, a stable family that clearly distinguished the roles of husbands and wives, men and women. In this arrangement the women in the imperial family were supposed to conform to what might be described as the bourgeois ideal. They were to be nurturing, modest, graceful, chaste, and intelligent. The people, however, often completely disregarded these messages and celebrated as they pleased, setting out displays of sea bream (*tai*), storks, turtles, and isles of youth (*hōraisan*)—all familiar signs for long life and prosperity which could be found in most popular marriage ceremonies. They also dressed up the elderly as the old man and woman of Takasago, or fashioned figures of the Takasago couple, the paired deities Izanami and Izanagi, and the coupled rocks of Futamigaura. These represented conjugal harmony, fertility, and no doubt sex.[104] Quite outrageously, at the time of the emperor's silver anniversary, which was often referred to as the Great Wedding (*daikon*), the people of at least one neighborhood in the provincial town of Saga made a visual pun and placed a giant radish (*daikon*) on a festival float. Forty neighborhood residents of all ages danced to the rhythms of festive music (*hayashi*) as they paraded to the Saga prefectural office with what would appear to be a fairly explicit sexual symbol.[105]

The police certainly tried to stop the most undisciplined forms of folk behavior. In the days leading up to the emperor's silver wedding anniversary celebration, for example, the Tokyo Metropolitan Police, frightened by what seemed to them the crazed atmosphere throughout the country, began to suppress popular festivities. According to the *Miyako shinbun*, the police were disturbed by the fact that so many people "in the cities and the countryside, both good and mean," were making preparations for celebrating "as if mad" (*kyōsuru gotoku*). They thus rejected a petition by the people of Yoshiwara that would have allowed dancing in the frenzied *niwaka odori* style over a period of five days; they would only allow one day of dancing.[106] Later, the Metropolitan Police Headquarters informed all police stations within Tokyo Metropolitan Prefecture to discourage such activities as the drawing of "floats, carts with dancers, and dancing *geisha*." At the same time, they encouraged the display of national flags and lanterns.[107]

In this tension between the new habits and beliefs imposed by the disciplinary regime and the old and often wild habits and thoughts of folk life, there is no doubt that various state apparatuses—most significantly, schools and the military barracks—were the most efficient in constructing the interiorized sense of being observed that was a necessary counterpart to the emperor's gaze in the production of Japan's society of surveillance. The completely docile behavior of schoolchildren throughout the country during these pageants—whether along the routes of the imperial progresses in the first half of the Meiji period or in nearly every village, town, and city during the era's second half—is both impressive and chilling in its consistency. But here we are moving into yet another topic: namely, the proliferation of a large number of institutions in Japan's modernity that made disciplinary training more than an irregular moment that coincided with the brilliant spectacles of the monarch.[108]

CHAPTER SIX

Epilogue

Toward a History of the Present

The imperial pageants are still with us. The emperor and his family continue to perform their ceremonials as if they were traditional—somehow timeless and without a history—and in so doing erase the memories of a past when national community was but the dream of a few elites and when, for the great masses of the people who lived in the place we identify as Japan, the emperor did not stand for the national totality. In the erasure of their own origins, the pageants encourage us to think as a nation, whether as Japanese people observing the ceremonials or as foreigners curious about the traditions, symbols, and culture of an "other" nation. The national ceremonials promote the production of knowledges and beliefs premised on an easy division between "us" and "them" as complete and unified wholes, with an almost invariable privileging of "ourselves," whoever we might be. Not only do these national pageants reinforce our sense of the national community's boundedness vis-à-vis other nations, they also usually disprivilege or occlude differences within the nation.

"Whose tradition?" was the interrogation of many minority women and men in Japan who I heard challenge the idea that the Shōwa emperor's funeral or the current emperor's accession rites (*sokui no rei* and *daijōsai*) could represent their own pasts and cultures. When I heard this critique during my visits to Japan in the winter of 1988–89 and the fall of 1990 to observe various activities associated with these recent imperial succession rites, including anti-imperial rallies and community meetings, it invariably came from clearly minoritized groups in Japan—for example, Okinawans, the *buraku* minority, descendants of former colonial subjects from Korea and Taiwan, and feminists. But if the arguments of this book can be taken seriously, anyone with affiliations to Japan might choose to learn from such critical perspectives, from their challenges to the taken-for-grantedness of national unity, dominant national memories, and the erasure, or at least marginalization, of the particularity of "local" experiences, histories, and knowledges.

I do not use "local" in only its strictly geographical sense, although that could certainly be one of its groundings. Rather, I mean to suggest all those knowledges that Foucault called "subjugated knowledges"— knowledges considered naive, low-level, or inadequate and that have been disqualified as legitimate knowledge. This was a kind of "popular knowledge" that was "particular, local, regional knowledge, a differential knowledge incapable of unanimity and which owes its force only to the harshness with which it is opposed by everything surrounding it."[1] As applied to modern Japan, I mean the infinite variety of heterogeneous knowledges subordinated by the civilizing and rationalizing mission of the nation-state or by the one pantheon of official gods. These would include such visionary knowledges as those of religious leaders like Nakayama Miki and Deguchi Nao, who drew from folk religion and their own experiences to challenge patriarchy, hierarchies, and the ravages brought forth by capitalism and the nation-state, as well as the now almost unrecoverable memories of peasants who rejected the claims of the modern regime.

From the Meiji period onward the modern state, guided by its leaders and supported by a vast network of institutions and people, became a memory machine. It transfigured the physical landscape, recast the emperor's body and the bodies of his family members, and set loose a profusion of other "mnemonic sites," ranging from tiny commemorative postage stamps to the emperor's spectacular capital cities and national pageants. The land, the imperial body, and many other sites were marked by signs that symbolized both the nation's timeless, unique, and splendid past and its prosperity, power, and capacity to progress. Yet the writing onto such sites of a dominant system of signs, meanings, and memories also involved the writing out, the erasure or marginalization, of alternative meanings and memories. As much as memory, in other words, the Meiji regime produced forgetfulness—a forgetfulness about both the origins of its own memory making and about all those other experiences that did not fit into the hegemonic project of the Japanese nation's modernity. "Whose tradition?" is an interrogation that urges all of us to problematize the arbitrariness, that is to say the politics, of national representation.

The Monarchy and Tradition

There is perhaps no better articulation of a modern view of the interrelationships among culture, tradition, the monarchy, and the nation than Mishima Yukio's "In Defense of Culture" ("Bunka bōeiron").[2] This essay was written in 1968, a time that Mishima characterized as mired in a culture crisis, when even the emperor had been reduced by bureaucrats and the media to an increasingly trivial "thing" (*mono*). Culture, in his estimation, had become a clutter of fragmented and limited objects to manage and put on display, like flower arrangements or the tea ceremony. And like artifacts exhibited in a museum, these objects offered culture as finite and objectifiable. Insofar as he identified his contemporary culture's tendency toward fragmentation, superficiality, images over affects, and signs over meanings, Mishima's descriptions anticipate those of recent theorists of the culture of late capitalism.[3]

Yet what distinguishes Mishima's diagnosis of the culture crisis in Japan, and what characterizes it as a product of modern Japanese history, is his call for the people to reinvigorate the national culture through the revival of what he called "the emperor as a cultural concept" (*bunka gainen toshite no tennō*). In this prescription he questioned neither the a priori concept of the national whole nor the choice of the emperor as the symbol of this assumed national totality. Mishima claimed that only the "invisible" emperor, a symbol that could not be seen or objectified in its wholeness, could serve as the source of creativity for the Japanese people. From his reading of the philosopher Watsuji Tetsurō he took the idea that while historically the Japanese state had often been disunified, the "emperor as a cultural concept" had consistently integrated the people. Like Watsuji he projected back into the remote past a unity that had been constructed in modern times and wrote as if the people had always already been bound together in a continuum that stretched back in time and across space.[4]

He described this emperor as an "invisible cultural concept" that continuously returned to serve as the symbol of the people's unity and the source of their creativity. Since this emperor perpetually returned as exactly the same emperor—"the emperor of every reign is truly the very person, the emperor, and the relationship with the Sun Goddess is not that of a copy to an original"[5]—but could never be seen as such, Mishima described it not as an object to be seen but rather as a "seeing thing" (*miru mono*). And when state power alienated the people from the nation, this emperor as a cultural concept could return as a revolutionary or even terrorist principle, for example when loyalists of Emperor Kōmei took Ii Naosuke's life in 1860 and when young military officers on 26 February 1936 attempted to overthrow the government that had taken the form of a "Westernized constitutional monarchy" (*seiyōteki rikken kunshu seitai*). What people in general referred to as "tradition" (*dentō*), he claimed, is precisely such a constantly returning and limitless source of creativity for the people.

Mishima wrote of the emperor as the locus of Tradition and as the symbol of the national totality as if it had always existed as such. Yet as this book has tried to argue, this emperor was a product of the late nineteenth and early twentieth centuries. Like what Mishima called the "emperor as a political concept" (*seiji gainen toshite no tennō*)—that is, a nineteenth- or twentieth-century emperor limited in time and space and a part of the established political order—the "emperor as a cultural concept" was a product of Japan's modernity, not of some undifferentiated and suprahistorical Tradition. While Mishima's plea for the defense of culture and of the monarchy as a "cultural concept" might appear to have been an oddly anachronistic reaction to the rise of mass society, consumer capitalism, the managed society, and the U.S. hegemony that had constructed what he saw to be an impotent monarchy, he was in fact groping for a classically modern resolution to the crisis of culture—one rooted in the apparent security of recovering origins and the timeless essences of the national community.

Mishima associated this emperor with the elegant and refined culture of the imperial court in Kyoto, with *miyabi*. Ignoring the fact that throughout most of history the life of the people had had little to do with the emperor, he claimed that the people's culture had almost wholly been produced in emulation of this court culture, or as he put it, "in mimicry of *miyabi*" (*miyabi no manebi*). His "emperor as a cultural concept" would correspond to the set of homologies that I have argued included the emperor's invisible body, the emperorship, and Kyoto, as well as Origuchi's notion of the *tennōrei*, the imperial spirit. And it would not be too farfetched to argue that it was at least in part produced through the pageantry, imagery, and the mnemonic sites described in this book.

But in order to move closer to the present and at least begin to think about and diagnose the present in terms of the past, I want to end by sketching the post-1912 relations between the "emperor as a cultural concept" and what I have described as the visible emperor, and by tracing the history of the imperial gaze up until the present. What became of the ceremonial style of governance in the years after 1912, of the relationship between Japan's two capital cities, of the emperor's two bodies, and of the emperor-centered system of visual domination?

Kyoto, as the center of Japan's authenticated past, continued to provide the main setting for public accessions. Thus the national ceremonials held for the accessions of both the Taishō (1915) and Shōwa (1928) emperors culminated in rites held within the Kyoto Imperial Palace. On these occasions even the Sacred Mirror, normally enshrined within Tokyo's Palace Sanctuary, traveled back to the ancient capital in the archaic-looking Feather Palanquin (*ohaguruma*).[6] The ancient capital also furnished one of the settings for the imperial death rites of 1914. After a grand funeral at Yoyogi in Tokyo, Empress Dowager Shōken's interment rites took place in Kyoto, as her mausoleum was constructed next to that of her husband, Emperor Meiji. And even following the death of the Shōwa emperor in much more recent times there have been partisans of Kyoto who have argued that as the city of Tradition the ancient capital ought to be used again as the location for imperial death and accession rites.

At the same time, the pull of Kyoto as the locus of Tradition clearly declined after Meiji's death, partly because the accomplishments of Japan's first monarch to reside in Tokyo increasingly came to be perceived as a part of national history. The city that during the Meiji period had signified the regime's modernity, progress, wealth, and power now also had a tradition. The Charter Oath, the Constitution, the revision of unequal treaties with the Western powers, and great victories in wars—all praised in eulogies following Emperor Meiji's death—were now benchmarks in the nation's glorious past and a part of the dominant national memory. Similarly, Meiji period renovations of Tokyo's ritual topography—the Imperial Palace, Nijūbashi, the Palace Plaza, Yasukuni Shrine, and the capital's many bronze statues of loyal imperial retainers—were no longer novel but tinged with a sanctity conferred upon them by age.

The great imperial pageants of Meiji, too, were becoming a part of the collective national past, and this added to perceptions of Tokyo as a place with history. One writer, who suggested shortly after Emperor Meiji's death that a shrine to Meiji should be built at Aoyama Military Parade Field, believed that the field had become "a sacred place" through its use during numerous national ceremonials. This was the spot, he reminded his readers, where Emperor Meiji had reviewed the troops that had fought in wars with China and Russia. It had been the location of the "unprecedented Triumphal Military Review," as well as of the reviews conducted in conjunction with the Constitution's promulgation and the silver imperial wedding anniversary. He noted that it was with the celebration for the Constitution's promulgation, "a great ceremony unparalleled in 3,000 years," that the emperor and empress had first ridden together in the new state ceremonial carriage. No other place, he concluded, so closely associated the emperor with "the imperial household, the nation, national prestige, and historical events."[7] In short, while still the center of contemporary progress, civilization, wealth, and power, Tokyo by the end of Meiji had also become a part of the past.

The new national monuments that emerged after Meiji's death continued to enhance the traditionalized dimension of Tokyo. Certainly, the greatest of these was Meiji Shrine, dedicated to Emperor Meiji and his consort. The movement to build a shrine to Meiji began immediately after it became publicly known that the Imperial Household Ministry would erect his mausoleum in Kyoto. The project's official start came in 1913 when the House of Councillors passed a resolution to build such a monument, and it was for the most part completed by 1920.[8] In the Treasure Museum, located north of the Main Sanctuary, one can even today see historical artifacts from the reign of Meiji that have been designated as "treasures": such objects as clothes worn by both the emperor and his consort, a map of the "Six Great Imperial Progresses," and even the state ceremonial carriage used at the time of the Constitution's promulgation. One might also mention the late-Taishō-to early-Shōwa-period monuments described in the introduction to this study that are located to the east of the shrine in what is now the Meiji Shrine Outer Garden.

The ceremonial style in government continued throughout the prewar period, intermittently affirming both the depth of the national past and the prosperity and progress of the national community. The greatest of such pageants came with the accession and death rites of 1914,

1915, and 1928 mentioned above and with the funeral for Emperor Taishō. By the time that Emperor Taishō died in 1926, it was apparently no longer felt necessary to conduct public imperial death rites in Kyoto, for the obsequies took place at Shinjuku, and the mausoleum was built in an outlying area of eastern Tokyo Prefecture. Finally, in 1940, came the climaxing national ceremonial of the pre-1945 regime: the 2,600th anniversary of the accession of Japan's first emperor, Jimmu. The Imperial Palace in Tokyo and a gigantic celebration hall on the Palace Plaza supplied the central arena for the national festival.

During these events newer media became even more effective in facilitating production of a sense of national simultaneity even as the demand for instantaneous coverage of the pageants became an engine for technological innovation. Radio broadcasting began in 1925, allowing electronic reportage of the Shōwa emperor's 1928 enthronement. But it should also be noted that the pageant that took place over nearly three weeks in November in turn stimulated the inauguration of the first on-the-scene radio reports to be broadcast simultaneously throughout the entire nation. This was accomplished by setting up microphones in eleven locations in Tokyo, Kyoto, and Ise to pick up local reports and then linking the broadcasts of the entire nation's radio stations.[9] According to a former announcer who took part in this nationwide radio broadcast, what mattered was not so much the on-the-scene reporters' accurately relaying what they saw as their producing the belief that everyone throughout the nation heard the reports at the moment when the activities occurred. In fact, he and the other announcers did not describe the pageantry as they witnessed it. When broadcasting the emperor's procession from Kyoto Station to the Ōmiya Palace, for example, he read from a prepared script that he had written in advance of the event, based upon information and illustrations supplied by the Imperial Household Ministry's officials. In order to create the script it had been necessary to estimate the length of time it would take for the procession to pass before him so that his description would match what he might expect to see at any particular moment. All such texts required the Imperial Household Ministry's advance approval. Microphones communicated a sense of the broadcast's "liveness" by picking up the sounds of horses' hooves and trumpets playing the "Kimi ga Yo," but the narration that listeners heard as "live" radio reports had already been written.[10]

Newspaper companies acquired the technology for wireless transmission of photographs in anticipation of the 1928 enthronement, and when the event finally took place it was captured in newsreels that could be flown by plane across the country. Thus as the *Tōkyō asahi* reported on 7 November, on the previous day it had used some eighteen airplanes to deliver "photographs, motion picture film, stereotypes, extra and evening editions, and more" throughout the empire to such major cities as Osaka, Nagoya, Kyoto, and Tokyo, to regions as dispersed as Tōhoku, Kyushu and Shikoku, and even to "far off Korea."[11] As in Meiji and then later in 1959 when the desire to watch the current emperor's wedding ceremonial touched off a nationwide rush to buy television sets, it is clear that in modern times imperial pageants have not only fostered the idea of national simultaneity, but they have also repeatedly stimulated the invention or application of technological innovations. These have continued to produce and reproduce the feeling of a shared temporality among the national community's members, even beyond the passing moments of the pageants themselves.

The symbolic crisis brought on by Japan's defeat in war was enormous, but the postwar government and the American occupiers almost immediately began reestablishing the monarchy as the symbol of the national community's unity through time, and in space. Though almost none of the Japanese people had ever been asked to express their "will," the new Constitution declared that the emperor was to be the "symbol of the State and of the unity of the people, deriving his position from the will of the people with whom resides sovereign power." And in a curious repetition of history, reminiscent of the Meiji period's first years when the Meiji emperor had traveled through the provinces while the palace in Tokyo lay in ruins, the Shōwa emperor set out from his burned-out city on numerous tours through the countryside. Between February 1946 (only about seven weeks after he had renounced his divinity on New Year's Day) and November 1947, the emperor took to the provinces no less than fifteen times,[12] and then continued to do so with great frequency until his final tour to Hokkaido in 1954. By the end of this last progress he had traveled to every major region in Japan, with the single and important exception of Okinawa,[13] site of the only land invasion of U.S. troops, which had lost at least one-fifth of its population to the war.

Moreover, the first national ceremonial of the postwar era was, as in Meiji, not simply orchestrated around the promulgation of a constitution;[14] its ritual forms closely followed Meiji precedents. Neither the nation's people nor the Allied Powers but the emperor himself promulgated the new Constitution, thus affirming that he in fact transcended it. The emperor then reported the Constitution's promulgation to the national gods in the palace's Inner Sanctuary (*kyūchū sanden*), a place, we should recall, that had been fabricated just prior to the Meiji Constitution's promulgation. An estimated 100,000 people gathered together on the Palace Plaza on this day, 3 November 1946, on none other than Emperor Meiji's birthday, to participate in the festivities. At least in terms of the modern ritual idiom that had been constructed and routinized since Meiji, it was as if little had changed in the divide across 1945. The reconstruction of the Imperial Palace, which had been destroyed by firebombings toward the close of the war, took a longer period of time but was completed in the 1960s after much public debate. Part of the controversy had to do with the appropriateness of using a "feudal" palace for a "democratic" imperial household.[15]

Yet in contrast to the Meiji years, when imagery and pageantry constructed a masculinized monarch who could be imagined to be the heroic ruler who directed government even as he transcended it, the postwar progresses, ceremonials, and imagery tended over time increasingly to emasculate the Shōwa emperor. This was part of the process of constructing him as a "symbolic emperor," as one who does not rule but who "merely" represents the national totality. Instead of the militarized, dynamic, and masculinized figure riding on his white horse, the monarch became a civilian dressed in Western-style suits and soft hat who engaged in such peaceful pursuits as marine biology, poetry, sports viewing, and, in 1975, even visiting Disneyland. His image became one of passivity. Indeed, by 1975 when asked at his first public press conference with the Japan Press Club if he had meant to imply that he felt a sense of responsibility for the war in stating during his trip to the United States that it had been a "most unfortunate war that I deeply deplore," he could not even accept agency for the words that he himself had uttered. Instead, he responded: "With regard to such subtleties of speech, since I have not studied such literary matters and have little understanding of them, I am unable to respond to such issues."[16]

Earlier, when he had talked with a group of foreign correspondents in Tokyo in 1971 on the issue of his war responsibility he had also represented himself as having always been incapable of acting as a knowing subject or agent in political affairs. Contrary both to his own image during the prewar and wartime years and to the image of the Meiji emperor that I have described, he suggested that as mere constitutional monarchs he and his grandfather had been uninvolved in matters of governance or, presumably, war making. "Following the wishes of the

Meiji emperor I have acted as a constitutional monarch," he said. "I acted as such [during the war] and at other times as well. In fact, while I have heard many comments concerning my role, there were really many things that I did not personally know."[17]

A resurgence in the performance of imperial pageants, or what might be described as part of the postwar revival of invented traditions, began toward the end of the U.S. Occupation and therefore under the direct auspices of the U.S. government. While it may seem ironic that the U.S. government was involved in the revival of "Japanese Tradition" and the imperial institution, the aims of U.S. cold war policy and those of conservative Japanese politicians such as Yoshida Shigeru were congruent with respect to reestablishing social control in postwar Japan.[18] As Prime Minister Yoshida Shigeru made clear, he wanted the ceremonial events of the imperial household to be not simply private affairs, but rather "national festivals" (*kokumin no saiten*) that would provide the nucleus for the "spiritual unity of the nation's people" (*kokumin no seishinteki tōgō*).[19]

The funeral of Empress Dowager Teimei (22 June 1951) was the first of such private rites of passage of the imperial family in the postwar years to be performed as a national pageant. Following the modern precedent that, as we have seen, had been established in the Meiji era, the funeral took place in Tokyo in a "Shinto" style, and over half a million people watched the funeral procession that wound through the capital's streets. Her body was then transported by train from Harajuku Station and interred next to the remains of the Taishō emperor in Tama, just west of Tokyo.[20] The empress dowager had in fact been one of the primary women involved in the construction of an image of the modern Japanese monarchy in her position as the wife of the Taishō emperor. As such she had participated in Japan's first imperial wedding in 1900, and as the wife of Emperor Taishō and mother of Hirohito she had been central to the production of an image of the imperial family as a nuclear family headed by a monogamous emperor and supported by a devoted, nurturing, and loving wife and mother. As the managing director of Kyōdō News Service eulogized shortly after Teimei's death in a piece entitled "Empress Dowager as a Mother," "Japan's recently deceased Queen Mother was a good wife and tender mother." She was a "Symbol of Japanese Womanhood," claimed another article written around the same time.[21]

From the 1950s onward public attention began to shift away from the war-blemished emperor to the more "innocent" Crown Prince

Akihito. Some within the government and the Imperial Household Agency tried to rejuvenate the imperial institution as the center of the national tradition, while at the same time reconstituting it as a politically harmless symbolic monarchy, safely distanced from war memories and standing for the Japanese people's commitment to peace and democracy. On 10 November 1952 the post-Occupation government conducted ceremonies to mark Akihito's coming of age and his investiture as heir apparent, and in 1954 the Shōwa emperor's postwar progresses drew to a close. Akihito's televised wedding to Shōda Michiko presented the imperial household not only as democratic—Shōda Michiko was not of the nobility—but also as part of a bright and cheerful present and future that could even be the center of romance.

And this was the source of Mishima's rage. In his view while even the pre-1945 regime under the Meiji Constitution had not truly liberated the "emperor as a cultural concept"—that is, had limited the emperor that might be a revolutionary force—postwar conditions had done even more damage. The emperor system had barely survived the U.S. Occupation and by the 1960s had become so enmeshed in mass culture, had so lost its dignity, that it had sunk to the level of the "emperor system of the popular weekly magazines."[22] At the moment in which he wrote, Mishima called for the reinvigoration of the invisible emperor so that it might become that revolutionary force, that source of creativity that had so frightened the established government at the time of the 26 February insurrection.

While Mishima was clearly mistaken in describing the "emperor as a cultural concept" as a suprahistorical representation of the national totality and of Tradition, he was absolutely correct in his judgment that the postwar imperial household was becoming an increasingly trivialized object. This is not to say that politicians, bureaucrats, the Imperial Household Agency, business interests, and the media have not described the imperial household as the locus of the national Tradition. Quite the opposite is true. Even through all the most recent televised imperial pageants—Hirohito's funeral (February 1989), the wedding of the current emperor's second son Prince Akishino to Kawashima Kiko (June 1990), Akihito's *sokui no rei* and *daijōsai* accession ceremonies (November 1990), and the wedding of Crown Prince Naruhito to Owada Masako (June 1993)—the ceremonials have been widely described as the very crystallization of Japanese Tradition. But as Mishima would surely have said, the Palace Sanctuary, the ancient-looking hairstyles, ritual paraphernalia, and the clothes have been treated as if they were museum artifacts on display. Clearly the force or weightiness of the belief in the imperial household as the center of Tradition has radically changed in a world in which images of the so-called symbolic emperor and his family are often like those of entertainment stars, and the media confer a kind of fake imperial aura upon major celebrities. By 1985 the media could even refer to the "cute" idol singer Matsuda Seiko's wedding as a "*goseikon*," a royal wedding, and the funeral of one of the Shōwa era's most popular singers Misora Hibari, as a "*gotaisō*." The latter term, normally reserved for imperial funerals, had been used only five months earlier for Hirohito's last rites.[23]

The Imperial Gaze

The changed status of the Japanese monarchy can also be gauged through a brief history of the imperial gaze. Recall that beginning with the progresses of the first two Meiji decades and culminating in the spectacular military reviews of the late Meiji period, the emperor was presented as the all-seeing monarch who could dominate the people through his sight. In Japan's modernity this disciplinary gaze not only became dispersed into an infinite number of sites—schools, factories, barracks, and almost every other manner of social organization—it also continued to be most ideally diagrammed in the post Meiji years in the imperial vision.

The image of the Shōwa emperor riding on his white horse in military uniform while examining his troops on Army Commencement Day (8 January), on his birthday (*tenchōsetsu*, 29 April), following army maneuvers, or on other days of national significance became all too familiar to those not only within Japan proper but throughout the empire and even the rest of the world. Schoolchildren too were mobilized to the area fronting the emperor's palace in order to submit their souls and bodies to the imperial look. These disciplinary ceremonials took place most regularly on Tokyo's Yoyogi Parade Grounds, the field that replaced the Aoyama Military Parade Field in 1909, or the Palace Plaza, yet the Shōwa emperor also traveled to distant places throughout the nation for the purpose of examining his military men and the people.

To be sure, there can be no denying that particularly in the last years of the Second World War in Asia and the Pacific, as John W. Dower points out, discontent and pessimism about the imperial regime became quite widespread. Graffiti reported on by the Thought Police, for example, often called for outright acts of sedition and resistance such as killing "the dumb emperor."[24] Moreover, there were certainly a few spectacular incidents that could be read as displays of resistance to the imperial gaze. In one widely reported episode, Private Kitahara Taisaku, a member of the *buraku* minority, broke out of formation during an imperial review that followed large-scale maneuvers in Nagoya (19 November 1927), ran over to the emperor himself and presented a petition protesting discrimination against his people. Yet such an incident involving the momentarily unruly body of a discontented soldier seems exceptional and stands in stark contrast to the much more familiar record and memory of bodies made docile by the observing monarch. In fact, as Kitahara remembered in his autobiography, the only reason he was able to break ranks and get as close to the emperor as he did, with not a single soldier or officer moving to obstruct his approach, was that the "40,000 troops who participated in the review and were inspected were held completely motionless by the emperor's authority. Of course, it was not only the rank and file soldiers but also the noncommissioned and commissioned officers, those who gave the commands and those who received the commands—all of them were shackled by the emperor's charismatic authority. I alone—only I was the exception."[25]

While it is not possible here to construct a rigorous genealogy of the imperial gaze in prewar and wartime Japan, I would also at least like to suggest the possibility that in the course of the post-Meiji years many national subjects began increasingly to imagine the emperor's gaze as the loving, forgiving, all-embracing, protective, and self-sacrificing look that would correspond to what Kanō Mikiyo has identified as the motherly dimension of the emperor.[26] This is not to say that the modern imperial gaze should be understood as *either* a motherly or patriarchal gaze, but that it was ambiguously gendered, as both the stare of the Patriarch and the loving look of the Mother.

Kanō has given us an account of one woman's experience of an imperial inspection that can be analyzed in precisely this way.[27] The testimony comes from Ōtomo Yoshie, who as a young girl had been selected from among students at the Kawasaki Girls' High School (*kōtō jogakkō*) to participate in a massive ceremonial that took place on the Palace Plaza on 15 December 1928. The event was one of many that had been planned in conjunction with the Shōwa emperor's enthronement in November. The central moment in the ceremony involved the emperor's inspection of some 80,000 boys and girls from Saitama,

Chiba, Kanagawa, and Yamanashi Prefectures, as well as Tokyo. Ōtomo's recollection of her own experience in the event is striking in that
she recalled herself as having been overwhelmed at least as much by the
protective and loving feelings that she imagined the emperor to have, as
he observed the mass of children's bodies, as by being able to see the
"awesome figure of the emperor dressed in his khaki military uniform
on the tall, tall platform." The emperor, she believed, pitied her and the
other suffering schoolchildren as he observed them marching, singing,
or waiting on the plaza in the bitterly cold rain. He shared in their
suffering when he took down the awning protecting himself from the
downpour and he declined to wear an overcoat against the cold. Here
she felt not so much the hard male stare of the Patriarch but rather a
self-sacrificing and almost motherly concern. "Oh emperor," she recalled, "was it because you perceived our coldness, facing the wintry
winds on the Plaza? Oh emperor, who refused an overcoat. Oh emperor, so gallant. The emperor of our Japan. Truly, we would not regret
giving our lives, if for this lord."

As for the postwar history of the Gaze, it is most crucially marked by
a shattering of the imperial panopticism and finally in a nearly complete
reversal in the vector of vision today. This transformation in the relationship of sight and power is perhaps most dramatically diagrammed in
the practice of *ippan sanga,* or the congratulatory visits of the public
onto the palace grounds to celebrate the New Year (2 January) and on
the emperor's birthday, 29 April during Shōwa's reign or 23 December
in the current Heisei era. Since 1948 when the practice began,[28] no
longer does the emperor as the actively seeing Subject or Agent cross
over Nijūbashi to gaze on the crowds from his lofty position on a horse
or high platform. Instead, the people cross over the bridge, penetrating
the palace's entrance to observe him as he passively waves to them and
utters a few predictable words from a veranda.

Moreover, from the late 1950s to today, coinciding with the accel-
eration of consumer capitalism and the proliferation of print and electronic media forms, what can only be described as a new kind of voyeurism has characterized the dominant relationship between the people
and the monarchy. Weekly magazines, newspapers, and television shows
conjecture about such matters as prospective marriage partners or the
births of babies. People chat over tea about scandalous business within
the imperial family—sex, former boyfriends, domestic violence. The eye
of the television camera exposed the buildings if not the interiors of the
palace's Inner Sanctuary (*kyūchū sanden*) to public view for the first time

in history in 1959 during the wedding of Michiko Shōda to the then crown prince, who is now the Heisei emperor, thereby helping to dispel the aura and demystify the space occupied by the imperial household. And in the last few years televisual and other popular media images of the Shōwa emperor's illness, death, and funeral, the current emperor's accession rites, and the weddings of the two princes—all these titillated and promised an unveiling, thus encouraging the people to understand themselves as royal watchers. Though certainly not as crudely or relentlessly as the British public scrutinizes their royal family, it is now the Japanese people who increasingly subject the emperor and his family to their inquisitive gaze, consuming royal news and images as they would for entertainers.[29]

I do not mean to suggest that Japan is no longer a disciplinary society or that the imperial household can no longer arouse feelings of national identity. Nevertheless, there is no doubt that the monarchy's position at the apex of a network of visual domination has been exploded. Power certainly continues to pervade the entire social body through disciplinization at its capillaries, the imperial household still masquerades as the center of the national Tradition, the people are subjected to a constant barrage of royal trivia and events that further reinforce the sense of living exclusively in a shared time and national community—but for most people in Japan today, the belief in the emperor-centered Tradition has a kind of flatness or uninspired quality to it. Power is now increasingly decentered and operates not while the emperor disciplines the people with his gaze, but as the people peep in on an increasingly de-auratized imperial family.

The political implications of this situation are ambiguous. On the one hand, the emperor's loss of aura throws open the possibility of rethinking the ideas of national or racial essence, unity, and purity that the emperor and imperial household have symbolized in modern times. In this sense, it is at least compatible with recent attempts by activists and scholars in Japan and elsewhere to question the homogeneity and seamlessness of "Japan." In other words, the query "Whose Tradition?" has been made possible at least in part by the very shriveling of this modern Tradition's aura. Yet it is also quite possible, on the other hand, that the general flattening out of culture, meaning, history, and memory—especially now that the postwar miracle of rapid economic growth has imploded on itself—may in fact be stimulating a new search for rootedness and authenticity in everyday life. The most undesirable end result of that pursuit might be found in trends that we have already seen rising in postindustrial and post–high economic growth Japan—namely, in neonationalism or other totalizing beliefs about community exclusiveness.[30] Moreover, we are still left to wonder how it is that despite the withering of aura and belief, and regardless of the recent demystification of the Nation and the monarchy, so many people still act as if they believe in the dominant narratives of the nation that were created in the time of Japan's modernity.

Notes

Chapter 1. Introduction: Inventing, Forgetting, Remembering

1. David Cannadine, "The Context, Performance and Meaning of Ritual: The British Monarchy and the 'Invention of Tradition,' c. 1820–1977," in *The Invention of Tradition*, ed. Eric Hobsbawm and Terence Ranger (Cambridge: Cambridge University Press, 1983), 101–64; for the quote, 120; Eric Hobsbawm, "Mass Producing Traditions: Europe, 1870–1914," in Hobsbawm and Ranger, eds., *The Invention of Tradition*, 271, 280. For a long list of books and articles in the invention-of genre, see Werner Sollors, ed., *The Invention of Ethnicity* (New York and Oxford: Oxford University Press, 1989), 238–39.

2. B. H. Chamberlain, *The Invention of a New Religion* (London: Watts and Co., 1912), 6.

3. Ibid., 11–12.

4. Ibid., 23–27.

5. Ibid., 17, 26–27.

6. Pierre Bourdieu, *Outline of a Theory of Practice*, trans. Richard Nice (Cambridge: Cambridge University Press, 1977), 78–79. Writing some thirty years before Chamberlain, Ernest Renan also highlighted the peculiar ways in which the French nation had been formed out of the process of remembering and forgetting: "Yet the essence of a nation is that all individuals have many things in common, and also that they have forgotten many things" ("What Is a Nation," trans. and annotated by Martin Thom, in *Nation and Narration*, ed. Homi K. Bhabha [London and New York: Routledge, 1990], 11). More recent theorists of nationalism such as Homi Bhabha and Benedict Anderson have also thought through Renan's observations on the necessary ties between memory/ forgetting and nationhood: see Bhabha, "Dissemination: Time, Narrative, and the Margins of the Modern Nation," in his *Nation and Narration*, 291–322;

and Anderson, *Imagined Communities: Reflections on the Origins and Spread of Nationalism*, 2nd ed. (London: Verso, 1991), 187–206.

7. Former prime minister Nakasone Yasuhiro has repeatedly expressed such ideas. For example, on 8 March 1986 he told the Budgetary Committee of the Diet's Lower House that Japan has had the same tradition and culture for nearly two thousand years and that the lives of the Japanese people have centered on the emperor throughout that history (Miura Hisashi, "Nakasone naikaku ni teishutsu shita 'tennō oyobi tennōsei ni kansuru shitsumon shuisho,'" in *Tennōsei no genzai to kōtaishi*, ed. Nihon Kyōsantō Chūō Iinkai Shuppankyoku [Tokyo: Nihon Kyōsantō Chūō Iinkai Shuppankyoku, 1988], 122). Umehara Takeshi, the very well-known scholar who was formerly director general of the International Research Center for Japanese Studies, has consistently defended the imperial institution as self-evident and, literally, natural. For example, in a forum for the magazine *Chūō Kōron* which has recently appeared in English translation, he maintained: "At a time when industrial civilization is threatening the world's natural balances, I think we need to take a fresh look at institutions that retain their ties to nature, of which the imperial institution is one" (Ueyama Shunpei, Umehara Takeshi, and Yano Tōru, "The Imperial Institution in Japanese History," *Japan Echo* 16 [Spring 1989]: 52).

8. Anderson, *Imagined Communities*, 5.

9. For example, in a key essay on the genealogical method Foucault has written:

Genealogy does not pretend to go back in time to restore an unbroken continuity that operates beyond the dispersion of forgotten things; its duty is not to demonstrate that the past actively exists in the present, that it continues secretly to animate the present, having imposed a predetermined form to all its vicissitudes. Genealogy does not resemble the evolution of a species and does not map the destiny of a people. On the contrary, to follow the complex course of descent is to maintain passing events in their proper dispersion; it is to identify the accidents, the minute deviations—or conversely, the complete reversal— the errors, the false appraisals, and the faulty calculations that gave birth to those things that continue to exist and have value for us; it is to discover that truth or being do not lie at the root of what we know and what we are, but the exteriority of accidents. "Nietzsche, Genealogy, History," in *Language, Counter-Memory, Practice,* trans. Donald F. Bouchard and Sherry Simon, ed. Donald F. Bouchard (Ithaca: Cornell University Press, 1977), 146.

10. Akasaka Norio, *Ō to tennō* (Tokyo: Chikuma Shobō, 1988); Amino Yoshihiko, *Nihon shakai to tennōsei* (Tokyo: Iwanami Shoten, 1988); Amino Yoshihiko, Ueno Chizuko, and Miyata Noboru, *Nihon ōkenron* (Tokyo: Shunjusha, 1988). This is not the place for an exhaustive listing or review of these books. Suffice it to say that even Amino's great body of scholarship—brilliant in its illumination of a decisive historical break in the cultural field that contained the imperial institution during the late thirteenth and fourteenth centuries— seems taken in by the myth of continuity. Ultimately, he draws a straight line between a rupture that took place over half a millennium ago and the present. Akasaka Norio was kind enough to contact me and to discuss several issues that I had taken up in the shortened Japanese version of this book (*Tennō no pējento*, trans. Lisa Yoneyama [Tokyo: Nihon Hōsō Shuppan Kyōkai, 1994]). At that time he pointed out that his later book, *Shōchō tennō to iu monogatari*

(Tokyo: Chikuma Shobō, 1990), which deals with the construction of the postwar "symbolic emperor," was in some ways a critique of this dimension of his earlier book.

11. Inose Naoki's *Mikado no shōzō* (Tokyo: Shōgakkan, 1986), for example, is incredibly rich in historical detail on the imperial institution in the late nineteenth and twentieth centuries. However, he appropriates Roland Barthes's (*The Empire of Signs,* trans. Richard Howard [New York: Hill and Wang, 1982], 30–32) "empty center" reading of Japan as a final, and a priori, explanatory principle.

12. Tsurumi Shunsuke, *An Intellectual History of Wartime Japan, 1931–1945* (London: KPI Ltd., 1986), 14–32; for the quote, 17.

13. John W. Hall, "Rule by Status in Tokugawa Japan," *Journal of Japanese Studies* 1.1 (Autumn 1974): 39–49.

14. Mary Elizabeth Berry, *Hideyoshi* (Cambridge: Harvard University Press, 1982). For the relevance of Hideyoshi's centralization policies to the Tokugawa system of rule, see esp. 237–41.

15. Ernest Gellner, *Nations and Nationalism* (Ithaca: Cornell University Press, 1983), 8–18; for the quote, 13.

16. Anthony Giddens, *The Nation-State and Violence* (Berkeley: University of California Press, 1987), 16.

17. Fukaya Katsumi, "Kinsei no shōgun to tennō," in *Kōza Nihonshi*, ed. Rekishigaku Kenkyūkai and Nihonshi Kenkyūkai (Tokyo: Tokyo Daigaku Shuppankai, 1985), 6:45–75, esp. 50–55, 70.

18. H. D. Harootunian, *Things Seen and Unseen: Discourse and Ideology in Tokugawa Nativism* (Chicago: University of Chicago Press, 1988); for the quotes, 34, 409.

19. Fukaya, "Kinsei no shōgun to tennō"; Amino Yoshihiko, *Nihon chūsei no hinōgyōmin to tennō* (Tokyo: Iwanami Shoten, 1984). In "In Name Only: Imperial Sovereignty in Early Modern Japan," *Journal of Japanese Studies* 17.1 (Winter 1991): 25–57, Bob Tadashi Wakabayashi argues that not only the samurai ruling elite but also many commoners had considerable knowledge about the emperor and his court during the Tokugawa period. He emphasizes particularly the emperor's ability to serve as a source of social prestige, whether through people tracing their lineages back to the imperial court or by the emperor's conferral of court ranks, official titles, and names that connoted imperial pedigrees. He does so in order to explain the resilience or continuity of the emperor and the imperial court throughout Japanese history. While he makes a strong case for the symbolic importance of the emperor for the ruling elite during the Tokugawa period, his evidence for commoners' knowledge does not seem to warrant a revision of the point made here—namely, that at the popular level, knowledge of the emperor in Japan was incomplete or fused with folk beliefs, and in many places did not even exist.

20. Quoted in Yoshida Kyūichi, "Meiji shonen no shūkyō ikki ni tsuite," *Nihon kindai bukkyōshi kenkyū* (Tokyo: Yoshikawa Kōbunkan, 1959), 53. For convenient summaries and analyses of antigovernment uprisings in the early Meiji years, see Sasaki Junnosuke, ed., *Yonaoshi* (Tokyo: Sanseidō, 1974), 332–85, and Stephen Vlastos, "Opposition Movements in Early Meiji, 1868–1885,"

in *Cambridge History of Japan*, ed. Marius B. Jansen (Cambridge and New York: Cambridge University Press, 1989), 5:367–431.

21. For the full interview see Tsurumi Shunsuke, ed., *Goishin no arashi*, revised ed. (Tokyo: Chikuma Shobō, 1977), 279–85; for the quote, 280.

22. Although I have not translated all the prayers shown on this print, these give a good sense of the sorts of benefits the craftspeople and their families expected from the emperor as Shōtoku Taishi. The print, "Shōtoku Taishi no Mikoto e shoshokunin ritsugan no zu," is collected in *Nishikie: Bakumatsu Meiji no rekishi*, ed. Konishi Shirō (Tokyo: Kōdansha, 1977), 5:6–7. I thank Urabe Manabe for helping me decipher some of the writing on the print.

23. Miyata Noboru, *Ikigami shinkō* (Tokyo: Haniwa Shobō, 1970), 42–110, esp. 42–75; also treated in idem, *Minzoku shūkyōron no kadai* (Tokyo: Miraisha, 1977), 9–53. Miyata's analysis of emperor worship is quite involved, and I have not felt it necessary to include all the details here. Suffice it to say that he deals with the originally magical and priestly roles of emperors, their theatrical qualities, their noneverydayness, Chikamatsu's emperor plays, and the Shinto/Confucian formalization of emperor worship.

24. Famous provincial shrines sometimes had ranks attached to them corresponding to court ranks. The Nagasaki notice, "Goyusho," and "Ōu jinmin kokuyu" are collected in Meiji Bunka Kenkyūkai, ed., *Meiji bunka zenshū* (Tokyo: Hyōronsha, 1967), 22:491–93; for the passages cited, 491.

25. On the establishment, development, and activities of *senkyōshi* and *kyōdōshoku*, see James Edward Ketelaar, *Of Heretics and Martyrs in Meiji Japan* (Princeton: Princeton University Press, 1990), 87–135; Umeda Yoshihiko, *Nihon shūkyō seidoshi: Kindai-hen*, revised and expanded ed. (Tokyo: Tosen Shuppan, 1971), 35–43; Helen Hardacre, "Creating State Shinto: The Great Promulgation Campaign and the New Religions," *Journal of Japanese Studies* 12.1 (Winter 1986): 29–63; Yasumaru Yoshio, *Kamigami no Meiji ishin* (Tokyo: Iwanami Shoten, 1979), 121–22, 181–95. For the *senyushi* in Mikawa, see Tanaka Nagane, "Junkō eshi furoku," collected in *Nihon shomin seikatsu shiryō shūsei*, ed. Tanigawa Ken'ichi (Tokyo: San'ichi Shobō, 1970), 13:660–61, 675; Fukuda Gidō, "Mikawa kuni dōyō jikki," collected in *Nihon shomin*, ed. Tanigawa, 13:671–72, 675. For the Nishi Honganji *monshu* example, see Yasumaru, *Kamigami*, 188–89.

26. What I mean by "mnemonic sites" would appear to bear some similarity to Pierre Nora's *lieux de mémoire*. He writes:

Thus, the method used consists of a concentrated analysis of the specific objects that codify, condense, anchor France's national memory. These can be monuments (the *château* of Versailles or the cathedral of Strasbourg); emblems, commemorations, and symbols (the tricolor of the French flag, the Fourteenth of July, the Marseillaise); rituals (the coronation of the kings at Reims) as well as monuments (such as the *monuments aux morts* in every French village or the Pantheon); manuals (a textbook used by all French children, a dictionary); basic texts (the Declaration of the Rights of Man or the *Code civil*); or mottos (for example, "Liberté, Egalité, Fraternité"). "Between Memory and History: *Les Lieux de Mémoire*," *Representations*, no. 26 (Spring 1989): 7–25; for the quote, 25.

27. The modern rulers' concern with ritual as a means of controlling the people can be traced back to the late Tokugawa period. Aizawa Seishisai of the

Mito School, for example, advocated in his *Shinron* (1825) a thoroughgoing system of rites centering on the emperor as ritualist. The system he envisioned extended down to the populace through famous provincial and village shrines (Yasumaru, *Kamigami*, 33–37). Bob Tadashi Wakabayashi has translated and introduced *Shinron* in *Anti-Foreignism and Western Learning in Early-Modern Japan: The "New Thesis" of 1825* (Cambridge: Harvard University Press, 1986).

28. All dates prior to the Meiji government's adoption of the Gregorian calendar on 1 January 1873 have been converted from the lunar calendar that was then in use.

29. Murakami Shigeyoshi, *Kokka shintō* (Tokyo: Iwanami Shoten, 1970), 154–60; idem, *Tennō no saishi* (Tokyo: Iwanami Shoten, 1977), 137–43. The guidelines for the standardization of shrine rituals at the local level were set down in piecemeal fashion beginning in 1872. By 1914 they were quite comprehensive and prescribed the annual major, middling, and small festivals for all shrines. As for the point that rites held at local shrines were supposed to correspond in general to rites held within the imperial household, see the list of correspondences in *Tennō no saishi*, 139–40.

30. A new set of holidays, sometimes falling on the same days as the prewar holidays, was established in 1948. See Murakami, *Tennō no saishi*, 1–21, 68–74, 76–86, 89–94, 125–27; Murakami Shigeyoshi, *Kōshitsu jiten* (Tokyo: Tokyodō Shuppan, 1980), 121–23.

31. Murakami, *Tennō no saishi*, 75. The two rites that had existed since ancient times were the *niinamesai* and the *kannamesai*. For a summary of rites centering on the imperial household, see *Tennō no saishi*, 45–106.

32. Ibid., 47–49, 53, 70, 108–20.

33. Tayama Katai, *Tōkyō no sanjūnen* (1917; Tokyo: Iwanami Shoten, 1981), 287–88. This book was a rather thinly veiled imitation of Alphonse Daudet's (1840–97) reminiscences of life in the French capital, *Trente ans de Paris* (1888). See Takamori Amao, "Kaisetsu," in the above edition of *Tōkyō no sanjūnen*. For an alternative translation, see Tayama Katai, *Literary Life in Tokyo, 1885–1915*, trans. with full annotations by Kenneth G. Henshall (Leiden: E. J. Brill, 1987), 248–49.

34. Ariizumi Sadao, "Meiji kokka to shukusaijitsu," *Rekishigaku kenkyū*, no. 341 (October 1981): 70.

35. Ōe Shinobu, *Yasukuni jinja* (Tokyo: Iwanami Shoten, 1984), 131.

36. See Chapter 3.

37. See Uchiyama Masao and Minomo Toshitarō, *Yoyogi no mori* (Tokyo: Kyōgakusha, 1981), 64, 68–70; Meiji Jingū Gaien, ed., *Seitoku kinen kaigakan hekiga* (Tokyo: Meiji Jingū Gaien, 1981); and of course one can literally see the Meiji Shrine Outer Garden itself.

38. See Chapter 5.

39. For "statumania" and *torii* "monumentalism," see Chapter 3. For the Kanda Shrine controversy, see Ogi Shinzō, *Tōkei shomin seikatsushi kenkyū* (Tokyo: Nihon Hōsō Shuppan Kyōkai, 1979), 563–73, and Yasumaru, *Kami gami*, 162–64.

40. See Chapter 2.

41. I have borrowed the term from Patrick H. Hutton, "The Art of Memory Reconceived: From Rhetoric to Psychoanalysis," *Journal of the History of Ideas* 48 (July–September 1987): 371.

42. Maruyama Masao, *Studies in the Intellectual History of Tokugawa Japan,* trans. Mikiso Hane (Tokyo: University of Tokyo Press, 1974), 330. Maruyama's translator adds: "The Tokugawa Bakufu governed with the philosophy that the people have to depend on the ruling class, and must not be informed about political matters. *Tami wa yorashimubekushite shirashimubekarazu:* 'The people should be made to depend upon [the Way] but not be informed about it.' This is based on a statement in the Confucian Analects (Book VIII, Chapter 9) that actually says that 'the people can be made to follow [the Way] but they cannot be made to understand it.' The Tokugawa rulers adopted the former interpretation" (330 n. 4).

43. These themes are developed in Yasumaru, *Kamigami,* and idem, *Nihon nashonarizumu no zen'ya* (Tokyo: Asahi Shinbun, 1977), i–iv, 5–81.

44. Michel Foucault, "The Subject and Power," published as an afterword to Hubert L. Dreyfus and Paul Rabinow, eds., *Michel Foucault: Beyond Structuralism and Hermeneutics,* 2nd ed. (Chicago: University of Chicago Press, 1983), 208–26; for the quotes, 212.

45. Yasumaru, *Kamigami,* esp. 145–79.

46. For these remarkable figures and attempts to reform folk practices in early Tokyo, see Ogi Shinzō, *Tōkei jidai* (Tokyo: Nihon Hōsō Shuppan Kyōkai, 1980), 98–101.

47. Kano Masanao, "Joron—tōchi taisei no keisei to chiiki," in *Kindai Nihon no tōgō to teikō,* ed. Kano Masanao and Yui Masaomi (Tokyo: Nihon Hyōronsha, 1982), 1:11.

48. See Carol Gluck's characterization of postwar reflections on the emperor system's ideology in *Japan's Modern Myths: Ideology in the Late Meiji Period* (Princeton: Princeton University Press, 1985), 4–6.

49. Sanjō Sanetomi, "Hokkaidō junkō no jōsōkō," collected in *Tennō to kazoku,* ed. Tōyama Shigeki (Tokyo: Iwanami Shoten, 1988), 48–49.

50. Lynn Hunt, *Politics, Culture, and Class in the French Revolution* (Berkeley: University of California Press, 1984); Mona Ozouf, *Festivals and the French Revolution,* trans. Alan Sheridan (Cambridge: Harvard University Press, 1988), esp. 197–216.

51. My usage of the "folklore of a regime" concept seems a bit broader than Maurice Agulhon's. He argues that

The "folklore" of a regime, in the general sense of the word, means the rituals, customs, and ceremonies to which it gives rise, ranging from the village electoral campaign to grandiose national funeral rites and from inaugural ceremonies for memorial monuments to presidential tours. And then, quite apart from all this, there is folklore pure and simple, without inverted commas—the traditional life of the towns and countryside which continued throughout the Republic but which must have been to some extent influenced, diverted or coloured by the new institutions. *Marianne into Battle,* trans. Janet Lloyd (Paris: Maison des Sciences de l'Homme; Cambridge: Cambridge University Press, 1981), 4–5.

52. For the nationalization of French local cultures as seen from a modern-ist's point of view, see Eugen Weber, *Peasants into Frenchmen* (Stanford: Stan-ford University Press, 1976).

53. From the title of Sean Wilentz, ed., *Rites of Power: Symbolism, Ritual, and Politics Since the Middle Ages* (Philadelphia: University of Pennsylvania Press, 1985).

54. Clifford Geertz, *Negara* (Princeton: Princeton University Press, 1980), 136.

55. Others have criticized Geertz's work along similar lines. For a recent and concise summary of several points made by Geertz's critics and an attempt to situate him between anthropology and history, see Aletta Biersack, "Local Knowledge, Local History: Geertz and Beyond," in *The New Cultural History*, ed. Lynn Hunt (Berkeley: University of California Press, 1989), 72–96. For an even more damning consideration of the conservative political implications of Geertz's privileging of culture over politics, see Vincent P. Pecora, "The Limits of Local Knowledge," in *The New Historicism*, ed. H. Aram Veeser (New York and London: Routledge, 1989), 243–76.

56. Geertz, *Negara*, 125, 9, 8, 10.

57. Ibid., 9.

58. Clifford Geertz, "Centers, Kings, and Charisma: Reflections on the Symbolics of Power," in *Culture and Its Creators*, ed. Joseph Ben-David and Terry Nichols Clark (Chicago and London: University of Chicago Press, 1977), 150–71; for the quotes, 168, 171.

59. Clifford Geertz, "Person, Time and Conduct in Bali," *The Interpreta-tion of Cultures* (New York: Basic Books, 1973), 404–8.

60. Itō Hirobumi, "Teishitsu seido kakuritsu no kyūmu" (11 September 1899), collected in *Zoku Itō Hirobumi hiroku*, ed. Hiratsuka Atsushi (Tokyo: Shunjusha, 1930), 136–39; for the quote, 137.

61. For a multilayered and provocative attempt to theorize and historicize the project of deconstructing memory, see Richard Terdiman, "Deconstructing Memory: On Representing the Past and Theorizing Culture in France Since the Revolution," *Diacritics* 15 (Winter 1985): 13–36. See also his later book on the subject of modernity and memory, *Present Past: Modernity and the Memory Crisis* (Ithaca: Cornell University Press, 1993).

62. For an overview and critique of interpretations of the emperor system as backward—including those of the *kōza* school and modernists such as Maruyama Masao—see Yasumaru Yoshio, "Kindai tennōzō no keisei," *Rekishi hyōron*, no. 465 (January 1989): 1–20, as well as his later book, *Kindai tennōzō no keisei* (Tokyo: Iwanami Shoten, 1992). Hirota Masaki has written an im-portant essay on the modernity of the post-Meiji emperor system from the perspective of its relationship to the modern system of discrimination in Japan: "Kindai tennōsei to sabetsu," in *Tennōsei o tou*, ed. Nihonshi Kenkyūkai and Kyoto Minka Rekishi Bukai (Tokyo: Jinbun Shoin, 1990), 129–57. For a de-tailed summary of Marxist writings on the emperor system and the *kōza* school's interpretation of it as a feudal remnant indicative of Japan's arrested develop-ment, see Germaine A. Hoston, *Marxism and the Crisis of Development in*

Prewar Japan (Princeton: Princeton University Press, 1986), 179–222. I first wrote on the modern invention of the Japanese monarchy in "Kindai Nihon ni okeru kokka-teki ibento no tenjō—1889–1912 no Tōkyō," *Yasō* 14 (February 1985): 126–40. I took up the issue of the imperial gaze and its centrality to Japan's modernity in "Kindai Nihon ni okeru gunshū to tennō no pējento: shikakuteki shihai ni kansuru jakkan no kōsatsu," trans. Yoshimi Shun'ya, *Shisō*, no. 797 (November 1990): 148–64.

63. John Whitney Hall, "A Monarch for Modern Japan," in *Political Development in Modern Japan*, ed. Robert E. Ward (Princeton: Princeton University Press, 1968), 11–64; for the quote, 64. I have written at more length on modernization theory and the monarchy in "Minshūshi as Critique of Orientalist Knowledges," *Positions* (forthcoming), and with Naoki Sakai in the introduction to a forthcoming volume on modernity and the emperor system.

Chapter 2. From Court in Motion to Imperial Capitals

1. For an excellent overview of the development of Japanese school excursions, see Yamamoto Nobuyoshi and Konno Toshihiko, *Kindai kyōiku no tennōsei ideorogii* (Tokyo: Shinsensha, 1973), 182–40.

2. Mark Peattie, *Nan'yō: The Rise and Fall of the Japanese in Micronesia, 1885–1945* (Honolulu: University of Hawaii Press, 1988), 109–11.

3. David Cannadine, "The Context, Performance, and Meaning of Ritual: The British Monarchy and the 'Invention of Tradition,' c. 1820–1977," in *The Invention of Tradition*, ed. Eric Hobsbawm and Terence Ranger (Cambridge: Cambridge University Press, 1983), 126–27; Bernard S. Cohn, "Anthropology and History in the 1980s," *Journal of Interdisciplinary History* 12 (1981): 251; Lewis Mumford, *The City in History* (New York and London: Harcourt Brace Jovanovich, 1961), 399–409.

4. John W. Reps, *Monumental Washington: The Planning and Development of the Capital Center* (Princeton: Princeton University Press, 1967); for the quote, 38.

5. Cannadine, "Meaning of Ritual," 127–28.

6. On the creation of New Delhi and the American and European models upon which it was based, see Robert Grant Irving, *Indian Summer: Lutyens, Baker, and Imperial Delhi* (New Haven: Yale University Press, 1981), esp. 53–90, 166–274.

7. Ibid., 86. For an immensely readable description of the original plans for Canberra and the difficulties in translating this plan onto the landscape, see K. S. Inglis, "Ceremonies in a Capital Landscape: Scenes in the Making of Canberra," *Daedalus* 114 (Winter 1985): 85–126.

8. Although this is basically the position that Henry D. Smith II takes in "Tokyo and London: Comparative Conceptions of the City," in *Japan: A Comparative View*, ed. Albert M. Craig (Princeton: Princeton University Press, 1979), 49–99, he also notes the important fact that Tokyo has had an "immense integrating influence on a national scale—socially, culturally, and politically" (71).

9. Roland Barthes, *Empire of Signs,* trans. Richard Howard (New York: Hill and Wang, 1982), 32.

10. *Tento,* a special issue of *Taiyō* 4 (1898): 40.

11. The description of this event is based on *Tento sanjūnensai zue,* a special issue of *Fūzoku gahō,* no. 163 (April 1898), esp. 13–31.

12. Inoue Yorikuni, "Tōkyō tento," *Tento,* 110.

13. Fukuoka Takachika, "Shinsei naru Tōkyō tento," *Tento,* 105–6.

14. Tokyo-to, ed., *Edo kara Tōkyō e no tenkai* (Tokyo: Tokyo-to, 1953), 82–118.

15. While population figures for Edo are only approximate since no concrete data exist for the large number of people attached to the *daimyō,* my point has less to do with exact figures than with tidal movements. For this estimate see Ogi Shinzō, *Tōkei shomin seikatsushi kenkyū* (Tokyo: Nihon Hōsō Shuppan Kyōkai, 1979), 54, who summarizes some of the generally accepted figures for the Edo population. In "The Edo-Tokyo Transition: In Search of Common Ground," in *Japan in Transition: From Tokugawa to Meiji,* ed. Marius B. Jansen and Gilbert Rozman (Princeton: Princeton University Press, 1986), 350–52, Henry D. Smith II somewhat downplays both the suddenness with which the *daimyō* left the city and the effects that this exodus had on the rest of the population and the economy. Nevertheless, there was undeniably a massive loss of population and an ensuing economic depression immediately preceding and following the Restoration.

16. See Ogi Shinzō, *Tōkei shomin,* 34–56, 577–88, for an analysis of Meiji period demographic trends and their social and cultural consequences. He argues that the post-Restoration population increase was to a large extent the result of heavy immigration. According to Ogi, this radically altered the characteristics of the Tokyo population and contributed to a breakdown of the traditional community. For a slightly different population estimate see Smith, "The Edo-Tokyo Transition," 356–57. According to his calculations the population was slightly more at both its peak and nadir. The translation of *shubiki-nai* as built-up area is Smith's.

17. Tokyo-to, ed., *Meiji shonen no bukechi shori mondai* (Tokyo: Tokyo-to, 1965), esp. 133–48, 162–84.

18. Fujimori Terunobu, *Meiji no Tōkyō keikaku* (Tokyo: Iwanami Shoten, 1982), 222; for photographs of some representative *daimyō* estates used as government offices, see Horikoshi Saburō, *Meiji shoki no yōfū kenchiku* (Tokyo: Maruzen, 1929), 138.

19. Herman Ooms, *Tokugawa Ideology* (Princeton: Princeton University Press, 1985), 57–62, 162–86. Ooms discusses Nikkō Tōshōgū and Kan'eiji in this thought-provoking book, but he is not attentive to the reconstruction of Edo and Edo Palace. This may be because he is only concerned with the "religious" bases of Tokugawa legitimation.

20. For the history and structure of Edo Castle I have consulted primarily Murai Masuo, *Edo-jō* (Tokyo: Chūō Kōronsha, 1964), esp. 80–133, 175–82; and William H. Coaldrake, "Edo Architecture and Tokugawa Law," *Monumenta Nipponica* 36 (1981): 235–84, esp. 239–53.

21. Murai, *Edo-jō,* 185.

22. During the Tokugawa period the structure that became the Akasaka Temporary Palace was part of the estate of one of the Tokugawa "Three Houses," the Kii Tokugawa (Minato Kuyakusho, ed., *Shinshū Minatokushi* [Tokyo: Minato Kuyakusho, 1979], 1445).

23. Quoted from Ichiki Shirō's autobiography, *Ichiki Shirō jiden,* in Tokyo Hyakunenshi Henshū Iinkai, ed., *Tōkyō hyakunenshi* (Tokyo: Tokyo-to, 1972), 2:100.

24. Internal petition (*naigi*), Sano Tsunetami, "Sento no ken," September 1878, Itō Hirobumi monjo, Kensei Shiryōshitsu, National Diet Library, Tokyo. Sano founded the Japan Red Cross, an extremely active patriotic association, and served at different times as home minister, Senate president, privy councillor, and minister of agriculture and commerce.

25. Isabella L. Bird, *Unbeaten Tracks in Japan* (New York: G. P. Putnam and Sons, 1880), 1:171–72.

26. It has been noted that the term *teito* came into frequent use from the late 1880s in Tokyo Hyakunenshi Henshū Iinkai, ed., *Tōkyō hyakunenshi,* 3:7–8.

27. The petition in its entirety is collected in Ōkubo Toshimichi, *Ōkubo Toshimichi monjo,* ed. Nihon Shiseki Kyōkai (Tokyo: Nihon Shiseki Kyōkai, 1927), 2:191–95; as well as in Tokyo-to, ed., *Edo kara Tōkyō,* 40–42.

28. While the character *ten* has a variety of meanings—among them, writings, rule, regulation, law, office, model, and ceremony or rite—Ōkubo Toshimichi definitely perceived the transfer of the capital as a spectacular "ceremonial act" that could help bring order to the troubled realm. When the emperor arrived in Tokyo on 26 November 1868, Ōkubo noted in his diary, *Ōkubo Toshimichi nikki,* ed. Nihon Shiseki Kyōkai (Tokyo: Nihon Shiseki Kyōkai, 1927), 1:187: "At two the arrival of the Imperial Palanquin; the procession magnificent; the Imperial Virtue resplendent; everyone, high and low, partaking in the celebratory drink; truly a great ceremony [*seiten,* having only the meaning of great ceremony] [which occurs] but once in a millennium; inexpressible jubilation. At the same time several thousand Imperial Soldiers, having quelled [the northern provinces] Mutsu and Dewa, are returning to Tokyo singing victory songs. Can this be a coincidence?"

29. Ōkubo, *Ōkubo Toshimichi monjo,* 193–94.

30. Ōkuma Shigenobu, "Tōkyō tento jijō," *Tento,* 98–100.

31. Smith discusses the Maejima plan in more detail in "The Edo-Tokyo Transition," 355–36. Maejima's petition, which was presented to Ōkubo Toshimichi and is dated 2 April 1868, is collected in Tokyo-to, ed., *Edo kara Tōkyō,* 51–54.

32. Collected in ibid., 56–60.

33. Kido noted that during a meeting held on 8 May 1868 among some of the leading figures in the government such as Iwakura Tomomi, Sanjō Sanetomi, Soejima Taneomi, and Fukuoka Takachika, "a plan which I have long advocated was adopted: to allow His Majesty to travel freely to all quarters of the land, coming frequently to Naniwa, setting up imperial living facilities and government offices here, and moving into the Nijō Palace after his return to Kyoto" (*The Diary of Kido Takayoshi,* trans. Sidney Devere Brown and Akiko

Hirota [Tokyo: University of Tokyo Press, 1983], 1:11). For the three-capital plan, see Tokyo Hyakunenshi Henshū Iinkai, ed., *Tokyo hyakunenshi*, 2:52.

34. Collected in Tokyo-to, ed., *Edo kara Tōkyō*, 83–84.

35. For an overview of imperial courts from their beginnings through the building of Japan's first planned imperial cities (*tojō*)—Fujiwara-kyō (court transfer 694), Heijō-kyō (court transfer 710), Nagaoka-kyō (court transfer 784), and Heian-kyō (court transfer 794)—see Kodama Kōta, ed., *Tennō* (Tokyo: Kondō Shuppansha, 1978), 106–17; and Paul Wheatley and Thomas See, *From Court to Capital* (Chicago: University of Chicago Press, 1978), 69, 103–58. The figures are from Wheatley and See, *From Court to Capital*, 105.

36. *Kojiruien*, teiōbu 1 (Tokyo: Kojiruien Kankōkai, 1932), 587–724, includes many examples of how these terms were used in a wide variety of texts, primarily Japanese.

37. Collected in ibid., 587.

38. Collected in ibid., 588.

39. Kodama, ed., *Tennō*, 135. One notable exception was Antoku's progress to Fukuhara in 1180.

40. Herschel Webb, *The Japanese Imperial Institution in the Tokugawa Period* (New York: Columbia University Press, 1968), ix.

41. For a complete table of major provincial outings from 1868 to 1947 based on an Imperial Household Agency list, see Taigakai, ed., *Naimushōshi* (Tokyo: Chihō Zaimu Kyōkai, 1971), 764–71. One reason why there is no agreement about the number of imperial provincial tours (*chihō junkō*) that occurred in any period is that the term itself is unofficial (see 771). Tanaka Akira, who apparently included as many small-scale provincial tours as he could find and called them all "tours" (*junkō*), has compiled a more comprehensive list than that found in *Naimushōshi*. According to his data there were 97 tours during the forty-five years of the Meiji period. Of these, 53 took place during the first two decades of the era, whereas 44 took place in the following twenty-five years. These figures might lead one to conclude that the first twenty years of Emperor Meiji's reign were only slightly more active than the last twenty-five. However, nearly half of the tours in the last twenty-five years were one-day excursions, whereas two-thirds of the tours in the first twenty years lasted more than a day (Tanaka, *Kindai tennōsei e no dōtei* [Tokyo: Yoshikawa Kōbunkan, 1979], 224–26).

42. In addition to the primary sources cited below, I have consulted partial descriptions in Irokawa Daikichi, *Kindai kokka e no shuppatsu* (Tokyo: Chūō Kōronsha, 1974), 2–30; Tanaka, *Kindai tennōsei*, 219–43; Obinata Sumio, "Tennō junkō o meguru minshū no dōkō," *Chihōshi kenkyū* 32 (February 1982): 1–16; and Sasaki Suguru, "Tennōzō no keisei katei," in *Kokumin bunka no keisei*, ed. Asukai Masamichi (Tokyo: Chikuma Shobō, 1984), 207–21; and the relevant entries in the chronologically arranged official history of Emperor Meiji's reign, Kunaichō, *Meiji tennōki* (Tokyo: Yoshikawa Kōbunkan, 1968–77), hereafter cited as *MTK*.

43. This is from a sixteen-point set of instructions sent out by the Home Ministry in Ōkubo's name to local officials along the route, "Endō no chihōkan kokoroe," collected in *Meiji tennō gojunkōroku*, ed. Fukushima-ken Kyōikukai

(Fukushima: Fukushima-shi, 1936), 13–14. Officials were to identify such individuals of merit and present them for imperial inspection at the prefectural offices.

44. *MTK*, 3:620–21, 655–56, 670.

45. Clifford Geertz, "Centers, Kings, and Charisma: Reflections on the Symbolics of Power," in *Culture and Its Creators*, ed. Joseph Ben-David and Terry Nichols Clark (Chicago and London: University of Chicago Press, 1977), 150–71.

46. Kodama, ed., *Tennō*, 102; and Murakami Shigeyoshi, *Tennō no saishi* (Tokyo: Iwanami Shoten, 1977), 179–82.

47. Murakami Shigeyoshi, *Kōshitsu jiten* (Tokyo: Tōkyōdō Shuppan, 1980), 171–72.

48. This episode is related in Obinata, "Tennō junkō," 6.

49. While the supposedly original Kusanagi Sword has been permanently housed at Atsuta Shrine since, according to the official history, the reign of Keikō (71–130), a replica (*katashiro*) of it is always kept near the emperor. In the prewar and wartime era, the sword and the jewel always accompanied the emperor on any overnight trips away from the palace (Murakami, *Kōshitsu jiten*, 70–71).

50. Murakami, *Kōshitsu jiten*, 203; and Rekishi Kyōikusha Kyōgikai, ed., *Shinpan hinomaru, kimigayo, kigensetsu, kyōiku chokugo* (Tokyo: Chirekisha, 1981), 21–26.

51. This testimony and the two following it are collected in Fukushima-ken, ed., *Meiji tennō gojunkōroku*, 107, 186, 179.

52. This is from an account that originally appeared in the *Tokyo nichi nichi shinbun*, which was then reprinted in the *Naniwa shinbun* and is now collected in full as "Tōhoku gojunkōki," in *Meiji bunka zenshū*, ed. Meiji Bunka Kenkyūkai (Tokyo: Nihon Hyōronsha, 1967), 17:339–400; for the quote, 353.

53. Obinata, "Tennō junkō," 6.

54. Kinoshita Naoe, *Zange*, in *Kinoshita Naoe chosakushū* (Tokyo: Meiji Bunken, 1968), 5:68–69,76–77.

55. Fukushima-ken, ed., *Meiji tennō gojunkōroku*, 110.

56. For examples of such official instructions see Tanaka, *Kindai tennōsei*, 227–28, and Obinata, *Tennō junkō*, 4.

57. For example, Irokawa, *Kindai kokka*, 24.

58. Geertz, "Centers, Kings, and Charisma," 153.

59. Sanjō Sanetomi, "Hokkaidō junkō no jōsōkō," in *Tennō to kazoku*, ed. Tōyama Shigeki (Tokyo: Iwanami Shoten, 1988), 48–49.

60. "Endō chihōkan kokoroesho," in ibid., 69–70; "Endō no chihōkan kokoroe," in Fukishima-ken, ed., *Meiji tennō gojunkōroku*, 13–14.

61. Taki Kōji, *Tennō no shōzō* (Tokyo: Iwanami Shoten, 1988), esp. 84–89.

62. "Tōhoku gojunkōki," 383.

63. Richard Wortman, "Rule by Sentiment: Alexander II's Journeys through the Russian Empire," *American Historical Review* 95 (June 1990): 745–71.

64. *MTK*, 3:728–29; 4:19–21, 224.

65. Ibid., 6:664–65, 685, 702.

66. Ibid., 2:698; 4:537; 5:143–44.

67. Ibid., 6:46–47.

68. The petition in its entirety is collected in Iwakura Tomomi, *Iwakura Tomomi kankei monjo,* ed. Otsuka Takematsu (Tokyo: Nihon Shiseki Kyōkai, 1927), 1:395–408; for the items from the petition cited, 405–6.

69. Nishigaki Seiji, *Oise mairi* (Tokyo: Iwanami Shoten, 1983), 20–21. This proposal for the creation of a national religion with two ritual centers and a sacred book written in an easily understood style was one suggestion for dealing with the threat of Christianity. The issue had been opened with an incredible plan to tattoo, brand, and condemn all Christians to hard labor.

70. "Kyōto hozon ni kansuru kengi," collected in Iwakura, *Iwakura Tomomi,* 1:482–90.

71. Ibid., 484–90.

72. For a discussion of Japanese imperial accession rites, see D. C. Holtom, *The Japanese Enthronement Ceremonies* (1928; Tokyo: Sophia University, 1972), esp. 45–111.

73. "Kyōto hozon ni kansuru kengi," 490.

74. *MTK,* 6:46–47, 55–56. For a description of the 1871 *daijōsai* see Murakami, *Tennō no saishi,* 114–20.

75. While exhibitions are a fascinating and important cultural phenomenon of modern Japan, this is certainly not the place for a detailed examination of them. Suffice it to say that Kyoto's exhibitions began in 1871 and continued through the Meiji era, reaching a climax with the Fourth National Industrial Exhibition of 1895. For a brief overview of Kyoto's exhibitions, see Umesao Tadao and Moriya Takeshi, eds., *Kyōto,* vol. 10 of *Meiji Taishō zushi,* ed. Asukai Masamichi et al. (Tokyo: Chikuma Shobō, 1978), 51–59; and Kyoto-shi, *Kamigyō-ku,* vol. 7 of *Shiryō Kyōto no rekishi* (Tokyo: Heibonsha, 1980), 46–47. For a chart showing locally sponsored exhibitions and their locations, in addition to a number of other significant facts, see the appendix to Kyoto Furitsu Sōgō Shiryōkan, ed., *Kyōto-fu hyakunen no shiryō,* vol. 2 (Kyoto: Kyoto-fu, 1972). For a highly original treatment of the politics of exhibitions within the global context of modernity, see Yoshimi Shun'ya's *Hakurankai no seijigaku* (Tokyo: Chūō Kōronsha, 1992).

76. The City Council of Kyoto, *The Official Guide-Book to Kyoto and the Allied Prefectures* (Nara: Meishinsha, 1895), 75.

77. For the draft which Itō and Inoue put before the Privy Council members I have used the text reproduced in Inada Masatsugu, *Meiji kenpō seiritsushi* (Tokyo: Yūhikaku, 1962), 2:1004–10. Inada has conveniently placed this draft side by side with the finalized version of the Imperial House Law for easy comparison. The official translation of the Imperial House Law can be found in *Japanese Government Documents,* ed. W. W. McLaren (1914; Washington, D.C.: University Publications of America, 1979), 1:145–53. I have been able to follow the debate within the Privy Council through the Privy Council's minutes, *Sūmitsuin kaigi gijiroku* (Tokyo: Tokyo Daigaku Shuppankai, 1984), 1:4–38.

78. Ibid., 9–10.

79. Ibid., 34–35.

80. Ibid., 35–36.

81. Ibid., 36–37.

82. Ibid., 37. At this point the Privy Council members voted on Higashikuze's proposal to merge Articles XI and XII. The motion failed, but the question of whether or not to merge the two articles was not the main issue anyway. The key question involved the location of the *sokui* rite. Thus the discussion continued.

83. Ibid., 37.

84. Ibid.

85. Ibid., 38.

86. While people such as Maejima Hisoka had indeed urged the move to the East in order to revive the declining city (see Maejima's petition in Tokyoto, ed., *Edo kara Tōkyō,* 51–4), that reason had been neither the sole nor primary one given.

87. *Sūmitsuin kaigi gijiroku,* 1:38.

88. The recommendation to combine Articles XI and XII came from the Temporary Office for the Survey of the Imperial Household (Rinji Teishitsu Torishirabekyoku). The Imperial Household Ministry established this office on 31 May 1888. The office was headed by Yanagihara Sakimatsu, a young but extremely influential figure in the creation of Japan's modern imperial ceremonies. On these points as well as the passing of the motion to combine Articles XI and XII without dissent, see *MTK,* 7:79, 188; *Sūmitsuin kaigi gijiroku,* 3:35. After the publication of my *Tennō no pējento,* the historian Takagi Hiroshi informed me that he had also written about the symbolic and ceremonial importance of Kyoto, and that like me he had argued that this attention to Kyoto was in large part inspired by European, and particularly Russian, models. While he does not place Kyoto in relation to the imperial progresses and to Tokyo, as I am trying to do here, Takagi's "Nihon no kindaika to kōshitsu girei: 1880 nendai no 'kyūkan' hozon," *Nihonshi kenkyū,* no. 320 (April 1989): 87–115, corroborates the argument concerning Kyoto that I first articulated in my 1986 dissertation. On several points he provides more detail. Takagi's work on Kyoto fits within his larger and important project of analyzing the Meiji period movement to preserve and even construct or invent various cultural artifacts representing Japanese Tradition; for example, see his "1880 nendai, Yamato ni okeru bunkazai hozon," *Rekishigaku kenkyū,* no. 629 (February 1992): 15–22.

89. *MTK,* 3:61–63.

90. The basic history of the planning and delays which preceded the rebuilding of the palace is covered in Nakajima Usaburō, *Kōjō* (Tokyo: Yūzankaku, 1959), 121–39.

91. Naikaku Kirokukyoku, ed., *Hōki bunrui taizen* (Tokyo: Naikaku Kirokukyoku, 1897), 1:37.

92. *MTK,* 5:174, 179.

93. Petition of Kawaji Kandō to Minister of the Left Prince Arisugawa no miya Taruhito, "Kōkyo gozōei ni kansuru kenpaku," June 1883, Sanjō-ke monjo, Kensei Shiryōshitsu, National Diet Library, Tokyo.

94. A copy of this petition is contained in volume 6 of the official 130-volume record of the palace construction: Kōkyo Gozōeishi Hensangakari,

ed., "Kōkyo gozōeishi," 1892, Shoryōbu, Imperial Household Agency, To-kyo. At various times in the 1870s Shishido had held such positions as vice-minister of justice, of religion, and of education, as well as senator (*genrōin gikan*) and envoy extraordinary and minister plenipotentiary to China. In 1887 he received the title of viscount (*shishaku*) and from 1890 to 1897 he sat in the House of Peers (*Konsaisu jinmei jiten: Nihon-hen* [Tokyo: Sanseidō, 1976], 539).

95. *MTK*, 6:84.

96. Nakamura Tatsutarō, "Kōkyo gozōei no koro," *Kenchiku zasshi*, no. 601 (July 1935): 861.

97. Yano Kōta Kinenkai, ed., *Sūji de miru Nihon no hyakunen* (Tokyo: Kokuseisha, 1981), 277.

98. In July 1883, the government reestimated the budget at 2.5 million yen, but this much smaller amount was for completion of what was originally intended to be a temporary palace. According to this scheme the government would have first constructed a temporary palace on the old Nishinomaru site and then built a permanent palace on the old Honmaru site at some later date. However, the government abandoned this plan and completed the Nishi-nomaru structure as the permanent palace at a cost of 4.9 million yen (Nakajima, *Kōjō*, 132-38).

99. For information on the planning of Tokyo during the Meiji period I am heavily indebted to the excellent book by Fujimori Terunobu, *Meiji no Tōkyō keikaku*. Based on exhaustive research in archival materials, it is written with broad vision and historical depth. It also includes a vast amount of illuminating primary sources.

100. Henry D. Smith II describes the Ginza brick town as a "showcase" in "Tokyo as an Idea: An Exploration of Japanese Urban Thought Until 1945," *Journal of Japanese Studies* 4.1 (Winter 1978): 53-54. See also Fujimori, *Meiji no Tōkyō keikaku*, 1-44.

101. Matsuda presented his plan to the Tokyo Assembly on 2 November 1880; see Fujimori, *Meiji no Tōkyō keikaku*, 84.

102. Cited ibid., 107. On the Matsuda plan and the influence of Kusumoto and Taguchi, see 79-109.

103. Fukuzawa publicized his views in an article, "Shufu kaizō to kōkyo gozōei to," that appeared in two parts on 7 and 8 June 1883 in the *Jiji shinpō*, the newspaper which he founded in March 1882; collected in *Fukuzawa Yuki-chi zenshū*, ed. Keiō Gijuku (Tokyo: Iwanami Shoten, 1960), 9:13-18.

104. Ibid., 16.

105. Cannadine, "Meaning of Ritual," 120-38.

106. Fukuzawa, "Shufu kaizō," 17.

107. Ibid.

108. On the Yoshikawa plan, see Fujimori, *Meiji no Tōkyō keikaku*, 110-38, esp. 123-25, 136.

109. Ibid., 139-54.

110. On this plan as well as two other German plans—one by one of the principal architects of modern Berlin, James Hobrecht, and the other by Ende—see ibid., 220-59.

111. For the Municipal Improvement Committee's plan, see ibid., 196–205.

112. For a fuller description of the buildings in the prewar Imperial Palace, see Nakajima, *Kōjō*, 151–55; and Murai, *Edo-jō*, 188–91. On Katayama's study and the importing of German palace interior decor and furniture, see Nakamura, "Kōkyo gozōei no koro," 123.

113. *Japan Weekly Mail*, 16 February 1889.

114. Erwin Baelz, *Awakening Japan: The Diary of a German Doctor*, ed. by his son Toku Baelz (1932; Bloomington: Indiana University Press, 1974), 80.

115. Nakamura, "Kōkyo gozōei no koro," 128.

116. Sanbō Honbu Rikugunbu Sokuryōkyoku, *Gosenbun no ichi Tōkyō-zu sokuryō genzu* (Tokyo, 1886; surveyed 1883). I thank Haga Hiraku of Kashiwa Shobō for first bringing this map to my attention many years ago. For a chart showing the buildings in this area at various points in history, see Maejima Yasuhiko, *Kōkyo gaien* (Tokyo: Kyōgakusha, 1981), 37–42.

117. On the movement of military facilities out of Tokyo's core, see Tokyo Toritsu Daigaku Toshi Kenkyūkai, ed., *Toshi kōzō to toshi keikaku* (Tokyo: Tokyo Daigaku Shuppankai, 1968), 58–59.

118. For a brief history of the Aoyama Military Parade Field, see Minato, ed., *Shinshū Minatokushi*, 538.

119. I have listed these institutions by the names by which they were known during the Meiji period. All presently continue to exist under slightly different names, though not necessarily in Ueno Park. See the list of Ueno's major institutions in Kobayashi Yasushige, *Ueno kōen* (Tokyo: Kyōgakusha, 1980), 54–55.

120. The Imperial Household Ministry retained jurisdiction over Ueno Park until 1924 when it gave the park as an imperial gift to the city of Tokyo (ibid., 48).

121. Irokawa Daikichi, one of the pioneering historians of popular thought and culture, offered this explanation long ago in *Kindai kokka e no shuppatsu*, 2–30, esp. 27–28, 29–30. The book even includes a map with the courses of the "Six Great Imperial Tours" superimposed on a map showing the centers of "Freedom and Popular Rights" strength. This is supposed to show that the courses of the progresses coincided with the regional strongholds of the movement. The map does initially give this impression—but only because the Meiji emperor rambled across nearly the entire country during the course of these progresses. In fact, a closer examination shows that the emperor did travel to major regions like Iwate, Aomori, and Hokkaido that were not such strongholds while he skipped over areas like southern Shikoku (especially Kōchi) that were. See map attached to *Kindai kokka*.

122. On these incidents, see Roger W. Bowen, *Rebellion and Democracy in Meiji Japan* (Berkeley: University of California Press, 1980).

123. These counts are according to *MTK*, 1:838; 2:70.

124. Murakami Shigeyoshi, *Kokka shintō* (Tokyo: Iwanami Shoten, 1970), 90–91.

125. On the timing and manner of the delivery of imperial portraits, see Yamamoto and Konno, *Kindai kyōiku no tennōsei ideorogii*, 71–74.

126. The following information on school ceremonies is from ibid., 58–129, 160–64, 402–13.

127. On the problem of two political centers in Russia, especially after the assassination of Alexander II in 1881, see the fascinating essay by Richard Wortman, "Moscow and Petersburg: The Problem of the Political Center in Tsarist Russia, 1881–1914," in *Rites of Power: Symbolism, Ritual, and Politics Since the Middle Ages,* ed. Sean Wilentz (Philadelphia: University of Pennsylvania Press, 1985), 244–71.

128. In 1940 Emperor Kōmei, the last emperor to reside permanently in Kyoto, was also enshrined here. This description of Heian shrine is based on the Kyoto City Council's official guide of 1895, *The Official Guide-book to Kyoto,* 58–60; and Murakami, *Kōshitsu jiten,* 210. The functional rather than literal translations of some of the structures follow John W. Hall, "Kyoto as Historical Background," in *Medieval Japan: Essays in Institutional History,* ed. John W. Hall and Jeffrey P. Mass (New Haven: Yale University Press, 1974), 3–38.

129. Heian Sento Kinensai Kyōsankai, *Heian jingū jidai matsuri gyōretsu zufu* (Kyoto: Murakami Shoten, 1895), unpaginated.

130. On Kyoto's modern history as described here, see Akamatsu Toshihide and Yamamoto Shirō, *Kyōto-fu no rekishi* (Tokyo: Yamakawa Shuppansha, 1969), 240–75; and Umesao and Moriya, eds., *Kyōto,* 13–84.

131. For a good and brief history of Ise Shrine see Nishigaki, *Oise mairi.* Helen Hardacre considers the role of *oshi* in popular Ise worship during the Tokugawa period in her wide-ranging article, "Creating State Shinto: The Great Promulgation Campaign and the New Religions," *Journal of Japanese Studies,* 12.1 (Winter 1986): 33–35. In "Kyōkai toshite no Ise," in *Hōhō toshite no kyōkai,* ed. Akasaka Norio (Tokyo: Shin'yōsha, 1991), 1–62, Yoshimi Shun'ya evocatively analyzes the reconstitution of Ise as a contestation between a "folkish memory" (*minshūteki kioku*) carried in the body, in such objects as Ise amulets, and in practices like the "pilgrimages of grace" (*okage mairi*) and a new set of practices and a new symbolic order generated and imposed by the Meiji state.

132. This and the following treatment of the founding of new shrines is not meant to be comprehensive. For an extremely detailed though uncritical history of the establishment of modern shrines with a national dimension, see Okada Yoneo, "Jingū-jinja sōkenshi," in *Meiji ishin shintō hyakunenshi* (Tokyo: Shintō Bunkakai, 1966), 2:3–182. On the shrines to Amaterasu, see 90–102.

133. Ibid., 80–4.

134. Ibid., 59–70.

135. Ibid., 13–59.

136. Ibid., 86–88.

137. Ibid., 103–10.

138. Murakami Shigeyoshi, *Irei to shōkon* (Tokyo: Iwanami Shoten, 1974), 28–51, 62–65. The early chronicler, Kamo Momoki, is cited in Kobayashi Kenzō and Terunuma Yoshibumi, *Shōkonsha seiritsushi no kenkyū* (Tokyo: Kinseisha, 1969), 21; for a list of currently existing *shōkonsha,* see 15, 213–22.

139. On this point as well as on the numerous contradictions and tensions that inevitably accompany national narratives, see the collection of essays edited by Homi K. Bhabha, *Nation and Narration* (London and New York:

Routledge, 1990), especially Bhabha's "Dissemination: Time, Narrative, and the Margins of the Modern Nation," 291–322.

140. The discussion concerning the incommensurability of Kyoto and Tokyo and the seam holding them together has been stimulated by Harry Harootunian's comments on an earlier draft of this book. Harootunian suggests that especially during the interwar years intellectuals such as Abe Jirō, Watsuji Tetsurō, Tanizaki Jun'ichirō, Izumi Kyōka, Nagai Kafu, and others turned to Edo or "Edo viewing" as a way of supplying an alternative past.

141. Though I would emphasize much more than he the importance of the nation-state and the state's agency in the process of disciplining memory, Richard Terdiman has argued that during Europe's "long nineteenth century," "history increasingly became the discipline of memory." He considers modern history to be a response to what he calls the "memory crisis" in Europe, a crisis inextricably related to the domination of the socioeconomy by commodities. While apparently preserving the past, this history in fact occluded "individual *dispossession* of the past" (*Present Past: Modernity and the Memory Crisis* [Ithaca: Cornell University Press, 1993], 31, emphasis in original).

Part 2 Overview

1. David I. Kertzer, *Ritual, Politics, and Power* (New Haven: Yale University Press, 1988), x.

2. Teofilo F. Ruiz in "Unsacred Monarchy: The Kings of Castile in the Late Middle Ages," in *Rites of Power*, ed. Sean Wilentz (Philadelphia: University of Pennsylvania Press, 1985), 109–45.

3. See my "Electronic Pageantry and Japan's 'Symbolic Emperor,'" *Journal of Asian Studies* 51 (November 1992): 824–50.

4. Yano Fumio, "Kyūtei no shoshiki o seitei shite eisei no teishiki to kōji ainaritaki gi," March 1891, handwritten copy in Rinji Teishitsu Seido Torishirabekyoku shorui, Shoryōbu, Imperial Household Agency, Tokyo.

5. *Daijinmei jiten* (Tokyo: Heibonsha, 1953); Takayanagi Mitsutoshi and Takeuchi Yoshizō, eds., *Nihonshi jiten*, 2nd ed. (Tokyo: Kadokawa Shoten, 1974).

6. *Jiji shinpō*, 10 February 1889.

7. Erwin Baelz, *Awakening Japan: The Diary of a German Doctor*, ed. Toku Baelz (1932; Bloomington: Indiana University Press, 1974), 82.

8. In *Japan's Modern Myths: Ideology in the Late Meiji Period* (Princeton: Princeton University Press, 1985), 42–48, 213–27, Carol Gluck describes two ceremonial events analyzed in this book—namely, the Meiji Constitution's promulgation ceremony and the Meiji emperor's funeral. The reader will thus find some overlap in our respective descriptions. Our treatments, however, differ significantly. While Gluck's book is a masterful overview of the complex production, diffusion, and transformation of modern Japanese ideology, as well as of what she considers to be that ideology's often discordant relation to social reality, she seems to be using these two events more for rhetorical flourish, to set off the beginning and end of her discussion with colorful events, rather than

because she sees such intermittent ceremonial occasions as intrinsically important. My point is that the pageantry was important in and of itself and that its significances need to be further examined.

9. Ubukata Toshirō, *Meiji Taishō kenbunshi* (1926; Tokyo: Chūō Kōronsha, 1978); for the phrase "epoch-making" event, 7; the three events described are the Constitution's promulgation, the crown prince's wedding, and Emperor Meiji's funeral: 23–25, 118–21.

10. David Cannadine, "The Context, Performance, and Meaning of Ritual: The British Monarchy and the 'Invention of Tradition,' c. 1820–1977," in *The Invention of Tradition*, ed. Eric Hobsbawm and Terence Ranger (Cambridge: Cambridge University Press, 1983), 120–38; for the domestic and international contexts which contributed to this effusion of ritual activity see esp. 120–32, 160–62.

11. Ibid., 133.

12. Bernard Cohn, "Representing Authority in Victorian India," in Hobsbawm and Ranger, eds., *The Invention of Tradition*, esp. 178–209; for the quote, 208.

13. One might think of this symbolic ordering on the physical landscape, the imperial body, and through pageantry as a working out, narrowing, and officializing of the worlds of the "seen" and the "unseen" that H. D. Harootunian has so powerfully described in his reading of late Tokugawa nativist discourse (*Things Seen and Unseen: Discourse and Ideology in Tokugawa Nativism* [Chicago: University of Chicago Press, 1988]).

14. This approach was pioneered by the Japanese anthropologist Yamaguchi Masao in such works as "Kingship, Theatricality, and Marginal Reality in Japan," in *Text and Context: The Social Anthropology of Tradition*, ed. Ravindra K. Jain (Philadelphia: Institute for the Study of Human Issues, 1977); and "Tennōsei no shinsō kōzō" and "Tennōsei no shōchō kūkan," in *Chi no enkinhō* (Tokyo: Iwanami Shoten, 1978), 333–98.

15. Pierre Bourdieu, *The Logic of Practice*, trans. Richard Nice (Cambridge, England: Polity Press, 1990), 68.

16. See Chapter 1.

17. Pierre Bourdieu, *Outline of a Theory of Practice*, trans. Richard Nice (Cambridge and New York: Cambridge University Press, 1977), esp. 87–158.

18. Pierre Bourdieu, *Distinction*, trans. Richard Nice (Cambridge: Harvard University Press, 1984), 548.

Chapter 3. Fabricating Imperial Ceremonies

1. "Kenpō happushiki roku," 1889, Shoryōbu, Imperial Household Agency, Tokyo.

2. Unless noted otherwise, this description of the ceremonies held in Tokyo is based on the following: Erwin Baelz, *Awakening Japan: The Diary of a German Doctor*, ed. Toku Baelz (1932; Bloomington: Indiana University Press, 1974), 81–83; Ikeda Terusuke, *Kenpō happushiki haikan gaikyō* (Chiba-ken: Shūeisha, 1889), 18–25; "Kenpō happushiki goshidai," *Fūzoku gahō*, no.

2 (March 1889): 1–7; *Japan Weekly Mail*, 16 February 1889; *Jiji shinpō*, 12 February 1889; *Yūbin hōchi shinbun*, 12 February 1889, morning edition; and *MTK*, 7:204–11.

3. The official translation of the "Imperial Speech on the Promulgation of the Constitution" is collected in *Japanese Government Documents*, ed. W. W. McLaren (1914; Washington, D.C.: University Publications of America, 1979), 1:133–34.

4. Baelz, *Diary of a German Doctor*, 82.

5. On 3 February the Imperial Household Ministry ordered the Tokyo Metropolitan Police to inform the newspapers of Tokyo to elect ten representatives from among themselves to attend the promulgation ceremony. On 6 February the representatives of the fifty-eight registered newspapers and magazines reported the names and newspaper affiliations of the ten representatives to the police. For this information, the names and affiliations of the five representatives of provincial papers, and the editors of the three foreign language papers, see Naikaku Kirokukyoku, ed., *Hōki bunrui taizen*, 2nd ed. (Tokyo: Naikaku Kirokukyoku, 1892), 1:16–19.

6. For example, see *Yūbin hōchi shinbun*, 4 February 1889, evening edition.

7. Ikeda, *Kenpō happushiki haikan gaikyō*, 1.

8. *Yūbin hōchi shinbun*, 8 February 1889, morning edition.

9. *Japan Weekly Mail*, 16 February 1889.

10. *Jiji shinpō*, 13 February 1889; *Yūbin hōchi shinbun*, 12 February 1889, evening edition; *MTK*, 7:218–19.

11. Yanagihara Sakimitsu, "Sueden koku kōtei heika ginkonshiki," 1882, Shoryōbu, Imperial Household Agency, Tokyo. The cover letter, written by Inoue and addressed to Nabeshima, is dated 22 December 1882.

12. "Kakkoku kinginkonshiki torishiraberoku," 1893, Shoryōbu, Imperial Household Agency, Tokyo.

13. *MTK*, 8:370–71, 375.

14. For the print media accounts see, for example: *Daikon nijūgonen shukuten kiji*, a special issue of *Fūzoku gahō*, no. 71 (April 1894): 6–8; *Japan Weekly Mail*, 17 March 1894; *Jiji shinpō*, 10 March 1894; *Tōkyō asahi shinbun*, 11 March 1894. For the official history see *MTK*, 8:384–86.

15. *MTK*, 8:385.

16. *Japan Weekly Mail*, 10 March 1894, 297; *Jiji shinpō*, 10 March 1894; *Kokumin shinbun*, 11 March 1894. The description from the imperial procession to the final events within the palace is based primarily on *MTK*, 8:386–88, and *Japan Weekly Mail*, 17 March 1894, 325–26.

17. Yamamoto Yokichi, *Japanese Postage Stamps* (Tokyo: Japan Travel Bureau, 1950), 98–159; Nihon Yūbin Kittesho Kyōdō Kumiai Katarogu Henshū Iinkai, ed., *1984 Nihon kitte katarogu* (Tokyo: Nihon Yūbin Kittesho Kyōdō Kumiai, 1984), 10–63.

18. The description of this imperial ceremony, unless otherwise noted, is based upon the following: *Kōtaishi denka gokeiji—chiyo no iwai*, a special issue of *Fūzoku gahō*, no. 211 (June 1900): 8–13; Kōno Kōzaburō, *Tōgū gokeijiroku* (Hiroshima: Kōno Kōzaburō, 1900), 17–21; and *MTK* 9:761–62, 813.

19. Kodama Kōta, ed., *Tennō* (Tokyo: Kondō Shuppansha, 1978), 57; Murakami Shigeyoshi, *Kōshitsu jiten* (Tokyo: Tōkyōdō Shuppan, 1980), 194.

20. For a description of the *judai* ceremony which preceded Haruko's installation as empress, see *MTK*, 1:941-42.

21. Fujinami Kototada, "Eikoku teishitsu shorei torishirabesho" (ca. 1880s), collected in *Hisho ruisan kenpō shiryō*, ed. Itō Hirobumi (1935; Tokyo: Hara Shobō, 1970), 3:38.

22. *MTK*, 9:694-95, 793. Itō's leadership in drafting the law and designing Crown Prince Yoshihito's wedding was no secret. For example, Hijikata Hisamoto, vice-president of the Imperial Household Investigations Bureau, noted this fact in an interview for the *Chūō shinbun* on 18 May 1900. Even a writer for the English language weekly, *The Japan Weekly Mail*, noted on 19 May 1900 that Itō was responsible for creating the religious marriage ceremony.

23. Itō Hirobumi, "Gokamon hōtōan," collected in "Itōkō zassan," vol. 2.1, ed. Rinji Teishitsu Henshūkyoku, 1916, Shoryōbu, Imperial Household Agency, Tokyo.

24. Baelz, *Diary of a German Doctor*, 124.

25. *Miyako shinbun*, 10 May 1900. This was an advertisement for, of all things, a medicine for safe childbirth. It will be discussed in more detail in Chapter 4, in "The Politics of Gendering and the Gendering of Politics."

26. Fujinami's role in designing the carriage is noted in *Kōtaishi denka gokeiji—chiyo no iwai*, 13; for the quote, *Japan Weekly Mail*, 19 May 1900.

27. *Chūō shinbun*, 11 May 1900; *Kōtaishi denka gokeiji—chiyo no iwai*, 52-3; *Miyako shinbun*, 10 and 11 May 1900; *MTK*, 9:813. According to its official report, the Association for the Celebration of the Crown Prince's Wedding was a group founded by the wealthy businessman Shibusawa Eiichi, Tokyo Governor Senge Takatomi, and Tokyo Mayor Matsuda Hideo (Tōgū Gokeiji Hōshukukai zanmu jimusho, ed., "Tōgū gokeiji hōshukukai hōkoku" [1909], excerpted in *Shibusawa Eiichi denki shiryō*, ed. Ryūmonsha [Shibusawa Eiichi Denki Shiryō Kankōkai, 1959], 28:692).

28. *MTK*, 9:814.

29. *Kōtaishi denka gokeiji—chiyo no iwai*, 14-23, 53-56; for Okazaki, 54.

30. Tokyo Hyakunenshi Henshū Iinkai, ed., *Tōkyō hyakunenshi* (Tokyo: Tokyo-to, 1972), 3:932.

31. The quote is from the official record of the construction project, "Yasukuni jinja seido torii no ki," in *Shiryōhen*, vol. 1. of *Yasukuni jinja hyakunenshi*, ed. Yasukuni Jinja (Tokyo: Yasukuni Jinja, 1983), 525-26.

32. Tayama Katai, *Tōkyō no sanjūnen* (1917; Tokyo: Iwanami Shoten, 1981), 29.

33. The 1974 survey, "Zenkoku torii no takasa besuto ten," is collected in Yasukuni Jinja, ed., *Shiryōhen*, 560.

34. Maurice Agulhon, "Politics, Images, and Symbols in Post-Revolutionary France," in *Rites of Power*, ed. Sean Wilentz (Philadelphia: University of Pennsylvania Press, 1985), 185.

35. The *Kenchiku zasshi* article, "Dōzō" (no. 253 [January 1908]: 35-36), also carries a list of Tokyo's fifteen most prominent public bronze statues as of that time.

36. Ishii Kendō, *Meiji jibutsu kigen*, reprinted as *Meiji bunka zenshū*, supplement vol., ed. Meiji Bunka Kenkyūkai (Tokyo: Hyōronsha, 1969), 63. This book's title is somewhat ambiguous and could alternatively be translated *The Origins of Things in Meiji*. Ishii also notes that the first bronze of a woman was that of Uryū Iwako, an important Meiji social worker.

37. Ubukata Toshirō, *Meiji Taishō kenbunshi* (1926; Tokyo: Chūō Kōronsha, 1978), 107.

38. Yasukuni Jinja, ed., *Yasukuni jinjashi* (Tokyo: Yasukuni Jinja, 1911), 195.

39. Kobayashi Yasushige, *Ueno kōen* (Tokyo: Kyōgakusha, 1980), 112.

40. Maejima Yasuhiko, *Kōkyō gaien* (Tokyo: Kyōgakusha, 1981), 112–14.

41. The dismantling of public statuary is mentioned in Maejima, *Kōkyō gaien*, 114–15.

42. Identifying a "first" event is a risky affair. Aside from a broad reading in the newspapers, magazines, diaries, memoirs, and general histories listed in my bibliography, I have also consulted the following chronologies: Yamaguchi Osamu, ed., *Zusetsu nenpyō*, vol. 17 of *Meiji Taishō zushi*, ed. Asukai Masamichi et al. (Tokyo: Chikuma Shobō, 1978); Iwanami Shoten Henshūbu, ed., *Kindai Nihon sōgō nenpyō* (Tokyo: Iwanami Shoten, 1968); Fujii Sadafumi, ed., *Meiji tennō gonenpu* (Tokyo: Meiji Jingū Shamusho, 1963); Kuwata Tadachika, ed., *Nihonshi bunrui nenpyō* (Tokyo: Tokyo Shoseki Kabushikigaisha, 1984); Tokyo Hyakunenshi Henshū Iinkai, ed., *Tōkyō hyakunenshi—bekkan* (Tokyo: Gyosei, 1980).

43. *Jiji shinpō*, 11 December 1894; and the official record of the celebration, Tsuchida Seijirō, ed., *Tōkyō-shi shukushō taikai* (Tokyo: Tsuchida Seijirō, 1895).

44. These figures were taken or calculated from Yasukuni Shrine's most recent official list of enshrinements in Yasukuni Jinja, ed., *Shiryōhen*, 317–29.

45. Very slightly altered from a translation by D. C. Holtom in his *Modern Japan and Shinto Nationalism* (Chicago: University of Chicago Press, 1943), 50.

46. I have relied upon the charts compiled by Ōhama Tetsuya, "Eirei sūhai to tennōsei," in *Kindai to no kaikō*, vol 3. of *Nihonjin no shūkyō*, ed. Tamura Yoshio et al. (Tokyo: Kōsei Shuppansha, 1973), 174–75. Ōhama's data are derived from the late Meiji official history of Yasukuni, Yasukuni Jinja, ed., *Yasukuni jinjashi*.

47. The description of Tōgō's return is based on *Gaisen zue—daiippen*, a special issue of *Fūzoku gahō*, no. 328 (November 1905): 10–19; Tōgō's speech is reproduced in full on p. 18, as well as in *MTK*, 11:359–61; my translation is a slightly modified version of one in the *Japan Times*, 23 October 1905.

48. This translation is taken from the *Japan Weekly Mail*, 16 December 1905. The original report was carried widely in the media: for example, *Gaisen zue—daisanhen*, a special issue of *Fūzoku gahō*, no. 331 (January 1906): 24–25; it may also be found in *MTK*, 11:426–27.

49. *Japan Weekly Mail*, 1 June 1895.

50. Before returning to Tokyo, however, the emperor took his Supreme

Command to Kyoto. There, in the capital of his ancestors, he visited the Fourth National Industrial Exhibition, a place in the city of the national past where the Japanese people could celebrate their progress and power. Then two days prior to his departure he worshipped at the mausoleums of several imperial ancestors, most notably that of his father, Emperor Kōmei. Having thus associated himself with national glories of both the past and the present, he left for Tokyo on 29 May. See *MTK*, 8:785–86, 821, 824–25.

51. The information on the decorating of the city and the actual triumphal return is based on *Japan Weekly Mail*, 25 May and 1 June 1895; *Kokumin shinbun*, 31 May 1895; *Miyako shinbun*, 21 May 1895; *Tōkyō asahi shinbun*, 31 May 1895.

52. *Kokumin shinbun*, 31 May 1895.

53. *Japan Weekly Mail*, 1 June 1895.

54. *Gaisen zue—daiippen*, 20–35; *Japan Times*, 24 October 1905.

55. *Gaisen zue—daiippen*, 1.

56. For this description of the plaza construction project I have synthesized the partial accounts given in *Gaisen zue—daigohen*, a special issue of *Fūzoku gahō*, no. 340 (May 1906): 17–18; *Kokumin shinbun*, 14 April 1906; and Maejima, *Kōkyō gaien*, 50–54. The moat was also filled in on the northern side of the plaza at Ōtemachi, but this entrance could not be made immediately available for public use.

57. Fujimori Terunobu gives a very concise and evocative account of Edo's closed nature and some early measures to open up the city in the early Meiji years in *Meiji no Tōkyō keikaku* (Tokyo: Iwanami Shoten, 1982), 125–31; he does not, however, discuss the relation between the city's structure and public ritual.

58. The *Kokumin shinbun*'s history of the undertaking (14 April 1906) cites these two tragedies as the immediate reasons for the construction project.

59. *Gaisen zue—daigohen*, 18.

60. "Rikugun gaisen kanpeishiki shorui," collected in *Meiji gunjishi*, ed. Rikugunshō (Tokyo: Hara Shobō, 1965), 2:1572–73.

61. *Japan Weekly Mail*, 5 May 1906.

62. This description of the review is based upon *Gaisen zue—daigohen*, 7–15; *Kokumin shinbun*, 1 May 1906; *MTK*, 11:538–41; *Japan Times*, 30 April and 1 May 1906; *Japan Weekly Mail*, 5 May 1906. The number of troops in the review has been corroborated with "Rikugun gaisen kanpeishiki shorui," 1570–71.

63. "Rikugun gaisen kanpeishiki shorui," 1574.

64. *MTK*, 11:540; *Kokumin shinbun*, 1 May 1906.

65. "Rikugun gaisen kanpeishiki shorui," 1573–75.

66. These times are recorded in the *Japan Times*, 1 May 1900.

67. Yasukuni Jinja, ed., *Shiryōhen*, 320.

68. Murakami, *Kōshitsu jiten*, 41, 39–40.

69. This description of the military reviews is taken from the annual *rikugun hajime* and *tenchōsetsu* entrees in Kunaichō, *Meiji tennōki* (Tokyo: Yoshikawa Kōbunkan, 1968–77), vols. 7–12. There is no entry for *rikugun hajime* for 1898, so I have assumed that the ceremony was not conducted.

70. *Gaisen zue—daigohen.*

71. These postcards can be consulted in Hibata Sekko, *Nihon ehagaki shichō* (Tokyo: Nihon Yūken Kurabu, 1936), no page; for a written description, see 91–97. An original print of the photograph used for the Triumphal Military Review's commemorative postcard can be found in the Tokyo Metropolitan Central Library's "Tōkyō-shitsu" and is labeled "Sanjūshichi-hachinen sen'eki gaisen kanpeishiki."

72. Nihon Yūbin Kittesho Kyōdō Kumiai Katarogu Henshū Iinkai, ed., *1984 Nihon kitte katarogu,* 152; *Gaisen zue—daigohen,* 41–44; *Kokumin shinbun,* 25 April 1906.

73. Michel Foucault, "Two Lectures," in *Power/Knowledge: Selected Interviews and Other Writings,* ed. Colin Gordon (New York: Pantheon Books, 1980), 105. The concept of the "gaze" and the related notion of "visibility" are central to much of Foucault's work. The following characterization of Foucault's comparison of the disciplinary society that emerged in the eighteenth century with the monarchical society that preceded it is based primarily on his *Discipline and Punish: The Birth of the Prison* (trans. Alan Sheridan [New York: Random House, 1977]), and "The Eye of Power" (in *Power/Knowledge,* 146–65). Martin Jay's "In the Empire of the Gaze: Foucault and the Denigration of Vision in Twentieth-Century French Thought" (in *Foucault: A Critical Reader,* ed. David Couzens Hoy [London: Basil Blackwell, 1986], 175–204) is a learned and evocative consideration of Foucault's use of the terms "gaze" and "visibility." It puts Foucault's critique of vision within the context of the emergence of a general denigration of sight, an "anti-ocular discourse," in twentieth-century French thought. See also Jay's *Downcast Eyes: The Denigration of Vision in Twentieth-Century French Thought* (Berkeley: University of California Press, 1993), 381–434.

74. Foucault, *Discipline and Punish,* 192.

75. Foucault, "The Eye of Power," 148.

76. Foucault, *Discipline and Punish,* 193.

77. Ibid., 205.

78. Ibid., 200, 201.

79. Ibid., 187–89.

80. Ibid., 217. Foucault quotes J. B. Treilhard, *Motifs du code d'instruction criminelle* (1808).

81. All of the medical bulletins are collected in *Meiji tennō gotaisōgō,* a special issue of *Fūzoku gahō,* no. 438 (October 1912): 7–14.

82. Ibid., 37.

83. These details of the rites within the palace are based on *Meiji tennō gotaisōgō,* 36–43. For a concise explanation of these rites, see Ihara Yoriaki, *Kōshitsu jiten,* enlarged ed. (1942; Kyoto: Toyamabō, 1959), 247–49.

84. Tokyo Hyakunenshi Henshū Iinkai, ed., *Tōkyō hyakunenshi,* 2:1207–8.

85. Quoted in ibid., 1211.

86. Harry D. Harootunian, "Introduction: A Sense of Ending and the Problem of Taisho," in *Japan in Crisis: Essays on Taisho Democracy,* ed. Bernard S. Silberman and H. D. Harootunian (Princeton: Princeton University Press, 1974), 3–28.

87. Natsume Sōseki, *Kokoro*, trans. from the Japanese and with a foreword by Edwin McClellan (Chicago: Henry Regnery, 1957), 245; Tokutomi Sohō, quoted in Carol Gluck, *Japan's Modern Myths: Ideology in the Late Meiji Period* (Princeton: Princeton University Press, 1985), 220.

88. *Tōkyō asahi shinbun*, 23 July 1912.

89. *Tōkyō asahi shinbun*, 10 August 1912.

90. See, for example, *Tōkyō asahi shinbun*, 30 July 1912.

91. See, for example, *Meiji tennō gotaisōgō*, 14–25.

92. Petition of Yanagihara Sakimitsu to Iwakura Tomomi and Sanjō Sanetomi, "Teishitsu gishiki no gi," May 1882, handwritten copy in Teishitsu gokihon shorui, Shoryōbu, Tokyo.

93. *Meiji tennō gotaisōgō*, 81–82; Ihara Yoriaki, *Kōshitsu jiten*, 250.

94. The description of the ceremonies on the thirteenth is based on the *Japan Times*, 14 September 1912; *Tōkyō asahi shinbun*, 14 September 1912; *Meiji tennō gotaisōgō*.

95. Yamaori Tetsuo, "Tennō no sōsō girei to sokui girei," *Rekishi kōron*, no. 62 (January 1981): 148–52.

96. Sakamoto Ken'ichi, "Kōshitsu ni okeru shinbutsu bunri," in *Meiji ishin shintō hyakunenshi*, ed. Matsuyama Yoshio (Tokyo: Shinto Bunkakai, 1968), 4:191–254. James Edward Ketelaar's *Of Heretics and Martyrs in Meiji Japan* (Princeton: Princeton University Press, 1990) is excellent on the anti-Buddhist movement of the early Meiji years and the later reconstitution of Buddhism as a quintessential part of "Japanese culture."

97. *Gotaisō zue*, vols. 1 and 2, special issues of *Fūzoku gahō*, nos. 135 and 136 (February and March 1897).

98. The description of the ceremonies on the fourteenth and fifteenth are based on the *Japan Times*, 15 September 1912; *Tōkyō asahi shinbun*, 15 September 1912; *Meiji tennō gotaisōgō*.

99. *Tōkyō asahi shinbun*, 13 September 1912.

100. *Meiji tennō gotaisōgō*, 89, 97.

101. Tanaka Mitsuaki, a powerful official within the Imperial Household Ministry, gave the names of the people involved in the decision to build Emperor Meiji's mausoleum in Kyoto to his biographer, Tomita Kōjirō; see *Tanaka Seizanhaku* (Tokyo: Aoyama Shoin, 1917), 388–89.

Chapter 4. The Monarchy in Japan's Modernity

1. A man of many talents, Suematsu was the first to translate a significant portion of the *Tale of Genji* into English and also translated several works of English literature into Japanese. See *Daijinmei jiten* (Tokyo: Heibonsha, 1953), 3:426–27; Asahi Shinbunsha, ed., *Nihon rekishi jinbutsu jiten* (Tokyo: Asahi Shinbunsha, 1994).

2. This is the *hō* of *hōgyo*, a term reserved for members of the imperial family.

3. Suematsu Kenchō, "Eikoku teishitsu shorei kansatsu hōkoku," no. 1, 1881, Shoryōbu, Imperial Household Agency, Tokyo.

4. Ernst H. Kantorowicz, *The King's Two Bodies* (Princeton: Princeton University Press, 1957), and R. E. Giesey, *The Royal Funeral Ceremony in Renaissance France* (Geneva: Libraire E. Droz, 1960).

5. This is Kantorowicz (*The King's Two Bodies*, 7) quoting from Edmund Plowden's *Commentaries or Reports*. Plowden's collection was compiled during the reign of Elizabeth I.

6. Quoted in ibid., 13.

7. In E. E. Evans-Pritchard, *Social Anthropology and Other Essays* (New York: Free Press, 1962), 192–212. For an overview of primarily but not exclusively anthropological work on divine kingship see Gillian Feeley-Harnik, "Issues in Divine Kingship," *Annual Review of Anthropology* 14 (1985): 273–313.

8. Origuchi's argument was most fully articulated in his famous article "Daijōsai no hongi" (1928), collected in *Origuchi Shinobu zenshū* (Tokyo: Chūō Kōronsha, 1966), 3:174–240. On the "imperial spirit," see especially 188–98; for the quote, 194. For a fuller but still concise explication of Origuchi's argument concerning the "imperial spirit" and some critiques of it, see Akasaka Norio, *Ō to tennō* (Tokyo: Chikuma Shobō, 1988), 221–34.

9. The official English language translation of the Imperial House Law can be consulted in *Japanese Government Documents*, ed. W. W. McLaren (1914; Washington, D.C.: University Publications of America, Inc., 1979), 1:145–53. The quote is from "Daijōsai no hongi," 174–75.

10. Marius Jansen, "Monarchy and Modernization in Japan," *Journal of Asian Studies*, 36 (August 1977): 611–22; for quote, 616.

11. David Anson Titus, *Palace and Politics in Prewar Japan* (New York and London: Columbia University Press, 1974), 13–49; for a table showing number of outings and figures, 48–49.

12. For the creation of the shrines, Murakami Shigeyoshi, *Tennō no saishi* (Tokyo: Iwanami Shoten), 55–67; for the rites, 68–106, 157–61.

13. In the inaugural issue of the illustrated magazine *Fūzoku gahō*, 10 February 1889, 2.

14. Suematsu Kenchō, "Eikoku teishitsu shorei kansatsu hōkoku," no. 4, 1881, Shoryōbu, Imperial Household Agency, Tokyo.

15. Irokawa Daikichi, *The Culture of the Meiji Period*, translation ed. Marius Jansen (Princeton: Princeton University Press, 1985), 255–59.

16. Walter Bagehot, *The English Constitution* (1867; Ithaca: Cornell University Press, 1966), 85–86.

17. *Chūō shinbun*, 11 May 1900.

18. These figures are from a report presented by the Imperial Household Ministry to the Cabinet Records Bureau (Naikaku Kirokukyoku) on 18 November 1891, *Hōki bunrui taizen*, 2nd ed. (Tokyo: Naikaku Kirokukyoku, 1892), 1:38–39.

19. For Tokyo see, for example, *Jiji shinpō*, 10 February 1889.

20. *MTK*, 8:389.

21. Ibid., 7:215.

22. For a brief description of the Chichibu Incident, including passing references to Miyakawa, see Roger W. Bowen, *Rebellion and Democracy in Meiji Japan* (Berkeley: University of California Press, 1980), 49–67.

23. A fellow Shinto priest from the same region, Tanaka Sen'ya, copied the letter, the "admonitory notice," and another notice informing Miyakawa that he had been absolved of his crime into his diary (Tanaka Sen'ya, *Tanaka Sen'ya nikki*, ed. Ōmura Susumu et al. [Urawa: Saitama Shinbunsha Shuppankyoku, 1977], 459–60).

24. *Tōkyō nichinichi shinbun*, 9 February 1889.

25. Suematsu Kenchō, "Eikoku teishitsu shorei kansatsu hōkoku," no. 7, 1881, Shoryōbu, Imperial Household Agency, Tokyo.

26. This is a common view found even in two relatively recent works in English: Carol Gluck, *Japan's Modern Myths: Ideology in the Late Meiji Period* (Princeton: Princeton University Press, 1985), 45; Edward Seidensticker, *High City, Low City* (New York: Alfred A. Knopf, 1983), 94. But there is reason to doubt the view that the *banzai* cheer did not exist until the late Meiji period. Note, for example, the following passage from Maejima Hisoka's recommendation of 1868 to transfer the capital from Kyoto to Edo: "If the great and bold decision to transfer the capital to Edo is made, if an order to take the imperial palanquin to the East is sent down, immediately the frost and snow in the mountains and the valleys of Kantō and Ōshū will disappear and the breath of spring will fill the air. The people will cheer and with cries of *banzai* in the background, they will begin preparations to greet the imperial palanquin" (collected in *Edo kara Tokyo e no tenkai*, ed. Tokyo-to [Tokyo: Tokyo-to, 1953], 52).

27. *Osaka asahi shinbun*, 23 October 1905.

28. *Japan Weekly Mail*, 16 February 1889.

29. For some pathbreaking work on pre-Meiji imperial and shogunal portraits, see Kuroda Hideo, *Ōe no shintai—ō no shōzō* (Tokyo: Heibonsha, 1993), 180–306.

30. This print is part of the Tanba Collection at the Kanagawa Prefectural Museum of Cultural History and has been reproduced in *Nishikie ni miru Meiji tennō to Meiji jidai*, ed. Tanba Tsuneo (Tokyo: Asahi Shinbunsha, 1966), 41.

31. Tanba Collection, Kanagawa Prefectural Museum of Cultural History; also reproduced in Tanba, ed., *Nishikie ni miru*, 80.

32. Ernest Satow, *A Diplomat in Japan* (1921; Rutland, Vt., and Tokyo: Charles E. Tuttle, 1983), 391.

33. William Elliot Griffis, *The Mikado: Institution and Person* (Princeton: Princeton University Press, 1915), 198–99.

34. Sasaki Suguru, "Tennōzō no keisei katei," in *Kokumin bunka no keisei*, ed. Asukai Masamichi (Tokyo: Chikuma Shobō, 1984), 181.

35. Tanba Collection, Kanagawa Prefectural Museum of Cultural History; also reproduced in Tanba, ed., *Nishikie ni miru*, 56.

36. *Tōkyō nichinichi shinbun*, 9 February 1889.

37. Kanō Mikiyo, "'Omigokoro' to 'hahagokoro': 'Yasukuni no haha' o umidasu mono," in *Josei to tennōsei*, ed. Kanō Mikiyo (Tokyo: Shisō no Kagakusha, 1979), 64–81.

38. As Alice Yaeger Kaplan puts it: "We need to realize how dependent the phallic fascist is on mother-nation, mother-machine, mother-war. I concentrate on mother-bound rather than father-bound feelings in fascism not because the

father-bound doesn't exist, but because mother-bound feelings do not, as I write, have an established place in political theory" (*Reproductions of Banality: Fascism, Literature, and French Intellectual Life* [Minneapolis: University of Minnesota Press, 1986], 11).

39. George L. Mosse, *Nationalism and Sexuality* (Madison: University of Wisconsin Press, 1985), 23; and Maurice Agulhon, *Marianne into Battle,* trans. Janet Lloyd (Paris: Maison des Sciences de l'Homme; Cambridge: Cambridge University Press, 1981), 183. Together these authors make the additional and important point that to become legitimate national symbols these feminized symbols needed to be chaste and modest women consistent with bourgeois ideals of respectability. For the gendering of the nation as woman in modern Hungary, see Martha Lampland, "Family Portraits: Gendered Images of the Nation in Nineteenth-Century Hungary," *East European Politics and Societies* 8.2 (Spring 1994): 287–316.

40. Kuroda, *Ō no shintai—ō no shōzō,* 276–303, esp. 287–88.

41. Satow, *A Diplomat in Japan,* 371. Satow seems to have been especially fascinated by the emperor's cosmetically whitened face, for in a second audience with the Meiji emperor he again noted, "It was so dark that we could hardly distinguish his dress, but his face, which was whitened artificially, shone out brightly from the surrounding obscurity" (400–401).

42. Though the stress on masculinization is mine, the discussion in this paragraph owes much to Sasaki Suguru's informative description of Emperor Meiji's image in "Tennō zō no keisei katei," 185–206; for the quoted material, see 191.

43. My interpretation of these portraits owes much to Taki Kōji's brilliant history and reading of them in *Tennō no shōzō* (Tokyo: Iwanami Shoten, 1988), 113–22, 157–77.

44. Cited in W. G. Beasley, *The Meiji Restoration* (Stanford: Stanford University Press, 1972), 326.

45. Tanba Collection, Kanagawa Prefectural Museum of Cultural History; also reproduced in Tanba, ed., *Nishikie ni miru,* 68.

46. In my possession. As with many other woodblock prints, the event depicted was in some particulars different from the print representation. In the "actual" parade the carriage's cover had been taken down. These discrepancies, however, are not of concern for my analysis. The print depiction was as real as the parade itself.

47. D. C. Holtom, *The Japanese Enthronement Ceremonies* (1928; Tokyo: Sophia University, 1972), 64. Actually, Emperor Taishō's consort happened not to participate in the 1915 ceremony. However, in 1928 Emperor Hirohito's wife did take part in his *sokui* (Richard Ponsonby-Fane, "Enthronement Ceremonies," *The Imperial House of Japan* [Kyoto: Ponsonby Memorial Society, 1959], 357).

48. Griffis, *The Mikado,* 229–31.

49. Fujinami, "Eikoku teishitsu shorei torishirabesho" (ca. 1880s), collected in *Hisho ruisan kenpō shiryō,* ed. Itō Hirobumi (1935; Tokyo: Hara Shobō, 1970), 3:50.

50. Suematsu, "Eikoku teishitsu shorei kansatsu hōkoku," no. 7.

51. Carol Gluck identifies Tokutomi Sohō as an important *"minkan* ideologue," that is, one of the many ideologues "among the people" who played an important role in the formation of late-Meiji ideology even though they were not formally affiliated with the government. For the quote, which Gluck cites to make a different point, see *Japan's Modern Myths,* 82.

52. *Kōtaishi denka gokeiji—chiyo no iwai,* a special issue of *Fūzoku gahō,* no. 211 (June 1900): 1.

53. Quoted in Arichi Tōru, *Kindai Nihon no kazokukan—kindai hen* (Tokyo: Kōbundō, 1977), 132.

54. Ibid., 134.

55. Ibid., 136.

56. See for example, Sharon H. Nolte and Sally Ann Hastings, "The Meiji State's Policy toward Women, 1890–1910," in *Recreating Japanese Women, 1600–1945,* ed. Gail Lee Bernstein (Berkeley: University of California Press, 1991), 159–60.

57. *Daikon nijūgonen shukuten kiji,* a special issue of *Fūzoku gahō,* no. 71, (April 1894): 12.

58. *Kokumin shinbun,* 10 May 1900.

59. *Miyako shinbun,* 21 February 1894.

60. *Miyako shinbun,* 10 May 1900.

61. Arichi, *Kindai Nihon no kazokukan,* 32–41; Yuzawa Yasuhiko, "Nihon no rikon no jittai," in *Kon'in no kaishō,* vol. 4 of *Kōza kazoku,* ed. Aoyama Michio et al. (Tokyo: Kōbundō, 1974), 331–43.

62. Except for the average, these figures are from Yuzawa, "Nihon no rikon no jittai," 332; I have calculated the average based on his data.

63. I have calculated the Tokyo figures from the marriage and divorce data compiled by Ogi Shinzō in his *Tōkei shomin seikatsushi kenkyū* (Tokyo: Nihon Hōsō Shuppan Kyōkai, 1979), 290.

64. *Miyako shinbun,* 11 March 1894.

65. Yuzawa, "Nihon no rikon no jittai," 344.

66. Ibid., 331–50.

67. *Miyako shinbun,* 20 February 1894.

68. *Kokumin shinbun,* 9 March 1894.

69. *Daikon nijūgonen shukuten kiji,* a special issue of *Fūzoku gahō,* no. 71 (April 1894): 1–2.

70. *Chūō shinbun,* 10 May 1900.

71. *Kokumin shinbun,* 10 May 1900.

72. *Chūō shinbun,* 19 April 1900.

73. For an overview of the historical and regional diversity in customary marriage rites, see Matsuoka Toshio, "Kon'in seiritsu no girei," in *Kon'in no seiritsu,* vol. 3 of *Kōza kazoku,* ed. Aoyama Michio et al. (Tokyo: Kōbundō, 1973), 260–81.

74. Murakami, *Tennō no saishi,* 169.

75. It was not until the 1890s that ideologues introduced a clearly formulated idea of the nation-state as a family into primary-school ethics textbooks. An early textbook enunciating this concept, written by Higashikuze Michitomi, was approved for use in 1890. In it Higashikuze explained that because the

relationship between the Imperial Ancestors and the people was like that of a main family to a branch family, or like that between a father and child, "the righteousness (*gi*) between the ruler and his subjects and the intimacy between father and child are absolutely the same" (quoted in Itō Mikiharu, *Kazoku kokkakan no jinruigaku* [Tokyo: Mineruva, 1982], 9). On government-approved ethics textbooks, see Wilbur M. Fridell, "Government Ethics Textbooks in Late Meiji Japan," *Journal of Asian Studies* 29 (August 1970): 823–34.

76. There is no dearth of scholarship on both the development of the image of the nation as a family and the corresponding equation made between loyalty and filial piety (*chūkō ipponron* or *chūkō itchi*). Some of the most important works are Ishida Takeshi, *Meiji seiji shisōshi kenkyū* (Tokyo: Miraisha, 1954), 1–215; Kamishima Jirō, *Kindai Nihon no seishin kōzō* (Tokyo: Iwanami Shoten, 1961), 249–346; Matsumoto Sannosuke, "Kazoku kokkakan no kōzō to tokushitsu," in *Kazokukan no keifu—sōsakuin,* vol 8. of *Kōza kazoku,* ed. Aoyama Michio et al. (Tokyo: Kōbundō, 1974), 55–78. For a summary of the *kazoku kokkakan* literature and an anthropologist's attempt to understand why the ideology was accepted at the popular level, see Itō Mikiharu's book cited above, *Kazoku kokkakan no jinruigaku.*

77. Nolte and Hastings, "The Meiji State's Policy toward Women," 154–55.

78. Sharon L. Sievers, *Flowers in Salt* (Stanford: Stanford University Press, 1983), 14–15.

79. There is an enormous body of literature on these topics, but I shall mention only Joan Wallach Scott's particularly lucid and explicitly poststructuralist call for the use of gender as a category of historical analysis: *Gender and the Politics of History* (New York: Columbia University Press, 1988), esp. 1–50.

80. In the author's possession.

81. Here I part slightly with Taki Kōji, who emphasizes more the suprahistorical and timeless quality of the imperial portrait.

Chapter 5. Crowds and Imperial Pageantry

1. Tanaka Sen'ya, *Tanaka Sen'ya nikki,* ed. Ōmura Susumu et al. (Uruwa: Saitama Shinbunsha Shuppankyoku, 1977), 532. Tanaka wrote the words contained within the quotation marks in red.

2. Ubukata Toshirō, *Meiji Taishō kenbunshi* (1926; Tokyo: Chūō Kōronsha, 1978), 23–24.

3. *Miyako shinbun,* 15 December 1895.

4. *Kokumin shinbun,* 6 May 1906.

5. Aizawa Kikutarō, *Zoku Aizawa nikki* (Sagamigahara: Aizawa Yoshihisa, 1966), 216.

6. For Miyatake's own reflections on the incident, see his 1951 essay, "Kore honmyō nari," in *Yo wa kiken jinbutsu nari,* ed. Yoshino Takao (Tokyo: Chikuma Shobō, 1985), 51–55.

7. Yasumaru Yoshio, *Nihon no kindaika to minshū shisō* (Tokyo: Aoki Shoten, 1974), 124.

8. Murakami Shigeyoshi, *Nihon shūkyō jiten* (Tokyo: Kōdansha, 1978), 298–310.

9. Ibid., 378–86; Yasumaru Yoshio, *Deguchi Nao* (Tokyo: Asahi Shinbunsha, 1977). A useful summary in English of Deguchi Nao's life and thought is Emily Croszos Ooms, *Women and Millenarian Protest in Meiji Japan: Deguchi Nao and Ōmotokyō* (Ithaca: East Asia Program, Cornell University, 1993).

10. Ōe Shinobu, *Heishitachi no Nichiro sensō* (Tokyo: Asahi Shinbunsha, 1988).

11. For a classically Durkheimian analysis of a national ceremonial, see Edward Shils and Michael Young, "The Meaning of the Coronation" (1956), in *Center and Periphery: Essays in Macrosociology,* by Edward Shils (Chicago: University of Chicago Press, 1975), 135–52. Such an approach has long been criticized. For example, both Christel Lane (*Rites of Rulers* [Cambridge: Cambridge University Press, 1981]) and Steven Lukes ("Political Ritual and Social Integration," in his *Essays in Social Theory* [New York: Columbia University Press, 1977], 52–73) have pointed out that this mode of analysis presumes a high degree of social consensus and tends to minimize the existence of social conflicts.

12. Benedict Anderson, *Imagined Communities: Reflections on the Origins and Spread of Nationalism,* 2nd ed. (London: Verso, 1991), 22–36.

13. W. G. Beasley, *The Modern History of Japan* (New York and Washington, D.C.: Praeger Publishers, 1963), 146, 185; Kuwata Tadachika, ed., *Nihonshi bunrui nenpyō* (Tokyo: Tokyo Shoseki Kabushikigaisha, 1984), 253–56.

14. Ernest Gellner, *Nations and Nationalism* (Ithaca: Cornell University Press, 1983), 127.

15. For a powerful critique of recent theorists' neglect of the specific ideas of nationalists in the "non-West" see Partha Chatterjee, *Nationalist Thought and the Colonial World: A Derivative Discourse?* (London: Zed Books, 1986) and *The Nation and Its Fragments: Colonial and Postcolonial Histories* (Princeton: Princeton University Press, 1993).

16. *Jiji shinpō,* 12 February 1889.

17. *Yamato shinbun,* 15 February 1889.

18. *Daikon nijūgonen shukuten kiji,* a special issue of *Fūzoku gahō,* no. 71, (April 1894): 18; *Jiji shinpō,* 9 March 1894; *Kokumin shinbun,* 9 March 1894; *Miyako shinbun,* 9 March 1894; *Tōkyō asahi shinbun,* 11 March 1894.

19. *Jiji shinpō,* 10 March 1894.

20. On the triumph following the Sino-Japanese War, see for example *Kokumin shinbun,* 31 May 1895; on the crown prince's wedding, see for example *Chūō shinbun,* 9 May 1900, and *Kōtaishi denka gokeiji—chiyo no iwai,* a special issue of *Fūzoku gahō,* no. 211 (June 1900): 67; on the celebrations following the Russo-Japanese War, see for example *Kokumin shinbun,* 3 May 1906.

21. Nishigata Tamezō, *Setsugekka—Nishigata Tamezō kaikōroku,* ed. Honma Jun'ichi and Tanaka Toshimarō (Niigata-ken, Sanjō-shi: Nojima Shuppan, 1974), 501–2. This is a diary in the loose sense of the term since Nishigata compiled the work from his notes and diaries toward the end of his life.

22. Ōe Shinobu, *Yasukuni jinja* (Tokyo: Iwanami Shoten, 1984), 124–27.

23. Yamamoto Takeyoshi, *Kindai Nihon no shinbun dokushasō* (Tokyo: Hōsei Daigaku Shuppankyoku, 1981), 409.

24. Ibid., 404–7.

25. Ibid., 87–88.

26. *Jiji shinpō*, 11 and 12 February 1889.

27. Haruhara Akihiko, *Nihon shinbun tsūshi* (Tokyo: Shinsensha, 1985), 69–71.

28. Aizawa Kikutarō, *Aizawa nikki* (Sagamigahara: Aizawa Yoshihisa, 1965), 131–34. Making a mistake that suggests his unfamiliarity with the term "promulgation," Aizawa also noted that in his first entries he had erroneously written "distribution" (*hanpu*), for "promulgation" (*happu*), when referring to the promulgation of the Constitution.

29. *Jiji shinpō*, 12 February 1889.

30. *Saga shinbun*, 23 February 1889.

31. On Kyoto, see *Jiji shinpō*, 12 February 1889; for Ubukata's town, see Ubukata, *Meiji Taishō kenbunshi*, 23–24.

32. Aizawa, ed., *Zoku Aizawa nikki*, 55.

33. *Saga jiyū shinbun*, 11 March 1895.

34. *Saga shinbun*, 15 May 1900.

35. Ibid.

36. *Kōtaishi denka gokeiji—chiyo no iwai*, 83–84.

37. Ibid., 75.

38. Aizawa, ed., *Zoku Aizawa nikki*, 115.

39. *Tōō nippō* (Aomori), 31 May 1895.

40. Aizawa, ed., *Zoku Aizawa nikki*, 116.

41. Ibid., 127–28.

42. Kobayashi Kenzō and Terunuma Yoshibumi, *Shōkonsha seiritsushi no kenkyū* (Tokyo: Kinseisha, 1969), 79–86; Ōe, *Yasukuni jinja*, 160–72.

43. *Tōō nippō*, 7 May 1895.

44. This example is given in Ōe, *Yasukuni jinja*, 182.

45. See *Yūbin hōchi shinbun*, 10 February 1889, morning edition; "Kenpō happushiki goshidai," *Fūzoku gahō*, no. 2 (10 March 1889), illustration between pp. 4 and 5.

46. Quote from *Japan Weekly Mail*, 16 February 1889; *Yūbin hōchi shinbun*, 10 February 1889, morning edition.

47. For several reproductions of representative prints, see Tanba Tsuneo, ed., *Nishikie ni miru Meiji tennō to Meiji jidai* (Tokyo: Asahi Shinbunsha, 1966), 55–57, 76.

48. Shimizu Yoshirō, ed., *Kenpō happu taiten nigiwai* (Tokyo: Maki Kinnosuke, 1889).

49. For two reproductions of representative prints, see Tanba, ed., *Nishikie ni miru*, 59, 62. On the other commemorative articles: *Jiji shinpō*, 7 March 1894; *Kokumin shinbun*, 8 March 1894; *Tōkyō asahi shinbun*, 4 March 1894.

50. Mizoguchi Sennosuke, *Daikon man nijūgonen goshukuten shōhō* (Tokyo: Ijitsudō, 1894); *Ginkon goshiki taiten no keiji* (Tokyo: Chūaidō, 1894).

51. *Kōtaishi denka gokeiji—chiyo no iwai*, 25, 49, 70; *Chūō shinbun*, 29 April 1900.

52. Teikoku Shōnen Shiseikai, ed., *Kōtaishi denka gokeiji kinenchō* (Tokyo: Teikoku Shōnen Shiseikai, 1900); for the bylaws, 295–97.

53. *Tōō nippō*, 8 May 1900.

54. *Kōtaishi denka gokeiji—chiyo no iwai*, 70, 79, 89.

55. *Tōō nippō*, 9 May 1900.

56. *Kōtaishi denka gokeiji—chiyo no iwai*, 78.

57. *Tōō nippō*, 8 May 1900.

58. *Tōō nippō*, 15 May 1900.

59. Tōgū Gokeiji Hōshukukai Zanmu Jimusho, ed., "Tōgū gokeiji hōshukukai hōkoku" (1909), excerpted in *Shibusawa Eiichi denki shiryō*, ed. Ryūmonsha (Tokyo: Shibusawa Eiichi Denki Shiryō Kankōkai, 1959), 28:692–95, 717–19.

60. Ishii Kendō, *Meiji jibutsu kigen*, reprinted as *Meiji bunka zenshū*, supplement volume, ed. Meiji Bunka Kenkyūkai (Tokyo: Hyōronsha, 1969), 62–63.

61. *Tōō nippō*, 16 February 1889.

62. Yamamoto Nobuyoshi and Konno Toshihiko, *Kindai kyōiku no tennōsei ideorogii* (Tokyo: Shinsensha, 1973), 65–66.

63. The record of ceremonies is given in ibid., 108.

64. *Saga jiyū*, 13 March 1894.

65. Hirade Kōjirō, *Tōkyō fūzokushi* (1899–1902; Tokyo: Yasaka Shobō, 1975), 26–27.

66. *Yūbin hōchi shinbun*, 6 February 1889, morning edition.

67. *Tōkyō asahi shinbun*, 7 February 1889.

68. *Miyako shinbun*, 29 May 1895.

69. Prior to 1898 the governor of Tokyo Prefecture had served as the city's mayor and there had been no independent Tokyo City Office. The new Tokyo City Office opened in October 1898.

70. *Chūō shinbun*, 23 April 1900.

71. Tanaka, *Tanaka Sen'ya nikki*, 532–33.

72. *Kōtaishi denka gokeiji—chiyo no iwai*, 75.

73. *Yūbin hōchi shinbun*, 5 February 1889.

74. From its beginnings in 1901 to at least the early 1930s, the Women's Patriotic Association tended to be an elite organization which "never built a solid local base, and thus did not carry out systematic organizational and educational activities on the hamlet level" (Richard J. Smethurst, *A Social Basis for Prewar Japanese Militarism: The Army and the Rural Community* [Berkeley: University of California Press, 1974], 46–47).

75. For example, the instructions which the Ministry of War sent to survivors of the war dead, whose deceased would be enshrined in Yasukuni in May 1906, informed them that the Women's Patriotic Association would receive them at the shrine. A copy of this notice is contained in *Gaisen zue—daigohen*, a special issue of *Fūzoku gahō*, no. 340 (May 1906): 21–22.

76. These figures are from Yui Masaomi, "Joron—tōchi kikō no kakuritsu to 'kokumin soshiki' ka," in *Kindai Nihon no tōgō to teikō*, ed. Kano Masanao and Yui Masaomi (Tokyo: Nihon Hyōronsha, 1982), 2:45, 48.

77. Young men's associations and military reservists' associations have been the subject of considerable study. See, for example, Kenneth B. Pyle, "The

Technology of Japanese Nationalism: The Local Improvement Movement, 1900–1918," *Journal of Asian Studies* 33 (November 1973): 51–65; Smethurst, *Prewar Japanese Militarism;* Yui Masaomi, "Joron—tōchi kikō no kakuritsu to 'kokumin soshiki' ka," 44–49.

78. *Tōō nippō,* 20 September 1912.

79. *Saga shinbun,* 15 May 1900.

80. Hirade, *Tōkyō fūzokushi,* 75.

81. *Miyako shinbun,* 10 May 1900.

82. For example, Carol Gluck, *Japan's Modern Myths: Ideology in the Late Meiji Period* (Princeton: Princeton University Press, 1985), 45–49; Tokyo Hyakunenshi Henshū Iinkai, ed., *Tōkyō hyakunenshi* (Tokyo: Tokyo-to, 1972), 3:16–28.

83. *Yūbin hōchi shinbun,* 10 February 1889, morning edition.

84. *Yūbin hōchi shinbun,* 8 February 1889, morning edition.

85. *Tōkyō asahi shinbun,* 5 February 1889.

86. *Jiji shinpō,* 12 February 1889.

87. Erwin Baelz, *Awakening Japan: The Diary of a German Doctor,* ed. Toku Baelz (1932; Bloomington: Indiana University Press, 1974), 81–82. Baelz's comments have often been cited to point out popular ignorance concerning the Constitution.

88. *Jiji shinpō,* 10 February 1889.

89. *Yamato shinbun,* 12 February 1889.

90. See, for example, *Miyako shinbun,* 11 March 1894.

91. James H. Foard discusses the Saikoku pilgrimage circuit and its possible contribution to the development of a sense of national identity during the Tokugawa period in "The Boundaries of Compassion: Buddhism and National Tradition in Japanese Pilgrimage," *Journal of Asian Studies* 41 (February 1982): 231–51.

92. Nishigaki Seiji, *Oise mairi* (Tokyo: Iwanami Shoten, 1983), esp. 194–97, 208. Nishigaki also offers estimates of two million and four million for the number of pilgrims in 1771 and 1830, respectively.

93. *Miyako shinbun,* 11 May 1900.

94. For such reports, *Tōkyō asahi shinbun,* 4 November 1898; *Kokumin shinbun,* 4 November 1898. For a description of the traditional "Cock Fair," see Hirade, *Tōkyō fūzokushi,* 140.

95. *Kokumin shinbun,* 2 May 1906.

96. *Kokumin shinbun,* 6 May 1906.

97. *Kokumin shinbun,* 3 May 1906.

98. *Hinode shinbun,* 29 September 1912.

99. Letter of Yamanaka Fusatoyu and Sakamoto Chiyozō to the branch office of the Imperial Household Ministry's Bureau of Mauesoleums (Shoryō-ryō Shutchōsho), December 1912, handwritten copy in "Meiji tennō taisō-roku," Shoryōbu, Imperial Household Agency, Tokyo.

100. *Meiji tennō gotaisōgō,* a special issue of *Fūzoku gahō,* no. 438 (October 1912): 97.

101. *Tōkyō asahi shinbun,* 1 June 1895.

102. Watanabe Gintarō, *Gotaisō goshashinchō*, vol. 2 (Tokyo: Shinbashidō Shoten, 1912), unpaginated.

103. "Ippan haikansha kokoroe," *Meiji tennō gojunkōroku*, ed. Fukushima-ken Kyōikukai (Fukushima: Fukushima-shi, 1936), 16–17.

104. Displays of such signs for long life, prosperity, conjugal harmony, and fertility could be found throughout the country for both the twenty-fifth wedding anniversary and the Crown Prince's wedding. See, for example, *Daikon nijūgonen shukuten kiji*, 16–18; *Kōtaishi denka gokeiji—chiyo no iwai*, 60–116.

105. *Saga jiyū shinbun*, 11 March 1894.

106. *Miyako shinbun*, 25 February 1894.

107. *Tōkyō asahi shinbun*, 8 March 1894.

108. I have begun to explore the military barracks as such disciplinary institutions in "Kindai Nihon ni okeru kenryoku no tekunorojii: guntai, 'chihō,' shintai," trans. Umemori Naoyuki, *Shisō*, no. 845 (November 1994): 163–76.

Chapter 6. Epilogue: Toward a History of the Present

1. Michel Foucault, "Two Lectures," in *Power/Knowledge: Selected Interviews and Other Writings*, ed. Colin Gordon (New York: Pantheon Books, 1980), 82. I do not mean to suggest that culture became completely homogenized in modern Japan. Since homogenization was an impossibility, Japanese nationalism, like successful nationalisms elsewhere, needed to foster the belief that the nation-state could countenance some degree of cultural pluralism. This contradiction in nationalism heightened as increasing numbers of heterogeneous populations became incorporated into the Japanese empire. The point here, however, concerns the subordination of the heterogeneous to the idea of national unity.

2. Mishima Yukio, "Bunka bōeiron" (1968), in *Mishima Yukio zenshū* (Tokyo: Shinchōsha, 1976), 33:363–401.

3. For the classic statement on postmodernism see Fredric Jameson, "Postmodernism, or the Cultural Logic of Late Capitalism," *New Left Review*, no. 146 (July–August 1984): 53–92. For postmodernism in Japan see Masao Miyoshi and H. D. Harootunian, eds., *Postmodernism and Japan* (Durham, N.C.: Duke University Press, 1989).

4. For a critique of Watsuji's thinking on this point see Naoki Sakai, "Seiyō e no kaiki/tōyō e no kaiki: Watsuji Tetsurō no ningengaku to tennōsei," *Shisō*, no. 797 (November 1990): 102–36.

5. Mishima, "Bunka bōeiron," 375.

6. On the accession ceremonies, see D. C. Holtom, *The Japanese Enthronement Ceremonies* (1928; Tokyo: Sophia University, 1972), esp. 45–111.

7. *Tōkyō asahi shinbun*, 10 August 1912.

8. Uchiyama Masao and Minomo Toshitarō, *Yoyogi no mori* (Tokyo: Kyōgakusha, 1981), 3, 36–37.

9. Kanō Mikiyo, "'Ittō kokumin' banzai!?" *Inpakshon*, no. 66 (10 October 1990): 13–14.

10. This personal account was given by Fujita Yoshinobu in *Asahi shinbun*, 10 November 1990.

11. Kanō Mikiyo, "'Ittō kokumin' banzai!?" 13–14.

12. Taigakai, ed., *Naimushōshi* (Tokyo: Chihō Zaimu Kyōkai, 1971), 770–71.

13. Kodama Kōta, ed., *Tennō* (Tokyo: Kondō Shuppansha, 1978), 135.

14. *Nippon Times*, 3 November 1946.

15. For an indication of the nature of the debate over the palace's rebuilding, see Nakajima Usaburō, *Kōjō* (Tokyo: Yūzankaku, 1959), 239–47.

16. The interviews are reproduced in Tsurumi Shunsuke and Nakagawa Roppei, eds., *Tennō hyakuwa* (Tokyo: Chikuma Shobō, 1989), 2:632–39.

17. Ibid., 529–30.

18. See John W. Dower, *Empire and Aftermath: Yoshida Shigeru and the Japanese Experience, 1878–1954* (Cambridge, Mass., and London: Council on East Asian Studies, Harvard University, 1979).

19. Quoted in Watanabe Osamu, *Sengo seijishi no naka no tennōsei* (Tokyo: Aoki Shoten, 1990), 182.

20. *Nippon Times*, 22 and 23 June 1951.

21. *Nippon Times*, 30 May 1951 and 2 June 1951.

22. Mishima, "Bunka bōeiron," 398.

23. Kamei Jun, *Kōshitsu hōdō no yomikata* (Tokyo: Iwanami Shoten, 1990), 14.

24. John W. Dower, *Japan in War and Peace* (New York: New Press, 1993), 101–54; for the quote, 126.

25. Kitahara Taisaku, *Senmin no kōei* (Tokyo: Chikuma Shobō, 1974), 134. In English, Mikiso Hane has introduced Kitahara in *Peasants, Rebels, and Outcastes: The Underside of Modern Japan* (New York: Pantheon Books, 1982), 163–71.

26. Kanō Mikiyo, "'Omigokoro' to 'hahagokoro': 'Yasukuni no haha' o umidasu mono," in *Josei to tennōsei*, ed. Kanō Mikiyo (Tokyo: Shisō no Kagakusha, 1979), 64–81.

27. Kanō Mikiyo, "'Ittō kokumin' banzai!?" 15–16.

28. Murakami Shigeyoshi, *Kōshitsu jiten* (Tokyo: Tōkyōdō Shuppan, 1980), 16.

29. The classic statement on the movie star–like quality of the postwar imperial household is Matsushita Keiichi, "Taishū tennōseiron" (1959), in *Tennōsei ronshū*, ed. Kuno Osamu and Kamishima Jirō (Tokyo: San'ichi Shobō, 1974), 1:282–90. I have written more extensively on the current monarchy's relationships with television, voyeurism, the culture of late capitalism, and contemporary politics in "Electronic Pageantry and Japan's 'Symbolic' Emperor," *Journal of Asian Studies* 51 (November 1992): 824–50.

30. See Fujitani, "Electronic Pageantry."

Bibliography

Manuscripts and Manuscript Collections

Itō Hirobumi monjo. Kensei Shiryōshitsu, National Diet Library, Tokyo.
Itō Hirobumi. "Gokamon hōtōan." In "Itōkō zassan." Vol. 2.1, edited by
   Rinji Teishitsu Henshūkyoku. 1916. Shoryōbu, Imperial Household
   Agency, Tokyo.
"Kakkoku kinginkonshiki torishiraberoku." 1893. Shoryōbu, Imperial
   Household Agency, Tokyo.
"Kenpō happushikiroku." 1889. Shoryōbu, Imperial Household Agency,
   Tokyo.
Kōkyo Gozōeishi Hensangakari, ed. "Kōkyo gozōeishi." 1892. Shoryōbu,
   Imperial Household Agency, Tokyo.
"Meiji tennō taisōroku." 1912. Shoryōbu, Imperial Household Agency,
   Tokyo.
Rinji Teishitsu Seido Torishirabekyoku shorui. Shoryōbu, Imperial
   Household Agency, Tokyo.
Sanjō-ke monjo. Kensei Shiryōshitsu, National Diet Library, Tokyo.
Suematsu Kenchō. "Eikoku teishitsu shorei kansatsu hōkoku." 1881.
   Shoryōbu, Imperial Household Agency, Tokyo.
Teishitsu gokihon shorui. Shoryōbu, Imperial Household Agency, Tokyo.
Yanagihara Sakimitsu. "Sueden koku kōtei heika ginkonshiki." 1882.
   Shoryōbu, Imperial Household Agency, Tokyo.

Newspapers and Magazines

NATIONAL DIET LIBRARY, TOKYO

Chūō shinbun (Tokyo, 1900).
Hinode shinbun (Kyoto, 1912).

Japan Times (Tokyo, 1900–12).
Japan Weekly Mail (Tokyo, 1889–1906).
Jiji shinpō (Tokyo, 1889–94).
Kokumin shinbun (Tokyo, 1894–1906).
Miyako shinbun (Tokyo, 1894–1900).
Osaka asahi shinbun (Osaka, 1905).
Saga jiyū shinbun (Saga, 1894–95).
Saga shinbun (Saga, 1889–1900).
Tōkyō asahi shinbun (Tokyo, 1889–1912).
Tōkyō nichinichi shinbun (Tokyo, 1889).
Tōō nippō (Aomori, 1889–1912).
Yamato shinbun (Tokyo, 1889).
Yūbin hōchi shinbun (Tokyo, 1889).

HOOVER INSTITUTION ON WAR, REVOLUTION AND PEACE,
STANFORD UNIVERSITY

Nippon Times (Tokyo, 1946 and 1951).

HITOTSUBASHI UNIVERSITY LIBRARY, TOKYO

Fūzoku gahō (Tokyo, 1888–1912).
Taiyō (Tokyo, 1898).

Collections, Commemorative Literature, Diaries, Official Publications or Records, Reminiscences, and Other Meiji Period Sources

Aizawa Kikutarō. *Aizawa nikki*. Sagamigahara: Aizawa Yoshihisa, 1965.
———. *Zoku Aizawa nikki*. Sagamigahara: Aizawa Yoshihisa, 1966.
Baelz, Erwin. *Awakening Japan: The Diary of a German Doctor*. Edited by Toku Baelz. 1932. Reprint, Bloomington: Indiana University Press, 1974.
Bird, Isabella L. *Unbeaten Tracks in Japan: An Account of Travels on Horseback in the Interior*. 2 vols. New York: G. P. Putnam and Sons, 1880.
Chamberlain, B. H. *The Invention of a New Religion*. London: Watts and Co., 1912.
The City Council of Kyoto. *The Official Guide-Book to Kyoto and the Allied Prefectures*. Nara: Meishinsha, 1895.
Daikon nijūgonen shukuten kiji. A special issue of *Fūzoku gahō*, no. 71 (April 1894).
"Dōzō." *Kenchiku zasshi*, no. 253 (January 1908): 35–36.
Fujinami Kototada. "Eikoku teishitsu shorei torishirabesho" (ca. 1880s). Collected in *Hisho ruisan kenpō shiryō*, edited by Itō Hirobumi. Vol. 3. 1935. Reprint, Tokyo: Hara Shobō, 1970.

Fujita, Yoshinobu. "'Sokui no rei' o watashi wa hōsō shita." *Asahi shinbun*, 10 November 1990.

Fukushima-ken Kyōikukai, ed. *Meiji tennō gojunkōroku*. Fukushima: Fukushima-shi, 1936.

Fukuzawa Yukichi, "Shufu kaizō to kōkyo gozōei to" (1883). In *Fukuzawa Yukichi zenshū*, edited by Keiōgijuku. Vol. 9. Tokyo: Iwanami Shoten, 1960.

Gaisen zue—daigohen. A special issue of *Fūzoku gahō*, no. 340 (May 1906).

Gaisen zue—daiippen. A special issue of *Fūzoku gahō*, no. 328 (November 1905).

Gaisen zue—daisanhen. A special issue of *Fūzoku gahō*, no. 331 (January 1906).

Ginkon goshiki taiten no keiji. Tokyo: Chūaidō, 1894.

Gotaisō zue. Vols. 1 and 2. Special issues of *Fūzoku gahō*, nos. 135 and 136 (February and March 1897).

Griffis, William Elliot. *The Mikado: Institution and Person*. Princeton: Princeton University Press, 1915.

Heian Sento Kinensai Kyōsankai. *Heian jingū jidai matsuri gyōretsu zufu*. Kyoto: Murakami Shoten, 1895.

Hirade Kōjirō. *Tōkyō fūzokushi*. 1899–1902. Reprint, Tokyo: Yasaka Shobō, 1975.

Ikeda Terusuke. *Kenpō happushiki haikan gaikyō*. Chiba-ken: Shūeisha, 1889.

Itō Hirobumi. "Teishitsu seido kakuritsu no kyūmu" (1889). In *Zoku Itō Hirobumi hiroku*, edited by Hiratsuka Atsushi. Tokyo: Shunjusha, 1930.

Iwakura Tomomi. *Iwakura Tomomi kankei monjo*. Edited by Ōtsuka Takematsu. 8 vols. Tokyo: Nihon Shiseki Kyōkai, 1927–35.

Kido Takayoshi. *The Diary of Kido Takayoshi*. Translated by Akiko Hirota and Sidney Devere Brown. Tokyo: University of Tokyo Press, 1983.

Kinoshita Naoe. *Zange*. In *Kinoshita Naoe chosakushū*. Vol. 5. Tokyo: Meiji Bunken, 1968.

Kitahara Taisaku. *Senmin no kōei*. Tokyo: Chikuma Shobō, 1974.

Kojiruien. Teiōbu 1. Tokyo: Kojiruien Kankōkai, 1932.

Kōno Kōzaburō. *Tōgū gokeijiroku*. Hiroshima: Kōno Kōzaburō, 1900.

Kōtaishi denka gokeiji—chiyo no iwai. A special issue of *Fūzoku gahō*, no. 211 (June 1900).

Kunaichō. *Meiji tennōki*. 14 vols. Tokyo: Yoshikawa Kōbunkan, 1968–77.

McLaren, W. W., ed. *Japanese Government Documents*. Vol. 1. 1914. Reprint, Washington, D.C.: University Publications of America, 1979.

Meiji Bunka Kenkyūkai, ed. *Meiji bunka zenshū*. 31 vols. Tokyo: Hyōronsha, 1967–74.

Meiji Jingū Gaien, ed. *Seitoku kinen kaigakan hekiga*. Tokyo: Meiji Jingu Gaien, 1981.

Meiji tennō gotaisōgō. A special issue of *Fūzoku gahō*, no. 438 (October 1912).

Miyatake Gaikotsu. "Kore honmyō nari" (1951). In *Yo wa kiken jinbutsu nari*, edited by Yoshino Takao. Tokyo: Chikuma Shobō, 1985.

Mizoguchi Sennosuke. *Daikon man nijūgonen goshukuten shōhō*. Tokyo: Ijitsudō, 1894.

Naikaku Kirokukyoku, ed. *Hōki bunrui taizen*. 2nd ed. Tokyo: Naikaku Kirokukyoku, 1892.

Nakamura Tatsutarō. "Kōkyo gozōei no koro." *Kenchiku zasshi*, no. 601 (July 1935): 114–28.

Nishigata Tamezō. *Setsugekka—Nishigata Tamezō kaikōroku*. Edited by Honma Jun'ichi and Tanaka Toshimaro. Niigata-ken, Sanjō-shi: Nojima Shuppan, 1974.

Ōkubo Toshimichi. *Ōkubo Toshimichi monjo*. Edited by Nihon Shiseki Kyōkai. 10 vols. Tokyo: Nihon Shiseki Kyōkai, 1927–29.

———. *Ōkubo Toshimichi nikki*. Edited by Nihon Shiseki Kyōkai. 2 vols. Tokyo: Nihon Shiseki Kyōkai, 1927.

Rikugunshō, ed. *Meiji gunjishi*. 2 vols. Tokyo: Hara Shobō, 1965.

Satow, Ernest. *A Diplomat in Japan*. 1921. Reprint, Rutland, Vt., and Tokyo: Charles E. Tuttle Company, 1983.

Shimizu Yoshiro, ed. *Kenpō happu taiten nigiwai*. Tokyo: Maki Kinnosuke, 1889.

Sūmitsuin kaigi gijiroku. Vols. 1 and 2. Tokyo: Tokyo Daigaku Shuppankai, 1984.

Tanaka Sen'ya. *Tanaka Sen'ya nikki*, edited by Ōmura Susumu et al. Urawa: Saitama Shinbunsha Shuppankyoku, 1977.

Tanigawa Ken'ichi, ed. *Nihon shomin seikatsu shiryō shūsei*. Vol. 13. Tokyo: San'ichi Shobō, 1970.

Tayama Katai. *Literary Life in Tokyo, 1885–1915*. Translated with full annotations by Kenneth G. Henshall. Leiden: E. J. Brill, 1987.

———. *Tōkyō no sanjūnen*. 1917. Reprint, Tokyo: Iwanami Shoten, 1981.

Teikoku Shōnen Shiseikai, ed. *Kōtaishi denka gokeiji kinenchō*. Tokyo: Teikoku Shōnen Shiseikai, 1900.

Tento. A special issue of *Taiyō* 4 (1898).

Tento sanjūnensai zue. A special issue of *Fūzoku gahō*, no. 163 (April 1898).

Tōgū Gokeiji Hōshukukai Zanmu Jimusho, ed. "Tōgū gokeiji hōshukukai hōkoku" (1909). Excerpted in *Shibusawa Eiichi denki shiryō*, edited by Ryūmonsha. Vol. 28. Tokyo: Shibusawa Eiichi Denki Shiryō Kankōkai, 1959.

Tōyama Shigeki, ed. *Tennō to kazoku*. Tokyo: Iwanami Shoten, 1988.

Tsuchida Seijirō, ed. *Tōkyo-shi shukushō taikai*. Tokyo: Tsuchida Seijirō, 1895.

Tsurumi Shunsuke and Nakagawa Roppei, eds. *Tennō hyakuwa*. 2 vols. Tokyo: Chikuma Shobō, 1989.

Ubukata Toshirō. *Meiji Taishō kenbunshi*. 1926. Reprint, Tokyo: Chūō Kōronsha, 1978.

Watanabe Gintarō. *Gotaisō goshashinchō*. Vol. 2. Tokyo: Shinbashidō Shoten, 1912.

Yasukuni Jinja, ed. *Shiryōhen*. Vol. 1 of *Yasukuni jinja hyakunenshi*. Tokyo: Yasukuni Jinja, 1983.

———. ed. *Yasukuni jinjashi*. Tokyo: Yasukuni Jinja, 1911.

Post-1914 Sources in Japanese

Akamatsu Toshihide and Yamamoto Shirō. *Kyōto-fu no rekishi*. Tokyo: Yamakawa Shuppansha, 1969.

Akasaka Norio. *Ō to tennō*. Tokyo: Chikuma Shobō, 1988.

———. *Shōchō tennō to iu monogatari*. Tokyo: Chikuma Shobō, 1990.

Amino Yoshihiko. *Nihon chūsei no hinōgyōmin to tennō*. Tokyo: Iwanami Shoten, 1984.

———. *Nihon shakai to tennōsei*. Tokyo: Iwanami Shoten, 1988.

Amino Yoshihiko, Ueno Chizuko, and Miyata Noboru. *Nihon ōkenron*. Tokyo: Shunjusha, 1988.

Arichi Tōru. *Kindai Nihon no kazokukan—kindai hen*. Tokyo: Kōbundō, 1977.

Ariizumi Sadao. "Meiji kokka to shukusaijitsu." *Rekishigaku kenkyū*, no. 341 (October 1981): 61–70.

Asahi Shinbunsha, ed. *Nihon rekishi jinbutsu jiten*. Tokyo: Asahi Shinbunsha, 1994.

Daijinmei jiten. Tokyo: Heibonsha, 1953.

Fujii Sadafumi, ed. *Meiji tennō gonenpu*. Tokyo: Meiji Jingū Shamusho, 1963.

Fujimori Terunobu. *Meiji no Tōkyō keikaku*. Tokyo: Iwanami Shoten, 1982.

Fujitani, T. "Kindai Nihon ni okeru gunshū to tennō no pējento: shikakuteki shihai ni kansuru jakkan no kōsatsu," translated by Yoshimi Shun'ya. *Shisō*, no. 797 (November 1990): 148–64.

———. "Kindai Nihon ni okeru kenryoku no tekunorojii: guntai, 'chihō,' shintai," translated by Umemori Naoyuki. *Shisō*, no. 845 (November 1994): 163–76.

———. "Kindai Nihon ni okeru kokka-teki ibento no tanjō—1889–1912 no Tōkyō." *Yasō* 14 (February 1985): 126–40.

———. *Tennō no pējento*, translated by Lisa Yoneyama. Tokyo: Nihon Hōsō Shuppan Kyōkai, 1994.

Fukaya Katsumi. "Kinsei no shōgun to tennō." In *Kōza Nihonshi*, edited by Rekishigaku Kenkyūkai and Nihonshi Kenkyūkai. Vol. 6. Tokyo: Tokyo Daigaku Shuppankai, 1985.

Haruhara Akihiko. *Nihon shinbun tsūshi*. Tokyo: Shinsensha, 1985.

Hibata Sekko. *Nihon ehagaki shichō*. Tokyo: Nihon Yūken Kurabu, 1936.

Hirota Masaki. "Kindai tennōsei to sabetsu." In *Tennōsei o tou*, edited by Nihonshi Kenkyūkai and Kyoto Minka Rekishi Bukai. Tokyo: Jinbun Shoin, 1990.

Horikoshi Saburō. *Meiji shoki no yōfū kenchiku*. Tokyo: Maruzen, 1929.

Ihara Yoriaki. *Kōshitsu jiten*. Enlarged ed. 1942. Reprint, Kyoto: Toyamabō, 1959.

Inada Masatsugu. *Meiji kenpō seiritsushi*. Vol. 2. Tokyo: Yūhikaku, 1962.

Inose Naoki. *Mikado no shōzō*. Tokyo: Shōgakkan, 1986.

Irokawa Daikichi. *Kindai kokka e no shuppatsu*. Tokyo: Chūō Kōronsha, 1974.

Ishida Takeshi. *Meiji seiji shisōshi kenkyū*. Tokyo: Miraisha, 1954.

Itō Mikiharu. *Kazoku kokkakan no jinruigaku*. Tokyo: Mineruva, 1982.

Iwanami Shoten Henshūbu, ed. *Kindai Nihon sōgō nenpyō*. Tokyo: Iwanami Shoten, 1968.

Kamei Jun. *Kōshitsu hōdō no yomikata*. Tokyo: Iwanami Shoten, 1990.

Kamishima Jirō. *Kindai Nihon no seishin kōzō*. Tokyo: Iwanami Shoten, 1961.

Kano Masanao. "Joron—tōchi taisei no keisei to chiiki." In *Kindai Nihon no tōgō to teikō*, edited by Kano Masanao and Yui Masaomi. Vol. 1. Tokyo: Nihon Hyōronsha, 1982.

Kanō Mikiyo. "'Ittō kokumin' banzai!?" *Inpakshon*, no. 66 (10 October 1990): 6–18.

———. "'Omigokoro' to 'hahagokoro': 'Yasukuni no haha' o umidasu mono." In *Josei to tennōsei*, edited by Kanō Mikiyo. Tokyo: Shisō no Kagakusha, 1979.

Kobayashi Kenzō and Terunuma Yoshibumi. *Shōkonsha seiritsushi no kenkyū*. Tokyo: Kinseisha, 1969.

Kobayashi Yasushige. *Ueno kōen*. Tokyo: Kyōgakusha, 1980.

Kodama Kōta, ed. *Tennō*. Tokyo: Kondō Shuppansha, 1978.

Konishi Shirō, ed. *Nishikie: Bakumatsu Meiji no rekishi*. Vol. 5. Tokyo: Kōdansha, 1977.

Konsaisu jinmei jiten: Nihon-hen. Tokyo: Sanseidō, 1976.

Kuroda Hideo. *Ō no shintai—ō no shōzō*. Tokyo: Heibonsha, 1993.

Kuwata Tadachika, ed. *Nihonshi bunrui nenpyō*. Tokyo: Tokyo Shoseki Kabushikigaisha, 1984.

Kyoto Furitsu Sōgō Shiryōkan, ed. *Kyōto-fu hyakunen no shiryō*. Vol. 2. Kyoto: Kyoto-fu, 1972.

Kyoto-shi. *Kamigyō-ku*. Vol. 7 of *Shiryō kyōto no rekishi*. Tokyo: Heibonsha, 1980.

Maejima Yasuhiko. *Kōkyo gaien*. Tokyo: Kyōgakusha, 1981.

Matsumoto Sannosuke. "Kazoku kokkakan no kōzō to tokushitsu." In *Kazokukan no keifu—sōsakuin*. Vol. 8 of *Kōza kazoku*, edited by Aoyama Michio et al. Tokyo: Kōbundō, 1974.

Matsuoka Toshio. "Kon'in seiritsu no girei." In *Kon'in no seiritsu*. Vol. 3 of *Kōza kazoku*, edited by Aoyama Michio et al. Tokyo: Kōbundō, 1973.

Matsushita Keiichi. "Taishū tennōseiron" (1959). In *Tennōsei ronshū*, edited by Kuno Osamu and Kamishima Jirō. Vol. 1. Tokyo: San'ichi Shobō, 1974.

Minato Kuyakusho, ed. *Shinshū Minatokushi*. Tokyo: Minato Kuyakusho, 1979.

Mishima Yukio. "Bunka bōeiron" (1968). In *Mishima Yukio zenshū*. Vol. 33. Tokyo: Shinchōsha, 1976.

Miura Hisashi. "Nakasone naikaku ni teishutsu shita 'tennō oyobi tennōsei ni kansuru shitsumon shuisho.'" In *Tennōsei no genzai to kōtaishi,* edited by Nihon Kyōsantō Chūō Iinkai Shuppankyoku. Tokyo: Nihon Kyōsantō Chūō Iinkai Shuppankyoku, 1988.

Miyata Noboru. *Ikigami shinkō.* Tokyo: Haniwa Shobō, 1970.

———. *Minzoku shūkyōron no kadai.* Tokyo: Miraisha, 1977.

Murai Masuo. *Edo-jō.* Tokyo: Chūō Kōronsha, 1964.

Murakami Shigeyoshi. *Irei to shōkon.* Tokyo: Iwanami Shoten, 1974.

———. *Kokka shintō.* Tokyo: Iwanami Shoten, 1970.

———. *Kōshitsu jiten.* Tokyo: Tōkyōdō Shuppan, 1980.

———. *Nihon shūkyō jiten.* Tokyo: Kōdansha, 1978.

———. *Tennō no saishi.* Tokyo: Iwanami Shoten, 1977.

Nakajima Usaburō. *Kōjō.* Tokyo: Yūzankaku, 1959.

Nihon Yūbin Kittesho Kyōdō Kumiai Katarogu Henshū Iinkai, ed. *1984 Nihon kitte katarogu* Tokyo: Nihon Yūbin Kittesho Kyōdō Kumiai, 1984.

Nishigaki Seiji. *Oise mairi.* Tokyo: Iwanami Shoten, 1983.

Obinata Sumio. "Tennō junkō o meguru minshū no dōkō." *Chihōshi kenkyū* 32 (February 1982): 1–16.

Ōe Shinobu. *Heishitachi no Nichiro sensō.* Tokyo: Asahi Shinbunsha, 1988.

———. *Yasukuni jinja.* Tokyo: Iwanami Shoten, 1984.

Ogi Shinzō. *Tōkei jidai.* Tokyo: Nihon Hōsō Shuppan Kyōkai, 1980.

———. *Tōkei shomin seikatsushi kenkyū.* Tokyo: Nihon Hōsō Shuppan Kyōkai, 1979.

Ōhama Tetsuya. "Eirei sūhai to tennōsei." In *Kindai to no kaikō.* Vol. 3 of *Nihonjin no shūkyō,* edited by Tamura Yoshio et al. Tokyo: Kōsei Shuppansha, 1973.

Okada Yoneo. "Jingū-jinja sōkenshi." In *Meiji ishin shintō hyakunenshi,* edited by Matsuyama Yoshio. Vol. 2. Tokyo: Shintō Bunkakai, 1966.

Origuchi Shinobu. "Daijōsai no hongi" (1928). In *Origuchi Shinobu zenshū.* Vol. 3. Tokyo: Chūō Kōronsha, 1966.

Rekishi Kyōikusha Kyōgikai, ed. *Shinpan hinomaru, kimigayo kigensetsu, kyōiku chokugo.* Tokyo: Chirekisha, 1981.

Sakai Naoki. "Seiyō e no kaiki/tōyō e no kaiki: Watsuji Tetsurō no ningengaku to tennōsei." *Shisō,* no. 797 (November 1990): 102–36.

Sakamoto Ken'ichi. "Kōshitsu ni okeru shinbutsu bunri." In *Meiji ishin shintō hyakunenshi,* edited by Matsuyama Yoshio. Vol. 4. Tokyo: Shinto Bunkakai, 1968.

Sasaki Junnosuke, ed. *Yonaoshi.* Tokyo: Sanseidō, 1974.

Sasaki Suguru. "Tennōzō no keisei katei." In *Kokumin bunka no keisei,* edited by Asukai Masamichi. Tokyo: Chikuma Shobō, 1984.

Taigakai, ed. *Naimushōshi.* Tokyo: Chihō Zaimu Kyōkai, 1971.

Takagi Hiroshi. "1880 nendai, Yamato ni okeru bunkazai hozon." *Rekishigaku kenkyū,* no. 629 (February 1992): 15–22.

———. "Nihon no kindaika to kōshitsu girei: 1880 nendai no 'kyūkan' hozon." *Nihonshi kenkyū,* no. 320 (April 1989): 87–115.

Takayanagi Mitsutoshi and Takeuchi Yoshizō, ed. *Nihonshi jiten.* 2nd ed. Tokyo: Kadokawa Shoten, 1974.

Taki Kōji. *Tennō no shōzō.* Tokyo: Iwanami Shoten, 1988.

Tanaka Akira. *Kindai tennōsei e no dōtei.* Tokyo: Yoshikawa Kōbunkan, 1979.

Tanba Tsuneo. *Nishikie ni miru Meiji tennō to Meiji jidai.* Tokyo: Asahi Shinbunsha, 1966.

Tokyo Hyakunenshi Henshū Iinkai, ed. *Tōkyō hyakunenshi.* 7 vols. Tokyo: Tokyo-to, 1972–73.

———, ed. *Tōkyō hyakunenshi—bekkan.* Tokyo: Gyosei, 1980.

Tokyo-to, ed. *Edo kara Tōkyō e no tenkai.* Tokyo: Tokyo-to, 1953.

———, ed. *Meiji shonen no bukechi shori mondai.* Tokyo: Tokyo-to, 1965.

Tokyo Toritsu Daigaku Toshi Kenkyūkai, ed. *Toshi kōzō to toshi keikaku.* Tokyo: Tokyo Daigaku Shuppankai, 1968.

Tomita Kōjirō. *Tanaka Seizanhaku.* Tokyo: Aoyama Shoin, 1917.

Tsurumi Shunsuke, ed. *Goishin no arashi.* Revised ed. Tokyo: Chikuma Shobō, 1977.

Uchiyama Masao and Minomo Toshitarō. *Yoyogi no mori.* Tokyo: Kyōgakusha, 1981.

Umeda Yoshihiko. *Nihon shūkyō seidoshi: Kindai-hen.* Revised and expanded ed. Tokyo: Tosen Shuppan, 1971.

Umesao Tadao and Moriya Takeshi, eds. *Kyōto.* Vol. 10 of *Meiji Taishō zushi,* edited by Asukai Masamichi et al. Tokyo: Chikuma Shobō, 1978.

Watanabe Osamu. *Sengo seijishi no naka no tennōsei.* Tokyo: Aoki Shoten, 1990.

Yamaguchi Masao. *Chi no enkinhō.* Tokyo: Iwanami Shoten, 1978.

Yamaguchi Osamu, ed. *Zusetsu nenpyō.* Vol. 16 of *Meiji Taishō zushi,* edited by Asukai Masamichi et al. Tokyo: Chikuma Shobō, 1978.

Yamamoto Nobuyoshi and Konno Toshihiko. *Kindai kyōiku no tennōsei ideorogii.* Tokyo: Shinsensha, 1973.

Yamamoto Takeyoshi. *Kindai Nihon no shinbun dokushasō.* Tokyo: Hōsei Daigaku Shuppankyoku, 1981.

Yamaori Tetsuo. "Tennō no sōsō girei to sokui girei." *Rekishi kōron,* no. 62 (January 1981): 148–152.

Yano Kōta Kinenkai, ed. *Sūji de miru Nihon no hyakunen.* Tokyo: Kokuseisha, 1981.

Yasumaru Yoshio. *Deguchi Nao.* Tokyo: Asahi Shinbunsha, 1977.

———. *Kamigami no Meiji ishin.* Tokyo: Iwanami Shoten, 1979.

———. "Kindai tennōzō no keisei." *Rekishi hyōron,* no. 465 (January 1989): 1–20.

———. *Kindai tennōzō no keisei.* Tokyo: Iwanami Shoten, 1992.

———. *Nihon nashonarizumu no zen'ya.* Tokyo: Asahi Shinbun, 1977.

———. *Nihon no kindaika to minshū shisō.* Tokyo: Aoki Shoten, 1974.

Yoshida Kyūichi. "Meiji shonen no shūkyō ikki ni tsuite." In *Nihon kindai bukkyōshi kenkyū.* Tokyo: Yoshikawa Kōbunkan, 1959.

Yoshimi Shun'ya. *Hakurankai no seijigaku.* Tokyo: Chūō Kōronsha, 1992.

———. "Kyōkai toshite no Ise." In *Hōhō toshite no kyōkai,* edited by Akasaka Norio. Tokyo: Shin'yōsha, 1991.

Yui Masaomi. "Joron—tōchi kikō no kakuritsu to 'kokumin soshiki' ka." In *Kindai Nihon no tōgō to teikō,* edited by Kano Masanao and Yui Masaomi. Vol. 2. Tokyo: Nihon Hyōronsha, 1982.

Yuzawa Yasuhiko. "Nihon no rikon no jittai." In *Kon'in no kaishō.* Vol. 4 of *Kōza kazoku,* edited by Aoyama Michio et al. Tokyo: Kōbundō, 1974.

Other Sources in English

Agulhon, Maurice. *Marianne into Battle.* Translated by Janet Lloyd. Paris: Maison des Sciences de l'Homme; Cambridge: Cambridge University Press, 1981.

———. "Politics, Images, and Symbols in Post-Revolutionary France." In *Rites of Power,* edited by Sean Wilentz. Philadelphia: University of Pennsylvania Press, 1985.

Anderson, Benedict. *Imagined Communities: Reflections on the Origins and Spread of Nationalism.* 2nd ed. London: Verso, 1991.

Bagehot, Walter. *The English Constitution.* 1867. Reprint, Ithaca: Cornell University Press, 1966.

Barthes, Roland. *The Empire of Signs.* Translated by Richard Howard. New York: Hill and Wang, 1982.

Beasley, W. G. *The Meiji Restoration.* Stanford: Stanford University Press, 1972.

———. *The Modern History of Japan.* New York and Washington, D.C.: Praeger Publishers, 1963.

Berry, Mary Elizabeth. *Hideyoshi.* Cambridge: Harvard University Press, 1982.

Bhabha, Homi K. "Dissemination: Time, Narrative, and the Margins of the Modern Nation." In *Nation and Narration,* edited by Homi K. Bhabha. London and New York: Routledge, 1990.

———, ed. *Nation and Narration.* London and New York: Routledge, 1990.

Biersack, Aletta. "Local Knowledge, Local History: Geertz and Beyond." In *The New Cultural History,* edited by Lynn Hunt. Berkeley: University of California Press, 1989.

Bourdieu, Pierre. *Distinction.* Translated by Richard Nice. Cambridge: Harvard University Press, 1984.

———. *The Logic of Practice.* Translated by Richard Nice. Cambridge, England: Polity Press, 1990.

———. *Outline of a Theory of Practice.* Translated by Richard Nice. Cambridge: Cambridge University Press, 1977.

Bowen, Roger W. *Rebellion and Democracy in Meiji Japan.* Berkeley: University of California Press, 1980.

Cannadine, David. "The Context, Performance and Meaning of Ritual: The British Monarchy and the Invention of 'Tradition,' c. 1820–1977." In *The Invention of Tradition,* edited by Eric Hobsbawm and Terence Ranger. Cambridge: Cambridge University Press, 1983.

Chatterjee, Partha. *Nationalist Thought and the Colonial World: A Derivative Discourse?* London: Zed Books, 1986.

————. *The Nation and Its Fragments: Colonial and Postcolonial Histories.* Princeton: Princeton University Press, 1993.

Coaldrake, William H. "Edo Architecture and Tokugawa Law." *Monumenta Nipponica* 36 (1981): 235–84.

Cohn, Bernard S. "Anthropology and History in the 1980s." *Journal of Interdisciplinary History* 12 (1981): 227–52.

————. "Representing Authority in Victorian India." In *The Invention of Tradition,* edited by Eric Hobsbawm and Terence Ranger. Cambridge: Cambridge University Press, 1983.

Dower, John W. *Empire and Aftermath: Yoshida Shigeru and the Japanese Experience, 1878–1954.* Cambridge, Mass., and London: Council on East Asian Studies, Harvard University Press, 1979.

————. *Japan in War and Peace.* New York: New Press, 1993.

Embree, John. *Suye Mura: A Japanese Village.* 1939. Reprint, Chicago: University of Chicago Press, Phoenix Books, 1964.

Evans-Pritchard, E. E. "The Divine Kingship of the Shilluk of the Nilotic Sudan" (1948). In *Social Anthropology and Other Essays.* New York: Free Press, 1962.

Feeley-Harnik, Gillian. "Issues in Divine Kingship." *Annual Review of Anthropology* 14 (1985): 273–313.

Foard, James H. "The Boundaries of Compassion: Buddhism and National Tradition in Japanese Pilgrimage." *Journal of Asian Studies* 41 (February 1982): 231–51.

Foucault, Michel. *Discipline and Punish: The Birth of the Prison.* Translated by Alan Sheridan. New York: Random House, Inc., 1977.

————. "The Eye of Power." In *Power/Knowledge: Selected Interviews and Other Writings,* edited by Colin Gordon. New York: Pantheon Books, 1980.

————. "Nietzsche, Genealogy, History." In *Language, Counter-Memory, Practice,* translated by Donald F. Bouchard and Sherry Simon, edited by Donald F. Bouchard. Ithaca: Cornell University Press, 1977.

————. "The Subject and Power." In *Michel Foucault: Beyond Structuralism and Hermeneutics,* edited by Hubert L. Dreyfus and Paul Rabinow. 2nd ed. Chicago: University of Chicago Press, 1983.

————. "Two Lectures." In *Power/Knowledge: Selected Interviews and Other Writings,* edited by Colin Gordon. New York: Pantheon Books, 1980.

Fridell, Wilbur M. "Government Ethics Textbooks in Late Meiji Japan." *Journal of Asian Studies* 29 (August 1970): 823–34.

Fujitani, Takashi. "Electronic Pageantry and Japan's 'Symbolic Emperor.'" *Journal of Asian Studies* 51 (November 1992): 824–50.

————. "Minshūshi as Critique of Orientalist Knowledges." *Positions* (forthcoming).

Geertz, Clifford. "Centers, Kings, and Charisma: Reflections on the

Symbolics of Power." In *Culture and Its Creators*, edited by Joseph Ben-David and Terry Nichols Clark. Chicago and London: University of Chicago Press, 1977.

————. *Negara*. Princeton: Princeton University Press, 1980.

————. "Person, Time, and Conduct in Bali." In *The Interpretation of Cultures*. New York: Basic Books, 1973.

Gellner, Ernest. *Nations and Nationalism*. Ithaca: Cornell University Press, 1983.

Giddens, Anthony. *The Nation-State and Violence*. Berkeley: University of California Press, 1987.

Giesey, R. E. *The Royal Funeral Ceremony in Renaissance France*. Geneva: Libraire E. Droz, 1960.

Gluck, Carol. *Japan's Modern Myths: Ideology in the Late Meiji Period*. Princeton: Princeton University Press, 1985.

Hall, John W. "Kyoto as Historical Background." In *Medieval Japan: Essays in Institutional History*, edited by John W. Hall and Jeffrey P. Mass. New Haven: Yale University Press, 1974.

————. "A Monarch for Modern Japan." In *Political Development in Modern Japan*, edited by Robert E. Ward. Princeton: Princeton University Press, 1968.

————. "Rule by Status in Tokugawa Japan." *Journal of Japanese Studies* 1.1 (Autumn 1974): 39–49.

Hane, Mikiso. *Peasants, Rebels, and Outcastes: The Underside of Modern Japan*. New York: Pantheon Books, 1982.

Hardacre, Helen. "Creating State Shinto: The Great Promulgation Campaign and the New Religions." *Journal of Japanese Studies* 12.1 (Winter 1986): 29–63.

Harootunian, Harry D. "Introduction: A Sense of Ending and the Problem of Taisho." In *Japan in Crisis: Essays on Taisho Democracy*, edited by Bernard S. Silberman and H. D. Harootunian. Princeton: Princeton University Press, 1974.

————. *Things Seen and Unseen: Discourse and Ideology in Tokugawa Nativism*. Chicago and London: University of Chicago Press, 1988.

Hobsbawm, Eric. "Mass-Producing Traditions: Europe, 1870–1914." In *The Invention of Tradition*, edited by Eric Hobsbawn and Terence Ranger. Cambridge: Cambridge University Press, 1983.

Hobsbawm, Eric, and Terence Ranger, eds. *The Invention of Tradition*. Cambridge: Cambridge University Press, 1983.

Holtom, D. C. *The Japanese Enthronement Ceremonies*. 1928. Reprint, Tokyo: Sophia University, 1972.

————. *Modern Japan and Shinto Nationalism*. Chicago: University of Chicago Press, 1943.

Hoston, Germaine A. *Marxism and the Crisis of Development in Prewar Japan*. Princeton: Princeton University Press, 1986.

Hunt, Lynn. *Politics, Culture, and Class in the French Revolution*. Berkeley: University of California Press, 1984.

Hutton, Patrick H. "The Art of Memory Reconceived: From Rhetoric to Psychoanalysis." *Journal of the History of Ideas* 48 (July–September 1987): 371–92.

Inglis, K. S. "Ceremonies in a Capital Landscape: Scenes in the Making of Canberra." *Daedalus* 114 (Winter 1985): 85–126.

Irokawa Daikichi. *The Culture of the Meiji Period*. Translation edited by Marius Jansen. Princeton: Princeton University Press, 1985.

Irving, Robert Grant. *Indian Summer: Lutyens, Baker, and Imperial Delhi*. New Haven: Yale University Press, 1981.

Jameson, Fredric. "Postmodernism, or the Cultural Logic of Late Capitalism." *New Left Review*, no. 146 (July–August 1984): 53–92.

Jansen, Marius. "Monarchy and Modernization in Japan." *Journal of Asian Studies* 35 (August 1977): 611–22

Jay, Martin. *Downcast Eyes: The Denigration of Vision in Twentieth-Century French Thought*. Berkeley: University of California Press, 1993.

———. "The Empire of the Gaze: Foucault and the Denigration of Vision in Twentieth-Century French Thought." In *Foucault: A Critical Reader*, edited by David Couzens Hoy. London: Basil Blackwell, 1986.

Kantorowicz, Ernst H. *The King's Two Bodies*. Princeton: Princeton University Press, 1957.

Kaplan, Alice Yaeger. *Reproductions of Banality: Fascism, Literature, and French Intellectual Life*. Minneapolis: University of Minnesota Press, 1986.

Kertzer, David I. *Ritual, Politics, and Power*. New Haven: Yale University Press, 1988.

Ketelaar, James Edward. *Of Heretics and Martyrs in Meiji Japan*. Princeton: Princeton University Press, 1990.

Lampland, Martha. "Family Portraits: Gendered Images of the Nation in Nineteenth-Century Hungary." *East European Politics and Societies* 8.2 (Spring 1994): 287–316.

Lane, Christel. *Rites of Rulers*. Cambridge: Cambridge University Press, 1981.

Lukes, Steven. "Political Ritual and Social Integration." In *Essays in Social Theory*. New York: Columbia University Press, 1977.

Maruyama Masao. *Studies in the Intellectual History of Tokugawa Japan*. Translated by Mikiso Hane. Tokyo: University of Tokyo Press, 1974.

Miyoshi, Masao, and H. D. Harootunian, eds. *Postmodernism and Japan*. Durham, N.C.: Duke University Press, 1989.

Mosse, George L. *Nationalism and Sexuality*. Madison: University of Wisconsin Press, 1985.

Mumford, Lewis. *The City in History*. New York and London: Harcourt Brace Jovanovich, 1961.

Natsume Sōseki. *Kokoro*. Translated and with a foreword by Edwin McClellan. Chicago: Henry Regnery, 1957.

Nolte, Sharon H., and Sally Ann Hastings. "The Meiji State's Policy Toward Women, 1890–1910." In *Recreating Japanese Women, 1600–1945*, edited by Gail Lee Bernstein. Berkeley: University of California Press, 1991.

Nora, Pierre. "Between Memory and History: *Les Lieux de Mémoire*." *Representations*, no. 26 (Spring 1989): 7–25.

Ooms, Emily Groszos. *Women and Millenarian Protest in Meiji Japan: Deguchi Nao and Ōmotokyō*. Ithaca: East Asia Program, Cornell University, 1993.

Ooms, Herman. *Tokugawa Ideology*. Princeton: Princeton University Press, 1985.

Ozouf, Mona. *Festivals and the French Revolution*. Translated by Alan Sheridan. Cambridge: Harvard University Press, 1988.

Peattie, Mark. *Nan'yō: The Rise and Fall of the Japanese in Micronesia, 1885–1945*. Honolulu: University of Hawaii Press, 1988.

Pecora, Vincent P. "The Limits of Local Knowledge." In *The New Historicism*, edited by H. Aram Veeser. New York and London: Routledge, 1989.

Posonby-Fane, Richard. "Enthronement Ceremonies." In *The Imperial House of Japan*. Kyoto: Ponsonby Memorial Society, 1959.

Pyle, Kenneth B. "The Technology of Japanese Nationalism: The Local Improvement Movement, 1900–1918." *Journal of Asian Studies* 33 (November 1973): 51–66.

Renan, Ernest. "What Is a Nation?" translated and annotated by Martin Thom. In *Nation and Narration*, edited by Homi K. Bhabha. London and New York: Routledge, 1990.

Reps, John W. *Monumental Washington: The Planning and Development of the Capital Center*. Princeton: Princeton University Press, 1967.

Ruiz, Teofilo F. "Unsacred Monarch: The Kings of Castile in the Late Middle Ages." In *Rites of Power*, edited by Sean Wilentz. Philadelphia: University of Pennsylvania Press, 1985.

Scott, Joan Wallach. *Gender and the Politics of History*. New York: Columbia University Press, 1988.

Seidensticker, Edward. *High City, Low City*. New York: Alfred A. Knopf, 1983.

Shils, Edward, and Michael Young. "The Meaning of the Coronation" (1956). In *Center and Periphery: Essays in Macrosociology*, by Edward Shils. Chicago: University of Chicago Press, 1975.

Sievers, Sharon L. *Flowers in Salt*. Stanford: Stanford University Press, 1983.

Smethurst, Richard J. *A Social Basis for Prewar Japanese Militarism: The Army and the Rural Community*. Berkeley: University of California Press, 1974.

Smith, Henry D., II. "The Edo-Tokyo Transition: In Search of Common Ground." In *Japan in Transition: From Tokugawa to Meiji*, edited by Marius B. Jansen and Gilbert Rozman. Princeton: Princeton University Press, 1986.

———. "Tokyo and London: Comparative Conceptions of the City." In *Japan: A Comparative View*, edited by Albert M. Craig. Princeton: Princeton University Press, 1979.

———. "Tokyo as an Idea: An Exploration of Japanese Urban Thought Until 1945." *Journal of Japanese Studies* 4.1 (Winter 1978): 45–80.

Sollers, Werner, ed. *The Invention of Ethnicity.* New York and Oxford: Oxford University Press, 1989.

Terdiman, Richard. "Deconstructing Memory: On Representing the Past and Theorizing Culture in France Since the Revolution." *Diacritics* 15 (Winter 1985): 13–36.

———. *Present Past: Modernity and the Memory Crisis.* Ithaca: Cornell University Press, 1993.

Titus, David Anson. *Palace and Politics in Prewar Japan.* New York and London: Columbia University Press, 1974.

Tsurumi Shunsuke. *An Intellectual History of Wartime Japan, 1931–1945.* London: KPI Ltd., 1986.

Ueyama Shunpei, Umehara Takeshi, and Yano Tōru. "The Imperial Institution in Japanese History." *Japan Echo* 16 (Spring 1989): 46–52.

Vlastos, Stephen. "Opposition Movements in Early Meiji, 1868–1885." In *Cambridge History of Japan,* vol. 5, edited by Marius B. Jansen. Cambridge and New York: Cambridge University Press, 1989.

Wakabayashi, Bob Tadashi. *Anti-Foreignism and Western Learning in Early-Modern Japan: The "New Thesis" of 1825.* Cambridge: Harvard University Press, 1986.

———. "In Name Only: Imperial Sovereignty in Early Modern Japan." *Journal of Japanese Studies* 17.1 (Winter 1991): 25–57.

Webb, Herschel. *The Japanese Imperial Institution in the Tokugawa Period.* New York: Columbia University Press, 1968.

Weber, Eugen. *Peasants into Frenchmen.* Stanford: Stanford University Press, 1976.

Wheatley, Paul, and Thomas See. *From Court to Capital.* Chicago: University of Chicago Press, 1978.

Wilentz, Sean, ed. *Rites of Power: Symbolism, Ritual, and Politics Since the Middle Ages.* Philadelphia: University of Pennsylvania Press, 1985.

Wortman, Richard. "Moscow and Petersburg: The Problem of the Political Center in Tsarist Russia, 1881–1914." In *Rites of Power,* edited by Sean Wilentz. Philadelphia: University of Pennsylvania Press, 1985.

———. "Rule by Sentiment: Alexander II's Journeys through the Russian Empire." *American Historical Review* 95 (June 1990): 745–71.

Yamaguchi Masao. "Kingship, Theatricality, and Marginal Reality in Japan." In *Text and Context: The Social Anthropology of Tradition,* edited by Ravindra K. Jain. Philadelphia: Institute for the Study of Human Issues, 1977.

Yamamoto Yokichi. *Japanese Postage Stamps.* Tokyo: Japan Travel Bureau, 1950.

Index

Compositor: Braun Brumfield, Inc.
Text: 10/13 Galliard
Display: Galliard
Printer and Binder: Braun-Brumfield, Inc.